REPRESENTATIONS: SOCIAL CONSTRUCTIONS OF GENDER

edited by:

RHODA K. UNGER

Sponsored by the Society for the Psychological Study of Social Issues

Baywood Publishing Company, Inc.
AMITYVILLE, NEW YORK

Library of Congress Catalog Number: 88-22003
ISBN: 0-89503-052-7 (Paper)
ISBN: 0-89503-057-8 (Cloth)

Library of Congress Cataloging-in-Publication Data
Main entry under title:

Representations: social constructions of gender/ edited by Rhoda K. Unger.
p. cm.
Includes bibliographies and index.
ISBN 0-89503-052-7
1. Feminism--United States. 2. Women--United States--Psychology.
3. Sex role--United States. I. Unger, Rhoda Kesler.
HQ1426.R47 1989
305.3--dc 19

88-22003
CIP

This book is dedicated to Nancy Datan (1941-1987) who in her life and work taught me a great deal about the reconstruction of reality. She gave from her heart as well as her mind and has left a Nancy-shaped hole in feminist scholarship.

Table of Contents

PART II

PART III

Foreword

It is a pleasure to bring *Representations: Social Constructions of Gender* to your attention. To begin to appreciate the complex and unusual character of this book—developed from an edited series of journal articles into a larger collection with a clear identity and emphasis all its own—one need only browse through the Table of Contents. "The divided lives of women in literature," "Case studies of agency and communion in women's lives," "A sense of humor," "Dialogue with Guatemalan Indian women," "Coping with rape," "Earliest memories: Sex differences and the meaning of experience," "Women's explanations for job changes," "Androgyny and the life cycle: The Bacchae of Euripides"—these are but a few of the topics represented in this diverse and interesting collection.

What, then, binds these essays together? First and foremost, this is a book of stories about women, about the conflicts, choices, and opportunities that are present in the lives of women, both real and imagined. Beyond that, this volume is a defense of intellectual complexity, differentiation, subtlety, and nuance. As the book's distinguished editor observes, all of the papers included are, in one way or another, compatible with the conceptual framework of "social constructionism:" a point of view that argues that people are not pawns of the social system into which they are born, but help to create and shape it. If, as Rhoda Unger points out, the prevailing wisdom in American psychology continues to call for a view of the self as stable and coherent, and continues to regard reason and science as able to "provide an objective, reliable, and universal foundation for conceptions of both the self and reality" (p. 4), then this book offers a dramatically different perspective. Unger believes that the world of the powerful, of society's "haves," is a place where rationality, reason, and science are each potential tools to be used in the service of justifying the *status quo*. She calls for a different paradigm, one that argues for the importance of the ongoing creation of new social realities.

But this book does more than provoke theoretical critique of the prevailing wisdom in American scientific psychology. Written by a distinguished group of scholars in women's studies, many of the articles selected for inclusion present alternative methods as well as findings that may move the study of sex and gender beyond its present concerns to a new level of analysis.

At yet another level, this book may be seen as a response to the ever changing and emerging women's movement of the last several years, a movement that has developed a clear and strong vision, an identity, and—in doing so—has occasionally found it necessary to stake out a set of ideological "rights" and "wrongs." Unger points out the danger of "minimizing the differences between particular groups of women by focusing only on the commonalities among them" (p. 10). The editor's response to this danger is to encourage openmindedness, the examination of neglected groups, and the tolerance of divergent points of view.

Thus, while you might conclude, on the basis of the book and chapter titles that this book is simply about women and women's lives, it is far more than that. It is a book about the development of social and political movements, the effect such movements have upon scholarship, the challenges that face scholarship with a political focus, and the continuing vigilance that is called for if such scholarship is to continue to develop and mature.

Finally, a word about the organization that has sponsored this book. The Society for the Psychological Study of Social Issues (SPSSI) is a 50-year-old organization of social scientists, committed to applying social science wisdom to the analysis and redress of social problems and issues. The work of SPSSI, as represented by the many books we have sponsored over the years, has consistently combined attention to the subtlety and complexity of social science knowledge with the determination to apply what we know to pressing social problems. Rhoda Unger's *Representations: Social Constructions of Gender* is very much in the spirit of this SPSSI tradition. I am therefore extremely pleased and proud that SPSSI has sponsored this book.

Jeffrey Z. Rubin
President, 1987–1988
Society for the Psychological Study of Social Issues
April 1988

Introduction

RHODA K. UNGER

Several years ago I was asked by the editors of a new cross-disciplinary journal to edit a series of articles on sex and gender for them. Since the title of this journal: "Imagination, Cognition, and Personality: Consciousness in Theory, Research, and Clinical Practice" was both enigmatic and intriguing, I saw this series as an opportunity to extend the parametric base of feminist psychology. Therefore, I sought work that appeared to be somewhat distinct from usual theory and practice within psychology—work that was on the cutting edge of feminist psychology. Not surprisingly, given the broad scope of the journal, many of these papers turned out to have an interdisciplinary outlook as well.

Although the thirteen papers that were published as part of the original series included a number of innovative approaches to the study of sex and gender, the series failed to reach many people who might have been interested in it. The lack of visibility of these articles may have been due to the newness of the journal, the low percentage of scholars of sex and gender who are aware of it, or to the reluctance of most psychologists to deal with interdisciplinary work. Since my purpose was to broaden both the conceptual and methodological base of feminist psychology, it was obviously not in the interests of either myself or the authors to have these papers pass into oblivion.

Fortunately, I was able to persuade the publisher of the journal that it would be valuable to collect the series of articles into a more easily accessible book. By this time, however, I had located a number of other papers that fit into its framework and had also recognized that the materials were more intellectually integrated than I had originally believed. This book is, therefore, not a simple reprinting of already published materials. Nine original articles have been added to the collection and integrated with the previously published materials in a theoretical synthesis that emerged while the series was being developed. For this reason, I have left much of the original introduction to the series intact and added this more current prologue as well.

As I reread the original articles in the series and as new papers arrived, I realized that, in many forms, the various authors were concerned with the telling of stories. The use of narrative is not a typical component of the dominant positivist empiricist paradigm within psychology which is concerned with the development of general rules for the prediction of human behavior [1]. It is, however, characteristic of social constructionism—a theoretical framework that is important for feminists in many disciplines outside of psychology, notably, anthropology, history, and literary criticism [2]. This theoretical framework is becoming increasingly important for the psychological study of gender as well. The chapters in this book exemplify the subject matter, techniques, and questions of this newer perspective.

According to Kenneth Gergen the assumptions of the social constructionist orientation include [3]:

1. The view that what we know of the world is determined by the categories (linguistic and conceptual) that we possess to define it. "Constructionism asks one to suspend belief that commonly accepted categories receive their warrant through observation. Thus, it invites one to challenge the objective basis of conventional knowledge" [3, p. 267].
2. The idea that the terms by which the world is understood are social artifacts, products of historically situated interchanges among people.
3. The belief that the degree to which a particular form of understanding prevails or is sustained across time is not fundamentally dependent on its empirical validity, but on the vagaries of social processes which must be understood in terms of historical events as well as through the analysis of psychological processes.
4. The view that forms of negotiated understanding are of critical significance in social life. For example, to treat the behavior of an individual or that of a group as involuntarily manifested as opposed to freely chosen has far-reaching consequences for the individual so designated.

Social constructionism as a form of postmodern philosophy challenges beliefs still prevalent in American psychology as well as American society. Flax suggests that these ideas [4], derived from the Englightenment, include: belief in the existence of a stable, coherent self; belief that reason and science can provide an objective, reliable, and universal foundation for conceptions of both the self and reality; belief that the knowledge acquired from the right use of reason will represent something real and unchanging; and belief that reason itself has transcendental and universal qualities. She further argues that by grounding claims to authority in reason, the conflicts between truth, knowledge, and power have been evaded and language can also be seen as unproblematic—as merely the medium through which representation of the world occurs.

Thus, a social constructionist theory of gender goes beyond the conception of gender as a cognitive variable. It is important to view gender as a major social category that functions in a complex variety of ways to influence behavior [5].

However, social constructionism means that we must continually question ideology and methodology that may deny gender its broader cultural and systemic meaning. Some of the issues that extend beyond cognitive mechanisms are: the many ways that different cultures negotiate issues of gender, the function of gender (as well as other race and class categories) as a social control mechanism, and the role of consciousness (in the sense of awareness of and reflection upon our own behavior) in mediating the effects of gender upon us all.

What is important here is that social constructionist does not permit us to define gender as a variable at all. Gender is constantly altered by social context: by culture, by cross-personal interactions, and by the consciousness of individuals themselves. It is an inconsistent and sometimes contradictory category [1].

Social constructionists see the individual as an active—albeit not always more rational—creator of his or her reality. I believe it is this perception that has led many of the contributors to this book (some of whom would probably not label themselves as social constructionists) to make use of one or another form of narrative material. Narrative material lends itself to the exposition of different versions of consciousness: that of its subject, its author, and, perhaps, that of the observer as well. It makes the fiction of one true reality harder to sustain.

This collection is not meant to be either inclusive or exclusive. It is too early in the development of the area to attempt to define a feminist methodology for psychology based upon social constructionism. I believe, however, that these chapters show the value a different theoretical perspective can have for the study of sex and gender. They show how gender has been problematized by feminist scholarship and introduce a new set of issues that have rarely been considered by more traditional treatments of sex and gender. In keeping with my belief in the value of multiple perspectives for psychology, the materials in this book can be used by the reader in several ways.

The chapters have been organized in a framework of several general themes important for the social construction of gender: the nature of women's consciousness in terms of public and private images; cultural constructions of women and men; innovative strategies for the reconstruction of sex and gender; and the personal and societal implications of the dichotimization of sex and gender. However, many of the chapters subsumed under one of these section headings could have been placed in others as well.

This material can also be read in terms of content area: androgyny; dual career issues; social change; humor; rape; attitudes about achievement; etc. Many chapters discuss concrete findings using a feminist framework. They demonstrate that feminist research has gone beyond theoretical critique. I believe, however, that the methodologies and ideological strategies employed are at least as important, than the particular topic addressed. I have chosen, therefore, to introduce each chapter briefly in terms of what I see as its place in the methodology and/or epistemology of the social constructionist paradigm of gender.

THE USES OF AN ALTERED EMPIRICISM

In one sense, these chapters exemplify the way theoretical changes can alter methodological practices and, hence, empirical conclusions [6]. Some of the research discussed here demonstrates that one can make use of traditional empirical methodology to question its underlying framework. For example, Volentine and Brodsky show that cognitions about women and men are constructed in the form of an interaction between the sex of the subject and the sex of the stimulus person. Using rather traditional research methodology, they found that there is no one universal conceptual reality. Identical information involving gender roles is evaluated differently depending upon the sex of the stimulus person and the sex of the observer. Unger uses a modification of a standard psychological measurement technique—a paper-and-pencil scale in which statements can be interpreted in several different ways—to evaluate individual differences in views about the relationship between the person and reality. She found that feminists have a less determinist conception about how the world works than do nonfeminists. This feminist construction of reality extends beyond attitudes involving the social, economic, and political equality of the sexes.

Slight alterations in methodological perspective can produce rather large effects in the area of gender. Thus, Sanders, Steil, and Weinglass demonstrate that the extent to which some religious women appear to be negative about traditional decisions for married career women differed depending upon whether objective or subjective measures were used. Subjective measures indicated more negativity than objective ones. Another subjective measure—the generation of social scripts—used by Frieze and her associates—showed that college women were able to imagine aspects of the housewife's daily life much more fully than other occupational roles available to today's women. The women were more informed about aspects of this role even though they were negative about it. The work of Frieze et al. raises the question of how much familiarity rather than affect influences women's future life choices.

LaFrance examined women's explanations for job changes using longitudinal methodology. There was little stability in reasons given for job changes when the same women's responses at different times in their lives were analyzed. The past appears to have been rewritten by a significant number of her respondents. A cross-sectional rather than a longitudinal survey of earliest memories by Schwartz also suggests that the past may be rewritten. She found that although women's subjective reality appears to be generally less positive than men's, women for whom mastery was not a current issue (those successfully enrolled in graduate school) did not differ from men in the number of mastery themes reported in their earliest memories, but did differ in this respect from undergraduate women still living at home. These studies illustrate the role of the current situation in structuring beliefs about past reality.

Stewart and Malley's findings also relate to the way situational constraints influence consciousness. They examined women in five different combinations of domestic and work roles in terms of how they described the way they gratified their basic needs. Their findings indicated that women can, generally, structure any life circumstance to permit opportunities for both love and work. The particular combination of roles chosen may be less important for life satisfaction than how the individual perceives her circumstances. However, they also warn that their conclusions are probably limited by the rather privileged group of women studied.

All of these studies attempt to involve the consciousness of the respondents by the use of several versions of research questions or through qualitative analysis of more extended responses than are usually elicited in laboratory research. In contrast, John and Sussman used a technique that seeks to intervene actively in the respondent's perception of reality. They used an ambiguous narrative between two sexually unspecified individuals in which clues to gender were available from an on-going dialogue. They found that subjects made assumptions about the heterosexual nature of the interaction even at the expense of role consistency and the integrity of the narrative. Their subjects inferred role reciprocity so that when one participant was inferred to be "male," the other automatically became "female." Subjects used gender stereotypes to form cognitive schemata by which to infer the sex of the participants and their sex assignments became more stable as they continued to respond to the narrative. These data demonstrate how social knowledge is constructed even at the expense of a loss of so-called objective information.

Towson, Zanna, and MacDonald's discussion of an impressive series of experimental studies on the self-fulfilling prophecy further elucidates mechanisms by which the gender-related expectancies of significant others are communicated to women (and others in low power positions). They show how behaviors consistent with sex-stereotypic expectations are rewarded and confirm beliefs in sex-related differences. Individuals incorporate such social beliefs in their self-presentation strategies, but may be unaware of the extent to which their behaviors are producing consequences that are harmful to themselves.

THE RECONSTRUCTION OF PSYCHOLOGICAL CONSTRUCTS

A number of chapters in this book question the nature of our society's assumptions about so-called masculine or agentic versus feminine or communal characteristics. Feminists have used the concept of androgyny as a way of transcending psychological theories that see masculinity and femininity as opposite and contradictory traits [7]. Bem, among others, has argued that gender is a social construction or schema that can be eliminated by extensive changes in the gender socialization practices of our society [8]. Androgyny is, however, also a social construction and as the careful theoretical analysis by Sedney indicates, a number of different conceptualizations have evolved using the same label. Sedney provides a taxonomy for the term that takes into account its different operational meanings as well as the levels of personality theory into which androgyny may be fitted. Her ironic conclusion is that although androgyny was originally offered as a way of envisioning alternatives to traditional sex-typing, much of the research on the concept has been constrained by existing professional and social biases. "What was designed to be a 'new' model has generated primarily 'more of the same' methods using fairly traditional scales that lead to results that often confirm old biases (p. 112)."

Both Crawford and Marlowe question assumptions about women's and men's humor. Marlowe reviews the literature on sex-related differences in humor looking at the social use of humor as well as developmentally based differences between the sexes. Her analysis of feminist uses of humor may be particularly valuable in a social constructionist framework. She suggests that what is funny is defined not only by social roles but by the institutional structure in which roles are embedded. The "new" feminist humor may be seen both as a way to strike back against social control and as a vehicle by which women can reconceptualize themselves.

Crawford describes findings obtained from more open-ended methodologies than are customarily used in studying humor. She asked people of both sexes about their perceptions of their sense of humor rather than impose an experimenter-defined "humor stimulus" on them. Men and women saw their own humor as serving different purposes. Women use humor to facilitate social interaction, to invite self-disclosure, and to share perspectives reciprocally. For these reasons, women's humor must be analyzed within its conversational context. Crawford charges that men's preferred style of humor (the use of set-pieces) is more easily adapted for laboratory study. Consequently, the professional literature on humor is a body of knowledge that focuses on the appreciation of "canned" humor while ignoring creativity and the social use of humor.

THE USE OF NARRATIVE FOR PSYCHOLOGY

I suggested earlier that traditional empirical methodologies can be adapted to social constructionist theory, but it is also true that new methodologies have evolved that broaden our psychological perspective. It is no accident that almost half the chapters in this book involve some form of narrative analysis. A synthesis of psychological and literary perspectives may be particularly rewarding for understanding aspects of gender. For example, androgyny probably has different meanings for each individual as well as for each theorist. Datan analyzes *The Bacchae* of Euripides from the standpoint of modern life-span developmental theory to give us a different perspective on the meaning of androgyny for different individuals. She suggests that the traits supposedly characteristic of the "other" sex may be more threatening to younger individuals than to those at a later life stage. She also notes that androgyny as a scholarly concept has been advanced and "forgotten" more than once because of its threat to prevailing perspectives.

Analyses of literary narratives are particularly valuable for exploring the consciousness of individuals. Psychology's experimental paradigms have difficulty in distinguishing between the self and the roles that self plays. Pope's analysis of literary themes makes the point that the roles constructed for women in our society frequently conflict with their own image of themselves. This conflict between social roles and self actualization is difficult to resolve and most resolutions are only partially successful. If the woman opts for portrayal of a traditionally female role, she is forced to ignore or deny her image of herself. If, on the other hand, she publicly acknowledges her true self, she is likely to be punished for failure in role-playing behavior. Self-actualizing women often lack external sources of validation as well and may be forced into fantasy. Pope's literary analysis is remarkably similar to my more psychological analysis of the "double-bind" [1].

Hartman gives us another view of women's private and public lives through her intensive analysis of the female protagonists in some of George Eliot's novels. Hartman argues that the heroic characters in Eliot's fiction—those who are able to enlarge their perceptual field to take in other selves—are, more often than not, women. She also argues, however, that although Eliot recognizes the pain attendant upon women's confinement to the domestic sphere in nineteenth century England, she was not able to imagine an alternative reality for them. Eliot's escape from women's private world was costly for her. As a result of her gendered upbringing and internalization of society's expectations, Eliot continued to feel herself a trespasser in the world of men throughout her life. Thus, she was able to grant her female characters perceptual clarity, but not the ability to alter their actual life circumstances except in limited ways.

Hartman's analysis involves the contextual aspect of feminist scholarship—the need to understand fictional works in terms of the historical and personal situation of the author. Helson's psychological analysis of a nineteenth century children's fantasy writer, Edith Nesbit, looks at the evolution of an author's fiction in terms of changes in life circumstances. Nesbit suffered a severe midlife crisis centered around losses in important familial relationships. Her fantasies changed at this time to themes of abandonment and their resolution and a search for the more rational parts of the self. She also created gatekeeper figures that embodied more female sexuality and androgynous symbolism than those of other (male) Edwardian fantasy writers.

The analysis of the imaginative work of women (a group once thought incapable of symbolic manipulation) may tell us much about the conflicts they experience. The conflicts between autonomy and dependency and between emotional and sexual expression and rationality are as salient today as they were in the nineteenth century. Women are still particularly likely to be caught in double binds by the mutually exclusive definitions of roles they are supposed to occupy.

Given the strength with which gender is embedded in our society, it is difficult to understand how transformation ever takes place. Snoek attempts to understand such change through the narrative of "ordinary women" who made major changes in their lives as a result of the Women's Liberation Movement. Through an extensive series of interviews, we see one such women, "Nancy," move from seeing herself as only a product of her roles to a view of herself as a more autonomous individual. Snoek argues that while Nancy's particular life experiences made her susceptible to personal change at this time, she would have been unlikely to have been able to do so without the supporting ideology of the women's movement and contact with a critical mass of women espousing this ideology. He suggests that feminism legitimized what had heretofore been seen as privately held complaints. In other words, feminism validated an alternative view of reality.

Howe uses women's narratives in still another way to examine changes in their perceptions. As an exercise in her courses in women's studies, she asked students to obtain biographies of their mothers. This project produced changes in daughters' views of their mothers in terms of a greater sense of the mothers' personhood, the greater expression of authenticity by both mother and daughter, and the recognition of the role of social context in the construction of women's lives.

Personal change appears to be facilitated by the recognition that other perspectives are as valid as one's own. Women writers have increasingly become interested in speculative fiction, a field long dominated by men. Fine, Kidder, and Boell survey futuristic images constructed by professional writers and social scientists. Speculative fiction offers an opportunity to explore a variety of alternative lifestyles in a non-threatening context since the ambience of such fiction is, by definition, *not* here or *not* now. Organized thematically, some of the gender arrangements discussed by this literary genre include: explanations for sex differences (or the absence of such differences), organization of labor, and criticism of current gender arrangements. However, Fine and her colleagues also found that what one can imagine about the future is constrained by what exists in the present. Nevertheless, the use of various kinds of speculation provides one valuable advantage over present day social science methodology. The arrangement of reality is limited more by the imagination of the respondents than by the imagination of the investigator as he or she structures research questions.

FEMALES ARE NOT A GLOBAL CATEGORY EITHER!

Recently, feminist scholars [9] have warned us that we risk minimizing the differences between particular groups of women by focusing only on the commonalities among them. This risk is reduced by spotlighting the experience of particular women. It is important, however, to keep in mind that the reality that feminist social scientists are constructing is largely limited to the perceptions and circumstances of white, middle-class, Western women. There is no reason to believe that other groups of women deal with gender-related realities in the same way.

Fine's article represents both a departure from conventional empirical methodology and a focus on a woman from one underrepresented group—those who are poor and black. Fine describes an encounter in a rape-counseling situation in order to explore the phenomenology of a rape victim in terms of her methods of coping and control. She argues that the established hierarchy of control sanctioned by mental health experts vitiates the strategies of those with low personal power. Encouragement of active individualistic strategies when change is unlikely places the victim at risk and reinforces existing power inequities. This chapter considers race and class as well as sexual issues. It focuses on the differential consciousness of victims and nonvictims, illustrating how different styles of coping can be evaluated only in terms of the context of the individual's life. One critical issue that is raised for clinical practitioners is whether self-disclosure is helpful in producing the structural changes necessary for the empowerment of members of some social groups.

Lykes also employs consciousness in her discussion of another underrepresented group—Guatemalan Indian women—to raise a critical ethical issue for psychologists. She points out that even such a positive safeguard as "informed consent" (the process by which prospective subjects of a study are told about its procedures and potential outcomes) has embedded within it assumptions about the power of the researcher to control the topics to be studied and the methods used. In her attempts to do collaborative research about the experiences of refugee Indian women, her written informed consent form proved to be a barrier cancelling out prior mutual trust. These women perceived that a written contract of any form reduced their ability to negotiate power differentials which could not be obviated simply by the good will of the investigator.

Fine and Lykes' chapters are particularly useful because these researchers tell us a great deal about themselves as well as about their respondents. These and other papers in this book illustrate one of the best qualities of feminist scholarship—its self-reflexive nature. Feminists make no pretense of being impartial, objective observers. Our definition of context includes that of the researcher as well as the respondent.

THE LIMITS OF SOCIAL CONSTRUCTIONISM

Farganis' contribution to this volume serves several purposes. Her analysis of Margaret Atwood's *The Handmaid's Tale* provides us with yet another example of women's consciousness—this time in a dystopia in which women's reproductive role has become their primary reason for existence. Farganis explores the limits to which the self can be constructed. But, she also provides us with some valuable caveats about the uses to which social construction may be put.

An important issue for her is who has the power to define social reality. In Atwood's story, reality has been reconstructed by religious fundamentalists. Women's sexuality and ability to reproduce have been placed solely at the service of the state. Farganis warns us that a social constructionist position that asserts that anything can be constructed can lead to an invasion of both the private and the personal by so-called outside experts. She argues that social constructionism demystifies biology and can be used to legitimize the appropriation of women's bodies for the purposes of others more powerful than themselves.

It is a large conceptual leap from social constructionism to the "Baby M" case. However, Farganis' discussion suggests that we must continue to examine the assumptions and implications of social constructionism for gender. There are many unresolved issues that are particularly relevant for those of us in psychology. For example, chapters in this book examine a variety of subjects for their narratives such as: fictional characters, authors of fiction, maternal biographies, and extensive interviews with "real" people. Everyone's life is equally important to themselves, but are there any criteria by which we decide whose life is best suited for intense public scrutiny? In other words, if we are dealing with multiple perspectives of reality, whose reality is most useful? And, if we apply some form of utilitarian criteria—useful to whom and why?

Social constructionism can also lead to an extreme relativistic position. For example, if individual lives can only be understood in terms of their particular historical and personal context, what are the implications of this theoretical framework for psychology as a scholarly discipline? Is it possible to establish any general rules for the prediction of behavior? Such an extreme idiographic approach could lead to the disappearance of all forms of empirical research currently used in psychology. With what, then, can we replace such useful psychological concepts as reliability and validity?

To state that meaning is situationally based does not imply that no consensual agreement about meaning is possible. It is important, however, to emphasize that consensual agreement can exist only for the here and now and is always limited by who asks what questions. Insomuch as women are part of all society, feminist thinking cannot be free from culture-bound modes of understanding.

The understanding of meaning as contextual helps to explain why social problems that have apparently been solved rarely stay solved. "When we intervene to ameliorate some social problem, we cannot hope to change just what we want and nothing else" [10, p. 16]. The solutions we find may benefit some groups, but prove harmful to others. Problems reappear when new spokespersons emerge from a different disadvantaged group to articulate the issue anew. Of course, such spokespersons must also have the power to establish their definitions as socially problematic.

The self-reflexive aspect of social constructionism is extremely valuable for illustrating the proximal nature of solutions to both social and scientific problems. Feminists are probably no more objective than any other scholars, but we appear to be more aware that we are speaking only with our own voice. We need to be suspicious of any canon that claims a reality that will "rescue" us from contradiction and differences. I hope that this book shows that there are no easy answers. "Feminist theory, like other forms of postmodernism, should encourage us to tolerate and interpret ambivalence, ambiguity, and multiplicity as well as to expose the roots of our needs for imposing order and structure. . . . If we do our work well, 'reality' will appear even more unstable, complex, and disorderly than it does now. In this sense, perhaps Freud was right when he declared that women are the enemies of civilization" [4, p. 643].

REFERENCES

1. R. K. Unger, Psychological, Feminist, and Personal Epistemology: Transcending Contradiction, in *Feminist Thought and the Structure of Knowledge*, M. Gergen (ed.), New York University Press, New York, in press.
2. J. Stacey and B. Thorne, The Missing Feminist Revolution in Sociology, *Social Problems*, *32*, pp. 301-316, 1985.
3. K. J. Gergen, The Social Constructionist Movement in Modern Psychology, *American Psychologist*, *40*, pp. 266-275, 1985.
4. J. Flax, Postmodernism and Gender Relations in Feminist Theory, *Signs*, *12*, pp. 621-643, 1987.
5. K. Deaux and B. Major, Putting Gender into Context: An Interactive Model of Gender-related Behavior, *Psychological Review*, *94*, pp. 369-389, 1987.
6. R. K. Unger, Through the Looking Glass: No Wonderland Yet! (The Reciprocal Relationship between Methodology and Models of Reality), *Psychology of Women Quarterly*, *8*, pp. 9-32, 1983.
7. S. L. Bem, The Measurement of Psychological Androgyny, *Journal of Consulting and Clinical Psychology*, *42*, pp. 155-162, 1974.
8. ——, Gender Schema Theory and Its Implications for Child Development: Raising Gender-aschematic Children in a Gender-schematic Society, *Signs*, *8*, pp. 598-616, 1983.
9. M. Culley and J. E. Butler, Black Studies and Women's Studies: An Overdue Partnership, in *Toward a Balanced Curriculum*, B. Spanier, A. Bloom, and D. Boroviak (eds.), Schenkman Publishing Company, Cambridge, 1984.
10. J. E. McGrath, Continuity and Change: Time, Method, and the Study of Social Issues, *Journal of Social Issues*, *42*:4, pp. 5-19, 1986.

PART I

Women's Consciousness: Public and Private Images

The chapters in this section illustrate some of the complex issues raised when one considers various aspects of consciousness. Although consciousness is a very popular term in psychology these days, there is little agreement about what is implied when the word is used. In these papers, consciousness is examined in terms of women's awareness (which may be multilayered or even contradictory), by their subjective response (as either interpreted by themselves or another), and by the role of self-knowledge (or lack thereof) in altering personal reality.

An important contribution of these chapters is their focus on situational context as a determinant of consciousness. Thus, Pope focuses upon the lives of women in literature. She discusses such issues as the distinction between oneself and one's role, the hidden versus the public actor, and the extent to which one acts upon oneself to produce the image that others expect. Helson explores, in depth, the relationship between the life and work of one early female fantasy writer, Edith Nesbit. She looks at changes in her life circumstances and the way it was reflected (probably largely unconsciously) in her subsequent creative efforts. She notes that developmental change appears to be more evident in Nesbit's creative fantasies than in her overt behavior. Howe, in contrast, analyzes students assigned to write their mothers' biography rather than professional writers. Her findings suggest that the reconstruction of the past life of someone important to oneself can have important effects in changing present relationships.

Both Snoek and Stewart and Malley consider aspects of self-consciousness and personal change. Stewart and Malley suggest that objective personal circumstances (in terms of various work and family role combinations) may be less important for women's life satisfaction than how they perceive these circumstances. Their work exemplifies the active role of the individual in structuring personal reality, but may be limited by the privileged group of women that they studied. Snoek also suggests that individuals may restructure their reality, but warns that such restructuring may first require public validation that personal problems are not just the responsibility of the individual enduring them.

In the most traditionally social psychological paper in this section, Towson and her associates analyze the problems raised for individual women by expectations about members of her group. Individuals with whom the woman interacts may communicate their expectations and produce gender-consistent behavior by way of what has become known as the "self-fulfilling prophecy." This process represents an excellent example of what social constructionists mean by negotiated understanding. One unresolved issue here is the extent to which conscious awareness of such social mechanisms alters the individual's response to them.

Some of the questions raised by these chapters include: Do women possess a public and a private awareness? How do we measure these different forms of consciousness? If women's awareness is more bifocated than men's, how can we account for this difference? What impact does multiple awareness have upon women's lives? Are different perceptions about personal reality available to the individual at any time or are they evoked by particular circumstances? What is the relationship between insight and the quality of one's life? Is insight necessary for personal change to occur? What limits exist for the individual in the reconstruction of her reality? Do universal biological realities lead to the similar construction of different psychological norms for females and males across time and place? How generalizable are women's realities across culture, race, or social class?

FURTHER READINGS

Apfelbaum, E. Relations for Domination and Movements for Liberation: An Analysis of Power between Groups, in *The Social Psychology of Intergroup Relations*, W. G. Austin and S. Worchel (eds.), Brooks/Cole, Monterey, 1979.

Dion, K. L. Women's Reactions to Discrimination from Members of the Same or Opposite Sex, *Journal of Research in Personality*, *9*, pp. 294-306, 1975.

Kahn, A. S. and J. D. Yoder. Psychology and Feminism: From Social Change to Psychotherapy, unpublished paper, 1987.

Laws, J. L. The Psychology of Tokenism: An Analysis, *Sex Roles*, *1*, pp. 51-67, 1975.

Rosenthal, N. B. Consciousness Raising: From Revolution to Re-evaluation, *Psychology of Women Quarterly*, *8*, pp. 309-326, 1984.

Sherif, C. W. Needed Concepts in the Study of Gender Identity, *Psychology of Women Quarterly*, *6*, pp. 375-398, 1982.

CHAPTER 1

Sex in Psychological Paradigms—from Behavior to Cognition

RHODA KESLER UNGER

Once upon a time I was a confirmed behaviorist. In principle, this meant that I believed effects derived from orderly determinist causes, that the subjective aspects of behavior were irrelevant, and that the best studies required maximal distance between experimenter and subject. In practice, this meant that my first major research, my doctoral dissertation, involved making lesions in the caudate nucleus of rats and examining their effects upon temporal and spatial alternation by means of operant conditioning procedures. If I thought of sex professionally at all, I saw it as a variable which could neither be manipulated nor controlled and therefore of very little scientific interest. Even the rats were male.

In some ways my assumptions at that time about the lack of scientific value in the study of sex reflected the state of psychology as a whole. Buss has described psychology as having undergone a paradigm shift in recent years: from a view that reality constructs the person (assuming an invariant stable set of causal variables whose past actions determined present behavior) to a view that the person constructs reality (acknowledging the important function of the persons' view of themselves and their circumstances in formulating their behavior) [1]. In theory and in research, the study of sex and gender exemplifies this shift in perspective.

For those who are unfamiliar with recent work in this area a brief discussion may be useful. First, researchers in the area became dissatisfied with the data base on which assumptions about sex differences were based [2-4]. Still later, they questioned whether sex differences were anything more than a description of behavior rather than an explanation for it [5]. The recognition that sex was more than a mere biological dichotomy—female or male—brought into the social sciences a number of new terms about whose definition there is not yet complete agreement. These terms illustrate some of the complexities that have been brought to what was previously thought of as a discrete organismic variable.

It has been found necessary to discriminate between sex as a subject variable–what males and females do or say about themselves or others (the traditional area of sex differences)–and sex as a stimulus variable–how people respond to a stimulus person who is either female or male [6]. It is also necessary to distinguish between sex and gender–referring to those characteristics assigned to a particular sex by sociocultural assumptions and practices [5]. For convenience, these can be termed masculinity and femininity if it is recognized that different cultures recognize different trait constellations as appropriate to one or the other sex [7]. The extent to which the relationship between sex and gender is biologically programmed is unknown due to the fact that virtually no aspect of the human environment is sex-blind [8]. A few studies indicate, however, that under some circumstances self-ascribed gender traits or sexual preferences can be a better predictor of behavior than biological sex [9, 10].

Analysis of the effects of sex and gender is made more complex by findings that suggest that perception of one's own gender identity can serve as a cognitive cue for various instrumental and expressive behaviors [11]. An extensive and controversial literature has developed on such issues as the extent to which instrumentality and expressiveness encompass the domain traditionally assigned to masculinity and femininity [12, 13]; whether a personality constellation combining traditional masculine and feminine traits (known as androgyny) predicts behavior associated with sex-typing in our society [14, 15]; and the degree of relationship between personality traits and socially prescribed sex-typed roles [16, 17].

The term sex-role is also being reexamined by the new psychology of sex and gender. As Carolyn Sherif has noted the concept of sex-role is a curious one because it is one of the few concepts (if not the only one) that uncritically couples a biological term with a sociological one: "Thus, the concept suffers double jeopardy from myths about sex smuggled in uncritically and from denotative confusions in the sociological concept of roles." [17, p. 392] Theorists in the area have questioned the extent to which sex roles are internalized [18], the extent to which so-called sex stereotypes are actually stereotypes based on the differential distribution of females and males in various social roles [19], and the degree to which fears that are widely believed related to gender such as fear of success among women may actually be fear of role deviant behavior [20]. As in all cultures, sex roles serve both a normative and a prescriptive function–they define behaviors that are considered both typical and desirable [21].

Interest in sex roles has forced psychologists to take a look at the world outside of the laboratory. "Traditional" sex differences are more likely to appear in the real world than in the laboratory and are more likely to appear in public than when people believe themselves to be unobserved [22]. A major factor that is probably responsible for these differences is the role of differential status in the regulation of interpersonal relationships. A number of theorists and researchers have dealt with sex as an ascribed status characteristic. There have been repeated suggestions that relationships between the sexes parallel relationships between people of the same sex who possess different degrees of social power and status, in which the more powerful person assumes control and the less powerful defers [23-25].

Still other research indicates that sex is a significant label in the categorization of others as well as the self. Sex is the category chosen first by most people when asked for a description of an individual with whom they have had a brief interaction [26]. People will also choose sex in a problem solving task involving the selection of a particular individual from a group that is differentiated in a number of stimulus characteristics even when sex is a statistically less valuable cue than some other qualities of the members of the group. Individuals are more likely to be given a deviant label or even their normal behaviors may be described as deviant if they are viewed as distinctive within a group [27, 28]. People selectively describe their own properties as distinctive depending on their statistical probability within particular reference groups. Thus, when asked "Who are you?," both children and adults respond with sex-related categories when these characteristics are rare in members of their families or within their classrooms [29].

In sum, the work summarized above represents the other side of the paradigm characterized earlier as "the person constructs reality." In the new psychology of sex and gender, maleness and femaleness are viewed largely as social constructs that are confirmed by sex-characteristic styles of self-presentation and the differential distribution of females and males into different social roles and statuses and maintained by intrapsychic needs for self-consistency and the need to behave in a socially desirable manner. Most of the work to be presented in this volume derives from this paradigm.

At this point some readers may have noticed an omission of two areas from this discussion—the psychology of women and feminism. Indeed, much of the work in this series and in the field as a whole focuses on the behavior of women in general or upon the unique personal experiences of particular women. This is partly a response to the relative neglect of these areas within traditional disciplines, but also reflects the "state of the art" as it exists today. There is no *a priori* reason why the psychology of sex and gender needs to focus on women. In fact, the work of Joseph Pleck provides similar analyses with a focus upon men [21]. Since, however, particular life experiences of the investigators may predispose them to certain aspects of the lives of their subjects it is perhaps not surprising that most of the work in the field is conducted by women about women [30].

Some of the chapters in this book derive from a feminist perspective although this theoretical orientation was neither necessary nor sufficient for inclusion.

Since feminism is a controversial term–indicating for some a lack of objectivity in scholarship–it may be useful to offer a limited exploration here (Feminism probably has as many definitions as there are feminists, as might be claimed for psychology and psychologists). The feminist perspectives offered by some contributors to this volume include: willingness to accept women's personal experiences as valuable data; unwillingness to make value judgments about the relative worth of particular gender-related traits with a preference for androgyny as a combination of the strengths of both sexes; desire to expand existing scholarly bodies of knowledge by considering and including information from and about women; and awareness that integration of such information will benefit both sexes and society as a whole. Feminist theorists of either sex appear to be more aware of the role of power and status inequities within social and disciplinary groupings and to be more sensitive to the role of hidden assumptions in values and ideology in formulating what we believe we know about the world [31]. In the final analysis, however, we are probably no more active in constructing reality than are others proceeding from different ideological points of departure.

Does a belief that gender is largely a product of social construction mean that I am no longer a behaviorist? Yes, but it certainly does not mean a complete abandonment of all long-term antecedents of sex-related behaviors. Some physiological and early experiential factors are probably important in behaviors that are more characteristic of one sex than of the other. One cannot, however, make global generalizations in this area. Each behavior must be examined in terms of how it is influenced by self-awareness, role prescriptions (and the degree to which each role is internalized), group composition (and how one apprehends one's membership in the group), etc. as well as in terms of past realities in whatever form. There is a need for a dialogue between both paradigms.

Those who study consciousness may be particularly helpful in expanding the field. The traditional question, whether men and women are different, no longer suffices. The sexes are likely to be as different as they believe themselves to be. If sex and gender are viewed as "inside the head" phenomena, innovative strategies are required to determine how they function "out there."

REFERENCES

1. A. R. Buss, The Structure of Psychological Revolutions, *Journal of the History of the Behavioral Sciences*, *14*, pp. 57-64, 1978.
2. J. A. Sherman, *On the Psychology of Women*, C. C. Thomas, Springfield, 1971.
3. E. E. Maccoby and C. N. Jacklin, *The Psychology of Sex Differences*, Stanford University Press, 1974.
4. A. Frodi, J. Macaulay, and P. R. Thome, Are Women Always Less Aggressive than Men?, *Psychological Bulletin*, *84*, pp. 634-660, 1977.

5. R. K. Unger, Toward a Redefinition of Sex and Gender, *American Psychologist*, *34*, pp. 1085-1094, 1979.
6. K. E. Grady, Androgyny Reconsidered, in *Psychology of Women: Selected Readings*, J. H. Williams (ed.), W. W. Norton, New York, 1979.
7. P. R. Sanday, *Female Power and Male Dominance: On the Origins of Sexual Inequality*, Cambridge University Press, Cambridge, 1981.
8. R. K. Unger, *Female and Male: Psychological Perspectives*, Harper and Row, New York, 1979.
9. S. L. Bem, Sex-Role Adaptivity: One Consequence of Psychological Androgyny, *Journal of Personality and Social Psychology*, *31*, pp. 634-643, 1975.
10. S. C. Nash, The Relationship among Sex-Role Stereotyping, Sex-Role Preference, and the Sex Differences in Spatial Visualization, *Sex Roles*, *1*, pp. 15-32, 1975.
11. S. L. Bem, Gender Schema Theory: A Cognitive Account of Sex Typing, *Psychological Review*, *88*, pp. 354-364, 1981.
12. J. T. Spence and R. L. Helmreich, Masculine Instrumentality and Feminine Expressiveness: Their Relationship with Sex Role Attitudes and Behaviors, *Psychology of Women Quarterly*, *5*, pp. 147-163, 1980.
13. H. Markus, M. Crane, S. Bernstein, and M. Siladi, Self-schemas and Gender, *Journal of Personality and Social Psychology*, *42*, pp. 38-50, 1982.
14. K. Deaux, From Individual Differences to Social Categories: Analysis of a Decade's Research on Gender, *American Psychologist*, in press.
15. M. C. Taylor and J. Hall, Psychological Androgyny: A Review and Reformulation of Theories, Methods, and Conclusions, *Psychological Bulletin*, *92*, pp. 347-366, 1982.
16. J. T. Spence, K. Deaux, and R. L. Helmreich, Sex Roles in Contemporary American Society, in *Handbook of Social Psychology* (3rd edition), G. Lindzey and E. Aronson (eds.), Addison-Wesley, Reading, Massachusetts, 1983.
17. C. W. Sherif, Needed Concepts in the Study of Gender Identity, *Psychology of Women Quarterly*, *6*, pp. 375-398, 1982.
18. D. R. Kaufman and B. L. Richardson, *Achievement and Women: Challenging the Assumptions*, The Free Press, New York, 1982.
19. A. H. Eagly and W. Wood, Inferred Sex Differences in Status as a Determinant of Gender Stereotypes about Social Influence, *Journal of Personality and Social Psychology*, *43*, pp. 915-928, 1982.
20. F. Cherry and K. Deaux, Fear of Success versus Fear of Gender-Inappropriate Behavior, *Sex Roles*, *4*, pp. 97-101, 1978.
21. J. H. Pleck, *The Myth of Masculinity*, MIT Press, Cambridge, 1981.
22. R. K. Unger, Sex as a Social Reality: Field and Laboratory Research, *Psychology of Women Quarterly*, *5*, pp. 645-653, 1981.
23. M. E. Lockheed and K. P. Hall, Conceptualizing Sex as a Status Characteristic: Applications to Leadership Training Strategies, *Journal of Social Issues*, *32*, pp. 111-124, 1976.
24. N. M. Henley, *Body Politics*, Prentice-Hall, Englewood Cliffs, New Jersey, 1977.

25. R. K. Unger, The Politics of Gender: An Examination of Parallelisms, in *Psychology of Women: Future Directions of Research*, J. A. Sherman and F. L. Denmark (eds.), Psychological Dimensions, New York, 1978.
26. K. E. Grady, The Belief in Sex Differences, paper presented at the Meeting of the Eastern Psychological Association, Boston, April, 1977.
27. E. J. Langer and L. Imber, Role of Mindlessness in the Perception of Deviance, *Journal of Personality and Social Psychology*, *39*, pp. 360-367, 1980.
28. S. E. Taylor and S. T. Fiske, Salience, Attention and Attribution: Top of the Head Phenomena, in *Advances in Experimental Social Psychology* (vol. 11), L. Berkowitz (ed.), Academic Press, New York, 1978.
29. W. J. McGuire, C. V. McGuire, and W. Winton, Effects of Household Sex Composition on the Salience of One's Gender in the Spontaneous Self-Concept, *Journal of Experimental Social Psychology*, *15*, pp. 77-90, 1979.
30. R. K. Unger, Advocacy versus Scholarship Revisited: Issues in the Psychology of Women, *Psychology of Women Quarterly*, *7*, pp. 5-17, 1982.
31. R. K. Unger, Through the Looking Glass: No Wonderland Yet!, *Psychology of Women Quarterly*, *8*, 1983.
32. S. Z. Volentine and S. L. Brodsky, Personal Construct Theory and Stimulus Sex and Subject Sex Differences, *Imagination, Cognition, and Personality: The Scientific Study of Consciousness*, *3*:3, pp. 235-246, 1983-84.
33. D. E. Smith, A Sociology for Women, in *The Prism of Sex: Issues in the Sociology of Knowledge*, J. A. Sherman and E. T. Beck (eds.), University of Wisconsin Press, Madison, 1979.
34. J. Bernard, *The Female World*, The Free Press, New York, 1981.
35. C. Pearson and K. Pope, Consciousness in the Feminist Novel, *Imagination, Cognition, and Personality: The Scientific Study of Consciousness*, *1*, pp. 185-192, 1981-1982.
36. M. Fine, Coping with Rape: Critical Perspectives on Consciousness, *Imagination, Cognition and Personality: The Scientific Study of Consciousness*, *3*:3, pp. 249-267, 1983-84.

CHAPTER 2

The Divided Lives of Women in Literature

KATHERINE V. POPE

> I am wrapped in lies which
> do not penetrate my soul.
> As if the lies I tell were
> like costumes.
>
> Anaïs Nia.
> *House of Incest*

The discovery of the discrepancy between the self and the female role is made early on, whenever the girl child discovers that she is supposed to be pure and selfless and is not. Guilt feelings about having a wilful self and the determination to "be good" permeate the diaries of young girls such as Anne Frank and the thoughts of young fictional characters like Jane Erye. Later on, when the young woman begins to relate to men, the need to act out the appropriate, female role becomes a financial and social matter as well as a moral one. In George Meredith's novel of 1879, entitled *The Egoist*, Clara Middleton initially falls in love with and becomes engaged to Willoughby Patterne because in the eyes of society he is "the great match of the county." [1, p. 291] The idolized Willoughby turns out to be complacent, weak, ignorant, and even potentially cruel. Furthermore, he expects Clara to worship him like the others, indeed to be a "mirror of himself," and totally his, "every thought, every feeling." [1, pp. 38, 49] Clara is horrified with the situation in which she finds herself and is caught between her sense of duty to the social role she is assigned and her own instincts. The essence of the conflict is, in Meredith's words, "a dispute between the conventional idea of obligation and an injury to her nature." [1, p. 250]

Initially, Clara has no one to sympathize with or to validate her perceptions. Clara's father, for example, who is motivated by a selfish desire for the luxurious life of Patterne Hall, accuses Clara, when she makes a genuine plea for freedom and honesty, of being "mad as Cassandre," and the "epitome . . . of all the contradictions and multibilities ascribed to women from the beginning!" [1, pp. 359, 360] As for the others, Clara experiences that "horrible isolation of secrecy in a world amiable in unsuspectingness." [1, p. 224] Prior to her ultimate departure from the suffocating garden world of Patterne Hall and from the obtuse Adam who presides over it, Clara considers accepting the split life, and she wonders if it is possible to act out a false role of the devoted wife and to preserve her true self at the same time. She asks, "Can a woman have an inner life apart from him she is yoked to?" [1, p. 163]

The answer to the question is, of course, yes. The psychic energy and imagination that it takes to create the image is much greater, however, because of the greater degree of intimacy with those for whom she plays the part. The protagonist in Dorothy Bryant's recent novel, *Ella Price's Journal*, is a middle class, middle aged woman who returns to college in order to relieve the boredom of her life at home. Through her experiences at school, Ella develops a new sense of autonomy. She knows that her newly emerging ideas and feelings would threaten her husband and daughter, and therefore, during the time that she spends with them, she elects to "keep smiling and nodding" and "avoiding any subject that would lead to trouble." [2, pp. 72, 73] Anne Sexton, in her poem, "The Farmer's Wife," describes a woman who has had time to develop a completely separate inner life, which makes it possible for her to fulfill the role of the compatible wife and to endure years of an unfulfilling marriage:

> . . . she had been his habit;
> as again tonight he'll say
> honey bunch let's go
> and she will not say how there
> must be more to living
> than this brief bright bridge
> of the raucous bed or even
> the slow braille touch of him
> like a heavy god grown light,
> that old pantomime of love
> that she wants although
> it leaves her still alone,
> built back again at last,
> mind's apart from him, living
> her own self in her own words
> and hating the sweat of the house
> they keep when they finally lie
> each in separate dreams
> . . . . [3, p. 27].

As these literary examples suggest, the fictional woman may act out the restrictive, socially acceptable image as a way of protecting the male or as a way of avoiding conflict and social abuse. She also may assume a more aggressive attitude toward the dichotomy, using it to attain financial and social power. Daniel Defoe's eighteenth-century protagonist in his novel, *Moll Flanders*, is a brilliant and dynamic creator of her own social image and achieves great social and financial rewards as a result. Born in Newgate prison and immediately separated from her mother, Moll finds herself on her own in the world. As she grows up, she comes to understand that an eighteenth-century woman's greatest financial and social rewards come from an admiring male, and she therefore learns to act out the ideal of womanhood held by the economically and socially powerful characters with whom she must deal. She finds it prudent not even to reveal to them her true name. In accordance with the male ideal of what a woman should be, Moll appears innocent, weak, dependent, and blindly adoring, while in actuality she is experienced, strong, self-sufficient, and keenly aware of the realities of the world. ". . . Let them say what they please of our sex not being able to keep a secret," she remarks, "my life is a plain conviction to me of the contrary. . . ." [4, p. 350] A major cause of the split between the inner and the outer lives of traditional women is the ideal of female purity, to which Moll Flanders directly addresses herself, having learned from her own experience "how necessary it is for all women who expect anything in the world, to preserve the character of their virtue, even when perhaps they may have sacrificed the thing itself." [4, p. 147]

The fictional woman, like her real life counterpart, often sees the dichotomy between the self and the public image as a private joke, which she may or may not share with other women. Much of women's humor is based on the incongruity between the inner and outer self, between reality as women perceive it and the myths of male superiority, for example. Women's humor also exposes the myths of ideal womanhood which require that a woman pretend to be different from, often less than, what she is. In one of a series of essays, entitled *Crazy Salad*, the contemporary writer Nora Ephron describes with wit and candor the endless details involved in fulfiling the female image:

> . . . we learned that the way you sat, crossed your legs, held a cigarette, and looked at your nails—the way you did those things instinctively was absolute proof of your sex . . . I thought that just one slip, just one incorrect cross of my legs or flick of an imaginary cigarette ash would turn me from whatever I was into the other thing [5, p. 1].

Because this kind of humor has traditionally been very private, those of us who grew up female, particularly in the South, knew it not only as an oral traditional, but as a major characteristic of the older women, including the most elegant of ladies, with whom we spent our childhoods. Their remarks—about men, sex, marriage, their own socially designed facades and those of other women—varied in style from sharp wit to earthy and even bawdy comedy. Even now, I feel it would be inappropriate to repeat the humorous "asides"—made to themselves, to each other, and to the children (who heard or overheard)—with which the older women in my life punctuated their lives with men in conventional society.

This awareness of the split may be expressed in humorous terms, but it is often accompanied by bitter irony and even deep rage. The divided life itself may even become an act of revenge on those who require and then believe it. Sophia Tolstoy writes in her diary of her husband Leo's coldness toward her, which caused her to feel rejected and even invisible. While on the surface she appears to accept his treatment of her, she resolves, "Gradually I shall retreat into myself and shall poison his life." [6, p. 139]

When the tension of maintaining the dichotomy between the self and the social role becomes unbearable, the fictional woman may endeavor to deny or even to rid herself of the separate inner self, or she may withdraw into the inner self and separate herself finally from the social role and from the world that requires it. George Meredith documents in *The Egoist* the heroic struggle of a woman to express herself in a world that would cast her in an alien role, but he also appreciates how after a long period of playing the socially defined female part, the real self can essentially give up and disappear. He writes,

> Maidens are commonly reduced to read the masters of their destinies by their instincts; and when these have been edged by over-activity, they must hoodwink their maidenliness to suffer themselves to read: and then they must dupe their minds, else men would soon see they were gifted to discern. Total ignorance being their pledge of purity to men, they have to expunge the writing of their perceptives on the tablets of the brain: they have to know not when they do know. The instinct of seeking to know, crossed by the task of blotting knowledge out, creates that conflict of the natural with the artificial creature to which their ultimately-revealed double-face, complained of by everdissatisfied men, is owing. Wonder in no degree that they indulge a craving to be fools, or that many of them act the character [1, p. 167].

The traditional woman's denial of the existence of her separate self often results from her belief that any alternative life would be either impossible or even less fulfilling than her present confined and fragmented state. She is taught that "out there" she will be even less happy, have even less choices, and be even more lonely. Thus she will struggle throughout her life to fit her foot into a glass slipper that is too small, and be unable even to admit to herself or to tell anyone about the pain for fear they will find out that she does not fit as she has been taught she should. Sophia Tolstoy's diary records a tragic example of the denial of the alienated self. In it she recounts her intense emotional suffering that resulted from being married to a cold and preoccupied man, suffering that eventually lead to a mental breakdown. At times, however, she insists that no problem exists: "It makes me laugh to read over this diary. It's so full of contradictions, and one would think I was such an unhappy woman. Yet is there a happier woman than I? It would be hard to find a happier and more friendly marriage than ours. Sometimes, when I am alone in the room, I just laugh with joy, and making the sign of the cross, say to myself, 'May God let this last many, many years. . . .'" [6, p. 144]

Furthermore, the female character who is continually discounted, ignored, and instructed by those around her comes to doubt the validity of her separate self. In Gothic novels, for example, the female protagonist, who perceives the evil before anyone else, has difficulty dealing with the mysterious forces and events that threaten her life because the others tell her that she is just imagining things, and she, initially at least, believes them. The woman in Charlotte Perkins Gilman's *The Yellow Wall-paper* is isolated in the upstairs room of the country lodgings where her husband has taken her for a vacation, and she continues to defer to his judgment about what is best for her until his confinement of her so disorients her that she resorts to crouching round and round the room, peeling off the wallpaper in an effort to free the woman she perceives to be trapped there. In the beginning of the story, the protagonist explains that her husband, John, who is "practical in the extreme," is

> . . . a physician, and *perhaps*–(I would not say it to a living soul, of course, but this is dead paper and a great relief to my mind)–perhaps that is one reason I do not get well faster.
>
> You see he does not believe I am sick!
>
> And what can one do?
>
> If a physician of high standing, and one's own husband, assures friends and relatives that there is really nothing the matter with one but temporary nervous depression–a slight hysterical tendency–what is one to do?
>
> My brother is also a physician, and also of high standing, and he says the same thing.

She explains how she disagrees with their ideas and believes that "congenial work, with excitement and change would do me good."

> I did write in spite of them; but it *does* exhaust me a good deal–having to be so sly about it, or else meet with heavy opposition.
>
> I sometimes fancy that in my condition if I had less opposition and more society and stimulus–but John says . . . [7, p. 160].

Thus, the split between the woman's perceptions and consensus reality is blamed on the self, and the woman goes mad, or even kills herself, like Edna Pontillier in Kate Chopin's *The Awakening*.

The opposite danger is that, in a desperate bid for freedom and selfhood, she may retreat into the inner self and detach herself from the external world entirely. The female character who experiences years of brutalized feelings, dismissal, and disapproval, may become deadened to human relationships, as does Helene, in Joyce Carol Oates's contemporary novel, *Wonderland*. At the end of the novel, when Helene suddenly senses that her involvement with anything outside herself has ended, she is ecstatic: "Good! It was good! Her heart was pounding fiercely. The erotic glow in her loins, so teasing and warm, had spread lightly through her body now, light as May air, harmless. She was fulfilled. She was free of the man who hurried beside her, who could not love her now, and she was free of her husband, her daughters, the people in the park, her own youth. It was over: the tyranny of her body, the yearning for other bodies, for talking and touching and dreaming and loving. She had freed herself. It was over for her." [8, p. 424]

Finally, the female character who continues to live the divided life may develop a world of fantasy and daydreams, an imagined world in which, in effect, either the self or the role temporarily disappears. The appeal of romantic escape literature and dreams is that the woman can imagine herself to be all that society requires–pure, sexy, nurturing, beautiful, emotional, weak, etc.–and adequately rewarded for being perfect. Thus, she is relieved not only of the guilt and anger but also of the psychic demands of her real life struggle to be what she is not. Certain fictional women actually live in three time-space realms–the inner life, the public image, and the fantasy world–and the imagination is responsible for creating both the second and the third. In Katherine Mansfield's short story, "The Tiredness of Rosabel," the protagonist is a lonely young woman who lives in a dingy, gas-lit room; by day she is required to be a deferring, pleasant, dedicated worker in a milinary establishment. Because she serves rich young couples in the shop and because she has internalized the conventional myths about their ideal lives, she daydreams throughout the story about being a happy, wealthy ideal woman with a loving, rich husband, a house full of rooms with fires and roses and a French maid to serve her, dinners at elegant hotels, and more.

As I explained in an article entitled, "Consciousness in the Feminist Novel," which was published in this journal in the spring of 1982, the fictional woman also may imagine her real self acting spontaneously, free of her socially restrictive role. One of Joanna Russ's characters in her science fiction novel, *The Female Man*, vents her anger by imagining Jael, a future woman, who kills obnoxious, chauvinistic men without guilt. In Erica Jong's *Fear of Flying*, Isadora Wing fantasizes making love in public to a Black woman who is also a famous writer. This kind of fantasizing about what the real self would do can be the beginning of the healing process as the woman begins to imagine the life that fits her and that she wants to live.

The subject of the divided lives of women in literature has other dimensions and implications which I do not have room to explore here. Some of these issues and others regarding the divided life are dealt with in greater detail in *The Female Hero in American and British Literature*, which is much more of a psychological study than the title suggests [9].[1] One interesting effect of the divided life, for example, is that the woman with great energy and intelligence is directed by society to apply those dynamic human qualities to her restricted

[1] *The Female Hero in American and British Literature* uses literary examples to define the psychological stages of a woman's life journey.

conventional life. Specifically, the woman with the skills to run a large company traditionally devoted all her psychic energy and abilities to living for and *through* the members of her immediate nuclear family, usually no more than three people. The results in literature and in popular culture, as in real life, tend to be either ridiculous or frighteningly destructive. In Philip Roth's modern novel, *Portnoy's Complaint*, the overbearing mother is somewhere in between. Jane Austen's eighteenth-century protagonist in the novel, *Emma*, is also aggressive and intelligent but uses her abilities in the social behavior appropriate to women, manipulating the lives of those in her immediate social world with almost disastrous results. Alexander Pope's Belinda in *The Rape of the Lock* is one well-known example of the woman who devotes all her artistic imagination to creating an attractive physical appearance. Isadora Wing, in Erica Jong's *Fear of Flying*, remarks: "When I think of all the energy, all the misplaced artistic aggression which my mother channeled into her passion for odd clothes and new decorating schemes, I wish she had been a successful artist instead." [10, p. 149]

The psychological value of these fictional portraits, to which those of us who read and study and write and teach literature as well as those who use it as a tool of therapy will attest, is that it provides a source of identity and validity for the woman who is struggling with debilitating and alien cultural assumptions about herself. These fictional portraits are a form of realistic fantasy, a therapeutic vehicle through which women recognize their own situations and validate their own perceptions. The therapeutic value of literature by and about women results from the fact that in the fictional accounts the self behind the role is more visible than it is in the everyday world of appearances. Furthermore, the explicit statement that accompanies the imagery helps the reader to understand her own behavior and that of others. The reader sees herself as not alone in her experiences. She also comes to understand that, as with Blacks and others out of power in society, what appears to be weak, evil, or crazy behavior is not proof of society's negative definition of women but a consciously created image devised to protect and benefit the self. And as Simone de Beauvoir points out in *The Second Sex*, "To *make* oneself an object, to *make* onself passive, is a very different thing from being a passive object." [11, p. 379] Finally, the reader also sees the ways in which the social role, which she has been told is beneficial to her, is in fact detrimental.

Literature as a vehicle of therapy for women is more important than for others out of power in society—racial minorities and the lower classes—because while the others return at the end of the day to their own communities to acknowledge the role playing, the woman continues to live intimately with those for whom she plays the role of the pure, selfless, nurturing, emotional, passive daughter, wife, and/or mother, and often is unable to confide in anyone. Moll Flanders confides only in the reader. In turn, the fictional characters and their creators may act as friends, a kind of support group, for the reader, who communes with her own true feelings only in the process or as a result of reading the story. She may, like Ella Price, in

Bryant's *Ella Price's Journal*, discover in the process of reading how she really feels. The middle aged Ella writes in the journal that she keeps for her English class: "Sometimes I feel bitter about being a woman. Maybe it's just these books I'm reading, but I don't think so. I think I've always felt that way. But I never said anything because I was afraid of what people would think." [2, p. 62] As Charlotte Perkins Gilman's protagonist in *The Yellow Wall-paper* and Bryant's Ella Price suggest, writing often serves a similar therapeutic purpose.

The increasingly visible female point of view in our society has also made it possible to more fully understand and appreciate that self that previously was hidden not only from the world but often from the woman herself. The woman who insists upon healing the split between the female self and a woman's role in the world is perhaps best symbolized by the child in the fairy tale of the emperor's new clothes, who speaks out honestly of her own as well as of the male's demythologized nakedness. George Meredith and a growing number of men in our own world are beginning to understand how degrading it is for *them* to live in a society of disguised women. Meredith would undoubtedly urge men to read literature by and about women, realizing that the full selfhood of women publicly expressed and nurtured is essential if men are to be fully developed human beings as well. He writes in *The Egoist*: "Supposing you want it done wholly [the civilizing of men], you must yield just as many points in your requisitions as are needed to let the wits of young women reap their due harvest and be of good use to their souls. You will then have a fair battle, a braver, with better results." [1, pp. 167-168]

REFERENCES

1. G. Meredith, *The Egoist*, Houghton Mifflin Company, Boston, 1958.
2. D. Bryant, *Ella Price's Journal*, New American Library, New York, 1972.
3. A. Sexton, *To Bedlam and Part Way Back*, Houghton Mifflin Company, Boston, 1960.
4. D. Defoe, *Moll Flanders*, Washington Square Press, New York, 1966.
5. N. Ephron, *Crazy Salad: Some Things About Women*, Bantam Books, New York, 1980.
6. S. Tolstoy, Sophia Tolstoy (1844-1919), in *Revelations: Diaries of Women*, M. J. Moffat and C. Painter (eds.), Random House, New York, 1975.
7. C. P. Gilman, *The Yellow Wall-paper* in *Who Am I This Time? Female Portraits in British and American Literature*, C. Pearson and K. Pope (eds.), McGraw-Hill Book Company, New York, 1976.
8. J. C. Oates, *Wonderland*, Fawcett Publications, Greenwich, Connecticut, 1971.
9. C. Pearson and K. Pope, *The Female Hero in American and British Literature*, R. R. Bowker, New York, 1981.
10. E. Jong, *Fear of Flying*, Holt, New York, 1974.
11. S. de Beauvoir, *The Second Sex*, Knopf, New York, 1957.

CHAPTER 3

E. Nesbit's Forty-First Year: Her Life, Times, and Symbolizations of Personality Growth

RAVENNA HELSON

GENDER, LITERATURE "FOR CHILDREN," AND MIDLIFE INDIVIDUATION IN AUTHORS

If one analyzes themes and characters in the best imaginative literature for children, one finds that heroic and comic stories are written more frequently by men and "tender" stories by women [1]. But stories vary also with historical period, and so does the nature and amount of difference in books by men and women [2]. In all periods there has been overlap: some women have written about aggression and achievement, some men about relationship. Yet "tender" stories by men, such as *The Wind in the Willows* or *Charlotte's Web*, are not the same as those by women, such as *Heidi, The Secret Garden,* or *The Children of Green Knowe*. The almost equal participation of men and women in children's literature has contributed to a valuable diversity of stories. There are "fantasies" for every reader.

Imaginative literature for children is not only varied but also rich. Its richness is related, I believe, to the fact that the stories are so often produced out of the authors' frustrations, disappointments and yearnings. Many have been written after personal crises in middle-age. For example, Charles Kingsley wrote one of the first fantasies for children, *Water Babies*, at age forty-six, when he was in a particularly thorny phase of his career as clergyman and academic [3]. Louisa Molesworth, late Victorian, wrote her best-known fantasies immediately before and after dissolving her marriage at age forty. Frank Baum began writing for children at age forty-one, after a serious heart condition forced him to give up his work as a salesman. *The Wonderful Wizard of Oz* appeared two years later. These and other stories illustrate very clearly what Jung described as the individuation process, in which the ego establishes a relationship to childish, shadowy, and contrasexual parts of the psyche, and to the psychic totality referred to as the *self* [4]. If the process goes well, there is a sense of new potential and growth, a "rejuvenation" of personality, and the stories are symbolized in ways that make them appropriate for children. To the extent that what has been repressed or underdeveloped is not the same in men and women, their individuation stories may be expected to show different patterns. The differences are instructive, but so are the similarities, and the individuality of each story is the most important of all.

This chapter examines portions of the life and work of an Edwardian author, E. Nesbit. Although she was a professional writer and journalist from the age of twenty-one, she produced nothing very good until she was forty. Between the ages of forty and fifty she wrote half a dozen books that make her one of the outstanding contributors to children's literature. Her most original works are not characteristically feminine, but I will try to show that some of her problems and sources of imagery were directly related to sex and gender. Her life, work, and the reception of her work were influenced by her culture in many ways, including its attitudes toward gender roles. And yet, her life story and the appeal of her work transcend gender, and I shall try to convey that also.

There is an excellent biography of E. Nesbit by Doris Langley Moore [5], all the more useful because it is written without psychological theory in mind. There are also Nesbit's own recollections of her childhood [6]. She was an extravert with an interesting life and a prolific output. Here I will focus on material that lends perspective to an understanding of her middle-age and to the series of three outstanding fantasies written at this time.

YOUNG ADULTHOOD

Anybody who attended meetings of the Fabian Society in London in the 1880's or 1890's would have known Edith Nesbit Bland and Hubert Bland. Edith was an attractive woman with quick, birdlike movements of the head and a direct, sympathetic manner. She was bohemian, aesthetic, boyishly feminine. Her husband Hubert had a charming and impressive manner. Edith much admired his physical strength, his intellectuality, and skill in debating. The Blands were Socialists. In the area of sexual mores Hubert held strong conservative views for people in general; he himself was an inveterate philanderer. For example, the youngest of the Blands' four children had actually been born to Alice Hoatson, nicknamed "Mouse," a friend of Edith's who lived in the family and served as housekeeper. It wasn't all Hubert's fault that the Blands' marriage was tempestuous. Edith had emotional outbursts and eccentricities that were hard on the family.

Both Edith and Hubert enjoyed the company of fellow intellectuals and artists, and they entertained a lot. George Bernard Shaw, H. G. Wells, and many other Edwardians whose names one knows were among their close friends. Edith had a flair as a hostess, even when the Blands were quite poor, which they were for a long time. Soon after they married, (Edith seven months pregnant), Hubert contracted smallpox, and while he was critically ill, his business partner ran off with all his money. Soon after he recovered, he got a second case of smallpox. Edith was the sole provider for her husband and baby until Hubert began to take up journalism too. Adversity at this stage in Edith's life called out her courage and strengthened her endurance. But the habit of having to write a great many greeting cards, songs, horror stories, sentimental love stories, children's stories, and whatever would bring in money was probably one factor in the superficiality of most of her work.

She did not have disciplined work habits. She would delay writing until she had to shut herself off and work without stopping to meet a deadline. She could work this way because she was a very fluent writer, really too fluent for the best interests of her art.

Although Edith had serious aspirations as a novelist and especially as a poet, she did not believe in baring her soul before the public. In her view, this meant that she wrote "dramatic lyrics." Her sympathetic biographer, Doris Moore, describes her poetry as extravagantly artificial [5].

Edith craved attention, admiration, and affection. When a business meeting got too dull, she was the kind of woman who might interrupt the speaker to ask for a glass of water. She sent her books to eminent people and exchanged letters of mutual admiration. She was hurt if a friend, under her questioning, was reluctant to accord her a high rank as poet.

This narcissism and emotional dependence would seem to have had their origins in her childhood experience. She was the youngest of six children. Photographs show her to have been a darling child, and there is evidence that she often received attention and affection. But a brother died when she was in her infancy, and her father died of a lingering illness before she was four. After he died, his widow assumed financial control of the respected agricultural college of which he had been president. Then an older sister of Edith's developed tuberculosis and required considerable attention. So it is clear that in Edith's early years her mother had many preoccupations and was probably not a calm and consistently attentive "self-object." [7]

From earliest childhood, Edith suffered from fears. She describes a skit her brothers and sisters put on when she was about three. "I was the high-born orphan whom gypsies were to steal," she says, "and my part was to lie in a cradle, and at the proper time be carried away shrieking. I understood my part perfectly . . . and had rehearsed it more than once." Being carried away by her favorite sister was no reason for alarm. "Unfortunately," she continues, "there had been no dress rehearsal, and when on the night of the performance, the high-born orphan found itself close to a big black bonnet and a hideous mask, it did scream to some purpose, and presently screamed itself into some fit or swoon, was put to bed and stayed there for many days which passed dreamlike. But that old woman haunted my dreams, [and] haunts them still. . . ." [6, p. 51]

There were other incidents of this sort, phobias, and chronic night fears. From the age of seven she was sent off to one boarding school after another, first in England, later in France and Germany. She hated them all, longed to be with her mother, had frequent temper tantrums, could not do arithmetic, and continued to suffer from fears about skeletons, mummies, houses collapsing, and being buried alive. She was acutely sensitive to representations suggesting abandonment or of being overwhelmed by the unconscious.

Edith had written stories and poems from an early age. As she grew into adolescence and young adulthood, she adopted the attitude of taking conventional poses in what she wrote, rather than "baring her own soul." This must have been an effective means of controlling her emotions.

EARLY MIDLIFE

When Edith was thirty-six, her brother Alfred died, only four years older than she. His death may have influenced her, two years later, to write a series of recollections about her childhood. Most of her sketches treat the fears that I have mentioned and her unhappiness at school. The most pleasant of the recollections are about playing pirates and explorers with her brothers during several summer vacations in Brittany. In the course of writing these sketches, she found that memories began to flow in unexpected abundance and vividness–this was in 1898, when she was thirty-nine.

Soon after, she began what was to be her first great success. The Bastable stories were published first in adult magazines and later made into a book called *The Story of the Treasure Seekers*. These stories drew on her adventures with her brothers. The narrator is the eldest boy among six Bastable children, though there is an amusing pretense of disguising his identity.

Interlude: Peer Groups and Comic Style

In these real-life stories of imaginative children, E. Nesbit already showed two of the features for which she is well-known. One is the group of child characters. Victorian authors had used one child or a pair of children as central characters, and a relationship to admirable adults (usually female) figured prominently. In Edwardian fantasy, the child or animal peer group became pervasive, with adults cast in peripheral or villainous roles. Think of *The Jungle Book, Peter Pan, The Wind in the Willows*, and most of Beatrix Potter. This constellation was probably related to the loss of confidence in authority and the problems in sex roles that were painful in this era [2]. The group of child characters is so central in

E. Nesbit's work that it is considered one of her contributions to children's literature. In her case, the exclusion of adults may have been, in part, a revenge for their abandonment of her. (This motivation could be attributed to several other Edwardian authors as well.) More importantly, it expresses the absence of adults as felt resources of personality. Instead there are internalized sibling figures and childhood ego states.

The second feature of these stories is that they are comic. In children's literature, the merely pleasant story may be written by men or women, but the highly comic story is usually written by men. The reason is that the usual plot is about pretending to be heroic and manly by exhibitionism and wish-fulfillment (as a little boy might do) rather than by actually being heroic through discipline, endurance, courage, and goal-direction. The comic story usually mocks both the heroic ideal and the unheroic aspirant to glory. Ambivalence about masculine identity is an important complex in men, but as women are not expected to be heroes, their failings in this respect do not arouse in them the intense, contradictory, and complex feelings that are expressed in the creative comic story. However, women may have urethral-phallic impulses that cannot be acknowledged. They may be critical of the discrepancy between male pretensions and performance, or resentful of male bullying. Fond as E. Nesbit was of her siblings, she had suffered from their teasing on numerous occasions. The boys loved to frighten her by running after her with a scary calf's head, and once they thought she looked so much like a flower in her new party dress that they planted her in the garden. An important source of humor in *The Story of the Treasure Seekers* was probably a little sister's pleasure at "creating" her siblings, mocking them a bit, taking on her big brother's preadolescent voice, and then pretending to disguise his identity as narrator at the same time she fused with it and asserted it. There is also in the story a father who can't support the family. The family home is saved not by the mock-heroic attempts of the children but by the dead mother's "Indian uncle." This suggests aggressive humor directed both at Hubert's failures in the masculine role of provider and also at the brothers, whose repeated borrowing for ventures that never worked out had been responsible for Mrs. Nesbit's eventual loss of her home [5]. The theme of seeking treasure to save the home will recur.

SUCCESS AND HARD TIMES

The Bastable stories elevated E. Nesbit's status as an author. Hubert was becoming better known also, and early in 1899 the Blands bought Well Hall, a manor house with an ancient moat, orchard, ghost, and authentic Tudor outbuilding. The move to Well Hall must have seemed a very happy milestone, a sign that Edith and Hubert had achieved a position in status-conscious

Edwardian society. However, misfortunes began at once. And this was E. Nesbit's forty-first year.

First, the house was in worse shape than the Blands had realized. Much time, effort, and money were required to make it livable.

Then, Edith had a miscarriage or a stillborn child. Her last birth had been a stillborn, and she had been broken-hearted, refusing to give up the little body until forced to do so. This time she was especially grieved because she felt that she would never be pregnant again. Soon after this misfortune, Alice Hoatson gave birth to a child which for the second time turned out to have been fathered by Hubert. Edith again adopted the baby. The same month Edith's oldest sister, her "second mother," died.

After this, a physician who came to examine Edith told her that she must prepare for an immediate operation for cancer, and that her chances of recovery were remote. Three days later a specialist found the diagnosis to be entirely mistaken. The intervening week-end was carried off with the quiet drama of social entertaining as usual.

Finally, Edith's beloved son Fabian, very much like herself in personality, had a tonsillectomy just before his sixteenth birthday. The operation was performed at Well Hall. He was anesthetized, and never regained consciousness. After all else failed, Edith put hot water bottles and his sixteen candles around him but could not bring him back to life.

After Fabian's death, Edith was distracted, remorseful, bitter, and incapable of work or social activity. In her grief she cried out her outrage at the injustices she had suffered, and the children overheard secrets that until then had been well kept. It is my central thesis that the pressure of these misfortunes at this point in her midlife brought about an introversion of libido, the effects of which may be seen in the fantasy that she now began to write.

FIVE CHILDREN AND IT

E. Nesbit's new stories appeared in Strand Magazine in 1901, and were later published as the book, *Five Children and It*. The stories are about four children and a baby whose parents have taken a house for the summer. The children are thrilled to be in the country, so our attention is displaced a bit from the "real-life" details of the setting. The house is painted white, but it is said to be quite mediocre. It may be taken as a self-image. It is located on the edge of a hill, between a sand-pit and a gravel quarry. At the bottom of a long incline there are lime kilns and a big, red brewery. If setting conveys mood, the mood here is depressed, even hellish. In comic style, E. Nesbit says that at sunset "the limekilns and oast-houses glimmered and glittered till they were like an enchanted city of the Arabian Nights." This suggests a place of wonders, but also where Scheherazade had to tell 1,001 serialized stories before she was reprieved from execution.

The children are digging a deep hole in the gravel-pit when they begin to find bits of shells. Their father has told them that long ago the gravel-pit was a seashore. Then they find in the hole a creature who identifies itself as a Psammead, or sand fairy. It has "eyes" on retractible horns like a snail, ears like a bat, a tubby furry body like a spider, rat-like whiskers, and hands and feet like a monkey. Despite being this puzzling mixture of creatures usually thought ugly, the Psammead has an irritable dignity. He can grant wishes, although he has to swell his body up very large to do this and finds it tiring. He has one great fear, of getting wet. That would kill him. His wishes last only until sunset. After that things that have been wished for turn to stone. He grants the children one wish a day.

The book consists of a series of adventures in which the children get their wish but find that in various humorous ways it has led them into frustration or danger. Of course, getting her wish and then having everything turn out wrong is what happened to E. Nesbit at Well Hall. At one level, the theme is as depressed as the setting. But as one reads along, the stories are quite funny. They are also interesting, because the wishes explored and the consequences of their fulfillment evoke pleasure, excitement, and anxiety.

Five Children and It is dedicated to John Bland, the new baby born to Alice Hoatson, so a story about the baby is worth special attention. In this story one of the children becomes impatient with the baby, says nobody really wants it—otherwise the children wouldn't have to be taking care of it—and wishes (thoughtlessly) that everybody *did* want it. The Psammead has appeared unexpectedly, so this is the wish granted for the day. After staving off several people who want the baby, the children meet a band of gypsies who are determined to have it. The situation has become grim when the sun sets and all but one of the gypsies lose interest. The gypsy woman who remains is portrayed sympathetically. She still loves the baby but does not want to steal it, even though she has lost her own children.

The theme of the baby's not being wanted and then wanted so much that it was kidnapped by gypsies seems to refer to what Silvan Tomkins [8] would call a negative-affect "nuclear scene" created from E. Nesbit's early childhood experience and now amplified by recent traumata with analogs and "anti-analogs"—the latter being idealized scenes which capture the perfect negation of old dangers and disappointments and imply positive and active coping strategies [9]. The complex preconscious manipulations of the comic artist are apparent.

The Psammead

The Psammead is E. Nesbit's most original creation, and as he has a part to play in three of her books, it is important to try to understand what it is that has been discovered in this hole in the gravel-pit that was once a seashore. The

Psammead controls admission to a world in which wishes are marvelously gratified and impossible dangers confronted. Thus he seems to be a gatekeeper to the unconscious. There are many characters in myth, dream, and fantasy that personify processes that go on at the threshold between everyday consciousness and altered states of consciousness. Some of them are toll-collectors, border guards, ferrymen, door-keepers—guardians of the threshold.

Frightening or austere aspects of the gatekeeper express the idea that the ego may be paralyzed or "turned to stone" if it enters the alien region without the right protection. Because of E. Nesbit's high anxiety, this protection was very important. The rules of the Psammead's magic—one wish a day, magic stops at sunset—served to control the exploration of wishes. Of course, gatekeepers are often portrayed as treacherous tricksters, sometimes because one is allowed through and then gets into trouble. The children were suspicious of the Psammead for this reason.

The ugliness of most gatekeepers, and certainly of the Psammead, may be understood in relation to Jung's statement that the shadow stands at the threshold of the unconscious. Jung said that the individuation process usually started with midlife depression and unpleasant awareness of oneself and of life that one would prefer not to think about. But of course this kind of knowledge is essential if one is to develop, and acquaintance with the shadow may bring wisdom and possibilities of growth.

This whole set of ideas is implicit in the Psammead. It is a mixture of snail, bat, rat, spider, and monkey—creatures with preponderantly unpleasant connotations, but in myth and folklore most of them have positive value too. In terms of Jungian type theory [10], the Psammead's seclusiveness, heavy rationality, and polymorphic animality express the inferior opposites of E. Nesbit's extraverted feeling and intuition. But the children *converse* with the Psammead, and in time they learn that he is philosophically sophisticated ("time is a figment of the imagination") and shrewdly down-to-earth. When the imaginative and well-read children ask him for wealth "beyond the dreams of avarice," he says, "I can't go beyond dreams, you know! How much do you want, and will you have it in gold or notes?" And after they choose gold, he tells them to hurry out of the sandpit or they will be buried in guineas when he starts to work. This earthiness in the treatment of magic, along with the rules of magic, are features much commented upon and admired in E. Nesbit's work. Their effectiveness seems to come from the liveliness of inferior functions brought into play.

Jung said that acquaintance with the shadow brings wisdom. The main wisdom in *Five Children and It* is increased awareness of shadowy thought processes and the illusory appeal of wish-fulfillment: getting what they want through the Psammead repeatedly involves the children in misery and complications. In a later book, the Psammead becomes a guide in further explorations.

The Psammead is not merely a guardian of the threshold; he himself, with considerable effort, brings about the wished for conditions. Thus he represents a creative process that operates *at the threshold*, and this means a comic process. The comic figure is trapped between greed and anxiety at the threshold where it cannot "grow up" or become differentiated, but does manifest great versatility and dexterity. This is the world of the preconscious with its hypnogogic illusions, distortions, and double meanings. Magicians and clowns play with these processes as on a tightrope, emotions superficial (must not get wet), rules used as a balancing stick.

The threshold region is often depicted with sexual symbolism. Comic fantasy by male authors often has a hero with phallic characteristics (Pinnochio, Dwarf Longnose, Peter Pan). Sexual experience is a dramatic and familiar gateway to altered states of consciousness, and of course the penis symbolizes change of state particularly well. A vivid example is Alice's fall down the rabbit hole and her extreme changes in size as she tries to enter the locked door at the bottom. If the unconscious is represented as a womb and the barrier is personified, the gatekeeper, in a man's fantasy, is likely to be a symbol of maternal entrapment, such as the witch in Andersen's story, "The Tinder Box," or of paternal treachery, such as the false father in "Aladdin and His Wonderful Lamp." A relationship between central character and gatekeeper does not develop.

In E. Nesbit, the symbolism works out differently because she was female, and this is one reason for the novelty of the Psammead. The Psammead is located in a gravel pit. It has antennae that can extend or contract, and of course a snail's antennae are not really "eyes" but sensitive organs of touch. It has a tubby body that swells up in the process of gratifying the wishes of others. These and other details suggest that the Psammead is the underside of the female author as creator. Spiders, of course, spin "yarns."

Another woman author, well-known to E. Nesbit, had created fantasies in which children developed a relationship with a cuckoo (*The Cuckoo Clock*) and a lame raven (*The Tapestry Room*), who were first gate-keepers and then guides to inner worlds. This was Louisa Molesworth. Though it is reasonable to find that women's fantasies show a relation to their bodies and sexual experience, critics who have suggested a resemblance between the characters of Nesbit and Molesworth have not identified this as the source of similarity. Jung would describe their creatures as examples of a theriomorphic (earthy, primitive) animus. In his theory, the animus is a woman's guide to the unconscious.

In E. Nesbit's first famous fantasy, the children continue to represent her conscious personality with its absence of strong mature identifications. The Psammead is a representative of a variety of preconscious functions and processes, but he has also a perspective of centuries that makes him a primitive version of Philemon, the old man so important in Jung's experience of his psychic depths [11]. I think the conversations between the children and the Psammead represent what Jung called the transcendant function, a sustained communication between conscious and unconscious [12]. Once begun, the process continued, though new forces came into play.

THE PHOENIX AND THE CARPET

Five Children and It brought much public applause. The success was exhilarating, and the contact with the unconscious may have fired the author with new energies, because her next series of stories, later published as *The Phoenix and the Carpet*, was not depressive but manic.

It begins with the children setting off fireworks prematurely in their room. The damaged rug is replaced with a second-hand Persian carpet that, when unrolled, is found to have an egg-shaped stone in it. During an attempt on the part of the children to make magic with burnt offerings and sweet smells, the stone egg falls into the fire and hatches into the Phoenix. As the carpet proves to be of the flying variety, it takes the children and the charming, vain, self-congratulatory Phoenix on a number of adventures, including several visits to an ocean isle and subterranean locations. The Psammead, though he is called upon several times, never actually makes an appearance. The book has episodes more brilliant than anything in *Five Children and It*, but it is looser, coarser, and some chapters are rather silly. (At this point, the carpet, symbol of the weavings of the imagination, is discovered to have worn thin.) Towards the end of the book there is renewed vigor and control, with undoing of massive destruction by fire and rich gifts for all.

The phoenix, immortal bird that arises out of its own ashes, would seem to be an appropriate symbol for E. Nesbit's renewal of creative spirit after her many misfortunes. Her story also reminds one of the Icarus myth because of the conjunction of fire, flying, and water. Phoenix symbolism and the story of Icarus have in common the theme of ascension and movement from high to low, or vice versa, through phases of fire, air, and earth or water. The book seems to celebrate the ability to dip down to indulge tabooed impulses or curiosities and to fly away not only unharmed but energized (inflated). But fear and anxiety play an important role in maintaining the cycle. One remembers Icarus' last anguished cry to his father for help as his wings failed and he fell to the sea: people with an "Icarus complex" have lofty ambitions but lack self-sustaining powers (mature adult identifications), and the fate they risk is succumbing to their unconscious destructive tendences.[1]

E. Nesbit had a cycloid temperament, but there was probably something reactive about the mania in *The Phoenix and the Carpet* because her mother had

[1] It is unfortunately beyond the scope of this chapter to amplify the usefulness of the concept of the Icarus Complex in understanding E. Nesbit. See the review of the literature in Wiklund [13], especially the work of Fried, Murray, and Vaessen, and Wiklund's discussion of another woman author of comic fantasy for children, Astrid Lindgren.

recently died. In the last chapter of *Five Children and It*, an attempt to give jewels to the mother failed. In *The Phoenix and the Carpet*, the children are finally successful in salvaging a treasure and returning it to a mother figure in time to save the family home. They give their actual mother gifts, too. I regard these as attempts to restore value to the mother and to invest libido in a mother-identified personality. The manic energy may have accomplished something besides denial and defense, because the feminine self figures prominently in the last book of the series, *The Story of the Amulet.*

THE STORY OF THE AMULET

The third book of fantasy contrasts with the previous two in having a much more complicated and unified plot. Of all her books this is the one that E. Nesbit took the most trouble in writing. The plot and the order of emergence of different kinds of characters suggest that interrelated processes of confrontation and differentiation were going on in her psyche. Much of the material came from consultations with Wallis Budge, Keeper of the Egyptian and Assyrian Antiquities at the British Museum. They soon became friends, and then something more than friends. At one point Edith asked Budge to take her away from her marriage to Hubert. Budge was attracted to Edith and fond of her but he felt that his position at the British Museum precluded such an action. Extraverted feeling type that she was, Edith projected her thinking function on men, but now *The Story of the Amulet* involves, among other themes, the attempt to strengthen the thinking function in her own psyche.

At the beginning of the book, the four older children have been left with an old nurse. The father is away on duties as a war correspondent in Manchuria, and the mother is sick and has taken the baby with her to Madeira. The children find the Psammead in a pet shop. They buy him to remove him from this indignity. This is an important beginning, because in *The Phoenix and the Carpet* the Psammead was kept out of sight and used by the Phoenix to get the children out of jams in a cavalier, manipulative way. Now the Psammead regains his presence and austerity. Gratification of the children's own wishes is precluded, (though the Psammead still grants wishes of others when expressed in his presence, as his nature compels him to do). At once he puts them in touch with a higher form of magic than they have known before. They buy an amulet that he has observed in a curio chip. It is described as smooth, red, and softly shiny. In Wallis Budge's book on *Amulets and Superstitions* [14] this exact one is described as a Tjet, the vulva of Isis. (Scholars now call it the knot or girdle of Isis.) Isis, of course, was the Egyptian goddess much beloved for her resourcefulness and faithfulness as wife and mother. When Set tore her husband Osiris to pieces and scattered them, she found the pieces (all but one) and restored them. On another occasion she brought her son Horus back to life. Isis was a figure that would have appealed very much to E. Nesbit.

Back home, the children turn out to have only half of the amulet. The whole amulet, the Psammead tells them, would give generativity, integration, their heart's desire. But half an amulet is not without value: it will take them wherever they want to go to search for the other half. The "heart's desire" of the children is to bring back their parents and the baby. So now it is clear that this is a quest story, one that will describe E. Nesbit's search for the parts of herself that she does not know, with the hope of restoring the guiding factors in her personality and bringing a sense of renewed growth potential.

The amulet has strange marks on it that the Psammead says are important to be able to read. So the children take the amulet to a "poor learned gentleman" who lives upstairs. He is a scholar and says that the marks are pronounced "Ur Hekau Secheh" and that this is a Name of Power. (The term "Ur Hekau" was applied to an instrument used in the ancient mystic ceremony of "opening the mouth of the mummy," which served to establish communication between living and dead and to provide a dwelling place for the "double of the deceased." Wallis Budge had written about this. The symbolism is quite relevant to the story, if one regards the scholar as somewhat mummified.)

Under the instruction of the Psammead, the children sit down in a circle, put the half-amulet in the middle, and call out the Name of Power. The room becomes very quiet and very dark, and then a light comes and a serious sweet voice begins to speak. It tells them that they will have to go back in the past to find the other half of the amulet.

At this point there are already two important new characters. One is the poor learned gentleman, too gentle and dreamy to remember to eat his pork chops. He represents E. Nesbit's undernourished thinking function. The second is the voice of the amulet, which I take to be that of the Self, the whole feminine psyche.

The children's first venture (through an arch that appears when they hold up the amulet) takes them to a primitive village in very ancient Egypt. They manage to get inside a hut with a little maze inside that contains the amulet, but attackers appear, and they make a quick retreat to London.

Then they go to Babylon and ask to see the King, but he is away until evening fetching home his fourteenth wife. (The King and Hubert appear to have characteristics in common.) That evening three of the children commit sacrilege by asking the King directly for the other half of the amulet, and he condemns them to "the deepest dungeon." They have been separated from the youngest child, who has both the amulet and the Psammead, so the dungeon is deep indeed. However, the children call out their name of power and also a name they have heard the King use. A terrible fellow with a human-appearing body and an eagle's head appears. He is Nisroch, Servant of the Great Ones. I think he represents male power of the kind they have challenged or offended, and that this power can be terribly destructive to women if they turn its energy against themselves, as guilt or fear. But the children have called out "Ur Hekau Secheh" and are engaged in the mission of communicating with the past (or unconscious), so Nisroch serves this mission. The eagle's head suggests the power of vision. Nisroch obliterates a wall and brings into view the chamber of E. Nesbit's shadow, the imperious, irrational, narcissistic (but still rather likeable) Queen of Babylon. The missing youngest child, the Psammead, and the half-amulet are with the Queen. This shows the great importance of the Queen for the quest. In the next adventure the Queen erupts from the past into London (because she had wished to do so "on her husband's next hunting trip" in the presence of the Psammead) and she causes a lot of very funny trouble in trying to retrieve her jewelry from the British Museum before another wish causes her visit never to have happened.

The children, the Psammead, and the poor learned gentleman go together to Atlantis, where they see the temples of Poseidon and observe priests, kings, and bulls. Great waves break upon the land, a volcano begins to erupt, and they escape at the last nick of time. The primitive force of the masculine remains very dangerous and still impossible to assimilate.

On a trip to ancient Egypt the children encounter a somewhat sinister priest of Amen who becomes interested in them when he discovers that they can control fire (with a cigarette-lighter). Thus a power-oriented animus figure has energed in human form to take part in the main plot. After several other adventures, the priest erupts into their life in London, and a struggle ensues. He has the half-amulet like theirs, but the apparent twain merge into one still incomplete half (children and priest are both desirous). As the priest has a somewhat unscrupulous passion for knowledge, his joining forces with the children adds intensity to the quest. However, the Psammead keeps him from taking over. Because of common interests, priest and poor learned gentleman are drawn to each other. At the scholar's suggestion, priest and children together find the amulet by going back to a very ancient past when it was "whole and unguarded." They do not tarry, because there is strong magic at this claustral place at the dawn of life, and death is all about.

The denouement is swift. The children receive a telegram that their father and mother are returning home with the baby. The priest and scholar, with the help of the amulet—again impressively described—become one person. The children give the amulet to the scholar-priest. The scholar-priest politely wishes that the Psammead could obtain his own wish to go back forever to the sands of the past, so the Psammead does. Everyone seems to have obtained their "heart's desire," but there is an unsatisfactory lack of relationship between the reunited family and the now impassioned animus "upstairs" with the amulet. One realizes that the reinstatement of "the three"—mother, father, and child—may be a regressive dream of the narcissist, and not a strong position at all. We shall return to the consequences for E. Nesbit presently.

The Story of the Amulet is E. Nesbit's most differentiated treatment of the individuation quest. Unlike most Edwardian fantasy, it has important characters who are human and adult, even if frail. It differs from *Five Children and It* in being much less defended by ambivalences and negations; it has more daring and a farther reach. It differs from *The Phoenix and the Carpet* in its lack of exhibitionism and manic defense, and in its sustained direction. Note that the characteristics of the style are related to the psychological content of the story: it is concerned with increasing awareness of imperious and eccentric emotional states not well integrated into the personality (the author's shadow), an attempt to strengthen the thinking and planning functions (animus), and a vision—though flawed—of the possibilities of integration and renewal of personality through the Self.

E. Nesbit was now forty-seven. In the next two years she published several more books that show that she still had intermittent connection with the unconscious. Parts of these books are fascinating. But she seemed to have become ambivalent about the importance of the imaginative world and more concerned with love and responsibility (*The Enchanted Castle, The House of Arden, Harding's Luck*). Though these attitudes were probably a sign of personality growth, they may have led to changes in style and new characters that were not entirely successful. She never again wrote with the tautness that was the black-edged gift of the Psammead.

Did her quest make a difference in her life? Doris Moore describes E. Nesbit, approaching fifty, as still having the caprices and petulances of a child. On a trip to France, for example, shortly after the wedding of her daughter, she surprised custodians by taking a swim in the fountains at Versailles. Her bad moods were known to her household as "the Blights." But Moore quotes a letter Nesbit wrote to a young friend to show that she engaged in much self-examination about her temper and was working persistently to reduce its harmful effects.

The Queen of Babylon is so vividly and empathetically realized in *The Story of the Amulet* that one feels her creation may have changed the relationship between E. Nesbit and this shadow queen. But the passive, dreamy scholar and the dark priest were less life-like. In outer life, E. Nesbit had withdrawn some of her dependence on Hubert and Wallis Budge. Her conscious personality, however, was not able to take over the animus energies that now carried the power for personality change. This is the meaning, I believe, of the scholar-priest's being left "upstairs" with the amulet.

What happened was a cruel and unusual animus possession. Within a year after publication of the *Amulet* in 1907, E. Nesbit, who had never been able to do arithmetic, was engrossed in trying to learn mathematics so as to prove by cipher and Napierian logarithms that Bacon wrote the works of Shakespeare. She bought expensive rare books, studied Latin, and was undaunted by the antipathetic reactions of friends who thought the time, energy, and money that she poured into this pursuit was injurious to her creative productivity, responsible for considerable and long-lasting financial difficulties, and incomprehensible in one with a sensitive appreciation of Shakespeare and no capacity whatsoever for mathematics. Like a curse in a fairy tale, this passion lasted for ten years.

When Hubert died in 1914, Edith was devastated. She had no life-partner, no money, no work, no health, no children near, and World War I was grimly depressing. But three years later, a wonderful thing happened. At age fifty-nine she made a second marriage that was happy and peaceful. According to descriptions of her in her early sixties, a few years before her death, she was still charming, interested in almost everything, and deeply sympathetic to those with distressing problems. She retained her rapport with children, but was now less a child herself than a fairy godmother. She had become calmer, kinder, and more reserved. Moore quotes a friend from this time who felt that despite her social exterior she was "unworldly." She was often visited by an exceedingly amiable priest, the friend said, and "I gathered that she was often privately immersed in spiritual considerations, though she never at any time discussed them."

CONCLUSIONS

E. Nesbit grew up with strong fears of abandonment, poor impulse control, and, one may infer, ambivalence towards parental figures. However, there was also considerable achievement among her forebears and imagination among her siblings. Edith used what means her world offered to obtain the security and self-esteem that she needed so badly. She developed defensive patterns that would have kept her a "pseudo-writer"–one who writes to please an audience [15], had psychological processes of midlife not led her to closer contact with the unconscous.

Part of what Edwardian society offered her was a status as "modern woman." E. Nesbit was far from traditionally feminine in her literary ambition, use of her talent to support the family, friendships with men, love of sports and outings, and in her daring and adventurous spirit. On the other hand, home was precious to her. She was an erratic mother, but she shared the deep griefs of women over many ages after the death of a child. Her emotional dependence on Hubert and his compulsive philandering was a central aspect of her life and a painful exaggeration of traditional gender roles.

In some ways her work is "feminine." She could put babies into books as few other writers have known how to do, and her humorous domestic comments and attention to gender differences among siblings are those of a woman. In her experience of the unconscious, the Psammead served an important function, and I have argued that he was very much the creation of a woman. *The Story of the Amulet*, once analyzed, is clearly a woman's revelation of forces latent or ruling in her Psyche. But the basic characters in her three enduring fantasies are the immature children and the androgynous Psammead and Phoenix. No wonder that her work is not typically feminine. E. Nesbit had "both" family and career, but the inability to identify as an adult because of her dependence, emotional ambivalence, and boyishness is probably the basic dilemma underlying her comic style.

Works of creative fantasy usually emerge out of pain and limitation. This is particularly evident in Edwardian authors of fantasy for children, who all, male and female, had miserable childhoods, were severely handicapped in opportunities for mature identifications, and invented worlds of charm and delight without, or in opposition to, adult gender roles. E. Nesbit was one of those whose weakness and courage, limitation and imagination, made the Edwardian period a "golden age" in children's literature. Her fantasy is instructive today in another time of confusion and conflict in gender roles.

REFERENCES

1. R. Helson, The Creative Spectrum of Authors of Fantasy, *Journal of Personality*, *45*, pp. 310-326, 1977.
2. ———, Through the Pages of Children's Books and What a Psychologist Found There, *Psychology Today*, *7*:6, pp. 107-112, 1973.
3. ———, The Psychological Origins of Fantasy for Children in Mid-Victorian England, *Children's Literature III*, *3*, pp. 65-76, 1974.
4. C. G. Jung, The Relations between the Ego and the Unconscious, *Two Essays on Analytical Psychology (Collected Works 7)*, Princeton University Press, Princeton, New Jersey, 1966.
5. D. L. Moore, *E. Nesbit: A Biography*, Chilton, Philadelphia, 1966.
6. E. Nesbit, *Long Ago when I Was Young*, Watts, New York, 1966.
7. H. Kohut, *The Restoration of the Self*, International Universities Press, New York, 1977.
8. S. Tomkins, Script Theory: Differential Magnification of Affects, in *Nebraska Symposium on Motivation*, H. E. Howe, Jr. and R. A. Dienstbier (eds.), University of Nebraska Press, Lincoln, Nebraska, 1979.
9. R. Carlson, Studies in Script Theory: I. Adult Analogs of a Childhood Nuclear Scene, *Journal of Personality and Social Psychology*, *40*, pp. 501-510, 1981.
10. C. G. Jung, *Psychological Types (Collected Works 6)*, Princeton University Press, Princeton, New Jersey, 1971.
11. C. G. Jung, *Memories, Dreams, Reflections*, Randon House, New York, 1961.
12. ———, The Transcendent Function, *Collected Works 8*, Princeton University Press, Princeton, New Jersey, pp. 67-91, 1960.
13. N. Wiklund, *The Icarus Complex*, Department of Psychology, Lund, 1978.
14. E. A. W. Budge, *Amulets and Superstitions*, Oxford University Press, London, 1930.
15. H. Sachs, *The Creative Unconscious*, Sci-Art Publishers, Cambridge, Massachusetts, 1951.

CHAPTER 4

Telling Our Mother's Story: Changing Daughters' Perceptions of Their Mothers in a Women's Studies Course

KAREN G. HOWE

The role of mother in our society is characterized by complex and contradictory elements. Motherhood has been idealized and glorified at the same time that it is devalued as a profession. Images of motherhood in art, literature, film, advertisements, psychology and society have portrayed mothers in idealized, one-dimensional, polarized, and unrealistic ways, rather than as complex, multi-faceted human beings. These images of motherhood that pervade our society and our consciousness have shaped women's personal experiences as mothers, and daughters' perceptions of their mothers. As Rich discussed in her landmark book, *Of Woman Born*, motherhood exists on two levels: the societal institution and the personal experience [1]. Both levels have been influenced by myths and images, which also affect the relationship between mother and daughter.

This chapter discusses the societal images of motherhood, their effects on the daughter's perceptions of her mother, and how a mother biography assignment in a Women's Studies course changed the traditional and stereotyped view of the mother held by the students.

IMAGES OF MOTHERHOOD

Centrality of Motherhood

A major focus of the images of motherhood in our society is the centrality of the mother role to the woman's life and identity. One way to view the centrality is to examine Russo's concept of the "motherhood mandate" [2]. According to Russo, this refers to the social pressure on women to have at least two children, to "raise them well," and to keep any involvements in their own education, work, or public life secondary to this primary obligation. An example of this mandate is the common usage of the term "working mother." This term not only implies that women are not working when they are full-time homemakers, but also that a woman working outside the home is still primarily a mother, even in the work context. The parallel term "working father" is not a familiar one, since the father's primary obligation is seen as providing financially for the family.

A similar societal view is the "motherhood mystique" definition of motherhood discussed by McBride [3]. One aspect of this mystique is the idea that not only are children seen as the woman's primary obligation and responsibility, but also as her "ultimate fulfillment." Outside interests become secondary, or are seen as conflicting with the maternal role. McBride explains that the term "mystique" used here is similar to the "feminine mystique" term used by Friedan [4]: both describing social patterns which limit opportunities for women. In contrast, the father role is seen as part of a man's varied experiences, and is complementary, rather than incompatible, with other activities. Men are seen as fulfilled when they have lived long lives filled with many different experiences and achievements, rather than "ultimate fulfillment" through one activity.

An example of the exclusive absorption in childcare assumed by the social pressures of the motherhood mandate and the motherhood mystique is the following comment by a student in my Psychology of Women course:

> I've been thinking about our discussion in class and what my image of a Mom was. I am ashamed when I think of some of the things I thought and even said to her while growing up. I saw her as responsible for a number of undesirable chores from cleaning to changing diapers. I thought that was her whole life and it didn't seem like fun at all. So I got it into my head that life stopped when you become a Mom. You don't spend time with your friends or learn any more, you become a creature with no identity. The most important things were the kids and life revolved around them. And once those kids became mothers then life stopped for them and only revolved around *their* kids. I think that is why I felt this incredible push to get everything done that I've always wanted to do before I had kids.

This excerpt dramatically illustrates how the "ultimate fulfillment" image of motherhood fosters a one-dimensional perception of the mother and her interests.

Another societal image of motherhood in the same vein emerges from Oakley's analysis of the housewife and mother roles [5]. She discusses three components of a "myth of motherhood," which includes the ideas that motherhood is a natural and necessary experience for all women, that mothers need to have children for their own fulfillment as women, and that children need exclusive care from mothers in order to develop normally. As Oakley points out, myths serve to confirm traditional values, and this myth helps to perpetuate women's primary place as wife and mother, and reaffirms motherhood as the woman's most important responsibility.

These societal images—the motherhood mandate, the motherhood mystique, and the myth of motherhood—all emphasize the centrality of motherhood in the woman's life, and imply that outside activities detract from the quality of her mothering. In doing so, they also encourage a simplistic and one-sided view of women who are mothers.

The "Good Mother"

In addition to the centrality of motherhood, the defining characteristics of the "good mother" have been emphasized in psychological and social views of women. Contratto's interesting review of the history of views on mothers and mothering by twentieth-century psychological writers shows that even though beliefs about proper mothering changed over time, and on occasion contradicted each other, certain cultural themes were shared [6]. Mother was seen as "social sculptor," forming the citizens of the future, and her most important role was within the family as wife and mother, rather than in areas outside the home. Many of the writers focused on the natural or inherently maternal qualities of women, and highlighted the positive and/or negative effects of maternal behavior on the future development or behavior of their offspring. Contratto points out that in particular, post-World War II writers emphasized full-time mothering as crucial for the child's healthy development, at the same time warning of the dangers of bad mothering practices.

Social views of mothering have also defined the "good mother." As Lazarre has noted, while women are in reality diverse individuals, on the cultural level there is just one mythic image of the "good mother" [7]. Lazarre describes this image as follows: "She is quietly strong, selflessly giving, undemanding, unambitious; she is receptive and intelligent in only a moderate, concrete way; she is of even temperament, almost always in control of her emotions. She loves her children completely and unambivalently" [7, p. viii]. Similarly, in a study of mother-daughter relationships, Arcana describes the image of motherhood conveyed by the women she interviewed [8]: the perfect mother has constant sympathy and understanding, is constantly available and nurturant, despite any other factors, and is responsible for all aspects of the child's development.

Idealization

These descriptions of motherhood are idealized—they are not realistic or authentic descriptions of the motherhood experience. Yet these images persist and encourage one-dimensional portraits of mothers on societal and individual levels. The image of mothers in the media also contribute to and perpetuate such one-sided views. E. A. Kaplan's work on images of women in film discusses the unrealistic and idealized representations of mothers [9]. In her analysis of past and current films, Kaplan has found that mothers are usually portrayed in one-dimensional and polarized portraits. There are either Good (saintly, self-sacrificing, angelic) or Bad (evil, jealous, neglectful, sexual, transgressing, cruel, sadistic). In addition, Kaplan points out that in film, as in literature, the portrayal of the mother is usually from the child's perspective, particularly that of the son. There is a notable absence of the mother figure as portrayed from her own subjective viewpoint, which would be a vehicle for a more realistic representation of women and motherhood.

The idealization and polarization of images of motherhood in our society involve both cultural and psychological components. Chodorow and Contratto have discussed this theme in relation to the "fantasy of the perfect mother" [10]. They propose that children first know their mothers only in the capacity of mother, and develop a fantasy of a perfect, powerful mother. Later, the process of maturation should bring with it a recognition of the mother's subjective personhood. However, "people have trouble doing this and continue, condoned and supported by the ideology about mother they subsequently learn, to experience mothers solely as people who did or did not live up to their expectations" [10, p. 65]. Certainly the images of mothers discussed so far further contribute to this maternal fantasy. In a later paper, Contratto discussed how "psyche and culture merge here and reflexively create one another" [6, p. 170]. She describes how many women try to follow the powerful role prescriptions regarding motherhood, put forth by society and psychology; other women who want to explore alternatives define them as deviations from the prescriptions. Either way, the traditional norms are maintained and idealized; children are raised in environments shaped by these expectations, and are "culturally encouraged to maintain maternal idealizations" [6, p. 170].

An interesting demonstration of such maternal idealizations in contemporary adult women who are mothers themselves, is M. M. Kaplan's recent study of middle class mothers who were combining careers with motherhood. Through intensive interviews, Kaplan found that each woman had "a well-elaborated and *traditional* image of motherhood that affected her behavior and feelings about herself as a mother in dramatic ways" [11, p. 3]. These women described "good mothers" as selflessly devoted to their children, always enjoying their time with their children, and not allowing anything to interfere with their attention to the child, when at home. In addition, they felt that maternal anger, boredom, or impatience were unacceptable, and such negative feelings toward a child indicated "bad" mothering. A number of important themes emerge from these findings. Kaplan indicated that these images did not describe either the women's own mothers or their own mothering experiences, again suggesting the powerful influence of social messages and images. In addition, in their conversations, the women readily sorted maternal behaviors into the "good" and "bad" polarized images, yet according to Kaplan they also reported that they themselves rarely lived up to the "good mother" images. Rather than using their own experience to widen the definition of appropriate mothering, these women maintained the cultural image and felt that they did not measure up. Interestingly, Kaplan also reported that these mothers did not see their views within a social context, but felt they were discussing private visions of motherhood, not realizing how much that vision was shared with others and shaped by the culture.

The contrast between the idealized social image of motherhood and the more authentic personal experience has been eloquently described in "Anger and Tenderness," the first chapter of Rich's book, *Of Woman Born* [1]. Rich describes the often ambivalent, contradictory, and frustrating aspects of motherhood, as well as the overwhelming love and tenderness felt towards the children. In addition, she discusses the social taboos that have existed which prevent women from expressing these ambivalences, often encouraging them to experience them as personal inadequacies rather than responses to unattainable social images. In recent years, however, there have been growing numbers of accounts of the reality of the motherhood experience. As Rich states, "the words are being spoken now, are being written down; the taboos are being broken, the masks of motherhood are cracking through" [1, p. 5]. Such accounts are important for several reasons. In contrast to the emphasis on motherhood as the central and ultimate experience in a woman's life, as seen in societal images, these accounts more accurately portray motherhood as one aspect of a multi-faceted existence. Rich notes that "motherhood . . . is *one part* of a female process; it is not an identity for all time . . . it is not enough to let our children go; we need selves of our own to return to" [1, p. 18]. Thus, these accounts encourage a more complex vision of women who are mothers. In addition, they illustrate that the attempt to live up to the idealized images of "perfect mother" is a futile one—and clearly imply that the image of mother needs to be less idealized and less polarized to more accurately reflect women's experiences.

While such accounts of motherhood have been very important, by far the more widespread influence has been the societal image of the one-dimensional "good mother." When considering the mother-daughter relationship, the factors discussed so far converge to encourage daughters to see their mothers only as "mother," rather than as complex and multi-faceted women. In addition, researchers examining the psychological dynamics of the mother-daughter relationship have explored the complex ways in which that relationship is characterized by shared relational bonds, mutual identifications, and difficulties regarding separation and independence [12-16]. These factors further contribute to the daughter's view of mother being influenced by her own subjective perspective.

THE MOTHER BIOGRAPHY ASSIGNMENT

For the past seven years I have been teaching Psychology of Women at a state college. As in many other Women's Studies courses around the country, we sit in a circle, and students are encouraged to share with and learn from each other as well as from the instructor. We discuss reading material and use our personal experiences as women as illustrations, examples, or situations to analyze. I give the students a number of written assignments to encourage them to integrate personal experience with academic material, and the one that has the greatest impact on them is the mother biography assignment. It is based on a set of structured interview questions which I expanded from an exercise in Cox's book of readings on the psychology of women [17]. The questions elicit information about the mother's childhood experiences and influences, her relationship with her own parents, her work experiences, marriage, and interests. Students interview their mothers toward the end of the semester, record the answers, and write them up into a narrative of the mother's life. They also answer questions regarding their reactions to the interview and information learned, as well as regarding the nature of their relationship with the mother. If the student's mother is no longer living, the assignment can be done by interviewing relatives for the necessary information.

The Interview Questions

1. When and where were you born?
2. What were your parents like? (such as ethnic, religious, economic background).
3. What were the important influences on you as a child?
4. What was your relationship like with your mother? your father?
5. What is/was your relationship like with my father?
6. Did you work outside the home?
7. What are your main interests?
8. Are there some things that you have always wanted to do but never had the opportunity?
9. Student: Add two questions here of your own.

Questions Answered by Students

1. What are your earliest memories of your mother?
2. What is your relationship like with her—in the past and now?
3. What messages or advice did she give you about being a woman?
4. In what ways are you like or unlike your mother?
5. What have you learned from doing this biography assignment? Are there areas of your mother's life experience that you have learned about for the first time? Do you have any new understandings about your mother now?
6. How do you feel about you mother now?
7. What was your mother's reaction to being interviewed?
8. Other comments.

CHANGES IN DAUGHTERS' PERCEPTIONS

Beyond the Mother Role

The major and most dramatic effect of the mother biography assignment is to stimulate the daughter to see her mother as a *person*, separate from her identity as a mother. As we have seen, societal images of motherhood strongly encourage us to see our mothers primarily in that role. This assignment, within the context of the Psychology of Women course, encourages the daughter to consider her mother in a new light. The questions about the mother's early life force the daughter to see the mother as she was before she took on that role; the daughter must look at her, not with herself as the reference point, but with this young woman of the past as the reference point. The questions are very simple ones, but are rarely asked until the assignment. Thus, the daughter comes to see the mother in a new light:

> This assignment has given me great insight into my relationship with my mother. I have stepped back and seen my mother, really, for the first time.
>
> I feel as if I am meeting my mother for the first time.
>
> Most of the concrete information about my mother was not new to me. The more abstract things about her emotions, thoughts, and dreams were discovered for the first time.

The theme reflected here of seeing or meeting the mother "for the first time" is one commonly expressed in the mother biographies. Why is this view of the mother such a new one? Primarily because now the daughters are thinking about the mother beyond the role and its limited images. Thinking beyond the role allows the daughter to see her mother as a *person*, and the students recognize the importance of this new perspective:

> By writing my mother's biography, I was given the opportunity to look at her from a more objective view and see her as a person, rather than seeing her just in terms of her role as a wife to my father and a mother to me. I can see her as a person with a separate identity from her family. She is a person with her own needs to be satisfied and her own goals to be reached.
>
> I have learned to consider my mother as an individual with her own wants, needs, and desires. Instead, I used to see her as the "Mom" role and would place her in a stereotypic role. It's funny how all my life I have kept my Mom distant, depriving her of a personality or character. I stripped her of any individuality and only saw her as a role. Now, I'm beginning to see my mother as an individual with a life of her own.
>
> I realize now how little I've spoken with her about "her" and "her needs." I know very little about her as an individual, as a woman. I've always viewed her in a very selfish manner—"my mother," someone who has always been there for me. This assignment has given me great insight

> into my relationship with my mother. I believe I understand her much more now. I feel that we have gotten over a barrier, and will be able to relate to each other as women.
>
> I learned so much from doing this exercise. I learned that my mother isn't just my mother, she has a life and a personality, she is a woman and a person too. I experienced her fears, her doubts, which we don't like to think our mothers have. It was strange to see your mother in a new light, to talk to her like a friend. Now I hope our relationship can develop more as a friend to friend encounter rather than just the single dimension of the mother-daughter roles. We must have talked for hours and I was amazed and she was delighted every minute. I'm glad I had this journey to my mother's life.

These excerpts all reflect how the interview and biography encouraged the daughter to reflect on and focus on the mother's personhood. The sharing that goes on during the interview gives both women the opportunity to be more real, more authentic, less role-related in their interaction. The new perceptions of the mother appear to be refreshing and exciting to the daughters, and encourage a new kind of relating to occur. It is interesting to note that many of the daughters define this new sort of interaction as "friendship," suggesting an equality they feel lacking in the traditional mother-daughter relationship. By going beyond the roles, both women begin to relate to each other as *women*.

The next two excerpts further illustrate the theme of previously not knowing one's mother by using phrases related to darkness:

> I have not been close with my mother. I also kept her in the dark without allowing her to find the real me. She has also kept me in the dark, and when doing the biography she was a bit reluctant to answer my questions. I don't know if I will ever be best of friends with my mother, but I am aware of our situation and plan to slowly break away from the "game-playing."
>
> I've learned quite a lot from this assignment. I feel that I got to know my mother better as a person, not just a mother. This makes it easier for me to understand her. I feel a little closer to her now. I understand her better. I admire her now. I'm looking at her as a person now. I know our relationship will only grow from now on. This was a good thing for both my mother and myself. It opened a door for us that was closed and locked before. It's only open a crack but hopefully it will open a bit more a lot faster.

It is interesting to consider the phrases used in these excerpts in light of the societal images of motherhood discussed earlier. These excerpts reflect the blindness or darkness that is to a large extent caused by the role-playing involved in the mother-daughter relationship. Trying to live up to the societal images of "good mother" and "good girl," both parties have difficulty "seeing" each other as real people. In a similar vein, many of the terms used to describe the mother role and its societal images also conveyed the theme of non-authenticity: Rich discusses the "masks" of motherhood [1], McBride the "mystique of motherhood [3], Oakley the "myth" of motherhood [5].

Authenticity

Another aspect of the daughter's developing awareness of her mother's authentic self is her own growing self-disclosure. As the daughter starts seeing her mother beyond the mythic and stereotyped images, she also begins to go beyond her own image as the "good girl" or the "good daughter."As Arcana has pointed out [8, p. 7]:

> . . . being a *good* daughter depends on how closely we hold to the current standards for women. That is, no matter how loving we are, or how supportive—even financially—we are not meeting the expectations our mothers hold for us if we aren't proper women, in the now well-identified mode: passive, submissive, "pretty," not-too-obviously intelligent, and (at least potential) mothers and wives.

The greater authenticity on both parts contributes to the more equal nature of the relationship expressed in earlier excerpts, and both mother and daughter can relate as two individuals, rather than on the basis of ideals and expectations of motherhood and daughterhood. Such an interchange is portrayed frequently by students as a positive development:

> In doing this assignment I have seen a side of my mother that I rarely, if ever, see. I found out her past experiences and I truly felt for her. I can also see reasons now for why she is the way she is. I think I understand her a little better. I have to add that I enjoyed having the opportunity to talk to my mother in this way because this was one of the first times she has ever talked to me like an adult to adult. I even shared a few things with her that I would hide before and the relief of finally telling her was great.

The next excerpt was written by a student in her thirties who had a teenage daughter of her own, and beautifully captures the theme of developing authenticity for two sets of mothers and daughters, and also reveals the difficulty in holding on to it:

> I was aware of my own narcissism while questioning my mother. I think I wanted to discover more about myself than about her or through her—I'm forever searching to find myself. I found her remarkably unself-centered and was struck by the contrast. She revealed to me something that she said no one ever knew—"I never told anyone" she said. She cried bitterly when she told me. I cried with her and hugged her head. She, seventy-two, and never told anyone. It was at that moment that she became more a woman than my mother, or maybe just the woman. While writing this I recall a similar recent experience with my own daughter. We were arguing about something, I felt very vulnerable and I guess guilty and I revealed something about myself to her. She said to me, "You know Ma, I watch TV and see all those other people's problems—I never thought

> of you as having problems–you were just my mother." I'm back to thinking about my mother as my mother and I think my daughter has returned to thinking about me as her mother, but the awareness of the person is there. It's not total. It's a beginning, a starting point–something to build on, I hope it continues.

This excerpt also gives us the image of the three generations of women, linked together. Hammer has discussed how every transaction between a mother and a daughter is a transaction among three generations: the daughter, the mother who passes on her culture's messages about being female, and the mother's responses to her own mother's messages [15]. A number of students writing their mothers' biographies not only discovered their mothers in the process, but also their grandmothers. Some of the interview questions focused on the grandparents' influences on the mother when she was young, so a picture of that mother-daughter relationship emerged as well. This often resulted in the student becoming more aware of the generational connections, and stimulated an interest in getting to know the grandmother as a person as well:

> Doing this assignment, I have learned about my mother's life as a child–also about my grandmother and her childhood. I have realized not only how much my mother and I are alike, but how much my grandmother and I are alike. Now, I feel curious about my grandmother.

Social Context

A very important aspect of the mother biography assignment is the new attention paid by the daughter to the social forces that influenced her mother's life. Questions about the mother's early life, education, and decisions about marriage, children, and work illuminate the social expectations, restrictions, conflicts, and pressures that influenced the mother. Now the daughter can see that her mother had to deal with the same–if not stronger–social pressures on her development and behavior. Since these factors were discussed all semester in the Psychology of Women course, the daughters come to some understanding of the *social context* of their mothers' lives:

> After the biography, I understand why she is so traditional. For a long time, I couldn't understand why she didn't go to college. I didn't put her life in perspective from what she saw in *her* mother. Then I looked at her life, at her generation. Most of the women in her high school class became secretaries. And I'm looking at myself and thinking, a lot of my friends did not go to college–they were nurses, secretaries, dental assistants. So I think I've put things into perspective, and it's taken away that anger that I used to feel towards her for not being more independent. Now I understand why she didn't do it.

Students often report that they found out things they never knew about their mothers' past experiences, feelings, difficulties. Many times these involved restrictions or limitations that were placed on the mothers as young women, by their families or social pressures. The excerpts that follow illustrate this theme:

> I never knew my mother wanted to be an accomplished pianist.
>
> I never knew my mother had any ambitions outside of the family life. She wanted to be a teacher.
>
> This was the first time I've heard of her regretting not being a microbiologist.
>
> I never knew she wanted to take up so many hobbies.
>
> I never knew that she always just assumed that she would be only a wife and mother.
>
> I never knew that my mother had so much pressure from her parents and society to choose a typical woman oriented career.
>
> For the first time, I'm seeing my mother as such a product of her environment. Although she gave me some double messages growing up, at least I got two sides to look at; she wasn't given an option.
>
> I never knew the role her father played in her life.
>
> I did not realize what an unstable and unhappy family life she had when she was young.

When the students become aware of the social expectations that influenced the mother's experience, they focus more on her *womanhood*, rather than focusing on her in their individual, personal relationship from the daughter's perspective. Then the student can apply many course themes to the mother's experience. As discussed earlier, most of the students resist seeing their mothers as persons and women before doing the assignment, and many societal images of motherhood encourage and perpetuate such resistance. In the moving account of her mother's life, "Ruth's Song," Steinem suggests that this difficulty or resistance also stems from the daughter's concern that she will meet a fate similar to the mother's, if social rather than individual factors are involved. She wrote [18, p. 144]:

> I still don't understand why so many, many years passed before I saw my mother as a person and before I understood that many of the forces in her life are patterns women share. Like a lot of daughters, I suppose I couldn't afford to admit that what had happened to my mother was not all personal or accidental, and therefore could happen to me.

Once the daughter sees connections between her own situation as a woman and her mother's—a generation apart, but facing many similar influences in their lives—she can appreciate her mother in a new way, and also recognize and try to overcome limitations or restrictions in her own experience due to her status as a female. One student wrote:

> I've come to understand the major source of conflict in our relationship which was my fear of becoming like her. She has complied with society's prescribed roles for women, and therefore she has come to represent to

> me—my future in society, for she has been my role model. Now I understand that her role model was her mother who also complied . . . going back through each generation. Each being socialized according to the rules of a patriarchal society, originating from a time when women did not have any rights at all, and when they were seen as their husbands' possessions. It wasn't a weakness in my mother's character that caused her to choose roles of dependence and subservience. Society demanded women to conform to its system. . . . Now I know where the source of fear and anger comes from. I am happy to be like my mother and her mother and probably her mother . . . they have passed on to me many positive traits. It is society's definitions and roles which threaten me—not my mother. Somehow, I feel that I would prefer a lifetime battle with society compared to a lifetime battle with my mother.

In addition to becoming sensitive to social forces, students also become aware of the family influences on their mothers, and how these influences have affected them. In many cases, these awarenesses help transform a negative perception of the daughter's into a more positive one, through this new perspective. For example, one student had been concerned about her mother's apparently very strong involvement in family life, to the exclusion of other activities; when she found out about her mother's extremely unhappy home life as a child and adolescent, she developed admiration for the warm and close-knit family and home the mother had created. Another student was distressed at her mother's apparent obsession with food, until she found out about her mother's early experiences with poverty. A third student had been feeling under pressure from high expectations set by her mother, and had been perceiving such pressure in a negative light. During the interview, when she heard for the first time some details about her mother's early life, she interpreted the expectations in a new way:

> I also understand why she has a tendency to push me to strive for the best—to utilize my abilities to their fullest potential. She wasn't praised as a child, and as stated in the interview, her father didn't expect too much from her. She wanted him to expect more. She set out to prove herself. She's giving me something she never had: the awareness that my parents believe in me, and therefore, expect a lot. I no longer see her expectations as a threat; they are, rather, proof that she sees potential in me. My insecurity comes from not finding it within myself. She really is on my side, and she is not working against me.

A final excerpt illustrates many of these same themes. It was written by a student in her forties, who had immigrated to the United States with her mother from Lithuania, after World War II. As in previous excerpts, this daughter's understanding of her mother's social context, in this case wartime and refugee experiences, released feelings of appreciation and lessened feelings of anger. As a result, a new acceptance and admiration of the mother emerged:

> This has been a very valuable assignment because many thoughts and memories have transpired between the lines as well, and issues have come up about which I have not thought for a long time. It has helped me to

look at my mother more objectively because as I read this biography in "black and white" I am able to sharpen my image of her as a separate person and not just the mother I have needed for a long time. This exercise has helped me to see her as a woman who is a product of her background and some unfortunate circumstances. It has helped me to really think about the fact that in so many ways there simply were no choices.

I can also appreciate her strengths more because as I think about her life I can understand and emphathize how difficult it must have been for her to be a woman in her mid-thirties being homeless, uprooted with two small children and the constant stress and turmoil that surrounded her life as a refugee and immigrant. I admire her for the ways she coped and survived. Perhaps these are not totally new insights, but as I write this paper I feel so much more accepting of her, so much less angry–for the first time in many years, I look forward to her visit next summer hoping that I shall be able to reach out to her in the ways I have often wanted to but have been unable because of the "old" anger and blame.

CONCLUSION

The transformation of the daughter's perception of her mother through the biography assignment occurs within the context of a Women's Studies course, the Psychology of Women. Throughout the course, students learned to view many women's issues and roles within the context of the patriarchal society, and in writing the biography assignment they come to see their mothers and the mother-daughter relationship within that context as well. The more complex image of the mother as a multi-faceted person influenced by particular social forces represents an expansion of the daughter's earlier view of the mother from her own subjective viewpoint.

This new perspective that develops in a Women's Studies course, when the social context is taken into account, also characterizes feminist psychology and the feminist movement in general. In an article discussing the defining traits of feminist scholarship, Fine describes feminist psychology as "contextually valid" [19, p. 168], in contrast to traditional psychology which has focused on the individual independent of the social context. Similarly, in an article discussing the social context of the mother-daughter relationship, Westcott emphasizes the importance of analyzing the patriarchal social context since "the story of mothers and daughters takes place in the world of the father" [20, p. 16]. Such a social context includes the factors discussed earlier, such as the idealization and polarization of the mother images, and the presumed role incompatibility between maternal and other roles.

This process of focusing on the social context and thereby developing new perceptions has also characterized the consciousness-raising groups that have been part of the feminist movement over the past two decades. As reflected in the popular phrase, "the personal is political," consciousness-raising, whether it occurs in women's groups or Women's Studies courses, involves the examination of one's own experience in the social and cultural context of the patriarchal society and sexism. In one of her essays on feminism, Gornick eloquently described this process as follows [21, p. 49]:

> Thus, looking at one's history and experience in consciousness-raising sessions is rather like shaking a kaleidoscope and watching all the same pieces rearrange themselves into an altogether other picture, one that suddenly makes the color and shape of each piece startingly new and alive, and full of unexpected meaning.

As we have seen, when the daughter "rearranges" her perceptions of her mother and sees the *woman* in her, the vision of her mother and the relationship with her are transformed in new, positive, and unexpected ways.

In addition, the daughter learns about herself, as we have seen reflected in many of the excerpts from the students' mother biographies. While the mother biography assignment is a small scale example of biography writing, it is interesting to view it within the larger context of women writing biographies about women. In her article, "Daughters Writing: Toward a Theory of Women's Biography," Chevigny discusses the process of the recreation of the mother-daughter relationship that occurs when a woman writes another woman's biography [22]. Using her own experience as the biographer of the nineteenth-century writer Margaret Fuller, Chevigny describes the functions of empathy, identification, and separation that she experienced in writing about her subject, which she felt reflected her own experience with her mother. Chevigny argues that women can learn to know other women and themselves in more accurate ways than societal images generally allow when they write about other women and explore the psychological dynamics involved. She writes [22, p. 99]:

> Women's biography is simply a special case of our current study of women in which we work to recover our history and ourselves, each at least partly in terms of the other. In women's biographies, the intelligent grasp and flexible use of the dynamics of daughters writing is essential. Clearly, womankind has not been mirrored in culture in ways that provide us with adequate and confident self-definition; but, reaching across time, we can now begin to do that for each other when we create ourselves and our foremothers with the most scrupulous attention to each stage of our experience as it reveals itself.

Telling the mother's story through the biography assignment in a Psychology of Women course encourages the daughters to more accurately know their mothers, and in the process, to better know themselves as well. Societal images of mothers, which have long constructed and defined women's enactment of the mother role and the daughters' perceptions of them, become more visible and clear to the student interviewing her mother and writing the biography. The idealizations, the assumed incompatibility of multiple roles, the one-sided and simplistic views of mothers are factors which have influenced mother-daughter relationships, but are also difficult to perceive. The mother biography assignment, within the context of a Women's Studies course, helps students to perceive their mothers in new ways, and therefore develop new aspects of their relationships. Mothers emerge as multi-faceted and complex people, both mothers and daughters can explore and share more authentic feelings and experiences, and the social context is illuminated regarding the lives of both mothers and daughters, allowing more accurate and in-depth knowing of themselves and each other.

REFERENCES

1. A. Rich, *Of Woman Born: Motherhood as Experience and Institution*, W. W. Norton, New York, 1976.
2. N. F. Russo, Overview: Sex Roles, Fertility, and the Motherhood Mandate, *Psychology of Women Quarterly*, *4*, pp. 7-15, 1979.
3. A. B. McBride, *The Growth and Development of Mothers*, Harper and Row, New York, 1973.
4. B. Friedan, *The Feminine Mystique*, W. W. Norton, New York, 1963.
5. A. Oakley, *Women's Work: The Housewife, Past and Present*, Pantheon Books, Random House, New York, 1974.
6. S. Contratto, Psychology Views Mothers and Mothering: 1897-1980, in *Feminist Re-Visions: What Has Been and Might Be*, V. Patraka and L. A. Tilly (eds.), University of Michigan, Ann Arbor, 1983.
7. J. Lazarre, *The Mother Knot*, McGraw-Hill, New York, 1976.
8. J. P. Arcana, *Our Mothers' Daughters*, Shameless Hussy Press, Berkeley, 1979.
9. E. A. Kaplan, Mothering, Feminism and Representation: The Maternal in the Hollywood Melodrama, 1910-1940, paper presented at the Representations of Motherhood Seminar Series, Institute for Research on Women, Rutgers University, New Brunswick, New Jersey, December, 1985.
10. N. Chodorow and S. Contratto, The Fantasy of the Perfect Mother, in *Rethinking the Family: Some Feminist Questions*, B. Thorne and M. Yalom (eds.), Longman Press, New York, 1982.
11. M. M. Kaplan, A Motherload: Mothers' Images of Motherhood, paper presented at the Third Annual New Jersey Research Conference on Women, Douglass College, New Brunswick, New Jersey, May, 1985.
12. N. Chodorow, *The Reproduction of Mothering: Psychoanalysis and the Sociology of Gender*, University of California Press, Berkeley, 1978.
13. D. Dinnerstein, *The Mermaid and the Minotaur*, Harper and Row, New York, 1976.
14. J. Flax, The Conflict Between Nurturance and Autonomy in Mother-Daughter Relationships and Within Feminism, *Feminist Studies*, *4*:2, pp. 171-191, 1978.

15. S. Hammer, *Daughters and Mothers, Mothers and Daughters*, Quadrangle, New York, 1975.
16. J. Surrey, The Self-in-Relation: A Theory of Women's Development, *Work in Progress 84-02*, Stone Center Working Paper Series, Wellesley, 1984.
17. S. Cox (ed.), *Female Psychology: The Emerging Self*, 2nd edition, St. Martin's Press, New York, 1981.
18. G. Steinem, *Outrageous Acts and Everyday Rebellions*, Holt, Rinehart, and Winston, New York, 1983.
19. M. Fine, Reflections on a Feminist Psychology of Women: Paradoxes and Prospects, *Psychology of Women Quarterly*, *9*, pp. 167-183, 1985.
20. M. Westcott, Mothers and Daughters in the World of the Father, *Frontiers*, *3*:2, pp. 16-21, 1978.
21. V. Gornick, Consciousness, in *Essays in Feminism*, Harper and Row, New York, 1978.
22. B. G. Chevigny, Daughters Writing: Toward a Theory of Women's Biography, *Feminist Studies*, *9*, pp. 79-102, 1983.

CHAPTER 5

Case Studies of Agency and Communion in Women's Lives

ABIGAIL J. STEWART
JANET E. MALLEY

Most personality theorists—and many philosophers and theologians—argue that the ideal human condition provides individuals with the opportunity to form relationships with other people, and to perform meaningful work [1-3]. Feminist theorists, and others, have observed that women's condition, more often than men's, fails to resemble this ideal human condition [4, 5]. While there is considerable evidence that men and women differ in the value and significance they attach to relationships [6, 7], nevertheless men and women are involved in family relationships about equally often. In contrast, even in contemporary western cultures women are often faced with life circumstances in which there is little opportunity for socially-valued work. Women's relatively high access to relationships and low access to work (in contrast to men's access to both) must be taken seriously in any exploration of the ways in which women find satisfaction of the needs to love and work.

Because of women's relative exclusion from many social arenas, some women must hope to find more in their relationships than is usually possible—either because they can find no work, or because they can find no work which is challenging or personally validating (see [6], especially chapter 8). Thus, love has sometimes truly become a woman's "whole existence" [8]. Even women who work at well-paid jobs, from which they receive both social recognition and a sense of personal worth, do so in a wider social context in which employed women's work is devalued, and the quality of their relationships is suspect [9]. In short, all women's capacity to find satisfaction and meaning in relationships and work must be influenced—powerfully and directly, as well as more subtly and indirectly—by the social norms and ideologies which uniquely limit or constrain women's pursuit of happiness.

The consequences of a woman's relationships must also depend on the more specific context of her own life. Contemporary women's lives have a variety of shapes, partly because contemporary women vary widely in the ways in which relationships and family roles fit into their larger "life structure" (see [10] for a full discussion of different life patterns). These life structures are themselves partly defined by women's choices themselves, and partly defined by "unintended consequences" of choices. Thus, for example, a woman may choose to marry and may choose a particular husband, but marriage to that husband may result in pressures to limit her career involvement that she did not intend. Moreover, even among women whose lives appear to be structured in similar ways, there may be important differences. Thus, for some contemporary women with spouses and children (as for most men), family life has become "a thing apart," a sphere separate and unconnected to work; for others, it is still the whole of life; for still others, it is one central focus in a complex existence.

It is our assumption that, in principle, any life structure which provides for survival and reasonable freedom from discomfort could also provide adequate opportunities for "love and work" (always recognizing that the larger social context may limit the possibilities, regardless of life structure). For example, a woman who lives alone and works at a demanding job may have a highly-satisfying network of friendship or kin relations which meet her needs for connection [10, chapter 10; 11; 12]. Similarly, a woman who devotes herself fulltime to homemaking may find her family relationships intensely satisfying, and at the same time find her daily work challenging [10, pp. 157-163; 13]. On the other hand, a woman with a family and a career may find either or both fundamentally draining, tedious, or meaningless [14]. The experience, and the meaning of the experience, cannot be assumed.

Our exploration begins, then, with a recognition that while women's relationships are often central, they are not merely sources of connection and joy; they can be stressful. They may involve subtle devaluation or violent abuse. They may be demanding—of time, energy and emotional support—at the expense of women's own needs and interests. And they may, even if satisfying, be lost—leaving grief and emptiness in their stead. We recognize, too, that women's relationships can be important sources of strength. They may provide practical and emotional help or support. They may offer a woman a sense of being known, or understood. They may allow her to feel acceptable, lovable, and important. They may even allow her to feel helpful and competent.

Work situations, like relationships, are rich in both possibilities and in difficulties. It is not the mere presence of either work or relationships that affects women's emotional and physical well-being, but exactly how they operate, in combination with other features of a woman's life. In this chapter we will explore how women's family relationships, in combination with their work roles, may permit or impede gratification of the needs to love and be loved, and to perform meaningful work. Throughout this discussion we will treat both role activities which were freely chosen and those which were more imposed (e.g., employment opportunity) as having roughly equivalent consequences. Of course this overlooks some important differences between activities which are chosen vs. not, but we note that many features of chosen roles are not themselves chosen, and that some situations not chosen nevertheless have unexpected, desirable effects. As a strategic matter, in this chapter we will explore the ways in which apparently different life structures may be experienced similarly (as affording opportunities for agency and communion), and apparently similar structures may be experienced differently. We do, however, recognize the importance of the issue of choice, and will discuss it further.

We will begin by presenting a conceptual framework for understanding the psychological significance of work and family role activities. Then we will present case studies of several women's lives to determine both how well our framework fits their lives, and how we can develop and extend it to fit women's lives better.

A CONCEPTUAL FRAMEWORK FOR STUDYING LIVES: AGENCY AND COMMUNION

The broad human needs to love and work have been named variously by different thinkers after Freud [15, 16]. One useful set of terms was provided by Bakan, in his discussion of the "duality of human existence" [17]. Bakan suggests that there are two fundamental modalities: agency and communion. He defines *agency* as a modality which emphasizes the organism's individuality and separateness; and argues that agency is manifest in efforts at self-expression, self-control, and self-direction. (White's [18] concept of "competence" and Baruch, Barnett and Rivers' [10] concept of "mastery" are similar notions.) However, Bakan argues that "unmitigated agency," or agency without communion, is unhealthy. Thus, agency may be expressed in an undiluted drive to assert the self and control, or separate the self from, others. When this happens, the organism is ultimately vulnerable to illness.

We feel that it may also be important, particularly when studying women's lives, to consider the role of *indirect, or vicarious agency*. A number of theorists [6, 19, 20] have noted that some women direct their assertion not toward their own goals for themselves, but toward their goals for others (e.g., their children), or others' goals for themselves (e.g., their husbands'). Indirect or vicarious agency may permit some graditification of a woman's wish to feel competent, but at the same time it prevents some personal recognition and direct reward, distracts her from her own pursuits and goals, and may arouse resentment in the object of her assistance [5, 6, 21]. Indirect agency is, then, a way to "mitigate" agency, but it carries its own dangers and limitations.

In contrast to agency, Bakan proposes that the other "fundamental modality" is *communion*, or "the participation of the individual in some larger organism of which the individual is a part." Bakan indicates that "communion manifests itself in the sense of being at one with other organisms. . . [,] in the lack of separations. . . [,] in contact, openness, and union. . . [,] in noncontractual cooperation [17, p. 15]." Thus, communion includes affectionate and collaborative ties with others, which permit empathy, intimacy, and knowing and being known. Ideally, communion is experienced in a fully mutual relationship of mutual interdependence. However, intimacy *can* take place in an *asymmetrical* form–with one person providing more empathy and understanding than the other. Such relationships may leave the more empathic member depleted or drained [22]. Moreover, it is more often women than men who are on the "giving" end of asymmetrical relationships (with both other adults and children).

We argue, then, that the simultaneous, or balanced, presence of opportunities for direct agency and mutual communion provides women the greatest satisfaction and mental health (see [23] for a full discussion of these concepts in terms of existing empirical findings). Imbalance of agency and communion may lead to illness or tension (in the case of unmitigated agency) or to depression and despair (in the case of unmitigated communion). Moreover, direct agency is more satisfying than is indirect, both because it provides more social recognition and evokes less envy and resentment. Finally, mutual communion is more satisfying than is asymmetrical communion because it offers a sense of being understood and valued by an equal, as well as a sense of closeness and affection. In our study of divorcing mothers [24], we found that a balance of agency and communion was indeed an important predictor of women's mental and physical health. In this chapter, we will examine how useful the concepts of direct agency and mutual communion may be in case studies of women in a wider variety of life situations.

BALANCING AGENCY AND COMMUNION: PREVIOUS STUDIES

If family and work roles can be sources of satisfaction and frustration of needs for agency and communion, as well as of demands for asymmetrical communion and indirect agency, then the critical issue is not whether a woman has or lacks a particular role or relationship, but rather how that role or relationship fits into her overall life situation. Thus, Stewart and Salt found that marital and mothering status *per se* were not good predictors of one sample of young adult women's levels of stress [25]. However, the overall pattern of roles did mediate women's stress responses. Women who were never-married career women responded to life changes with physical illness (as men, with their general role imbalance in favor of agency, do). Married women with children who worked as housewives responded to life changes with depression, perhaps because of their role imbalance in favor of communion. Married women with careers, with and without children, showed no psychological or physical symptomatic response, perhaps because they were able to attain a balance of agency and communion. However, Stewart and Salt did not have any direct measures of agency and communion with which to explore these proposed explanations of their findings.

In a study of divorcing mothers, though, Steward and Malley did perform a content analysis of women's descriptions of their typical days at work and home in terms of agency and communion [24]. We found that women who reported high levels of agency and communion were significantly higher in overall well-being than women who were high in only one. Similarly, women reported the best physical health if they were high in both agency and communion. Interestingly, though, women who were *either* high *or* low (but equal) in agency and communion scored significantly lower in emotional distress than women high in communion and low in agency. Thus, "balanced agency and communion, regardless of level, predicted emotional health, balanced high agency and communion predicted well-being, and communion among those high in agency predicted physical health" [24, pp. 56-57]. Moreover, although the pattern of role combination (motherhood and no, part-time or full-time employment outside the home) was related to the agency-communion pattern, it did not itself predict emotional or physical health.

It was, then, agency and communion, not the presence or absence of roles, that was associated with the health outcomes. While this study certainly supported the importance of a balanced presence of agency and communion as a factor in women's life satisfaction and health, it was limited in that all of the participants were drawn from a study of divorcing families with school-age children. In addition, the concepts of direct vs. indirect agency and mutual vs. asymmetrical communion, were not explored. In this chapter, we will consider women in a wider array of life situations, and will broaden the conceptual framework being examined.

THE SOURCE OF THE CASE STUDIES

A further follow-up of the women involved in Stewart and Salt's [25] study was carried out when the women–initially sampled as alumnae of a competitive women's college–were about thirty-seven years old. For the purposes of this study, we selected ten women (out of 132 followed up), two of whom had experienced each of five different life structures for at least six consecutive years. Our only criteria in choosing women for this analysis were: their life was organized in a way which was reasonably common within this sample; and they had lived within the relevant life structure for several (six) years. The women included here were randomly selected from among those meeting these criteria. We selected two women for each of the life structures we studied, to help us focus on elements common to the two lives; in this way we hoped to minimize the chance that we would attach great importance to an entirely idiosyncratic feature of one woman's life. Our hope was that systematic analysis of a small number of cases would serve simultaneously to help evaluate our evolving conceptual framework and to develop it further.

The five life structures which occurred frequently enough to permit analysis were: never-married employed women; married employed women without children; married mothers who did not work outside the home; married, employed mothers; divorced, employed mothers. These five life situations were not equally common in the sample. The largest proportion of women (66%) were married, with children. Of those, 77 percent were employed outside the home at least parttime. Only 16 percent of the sample were never married, and all of these women were employed. Similarly, only 7 percent were married and childless; all but one of these women was also employed. Finally, by age thirty-seven, 12 percent of the sample were divorced mothers, and all of those women were also employed. Other life structures (e.g., married, but not employed and with no children, etc.) were very rare.

According to our review of the literature on stress and coping for women with various life patterns [23], some life patterns should lend themselves fairly readily to a balance of (direct) agency and (mutual) communion, while others should not. (Again, though, any individual can in principle structure any set of roles and relationships so that a balance of agency and communion can be achieved.) In women with three life patterns, imbalance is a particular risk: never-married workers, housewives, and working single parents. Never-married workers should be vulnerable to "unmitigated agency," in a direct form; housewives to unmitigated and asymmetrical communion, as well as to an excess of indirect agency; and working single parents should be in danger of a deficiency of mutual communion and—at least when under financial pressure—direct agency. In two other patterns (married working mothers, and married workers), a balance of agency and communion should be easier to achieve. We will use the case studies to examine in more detail precisely how and why this might be so. We should note, though, that the women in this sample are white, well-educated, and free from serious material need. Their life structures are in large part a function of informed, deliberate choice. For this reason, these women are not representative of other groups of women; they may in fact be those most able to define balanced lives within *any* one of the life structures.

We examined the ten women's open-ended responses to a number of written questions to assess their overall life satisfaction and the sources of stress and strength in their lives.

From the 1974 questionnaire, we examined the following questions:

- Please describe, in a brief paragraph, a typical week-day in your life right now.
- Looking back on the last ten years, what do you consider the high points/low points . . . of the last ten years.
- If you could do anything you wished in the next ten years, what would you do?

From the 1979 questionnaire, we examined these questions:

- If you had it to do over again, would you choose the same pattern with respect to your home versus career decision(s)? Why/why not? What would you change?
- High points/low points (as above).
- Which of the life structures (you've lived in since college) would you say is most naturally satisfying to you? Least?
- What do you find most satisfying, or rewarding, about your present family structure? most frustrating?
- Have you had any experience trying to combine working outside the home with raising children? If yes—best things? worst things? If no—why? best things about life-style you've chosen?
- How would you like to structure your family life in the next five years? ten years?
- If you could do anything you wished in the next ten years, what would you do?

From women's responses to these questions, we abstracted an overall view of their everyday life, stresses, and satisfactions over the fifteen years since their graduation from college. We hoped to use examination of particular women's experience to evaluate, modify, and elaborate our conceptual framework. In our accounts we have changed no essential information about these women, but we have given them fictitious names and have altered slightly or concealed some details in order to protect their privacy.

Never-married Workers

We examined the questionnaires of two women who had never married: Kate, a scientist; and Ellen, a teacher. Both had stable, successful careers, and both rated themselves, at thirty-seven, as "pretty happy."

Kate had pursued a classic academic career track since college. She had studied at top-ranking universities, and had achieved considerable recognition and status within her discipline. In 1974 (at 31) she described her typical day in highly-structured one-hour blocks, which included four hours of meals and rest or recreation, seven hours of sleep, and thirteen hours of work. She described her high points as, "the moments when I realize that I now do exactly as I please, no more and no less." Her low points occurred in the course of "attempts at professional collaboration." Kate's work focus was reflected in her discussion of her future, which was defined exclusively in terms of career goals. No important, continuing personal relationship was mentioned—as a reality or a wish—anywhere in the eight-page questionnaire written in 1974.

Five years later Kate expressed satisfaction with her life: "My best decision was to seek a lifestyle where I do what I like." Her high and low points included a number of personal events (buying a house, travelling, difficulties in a relationship with a student, sports), as well as professional ones. In evaluating her lifestyle she indicated that "I don't like to conform to the needs or wishes of others." She reported that she found it acceptable to live as she did—with "at most one adult," and expressed no dissatisfactions with her lifestyle. In fact, in discussing the future she said, "I could go on indefinitely as I am." Her future goals were again career goals, except she added "see the world. Tour. Live with and among people."

Kate's life seemed organized almost exclusively in agentic terms. She had many opportunities for self-expression and self-expansion, and she seized them. She described her life largely without reference to communal needs; by thirty-seven she seemed to give more importance to her non-work life, but still very little to relationships. In fact, the only relationship described in that questionnaire is an upsetting one with a student who was a "nut case." In short, Kate's life seemed to lack communion, but that lack was not one which distressed her at all—it seemed to suit her just fine.

Ellen's attitudes were a little different. In her questionnaire in 1979, Ellen indicated that if she had it to do over she "would have gotten married and had children." Moreover, she said that her reason for not combining child-rearing and career was "I'm not married and I'm not gutsy enough to be a single mother." Finally, she indicated that ideally she would like to "get married and have a child" in the next ten years.

Ellen reported, nevertheless, a number of deep satisfactions with her life. She said that her lifestyle "gives me lots of freedom. It forces me to take responsibility for my life." Moreover, her high and low points reflected a deep commitment not only to her work, but to her students as people, her parents, and new recreational activities. Ellen appeared to be experiencing increased doubt or dissatisfaction with her current life. Her low point was "Realizing I have only X number of productive years left and I feel I'm just starting to get a sense of what I honestly enjoy." And she said of her present family structure, "It's just beginning to feel a little lonely and empty." Thus, Ellen—unlike Kate—appeared to be experiencing some lack of "mutual communion." At this point, though, her opportunities for direct agency, and perhaps for asymmetrical communion and indirect agency, continue.

Housewives

The two housewives' lives were similar in some ways and different in others. They both had two children in 1979, and neither had worked for pay after they married (less than two years after graduating from college). Maureen lived in rural New England, though, and her family's income was rather modest (less than $20,000/year). Elaine lived in Europe (as she had for many years) and her family income exceeded \$75,000/year. The detailed texture of their lives reflects deeper similarities and differences.

Elaine had lived in three European countries and travelled to many more. She had had the financial, child care and leisure resources to pursue expensive hobbies (e.g., skiing) and many self-improvement courses. Nevertheless, she listed many stressful periods–tensions in in-law and other relationships, anxieties over family members' health, and difficulties in making family moves. Moreover, though she described herself as "very happy," and said the most satisfying thing about her family was "the support we all give each other," there were some signs of strain.

First, Elaine indicated that she would not live her life the same way if she had it to do over; instead, "I would have worked for a while after graduating from school and solidified my skills, instead of leaving, marrying and going abroad." Second, she indicated that it was a strain "having all of them dependent on me for so much all the time, and not being able, or seeing the opportunity, to do anything else." Finally, Elaine hoped to find a way to achieve a part-time job in the next five years, despite the complexities of doing so abroad. It appears, then, that Elaine was experiencing too many asymmetrical communal demands and too little opportunity for direct agency, despite the glamour and resources associated with her lifestyle.

Maureen's life is probably more representative of the life of other graduates–but it shared many of the characteristics of Elaine's. First, Maureen described herself as "very happy" and indicated she would not do things differently. She saw the strength of her lifestyle as "feelings of security, companionship, being needed" and said, "Basically, I like being home." Nevertheless, Maureen indicated that she had low points, too. "Can't organize this by year–it's pervasive. A feeling best described as the 'housewife blues'." She elaborated that she found it frustrating to have the "feeling that anyone could do what I'm doing–that my individuality and talent are not being used." Because of these feelings, Marueen was working toward increased involvement in local community theater, and planned to seek paid employment when her children were older.

Both of these women described themselves as very happy, and derived great satisfaction from their close family relationships. Nevertheless, they were–after nearly fifteen years of this lifestyle–experiencing some need to use their own talents, exercise their own agency. And in both one can detect a sense of being wasted, or under-used, at the same time that they are very necessary to their families.

Single Working Mothers

Marjorie and Andrea had both been divorced and raising children alone for almost ten years. Marjorie was a college professor, Andrea a free-lance consultant. Both earned modest professional salaries, supplemented by fairly substantial child support payments.

When reading their descriptions of their "typical day" in 1974 (when their children were under 10), one has a sense of extreme structure and busyness from early in the morning until children's bedtimes. (This pattern was also described by Weiss [26] as typical of single parents.) Thus Andrea wrote,

> Up at 7:30–begin nagging my son to rise, dress, etc. Fix breakfast. . . . Son leaves for school at 8:15, I for work at 8:30. . . . (after work) walk home, picking up son at babysitter's. . . . Fix dinner . . . (son) goes to bed around 8:00. Rest of evening: read, write letters, sew, balance checkbook . . . do the laundry. . . . Bed at 11:30 or so.

In 1974, while living this way, Andrea said "I'm pretty happy as I am," but indicated that she'd like more challenging work. By 1979, at thirty-seven, she indicated that she would make the same choices again in terms of her lifestyle, and said that "I feel both family and work are virtually essential, so that combining them is a necessity, not an option."

Andrea listed her son as a major source of satisfaction, and described her new job as an "ego boost." The difficulties she experienced focused very much on tensions in a new love relationship, which had ended just before she filled out the questionnaire. She expressed strong wishes for a relationship with a "wonderful man," and said "At the moment I don't find the absence of adult male companionship a serious problem . . . but in the long run I think I may really miss having a close relationship with a man." In short, her problem was attaining mutual communion. Her life was rich in agency and in asymmetrical, but close, connection with her son.

Marjorie's situation was very similar. In 1974 she described herself as "on the verge of career success" and "living a chaste, lonely life with my children." By 1979 she described herself as having "lots of admirers," and was continuing to publish in her field. She said of her lifestyle, "[I] like to work, like to go home again, love my children; I am absorbed by my children. . . . Still have freedom . . . am independent." On the whole, then, Marjorie found that her lifestyle offered her adequate agency and communion. However, she did complain, "Badly need help running the house, taking care of details of living. . . . Also on occasion wish I could share teenage raising responsibilities." In an effort to cope with the demands of her lifestyle, Marjorie said, "I have done it all myself–have become a superhuman efficiency machine." This "lack of support" Marjorie identified seems related to her sense that she might remarry, and that she needs "a wife." It may be that for Marjorie the communal lack took the form of the absence of help and advice rather than the more private or intimate sharing Andrea hoped for. Both felt that sharing some features of their life with another adult would fill a gap in their otherwise full and rewarding lives.

Married Working Mothers

In many ways, the married working mothers' lives were similar to the lives of the single working mothers; one big difference was that they did experience more mutual communion. However, they also seemed to have somewhat more difficulty balancing the various elements of their lives.

Marta and Irene had very different jobs and financial resources, but in some ways their lives were very similar. They were both married to men in fields similar to theirs, and they both had several children. While they both had demanding careers, the careers were quite different: at thirty-seven, Marta was struggling to establish herself in an academic field, subsisting on marginal part-time appointments while publishing and doing research. At the same age, Irene had worked for almost ten years as a scientist in a large company, for an excellent salary.

At thirty-one, Marta was sharing the care of two toddlers with her academic husband, while working on several research projects and teaching. Her day sounded both fragmented and very full. Early in the morning, she and her husband worked separately on the many tasks involved in starting the day.

> After breakfast I work in the upstairs study (read, write, prepare classes) for either one hour (if children are playing by themselves) or two and a half hours (if my husband is with them). The rest of the morning I spend with them. . . .

After lunch, she and her husband both worked for an hour while the children napped.

> In the busy time just before dinner, my husband is usually available for reading stories and keeping them amused. We eat dinner together between 5:30 and 6:30, bathe the children and have them in bed by 7. We watch the evening news, then work in the study till about 10.

Marta described high points deriving from her work, her marriage, and her children. She said of her work that the high points were in "discovery of myself as a scholar." Of parenting she indicated that the high points were "the experience of pregnancy and childbirth . . . and the joy of watching my children grow as individuals and as members of a family." She said of her marriage, "our married life has been so natural and so basic to my sense of myself that I find it hard to think of it as a 'point' or an 'activity.'"

Marta's low points were derived from work frustrations, miscarriages, and world problems. Her goals for the future included continued pleasure in her work and family roles: "Start a new and exciting research project. . . . Raise a couple of healthy and happy children. Enjoy my husband."

At thirty-seven Marta had found a new and satisfying direction in her career, and described herself as "very happy." She said that the pleasures of her life lay most in "companionship and support of husband, pleasures of raising and educating children." In addition, she pointed out that for her "stimulation of professional life combines well with very different demands of child-raising."

She expressed some sense of the difficulties, too. She said that the worst thing about combining career and family was "never enough time to relax," and elaborated that it is difficult "trying to meet everyone else's needs while still having time and energy for my professional life." In short, Marta did experience her life as offering her many opportunities for asymmetrical and mutual communion, and for direct and indirect agency. However, she sometimes found these various "opportunities" difficult to coordinate.

Things were, if anything, even more straightforward for Irene. She did mention that it was difficult to find "competent help," and she experienced "lack of time to get everything done, especially lack of time to be by myself." However, she mentioned that she had recently found "enough energy left over" to get involved in some community activities and a social life. Perhaps it is most accurate to say that for Marta and Irene the problem was attaining short-term, day to day balance; but the long run equilibrium seemed to be there.

Married Workers

According to the analysis outlined in this chapter, women with spouses and jobs they enjoy should have the best chance of experiencing mutual communion and direct agency, without experiencing asymmetrical communion or indirect agency. The key, of course, to whether this happens lies in the nature of the woman's job and her marriage.

Dorothy's day, in 1974, involved a long working day (as a lawyer), and time both alone and with her husband in the morning and the evening. In the morning, since Dorothy is an "earlier" person than her husband, they operate quite separately. In the evening,

> We eat late (8 p.m.) and my husband arrives just before dinner. Before he arrives I do laundry, cook, etc. After dinner he does the dishes and I read, pay bills, etc. We spend 9 p.m.-11 p.m. together, talking or reading.

Dorothy's work and her marriage had provided her with both high and low points, and at thirty-two she indicated that ideally she would like to "have a child and like it (I'm dubious)." Five years later, having decided against children, she wrote

> I might have chosen to have children earlier in my career/marriage before I became successful and set in my ways of freedom from this type of obligation.

She indicated that she did not try to add children to her life because "job suffers, children lack attention, nerves and health in a frazzle." Moreover, she viewed the positive features of her life style as including "satisfying career," "stable home life," and "sharing intellectual and cultural interests enough to be able to discuss what you consider important with someone near to you." In contrast, the negative element was "being primarily responsible for running home while dealing with career." (Presumably Dorothy's expectation was that adding children to her life would only add to this high demand for agency.) Dorothy described herself as "very happy," and hoped for no major changes in her life over the next ten years.

Melanie's situation was similar to Dorothy's, but different in a crucial way; at thirty-seven she still hoped she might one day have a child. She described a very similar life with her husband, and her job–though she worked in a "high tech" business–was as absorbing and gratifying as Dorothy's. Melanie explained that her husband often travelled on business. "If I'm in town I'll read or work in the evening, or do laundry. If he's home, we have a more leisurely dinner and read." Melanie indicated at thirty-two that her high points were travelling, working and being married; and she expressed the hope that in the future she would "continue what I'm doing now."

At thirty-seven she still described herself as "very happy," and said she would make the same choices again. She indicated that what was best about her life style was "freedom" and "my relationship with [my husband]." However, by this time Melanie felt that she would like to have children, and that their lack was an active frustration. Moreover, she indicated that she hoped to spend less time working in the future. Thus, Melanie was quite satisfied with the elements present in her life (which seemed to offer her considerable scope for both direct agency and mutual communion). Nevertheless, she seemed to be wishing for some other things too. Perhaps the experience of indirect agency combined with asymmetrical communion can not only frustrate needs, but also meet them–such as the need to give, or be generative.

It is clear, however, that Dorothy did not feel any lack of these opportunities. Perhaps it is relevant that Dorothy described as low points long, difficult illnesses in two of the past six years, and reported major distress resulting from her mother's physical and mental deterioration and a colleague's alcoholism. Perhaps Dorothy's capacities for asymmetrical communion and indirect agency were taxed too much by these other relationships for the similar demands of parenthood to feel attractive or feasible.

CONCLUSION

The particular concerns and stresses affecting these women's lives did seem to reflect the demands and opportunities for agency and communion more or less as we expected. No life structure was stress-free; no life structure precluded a satisfactory balance. However, the various patterns did each carry different risks. The single women without children were more vulnerable to a sense of "unmitigated agency;" the housewives to a sense of no direct agency at all. The single working mothers had some difficulties attaining mutual communion, and experienced some excess of demands for agency; and the married working parents had trouble coordinating the various agentic and communal elements of their lives. Finally, one of the married workers without children felt a need for the asymmetrical communion and indirect agency characteristic of the parental and adult daughter roles. This may suggest that indirect agency and asymmetrical communion—at least when combined with opportunities for direct agency and mutual communion—can be sources of a separate satisfaction (perhaps of a need for "generativity," in the Eriksonian sense), as well as stress.

We are struck by how generally happy and satisfied these women were with their lives. We feel it is important to emphasize both that this is true, and that we don't know how much these women's satisfaction depends on their exceptionally good education and generally high level of material resources, and their resulting capacity to control the definition of their life structures. Tangri and Jenkins, in a longitudinal study of college-educated women from 1967 to 1981, found both considerable stability and coherence in attitudes toward life roles and in actual role behavior [27]. Education and resources in that sample, as in this one, may permit women to shape their lives to meet their needs. Most of the women we have discussed chose to have or not to have their particular careers, their spouses, and their parenthood. Perhaps as a result, they have generally eventually found themselves in jobs and family situations they find rewarding. For that reason, the potential stresses deriving from tedious jobs and oppressive marriages were generally not a factor in these women's lives. For women with less choice—women with less education, with more traditional sex-role values, who married younger—life structures may not be so easy to fit to one's own needs.

Choices of marriage partners, careers, and parenthood are generally constrained by one's resources at the time they begin. Moreover, poverty and educational constraints must, more specifically, limit one's opportunities for agency. In addition, for parents, poverty creates a situation in which one's agency is rarely direct since one's children's material well-being depends on one's agency. Finally, poverty also can limit communion: the anxiety, self-doubt and hopelessness it engenders rarely enhance connections.

We believe, then, that the stresses we found associated with each life pattern would be intensified, and the rewards minimized, by poverty. Thus, women who are poor and live alone mostly do not experience great rewards for their agency; therefore, the absence of communion may be even harder to bear. Similarly, divorced or widowed working mothers who are poor are blocked from direct agency by the intensity of the demand to provide for their child. Thus they lack both mutual communion and direct agency. We believe that our analysis of life patterns in terms of the way in which various role and life structures readily provide for various human needs does apply far more widely than to the upper-middle class, well-educated, white women studied here. But the precise ways in which these same structures provide opportunities for poor women, black women, and other groups of women must also be studied.

In addition, the texture of men's lives in each of these life structures needs to be understood. The lack of ready opportunities for communion seems a far more serious problem for single, divorced, and widowed men [26, 28-32]. And the abundance of agency in their sex-role definition, work roles, and even in their family roles, adds up to a danger for many men. Finally, the father and adult son roles could offer men some opportunities for commuion and indirect agency, but often may not. Given the constraints of men's role norms, it seems clear that married men with families are in least danger of unmitigated agency. Only continuing development of a value and expectation of emotional and relational commitment and competence in men could help men find other life structures more bearable, or even rewarding.

Finally, individual personality probably plays an important role not explicitly addressed in this chapter. Marta and Irene differed in their satisfaction with being married career women without children; some of that difference probably derives from different strengths of their needs and capacities for agency and communion. Similarly, Andrea longed for mutual communion, while Marjorie, also a single working mother, did not. The degree to which a life pattern's opportunity structure fits the need structure of the individual's personality probably makes a big difference in the transformation of irritations and frustrations into yesterday's hassles or eternal bitterness or despair.

REFERENCES

1. S. Freud, The Future of an Illusion, in *The Standard Edition of the Complete Psychological Works of Sigmund Freud*, Vol. 21, J. Strachey (ed.), Hogarth, London, 1961. (Originally published 1927.)
2. ——, Civilization and Its Discontents, in *The Standard Edition of the Complete Psychological Works of Sigmund Freud*, Vol. 21, J. Strachey (ed.), Hogarth, London, 1961. (Originally published 1927.)
3. N. J. Smelser and E. H. Erikson (eds.), *Themes of Love and Work in Adulthood*, Harvard University Press, Cambridge, 1980.
4. S. Firestone, *The Dialectic of Sex: The Case for Feminist Revolution*, Morrow, New York, 1970.
5. J. Mitchell, *Women's Estate*, Penguin Books, Baltimore, 1971.
6. J. B. Miller, *Toward a New Psychology of Women*, Beacon Press, Boston, 1976.
7. C. Gilligan, *In a Different Voice*, Harvard University Press, Cambridge, 1982.
8. A. Ellis, *The American Sexual Tragedy* (2nd Edition), Lyle Stuart, New York, 1962.
9. A. R. Hochschild, *The Unexpected Community*, Prentice-Hall, Englewood Cliffs, New Jersey, 1973.
10. G. Baruch, R. Barnett, and C. Rivers, *Lifeprints: New Patterns of Love and Work for Today's Women*, New American Library, New York, 1983.
11. J. Birnbaum, Life Patterns and Self-esteem of Gifted Family-oriented and Career-committed Women, in *Women and Achievement: Social and Motivational Analysis*, M. Mednick, S. Tangri, and L. W. Hoffman (eds.), Hemisphere-Halstead, New York, 1975.

12. M. Adams, *Single Blessedness*, Basic Books, New York, 1976.
13. A. Oakley, *Women's Work*, Vintage Books, New York, 1974.
14. F. Hall and D. T. Hall, *The Two-career Couple*, Addison-Wesley, Reading, Massachusetts, 1979.
15. T. Parsons, *Social Structure and Personality*, Free Press, New York, 1970.
16. T. Parsons and R. F. Bales, *Family, Socialization and Interaction Process,* Free Press, Glencoe, Illinois, 1955.
17. D. Bakan, *The Duality of Human Existence*, Beacon Press, Boston, 1966.
18. R. W. White, Motivation Reconsidered: The Concept of Competence, *Psychological Review*, *66*, pp. 297-333, 1959.
19. J. Lipman-Blumen, Vicarious Achievement Roles for Women: A Serious Challenge for Women, *Personnel and Guidance Journal*, *53*:9, pp. 650, 1975.
20. J. Lipman-Blumen and H. Leavitt, Vicarious and Direct Achievement Patterns in Adulthood, *The Counseling Psychologist*, *6*:1, pp. 26-31, 1976.
21. A. R. Hochschild, The Sociology of Feeling and Emotion: Selected Possibilities, in *Another Voice: Feminist Perspective on Social Life and Social Science*, M. Millman and R. M. Kanter (eds.), Anchor Press/Doubleday, Garden City, New York, 1975.
22. D. Belle, The Stress of Caring: Women as Providers of Social Support, in *Handbook of Stress: Theoretical and Clinical Aspects*, L. Goldberger and S. Breznitz (eds.), Free Press, New York, pp. 496-505, 1982.
23. J. Malley and A. J. Stewart, Women's Work and Family Roles: Sources of Stress and Sources of Strength, in *Handbook of Life Stress, Cognition and Health*, S. Fisher and J. Reason (eds.), Wiley, New York, 1988.
24. A. J. Stewart and J. Malley, Role Combination in Women: Mitigating Agency and Communion, in *Spouse, Parent, Worker: On Gender and Multiple Roles*, F. Crosby (ed.), Yale University Press, New Haven, Connecticut, 1987.
25. A. J. Stewart and P. Salt, Life Stress, Life-styles, Depression, and Illness in Adult Women, *Journal of Personality and Social Psychology*, *40*, pp. 1063-1069, 1981.
26. R. S. Weiss, *Going It Alone: The Family and Social Situation of the Single Parent*, Basic Books, New York, 1979.
27. S. S. Tangri and S. R. Jenkins, Stability and Change in Role Innovation and Life Plans, *Sex Roles*, *14*, pp. 647-662, 1986.
28. W. Gove, The Relationships Between Sex Roles, Mental Illness, and Marital Status, *Social Forces*, *51*, pp. 34-44, 1972.
29. W. R. Gove and M. Hughes, Reexamining the Ecological Fallacy: A Study in Which Aggregate Dates Are Critical in Investigating the Pathological Effects of Living Alone, *Social Forces*, *57*, pp. 1157-1177, 1980.
30. J. Harrison, Warning: The Male Sex Role May Be Dangerous to Your Health, *Journal of Social Issues*, *34*, pp. 66-86, 1978.
31. S. Jourard, *The Transparent Self*, Van Nostrand, Princeton, New Jersey, 1971.
32. R. S. Weiss, *Marital Separation*, Basic Books, New York, 1975.

CHAPTER 6

A Case of Feminist Transformation: A Constructivist-Developmental Perspective

DIEDRICK SNOEK

INTRODUCTION

In 1979-80 I interviewed three women. Each of them, it seemed to me, had during the preceding decade made major changes in her life as a result of the Women's Liberation Movement. Given the difficulty many of us have in making any significant change in behavior or attitudes, with or without the assistance of therapists, I had been impressed by the Movement's apparent success in empowering women to make constructive, self-directed changes in their lives. Many made changes that seemed to be in a pro-human direction: They not only became more self-directed, but also acted in a way that affirmed our human connections with one another, the value of every human life, and the need to counteract racism and other forms of oppression. While I was aware of the anger towards men that was often part of these changes, my primary feeling was one of hope. My purpose in conducting these interviews was to learn as much as I could about the process of changing, the experiences that motivated the changes each woman made, and the costs and gains each woman counted as part of that process.

I had been trained as an experimental social psychologist, but in doing these interviews I had to deliberately set aside many of the values that had been imparted to me. I had been taught to believe that the purpose of psychological research was to discover functional relationships between theoretically meaningful variables. I had been told that it was useful to work only with variables that could be operationalized and quantified. Social psychology tended

Note: The interview reported in this chapter was collected as part of the Women and Social Change Project at Smith College, supported by a grant from the Andrew W. Mellon Foundation.

to focus on the individual's perceptions and behaviors to the exclusion of history or social context. I had been taught that social science should be value-free and that to that end it was better never to talk about any feelings I might have about the topic or its relevance to my own or my subjects' lives.

Unfortunately, after several years of this regimen I had become both bored and disgusted with much of what passed for social psychology at the time. I sought to renew my interest in psychology by seeking post-graduate training as a psychotherapist. What impressed me now was how hard people in therapy tried to "make sense" of their own stories, how much "sense" each client's life story made, and how little connection there seemed to be between the theoretical formulations which we employed to make sense of laboratory data, and the formulations which collaborating therapist-client teams constructed for accounting for the individual life stories. I began to re-read Allport's ideas about an idiographic approach to psychology, and White's attempt to synthesize the "study of lives" with the theories about personality, motivation, and social class available to him at the time [1, 2]. These formulations began to seem much more meaningful to me now that I had a lived experience of each client's attempts to come to terms with her own day-to-day experience.

What was most liberating for me was Sherif's 1979 essay on "Bias in Psychology" in which she brilliantly explained how the values that guided my training virtually guaranteed an androcentric (as well as a racist) psychology, one that was unconsciously oriented towards preserving existing dominance-subordination relationships [3]. It was in this spirit that I started this interview project. My goal in these interviews, therefore, was to provide data for a naturalistic description of personality change, based on the immediate reflections on women's lived experience. I selected women who were openly identifying themselves as feminists and whose activities justified the label "activists." I also learned either by direct questioning or by prior observation that each had made significant change in her own life [4].

The breadth of the questions I was asking invited complete self disclosure about virtually every relationship of importance to the subject of the study. The major question that remained was: Would women share that experience with me? Anyone who has any experience with interviewing will recognize that what we say is powerfully dependent on who is asking and how it is asked. The immediate results of my attempts to win cooperation were encouraging: Each woman I invited to participate agreed to participate, appeared willing to talk openly and at length, and welcomed my offer to let her review anything I wrote that quoted from the transcripts of her interviews.

One of these women was Nancy. I had known Nancy first as a faculty wife, then as a graduate student and budding academic, still later as a powerful "voice" in behalf of feminist causes. Nancy talked to me for a total of ten hours on five different occasions. In agreeing to be interviewed I am sure that Nancy spoke to me aware that I am a man, an ally of feminists, and a friend. She used references that assumed my acquaintance with American and English works of literature and explained herself in other ways that were no doubt subtly influenced by her perceptions of me. The interview took place ten years after the events she identified as key ones in influencing her to change her life. I had the advantage therefore of considerable reflection on her part; on the other hand the interviews reflect a point of view subtly different from what it would have been if we had talked immediately during and after the events she describes: It is a reconstruction. As we shall see, Nancy's experience of herself is organized around a primary identity of motherhood: how she resolves the tensions around a lasting loyalty to the values by which she was raised constitutes the main dynamic of the case. Although Nancy achieved a degree of correspondence between what she believes in and how she lives her life, she did not achieve all that she wanted. She still has to struggle almost daily against the oppressive assumptions and practices common to academic circles in the field of English literature. She also faces the disadvantages inherent in having entered her professional field in a period when openings for English professors had become a rarity and her age worked against her. She counts other costs as well.

I will first present Nancy's story in brief outline. In the following section we will examine Nancy's attitudes before, during and after her encounter with the Women's Liberation Movement and the changes she underwent as a result. In the final section I will argue that these changes amounted to a crisis characteristic of a developmental transition and suggest a constructivist-developmental interpretation.

NANCY'S STORY

When I first interviewed her, Nancy was fifty years old, married and the mother of three grown daughters. Born in 1930, she had grown up in a middle class household characterized by traditional family values and progressive political views. Her father earned a living as a company representative, but his avocation was music. Her mother kept house for the family, but also aspired to be a writer. In her teenage years Nancy began attending a Friends Meeting. This led her to participate in a Quaker work camp, where she met the man she later married. She went off to Antioch College. During her senior year there she married Michael and experienced an unplanned pregnancy; she finished her course work but not her senior project before the baby was born, followed her husband to Cambridge where he was a graduate student. The baby was a very demanding one and she completed her senior project, a novel, only with her mother's assistance in childcare. Nancy had two more children and spent the next fifteen years concentrating on rearing them. In the late sixties, in the midst of circumstances to be described below, she joined a women's consciousness-raising group. This group had its first meeting in the winter of 1970. The applicability of a feminist analysis of women's experience to her own life struck her forcefully:

> . . . it was obvious to me that this was the focus of an important political change, that I hadn't known that there was something like that . . . this was just like a thunderclap for me: It was really a very immediate recognition that this was the explanation. . . .

Ten years later Nancy had earned a doctorate in English literature and become a writer and teacher who spoke on women's issues in many different forums. In addition she had reorganized the shape of her marriage to reflect a dual career commitment in which she and her husband would sometimes spend months apart or maintain separate residences.

In her interview with me Nancy identified three key events as the ones that prepared her for a radical reorganization of her understanding of herself, her priorities and her position as a woman. The first of these was that in the preceding year Nancy's father announced that he was divorcing her mother and that he had no intention of providing continued financial support. Nancy thought it was likely that she would have to become her mother's principal financial support. Because she had little idea of what she would actually do to earn money, she decided to go back to school. She started to take courses at a nearby women's college in preparation for admission to graduate school. Her ambition at this time was limited to earning a Master's degree in English literature.

Second, Nancy decided to take part in a demonstration to protest the refusal of the local draft board to grant conscientious objector status to young men who were protesting the War in Viet Nam. The demonstrators were attacked, but the response of the Faculty Wives group to which she had belonged surprised her.

> . . . the day after we were attacked for demonstrating in front of City Hall, I was at the Faculty Wives' luncheon and I remember very distinctly that I was managed by some of those women so that I was deliberately prevented from talking to anybody (about it) . . . and it suddenly dawned on me that this was what it meant when people said they had been 'cut' socially, and I was totally outraged by it. I thought 'I have been polite all these years and have gone along because I didn't have anything to say, or didn't know I had anything to say.' It just suddenly changed the way I felt about what I was willing to go along with. Then, when I came home, the phone rang steadily and it was the newspaper, and people like that, wanting to know what had happened . . . and I realized 'I'm the one with the information!' I (also) realized that one of the reasons I had gone to the demonstration at all was that I had the opportunity there to make a statement with my body (on my own, without Michael) and that because nobody could retaliate against me I was also the logical person to make a statement about why we were there and what had really happened. So I gave the radio station a five minute talk which counteracted the statements of the people who had attacked us. . . . But with the whole adult world . . . and particularly the Smith world, I felt as if I had learned something terribly important about where conformity would get me, which was no place.

Third, her oldest daughter, Rebekah, who was then fifteen years old and who hated school, ran away from home. Some months later this daughter negotiated her return, but only on condition that her parents would not force her back to school. Her parents agreed, but instead of peace being restored, Nancy and Rebekah fought almost constantly. Witnessing these relentless battles, a good friend suggested that Nancy attend a women's consciousness-raising group that had just formed in nearby Amherst. Her participation in that group led to a process of examining her life and in particular to the awareness that "somehow I had gotten pulled into this idea that my role was taking care of everybody." Her relationship with her daughter contined to be painful, and within a few months Rebekah left home again, this time for good and with her parents' approval.

In the aftermath of this year of crisis, Nancy found herself resentfully listening in on her husband Michael's telephone negotiations for a new job. In graduate school Nancy had found professors who interested her greatly. Realizing how dependent she felt on Michael's decisions and also that she herself did not want to move, she came to a decision to stay in graduate school and continue living in her house. Michael took a job an hour's commute away. She conceived a dissertation that deeply challenged her creative energies and eventually earned her a doctorate. By this time, however, the job market for English Ph.D.'s had dried up and only temporary positions were available, particularly in schools that had just begun offering women's studies courses. Her husband's job was also again at an end and he gave up looking for teaching jobs in his field and came to a decision to study law; he began to commute to law school in Boston. Again Nancy came to a decision to accept whatever positions she could get and to become a sort of itinerant teacher and writer, while retaining her home in Massachusetts. In the succeeding years she has taught in a variety of places, usually in temporary or replacement positions, sometimes near her husband and sometimes not.

THEMATIC ANALYSIS

The suddenness with which Nancy experienced a re-orientation of her views and the emotional turmoil that accompanied the changes that occurred in her life during that time seem to characterize a developmental crisis. Three interrelated themes recur throughout Nancy's interviews: they concern Nancy's mother, Nancy's eldest daughter Rebekah, and Nancy's views of herself. In order to clarify the analysis I have arranged the things that Nancy has to say about each of these themes in terms of a simple chronological schema, separating attitudes she appears to have held as a young adult woman (pre-transition), the thoughts and feelings she describes during the period she joined the consciousness raising group (transition), and finally those that characterized her post-1970 life as a feminist activist and teacher (post-transition).

The Period Before the Transition

Asked to explain the chain of events that led to her rapid conviction that a feminist analysis was correct and required some changes in her life, Nancy turned to an account of her childhood years. She was the older girl among four children, with two older brothers and one younger sister. Her parents were both well-educated people of the middle class, born and raised in New England. Music, literature, political argument as well as constant talk about community matters, formed the backdrop to Nancy's early years in the small Connecticut town in which she grew up.

> "We were there, I think, because it was a good location for my father's business which took him as far as Danbury and Hartford and New Haven. And my mother was there because she wanted a place in the country where we could go swimming in the river and skiing in wintertime and where we could have a garden. . . . But-um- we were very important in the town, because we lived in the parsonage which was right next to the Episcopal church. We were a large family and my mother was very aware of the needs of children. . . . We had a little theatre group; we wrote the plays and put them on. My brother had a marionette theatre that he had made all the puppets for. The church was kind of a social focus: there were square dances in the basement and my father had a square dance band that played for these things. There was a church fair where we ran all of the games and did the book table and the gypsy fortune teller and the grab bag . . . I mean (laughs) we were . . . we did everything. . . . A lot of people thought my father was the minister. The minister kept changing and my father had decided that the Episcopal church had the best music. He played the violin and several other instruments, but he also learned to play the organ so that he could play in church and he was the director of the church choir. We all had to sing in the choir and he had (us singing) absolutely superb music, when there would be maybe only three people in church, including the minister's wife!

Besides her father's musical activities, the family also did a good deal of reading aloud, assigning parts to various members in a way that led to performances that were sometimes remembered for years afterward. Summers were spent at a beach house in Rhode Island. There were frequent guests and also, at various times, children who lived with the family while Nancy's mother provided them with a temporary home. One gets the impression that Nancy was quite happy amidst this crowd and enjoyed the good humor that was the dominant tone of this busy household. The family laugh, says Nancy, was known all over town and could be recognized instantly even in the darkness of a movie theater.

At the center of this busy enterprise stood Nancy's mother, the one who made it all possible, who opened her house to all who came, provided most of the labor necessary to keep it going, and who attended to the needs of the many children who made up this household.

Nancy took it upon herself to act as her mother's principal assistant. Of her mother Nancy says:

> She was an observer. I mean she was always a story teller, a wonderful story teller. She was aware of the lives of literally dozens of people who

> over the years actually lived in our house, who came to her with all their troubles, who had mothers who died or had conked out on them and some who were decidedly alcoholics and (who) really just weren't there. . . . I mean that some of them actually stayed with us every summer for six years in a row, or boarded with us while they went to a local school, because they had run away from home. . . . My mother maintained the same kind of abstract acceptance of all of them. I mean, I don't know whether any of them got . . . high-powered love from her. I think everybody just felt that she was there, they could eat . . . (laughs). You know, I mean that: It would be a place where they wouldn't get hassled. It was a shelter where they could come essentially any time. . . . The fabric of life was my mother's but it wasn't said that this was love or that this was a loving thing to do. . . .

We encounter in this passage the first instance of a distinction between care and love. Nancy's mother bestowed "care" on all those children, a kind of all-embracing acceptance and thoughtful attention on which they thrived, "but it was not said that this was love." Nancy was fascinated as well as troubled by her mother's attitude. She was dimly aware that her mother maintained a measured distance from everyone, a private and inviolable space at her emotional center that not even her eldest daughter and closest ally could penetrate.

> I think nobody knew what was at the center of my mother's life, and that's why she got up early in the morning and didn't want anybody else up. She would go for a walk. Also probably every day, she would get at least twenty minutes off in the woods or the backyard someplace. I don't know what she would do, because she certainly always had supper ready.

When I asked Nancy how she would describe her own relation to her mother, she replied:

> It wasn't personal . . . (pause) I felt I was a good friend of my mother's. I felt I was the one she could really count on to do the work . . . I felt valued by her. I felt we saw things the same way. You know, something about that complex humor was very reassuring.

And again later, speaking about the difference in her relation with her mother and that with her father, she says:

> It has something to do with love and with understanding. I mean that I make a distinction between those two (i.e. her parents). In this particular case (i.e. her views on religion) my philosophical stance is much more like my mother's, but I didn't adopt it because of pressure from her or for the love that I would get by being like that. It was a matter of indifference to her what I did. There was more interest from my father in my expressing my love by going along with him . . . and more of a struggle for me to try to find out where he stood, to think about it, and I felt more threatened by doing something different.

Despite this curious feeling that "it was a matter of indifference to her what I did," or maybe because of it, there are many indications that Nancy grew up deeply identified with her mother's values. As an adult, for example, she shares her mother's interest in writing and story-telling. She shares her mother's deep feelings about nature and seeks renewal in detailed observation of natural things. She herself says:

> I certainly do have a sense that I'm a continuation of my mother, in some ways, and that I'm not going to let what happened to her happen to me! But, I guess, I also have a lot of doubts about that. I mean that I am aware that she didn't get to do what she wanted to do with her life. . . . I've always tried to clean up particular trouble spots that I've identified because of watching her. And then I think: 'Well, okay, I'll be tidier about that than she was. And therefore I won't get set back as far as she was.'

She also describes herself as having very strict standards of what you had to be prepared to do if you were going to be a mother, an attitude that comes into full play when Nancy herself has children:

> I would not have had children at all if I hadn't decided that I had to be prepared to give . . . I had certain very strict standards of what you had to be prepared to do, if you were going to be a mother. (At this point, Nancy recounts stories of children who had been ill or had special needs) . . . So it was obvious to me that, if you had kids, they could be very sick. . . . And my mother, she did a lot. It was very clear that her feeling was that these kids had gotten a really raw deal, that they hadn't had full-time *mothering* . . . I mean this was why when I left home I just really did not see how you could, with my mother's values, possibly get free of that commitment. This is one reason why Tillie Olsen is so familiar to me; she feels the same way, you know: if you have a child in existence that child takes precedence. That's what one owes to the human race.

To summarize, Nancy's attitudes prior to her crisis may be characterized as follows: 1) I am a continuation of my mother, although 2) I am aware that she didn't get to do with her life what she wanted, so I'll try to avoid her mistakes, but 3) if one has children, those children take precedence.

The Transition Period

We hear the emotional turmoil Nancy was experiencing most clearly in relation to her daughter.

> Meanwhile Rebekah had been battling with the school. I think it's that Rebekah was a gifted child who was just not being given what she needed . . . and the science teachers were very uptight because they knew that Michael taught physics and Rebekah really had very damaging stuff on all her teachers who really did not know what they were talking about and Rebekah did, so it was just ugly. And she wanted to take shop and they thought that was just outrageous. And I was embarrassed (by the fear they showed when I even showed up) and I talked with them about it but accepted their explanation that girls couldn't possibly take shop . . . and Rebekah concluded, quite rightly, that the only way out was to *leave*,

that her parents were apparently too traumatized to deal with that school. I mean, I didn't want the town to feel put down, I did not want to exacerbate the whole thing. I really only wanted to mind my own business and go for my Master's degree. So, she left (on an archaeological dig and then to Mexico). . . . For a long time I could not answer the telephone at all, because I did not want to talk with Rebekah. I wished to wash my hands of her . . . I guess I was very angry that I was suddenly the enemy.

The first break in this crisis came when Rebekah agreed to try living at home again, but on condition that she not be expected to go to the town school, but instead allowed to weave on a loom her parents would acquire for her.

Rebekah had come home at Thanksgiving, threatening that she wouldn't come home if we didn't promise that she didn't have to go back to school. We arranged that she would be at home that winter, weaving, and that she would do a large share of the cooking for the family in exchange for living there. . . . So this lasted for about 2 or 3 weeks and then we began having these monumental battles, just as we had before she left. According to them, I spent every weekend crying saying that I had too much to do, that I had nobody to help me, that it wasn't fair . . . I mean I don't remember what they said, but that I did a lot of crying on Saturday mornings everyone in the family agrees to. And then we had a visit from our friends Gina and Ed and it was very good: the food was first-rate and we had really a wonderful family visit. In the course of that visit Gina said: "You know, you should find out about women's liberation . . . it will explain everything." She was sort of trying to mediate between Rebekah and me and she kept saying "You're both wonderful people and it's just ridiculous for you to be at each others' throats like this." . . . and sure enough there was a meeting that very night and Gina said: "Well, we will go and I'll go with you." . . . It was just a process of examining everything about how my life was and it was very clear to me immediately that they were right, that Rebekah was not my enemy, that somehow I had gotten pulled into this idea that my role was taking care of everybody, and that I *had* to do that and be in school and everything else. The whole problem I was having with my mother and my father changed drastically in its nature. It's even hard for me to remember what it had originally looked like, but a whole lot of places where I had blamed my mother for not having been a more supportive wife. . . . Like she wouldn't entertain my father's business associates and I always thought "Well, she really ought to have done that" . . . and my mother's feeling that she wanted to have time to write and my father's always saying "Oh, she never will. She'll put if off; she will always be doing something for other people." I suddenly realized that that was a kind of putdown that was based simply on her trying to do what the world expected of her, and what he expected of her, and then he was going to blame her for not doing it. All these things just suddenly began rearranging themselves in my head. I also began to realize that I had been writing papers ever since I went back to school: To see if I could *think* which I wasn't sure (up to then) that I could do."

And, finally, Nancy recounts how Rebekah solved the problem in their relationship:

> Rebekah decided that she wanted a job in construction and that she could get it by means of a friend who had a building cooperative in New Hampshire. Things with her didn't really settle down until about three and a half years later. . . . She wanted to be an architect and she was told by a woman who was her architecture teacher that it's a very difficult field for women and that she would be better off if she bought a house, if she could get anybody to help her with the payments, and do her own electrical work and her own rebuilding. So, she got me . . . it was the first time I really *talked* to her. And Rebekah explained that her life had been very difficult . . . and that all she needed from me was for me to persuade her grandmother to lend her the money for a downpayment on the house. So I did that.

We can summarize the perplexities Nancy is feeling in relation to her daughter as follows: 1) how can I account for the fact that having been a good mother, my daughter is treating me like an enemy? About her relationship with her own mother Nancy thinks: 2) I used to criticize her for being insufficiently supportive of my father, but now I see that she was being put down by him; and 3) my mother is being unfairly abandoned after years of devoted service to the family: I will have to come to her aid. Her attitudes to herself are also undergoing change: 4) I have always been willing to play the game, but confirmity will get me nowhere; and 5) I can be a competent spokesperson as well as anybody else (notably her husband Michael, who up to that time has been more active in political matters than she).

An intriguing story about having her portrait painted by a woman in her consciousness-raising group signals a transition in her understanding of herself:

> I really wanted my portrait done by somebody who knew something about my life. I (also) felt that for her to start to be an artist again—after having four kids—was similar to my going back to school. In a way she was making a statement with this painting that she could do that and that I existed. I mean, this was a big issue for me at the time: The way I looked, the way I was, or the way my life was, had not been recognized or even noticed. And so, when it seemed to me that she really was catching something about me, I was very excited. . . . (But) when she saw that she had ruined it she did not say to herself: 'Well, I almost had it before and therefore I will get Nancy to come over again and try it again.' She just said 'Oh, I ruined it' and that seemed to her some kind of fateful, deliberate undermining of herself by herself and she just felt terrible about it. She felt she had let me down, which she had in a way, but she didn't say to herself, 'Well, something happened this afternoon and next time I will really pull it off.' She took it as a kind of fateful defeat and that settled it.

We can hear the significance of "wanting her portrait done by someone who knew something about her life" as a self-affirmation. Clearly Nancy identified with the painter (another housewife and mother): re-telling the experience of the painter's defeat brought her to tears; however, she also saw that a "deliberate undermining of herself" is the painter's interpretation of the difficulty she is having. Nancy herself did not have to accept that explanation nor did she allow the painter's discouragement to undermine her own efforts to forge a life as a teacher and writer.

The Post-Transition Period

During much of this time Nancy was engaged in graduate study and working out a dissertation that explained the underlying linkages between the traditional ways in which English literature treated matters of racial heritage, sexuality, and gender. To recapitulate her thoughts on these topics is beyond the scope of this chapter. The interviews contain interesting sidelights on her newly developing conception of self:

> Kate Chopin's book *The Awakening* was very important to me. I didn't read it until about the time the Women's Movement was founded, but of course it's happening at the ocean . . . and one of the things she does in that book is that she learns to swim, which she relates to flying. I haven't talked about flying, but flying is very important too. I didn't start to fly until around 1969, but then I began flying in my dreams . . . it was quite something. At first I started with mostly little flights, you know, barely off the floor and I would make it maybe over a chair or a table, or from one room to another. . . . It was definitely not easy, but I was doing it and it was entirely my own power. And I was aware that I hadn't done that before and that it seemed that everybody else could do it. *The Awakening* was about that same sort of thing. (Interviewer: "But doesn't Edna Pontellier drown in the end?") Well, she didn't drown in this book: She is still swimming! Hell I could swim for days; I'm sure that she could too, if she felt like it. She'd probably get out to—who knows?—she probably found a whole new continent where everything was right. I am sure she did! How else do you explain that she turned up in 1970 or whenever it was. She obviously got somewhere!

Unlike the unhappy painter, Nancy experiences the power of self-authorship: Not only can she fly (in her dreams and, by extension, in the life of her imagination) but she can imagine Edna Pontellier's swim (and by extension her own excursion into a life of her own making) in any way she likes. About her mother she now says: "I still have to think carefully about re-connecting with my mother's mess, or with my father's mess for that matter." But about her daughters she comments:

> What I feel very proud about in relation to Rebekah and to the other kids also was that it was a primary commitment for them, as well as for me, to sort out what they could do with their lives that met . . . that they had to fight for but that they could get. I mean that Jennifer's an engineer, Katarina is working as an editor, and Rebekah has gone back to school to become an architect. And they all three have insisted on a kind of loyalty to the traditional world of women and have taken (advantage of) the opportunities that have been

opened for them, partly by their own efforts, but partly by the efforts of older professional women and by the Women's Movement generally.

Some of her most passionate thoughts come out in connection with a description of a visit she had with a group of women she got to know in Alabama during the time that she spent a year teaching there. All these women are divorced and they have formed a Displaced Homemakers Association:

> They had a lot of feelings about the fact that they had worked to free their kids up, they were aware that there were choices for their kids different from the choices they had had, and they felt their kids were blowing it, you know, still living with men who were impossible or still not taking the opportunity to get training that in fact their kids could have gotten, although they themselves could not. They felt that they were too old to pull that off, but wanted their kids to do it. Everybody's doing the best they can with it. I feel really much more impatient with their drinking themselves out of it, regularly. And only one of them has a really satisfying sexual relationship which she's got by simply deciding what's more important to her than her reputation. The others are locked into some kind of 'What will people say' thing. I also think that an obvious solution for older women is other older women, as sexual partners. And I did actually bring that up the last night I was there. One of the reasons I led them into it was that one of them was very reproachful of me because, she said, 'You're the only one in this room who is still married. You don't have our lives . . . we've got no husbands, we've got no financial security, we've got no sexual options that look okay, you just don't know how bad it is for us!

In another part of the interview she comments:

> It really seems like—and I think this is still true for a large part of the women's movement—more people have come to the conclusion that sexuality is just a luxury. They can't make decisions in their lives related to how they will get what they need sexually if they're going to make decisions in their lives about anything else. I mean that it's more important to figure out some way you can get some respect for your mind or some kind of way of earning money so that you don't have to take crap from the man that you've been living with.

To summarize, the post-transitional Nancy presents herself as a woman who conducts her life along self-chosen lines and keeps a careful boundary between herself and others. She has constructed a hierarchy of values such that she can say: 1) it is most "important to figure out some way you can get respect for your mind" or to earn a living; 2) in order to live by those priorities one may have to treat sexual expression as of secondary importance, although Nancy clearly values her sexuality; 3) she feels proud of her daughters as well as of herself for living out "a primary commitment to do what they could do with their lives" and 4) a continued "loyalty to the traditional world of women."

A CONSTRUCTIVIST-DEVELOPMENTAL INTERPRETATION

In an ambitious attempt to synthesize the cognitive-developmental theory of Piaget with later work on the development of social perspective by Kohlberg and of ego development by Loevinger, Kegan has proposed the following ideas as fundamental to a constructivist-developmental view [5-7]. First, at any stage of development, humans are motivated to make meaning. (This is the *constructivist* assumption.) Second, qualitative changes in our meaning-making schemata occur during the course of development. When our existing self-organization fails in its capacity to assimilate new experiences we are motivated to resolve discrepancies in our meaning-making schemata; a disequilibrium is created that calls for a new way of integrating experience. Thus, development proceeds by stages. The concept of "stage" has to be defined in terms of the underlying rules for meaning-making that can be inferred. (This is the *developmental* assumption.) Third, at any given developmental stage our meaning-making schema serve to unify thought and feeling. What this means is that both the *kinds* of feelings of which we are capable and *what* we have feelings about are intimately connected to the way we construct reality. Thus, for example, an infant can not suffer "separation anxiety" until it has attained some separation of self and other. Kegan writes that constructivist-developmental theory "neither subsumes affectivity to the cognitive realm, as traditional Piagetians tend to do, nor makes intellectual life the offspring servant of affect, as psychoanalysis tends to do" [7]. (We may call this the assumption of *cognitive-affective unity*.) Finally, the theory holds that what we experience as subject (our inner psychological organization) and what we experience as object (the contents of our experience: something or someone we can hold in mind, control, or relate to) changes systematically as a function of our developmental stage. (We may call this the assumption of *subject-object differentiation*.) The theory suggests "a series of qualitative reconstructions of the relationship between the subject and object of experience. The concept of self in this view refers both to the organizing principle in experience (the subject) and to the contents of experience (the objects)" [8]. Thus the infant lives in an undifferentiated state in which mothering is object and everything is subject. In this sense, an infant "is" its impulses, reflexes, and sensations, but a child at the next stage of development "has" perceptions, needs, and feelings.

These ideas are applicable not only to development during childhood and adolescence, but also characterize developmental progressions during early and middle adulthood. To state this another way, attaining the chronological age of adulthood (e.g. 21 years of age) gives no assurance that one has attained a "mature" post-adolescent mode of conceptualizing self and others. Neither does it mean that one has reached the end-point in human development. In the following I shall concentrate on the transition from stage 3 to stage 4, a transition that is frequently encountered in clinical work with adults in the early or middle adulthood era. In describing these stages and the transition between them I shall necessarily have to be brief in characterizing each. In illustrating this account with examples from the interviews with Nancy I hope to demonstrate the theory's usefulness for the psychology of adult development.

The dominant characteristic of Stage 3 is thought to be "interpersonalism." Replacing a self that is organized around stable needs and enduring habits but can only take one perspective at a time, the adolescent gradually acquires the capacity to take another's independent purposes into account as well as her own and so can enter into relations of mutuality, empathy, and reciprocal obligations. The self now participates in a shared reality (e.g. that of "our friendship" or of "our marriage"). Emotional life is therefore more complex, and ambivalence is no longer experienced as a conflict between what the self wants and what someone else requires, but as a conflict between several obligations. There is always an "other"—imagined or real—implicated in one's emotions:

> Often, at this stage, the repression of anger is a consequence of the fear of disrupting a relationship and losing the context for the psychologic of self. There are many reasons why people might find it difficult to express anger when they feel it, but it appears that persons in this psychologic undergo experiences, such as being taken advantage of or victimized, that do not make them angry because they cannot experience themselves as separate from the interpersonal context. Instead, they are more likely to feel sad, wounded, or incomplete [8].

Kegan, Noam and Rogers propose this stage includes much of the same phenomena as the ego-state that Loevinger describes as "conformist" and the moral reasoning stage Kohlberg describes as "interpersonal concordance orientation" [5, 6].

The way Nancy described herself in the pre-transition period (described above) fits the idea of an "interpersonal self." Nancy experienced herself as embedded in a conception of "motherhood" that was a continuation of her mother's values. The ambivalence she felt was experienced as a conflict between what she believed the role of mother demanded of her (or of any woman with children) and what she herself had hoped for in college, but could hardly articulate as a wish once she was a young mother: To have time for her writing. This wish would have been experienced as "selfish" and little anger was expressed about having to defer its fulfillment. There was no context to support her identity as a writer, although we may note here that Nancy made the attempt to set aside time for her writing by arranging to exchange childcare with another woman in Cambridge.

> The transition from stage 3 to stage 4, a development not seen until late adolescence or adulthood, eventually leads to a form of psychological independence or internal authority typically referred to as autonomy or identity formation [8].

Nancy clearly identified the experience that characterized the transition. Consider first the incident with the Faculty Wives group when she was an important witness and participant to a political event of high interest to the community. The lesson she drew from this experience (that "conformity will get you nowhere") implies a prior willingness to maintain good relations by suppressing her individuality to some extent. That "getting along" may require the subordination of self is the essence of Stage 3 interpersonalism. The experience of being "cut" socially did not fit well into this conception of how to get along with others. A disequilibrium had now been created that required a new psychologic. Her capacity to reflect on the source of her motivation and to take some distance from it and judge it inadequate to who she wanted to be signals the emergence of a new self organization.

The experience of "monumental battles" with her daughter, a relationship in which she suddenly experienced herself as "adversary" rather than Rebekah's mother was equally unsettling. She was aware of anger so deep that she could not answer the telephone for fear she would have to speak to her daughter. Remember that Nancy construed her relationship to her own mother as that of "good friend" and "the one she could really count on to do the work." It was only when she acknowledged her own unspoken assumption that "my role was to take care of everybody" and her own wish to be free of that compelling need that she began to understand the source for her anger and the true cause of the continual fighting over household responsibilities. Again, the developmental movement is one of "being" her needs and habits to "having" them and beginning to regulate their expression. She says, retrospectively, "I also began to realize that I had been writing papers ever since I went back to school: to see if I could think, which I wasn't sure (up to then) that I could do."

Nancy was equally puzzled about her parents' difficulties. She had understood by then that there were various strains in their relationship but that her father would break up the marriage and deny further financial responsibility was something she could not account for to herself. The way she saw it, her mother had done her "duty" of caring for the household (although "it was not said that this was love . . ."), but her father denied his "obligations" to the spousal relationship. Nor could she understand, at this point, her mother's refusal to sue for alimony. She therefore assumed, without being asked, that she would have to contribute to her mother's financial support. In material not quoted from the interviews, she re-examines her parents' character and the nature of their relationship and is able to estimate its costs to her mother. She stops blaming her mother for "not having been a more supportive wife" and understands her mother's insistence on a modicum of daily privacy in a new way. When I asked her to explain her earlier, somewhat puzzling remark that her mother had "cared" for everyone "but it wasn't said that this was love," she said—finally—"I don't think it is all that different . . . but my father thought so!"

Nancy experienced this transitional stage as an assault on her entire system of meaning, and showed unmistakable signs of depression. She felt unbearably lonely, deserted, and betrayed. ("I spent every weekend crying saying that I had too much to do, that I had nobody to help me, that it wasn't fair. . . .") This is an ego-state that Kegan et al. label "dependent depression," to distinguish it qualitatively from depressive states that characterize other transitions [8]. The emotions experienced during such a transition indicate the loss of the "interpersonal" self and signal the emergence of new more self-governing, but lonelier sense of self.

The authority to construct one's own life, a sense of self-dependence and self-ownership, is the hallmark of Stage 4. Instead of "being" one's relationships the self now "has" relationships and the feelings that depend on mutuality and reciprocity are now subordinated to a new sense of who one is and what one wants to become. Kegan, Noam and Rogers write [8]:

> The strength of stage 4 is its psychological self-employment, its capacity to own oneself, rather than having the pieces of oneself owned by various shared contexts; the sympathies that arise from one's shared space are no longer determinative of the self, but are taken as preliminary and mediated by the new self-system. But in this very strength lies a limit. Stage 4 is inevitably ideological, as Erikson recognized must be the case for identity formation—a truth for a faction, a class, a group. And stage 4 probably requires the recognition of a group (or persons as representative of groups)—either the tacit ideological support of American institutional life, which is most supportive of the institutional evolution of white middle-class males, or more explicit ideologies in support of disenfranchised social classes, gender, or races.

References to Nancy's growing sense of self-authorship abound. In her account of the incident with the portrait painter, we saw that Nancy was now aware both of the possibility of being held back by discouragement and self-limitation and of the possibility of choosing to persist, to imagine her life the way she wanted it to be, and to make decisions congruent with priorities she had set for herself. In rapid succession she made some critical decisions: To stay in her house, to go after the doctorate she wanted, to organize a feminist support group for women who were both mothers and intent on realizing other aims in their lives.

It is clear that Nancy's new sense of self incorporated her strong values about mothering. She continued to feel that children require an adult's commitment and was proud of the fact that her daughters have not only made use of professional opportunities that became more accessible during the seventies, but also remained loyal to "the traditional world of women." She tended to feel that the Women's Movement, in its pursuit of equal opportunity, had neglected serious questions about the nature of parenthood. She was most impressed by the theorizing of Chodorow, Dinnerstein, and Ruddick. Her thoughts were still on women who had been home-makers and who continued to bear the costs of that commitment during their post-divorce years. Listen, for example, to the following comments on her visit to Alabama:

> I just had a visit in Alabama with some people who are all members of the Displaced Homemakers Association. Of the group there are two alcoholics who know they are alcoholic; two who are on the borderline because drinking is the primary solution in Alabama; and all of them are political women working fairly hard on conventional politics, like the ERA. All of them were married to husbands who came to Alabama because there were jobs there; they're mostly Northerners who are unable to leave because they have kids there who have relationships or are married: They don't want the kids to be in a position of choosing between a mother who is in, say, New York and a father who's still in Alabama. They themselves have very small jobs with very little money—and most of that they drink up. And they have made different decisions about how to get their sexual needs met, but you know three of them told me there's just no way to get my sexual needs met and I just have to accept that. What they said was that there are certain things that are terribly important to them: That if they didn't have the opportunity to collect their husbands' Social Security when they retire, even though he has remarried, they wouldn't have any money at all. I came away from five days with those women totally bummed out: Mostly they just live very limited lives that they are hanging on to. One of them said to me: 'You just don't know how much energy it takes just to keep alive.' Their desperation was very depressing.

CONCLUDING REMARKS

Was it feminism or a transitional life crisis that accounts for the big changes in Nancy's life that occurred circa 1970? I believe we need not pose the issue quite so sharply. I would argue that feminism supported Nancy in her transition from an "interpersonal" to a more "self-governing" stance at a critical time in her life, because its more general analysis of the condition of all women legitimized what had hitherto been experienced as a privately held complaint. Because Nancy had grown up in a family with involvement in progressive politics and a concern for social justice, feminism also appealed to values of human equality and fairness that had informed Nancy's view of the world since at least her high school days. In this respect her development parallels that of other radical feminists whose activism (and experience of sexism) in the Civil Rights Movement was the prelude to the early call for a feminist consciousness [9].

However, Nancy was nearly forty years old at the time of the events described in this chapter. Clearly, up until that time the conditions in her life had prepared her for a more than adequate performance of the roles of spouse and parent, but had failed to support her psychological development in other ways. What was missing is reflected in Kegan's remark that the evolution of a stage 4 self "probably requires the recognition of a group" [8]. Psychological development does not take place in a vacuum. Not only do we require the personal emotional bonds with family and friends that provide a context in which we can explore and ultimately choose for ourselves what values, skills, and attachments we will make uniquely our own, but we also need the larger community's recognition of what it is *we may become*. The formulation of what is normative or acceptable for a person-of-our-kind plays a crucial role. Feminist writers have documented how difficult it was for a woman to make a deviant choice in a patriarchal society; the price one might have to pay to make a serious commitment to a career as an academic, for example, was frequently to live without a husband or children. In worse instances, a choice viewed as completely idiosyncratic might be called madness or criminality. So the paradox was that psychological conceptions of maturity called for the development of autonomy, but the terms in which autonomy was defined rested at bottom on a notion of development as a process of separating from others. Nancy's life illustrates how the development of self-governance may include the ability to engage in interactions which empower others and, simultaneously, oneself. It also shows how in the pre-1970 era this development was impeded by both psychological and socio-cultural constraints.

Kegan labels this self-governance state (stage 4 in his theoretical schema) as the "institutional" self, precisely because he recognizes its dependence on a supportive sociocultural context. He concedes that "the tacit ideological support of American institutional life . . . is most supportive to the institutional evolution of white males." That "tacit support" was unavailable to most women in pre-1970 American society. The emergence of feminism in the post-1970 era provides a new context for meaning-making: Nancy connected her personal struggles to a society-wide subordination of women's desires and feelings and felt empowered by the example of female peers to challenge the institutional barriers that kept her from a serious involvement in academic study and writing. To do this she had to develop a new sense of self that allowed her to transcend her former understanding of herself as having a primary obligation to children and family.

> Talk of 'transcending the interpersonal' often makes people uneasy who want to point out—and rightly I think—that other people should remain what is important to us throughout our lives. But others are not lost by an emergence from embeddedness in the interpersonal. . . . The question is always *how* 'other people' are known. The institutional balance does not leave one bereft of interpersonal relationships, but it does appropriate them to the new context of their place in the maintenance of a personal self-system [7].

The connection between personal (biographical) and political (social structural) factors in explaining why some women become feminists (and others resist this analysis of women's situation) continues to puzzle psychologists and social theorists alike. In a provocative article, Rosenthal has argued that the original ideological purpose of consciousness-raising was diffused when sex-role analysis replaced a more revolutionary emphasis on social-structural change and CR became mainly a vehicle for the development of feelings of self-worth and activities towards self-improvement [10]. The main point of her argument–that individual change becomes increasingly problematic if women's social circumstances remain the same–may certainly be conceded, but it is also true that radical feminist theory originally underestimated the depth of the personal roots for the values that women brought with them into the Women's Liberation Movement. Nancy felt deeply that her consciousness-raising group dealt principally with women's marital situation and her educated peers' attempts to enter the male-dominated professions, but failed to come to terms with the complex reality of their family-situations and relationships with children. The resolution she eventually worked out in her own life included both "a way in which you can get respect for your mind" and "a continued loyalty to the traditional world of women." However, she made it clear that both freedom of sexual expression and access to financial independence continued to be very problematic in the lives of many women of her age that she knew intimately.

Nancy counts Chodorow, Dinnerstein, and Gilligan among the psychological writers who have given most forceful expression to the phenomenology of women's experience. Yet the contributions of these theorists have often been denigrated by psychologists themselves. Gilligan, for example, has been criticized extensively both on ideological and methodological grounds [11, 12]. Thus, Linda Kerber, a historian, writes that "it cannot be surprising that themes of responsibility and care emerge in women's articulation of concern about abortion." But clinicians who work with women in all kinds of life transitions other than ones involving abortion find that Gilligan's formulation accurately describes many women's experience of their situation [13]. A second complaint is that Gilligan's conclusion–that women often define their identity through relationships of intimacy and care–appears to lend support to those who would wish to return to a society in which women are assigned "a separate sphere." Perhaps so, but the existence of a backlash against the Women's Movement should not deter us from describing the reality of women's experience. Conflicts between achievement and care are far more prevalent in women than in men and need to be both understood and explained. Gilligan herself has replied that to treat such conflicts as merely a sign of weakness "only reinforces the impression that women's fears are groundless" [11]. Moreover, she points out, there is an inconsistency in assuming, on the one hand, that women's predominance in the nurturance and care of young children is an accepted and cross-culturally universal fact" and, on the other hand, acting as if the psychological results of this situation for women's character development were of little or no consequence.

What contribution, if any, does a constructivist-developmental point of view make to our understanding of these issues? I think it is helpful for social psychologists to assume that the self can undergo qualitative re-organization. Gender role attitudes are anchored in our earliest experience and deeply affect how we view ourselves. If the possibility of developmental change did not exist, changes in such deep-seated attitudes could be brought about only by a fundamental personality re-organization ('brainwashing'). A developmental theory that builds on the human need for meaning-making permits us to view such a change in terms of a move to a new stage. The need to move from an "interpersonal" to an "institutional" self, as described above, will occur in every life. Without a feminist vision many women lack the social support necessary to legitimize their developmental need for a self that can experience the demands of multiple interpersonal relationships from a sufficiently autonomous stance to honor their own integrity and regulate these claims from a more self-serving perspective. A second implication of the developmental view is that we will be more ready for such ideological supports at some stages of our life than in others. For many women who were reared with rather traditional role expectations, feminism can serve to bring into focus experiences that do not fit into their existing self-schemata. This is more likely to happen during a transition from stage 3 to stage 4 than either before or after.

REFERENCES

1. G. W. Allport, *Pattern and Growth in Personality*, Holt, Rinehart and Winston, New York, 1961.
2. R. W. White, *Lives in Progress: A Study of the Natural Growth of Personality*, (3rd Edition), Holt, Rinehart and Winston, New York, 1975.
3. C. W. Sherif, Bias in Psychology, in *The Prism of Sex: Essays in the Sociology of Knowledge*, J. Sherman and E. T. Beck (eds.), University of Wisconsin Press, Madison, 1979.
4. J. D. Snoek, Mara: The Construction of a Professional Identity, in *Women Living Change*, S. Bourque and D. Divine (eds.), Temple University Press, Philadelphia, 1985.
5. L. Kohlberg, Stage and Sequence: The Cognitive-developmental Approach to Socialization, in *Handbook of Socialization: Theory and Research*, D. Goslin (ed.), Rand McNally, New York, 1969.
6. J. Loevinger, *Ego Development*, Jossey-Bass, San Francisco, 1976.
7. R. Kegan, *The Evolving Self: Problem and Process in Human Development*, Harvard University Press, Cambridge, 1982.
8. R. Kegan, G. Noam, and L. Rogers, The Psychologic of Emotion: A Neo-Piagetian View, in *New Directions for Child Development: Emotional Development*, D. Cichetti and P. Pogge-Hesse (eds.), No. 16, Jossey-Bass, San Francisco, 1982.
9. S. Evans, *Personal Politics: The Roots of Women's Liberation in the Civil Rights Movement and the New Left,* Alfred A. Knopf, New York, 1979.
10. N. B. Rosenthal, Consciousness Raising: From Revolution to Re-evaluation, *Psychology of Women Quarterly*, *8*:4, pp. 309-326, 1984.
11. L. Kerber, C. G. Greeno, E. E. Maccoby, Z. Luria, C. B. Stack, and C. Gilligan, On *In a Different Voice*: An Interdisciplinary Forum, *SIGNS: Journal of Women in Culture and Society*, *11*:2, pp. 304-333, 1986.
12. C. Gilligan, *In a Different Voice*, Harvard University Press, Cambridge, 1979.
13. J. B. Miller, *Toward a New Psychology of Women*, 2nd Edition, Beacon Press, Boston, 1986.

CHAPTER 7

Self-Fulfilling Prophecies: Sex Role Stereotypes as Expectations for Behavior*

SHELAGH M. J. TOWSON
MARK P. ZANNA
GLENDA MAC DONALD

Once upon a time, in ancient Greece, a sculptor called Pygmalion decided that since none of the local women measured up to his standards of feminine perfection, he would create his own ideal woman, a marble statue he named Galatea. When the gods saw how much Pygmalion loved Galatea, they brought her to life, "endowed with all of the characteristics and beauty envisioned by her creator" [1, p. 280], and she and Pygmalion lived happily ever after.

It is suggested, however, that instead of waiting for the gods, Pygmalion could have had his ideal woman merely by making a real woman aware of his expectations regarding gender-appropriate behavior. Rosenthal and Jacobson demonstrated that teachers' expectations for their students' academic performance had a significant impact on that performance [2], and subsequent studies have confirmed the self-fulfilling prophecy potential of expectations based on presumed knowledge about individual capabilities [3, 4]. Other studies suggest that expectations for behavior based on an individual's membership in a particular group can also function as self-fulfilling prophecies [5]. In the first of two studies conducted by Word, Zanna and Cooper, naive subjects acting as interviewers responded differently to black and white experimental confederates posing as job applicants [6]. In the second study, white experimental confederates interviewed white job applicant subjects, patterning their behavior on that elicited from the naive interviewers in the first study. In other words, they responded to half the white applicants as if they were black. When judges

* The research for this chapter was conducted while the first-named author was supported by an Ontario Graduate Scholarship.

blind to experimental condition scored the videotaped interviews, white applicants treated as blacks were perceived as significantly less adequate for the job, less calm and less composed than those treated as white.

Given this evidence, it seems reasonable to assume that sex-role stereotypes might also function as self-fulfilling prophecies. In an initial test of this possibility, Zanna and Pack asked female undergraduates to indicate their degree of agreement with eleven statements describing sex-role stereotypic traits and behaviors [7]. Three weeks later, the women were asked to form a first impression of a male partner on the basis of a self-description which indicated that he would be either desirable or undesirable as a date. Subjects also read their partner's responses to an "Opinion on Women" questionnaire, which indicated, for half the women, that his expectations for appropriate female behavior were very traditional. The other women expected to meet a man with more liberated views of appropriate female behavior. Each woman then completed a series of questionnaires, ostensibly for her partner to examine so that he could form a first impression of her. These questionnaires included the sex-role stereotype questionnaire completed at the initial experimental session and an anagram completion task supposedly measuring I.Q.

In this chapter, it was expected that the desirable male partner would be perceived as having much more personal reward power than the undesirable male partner [8, 9]. Therefore, women expecting to interact with the "loser" would have little motivation to conform to his image of the ideal woman and would describe themselves essentially as they had three weeks previously. However, women who expected to meet attractive, athletic, unattached and chauvinist men would portray themselves as more traditional while women paired with equally attractive but more liberated males would characterize themselves as more feminist. Examination of the change scores on the sex-role stereotypes questionnaire confirmed these predictions. In addition, women expecting to interact with more traditional men actually completed fewer anagrams on the bogus I.Q. test than those women anticipating a less traditional partner.

Would these women have responded differently if the anticipated contact had resembled a business rather than a social situation, in which the man's reward power involved concrete rather than personal resources? In order to explore this possibility, von Baeyer, Sherk and Zanna asked female undergraduates if they would pose as job applicants seeking a research assistant position [10]. The information given to half the women indicated that the man who would be conducting the job interview defined the ideal female employee in traditional, sex-role stereotypic ways: passive, gentle, sensitive, attractive, dependent. The other women expected an interviewer who stressed independence, assertiveness and equal work responsibilities as desirable female employee characteristics.

Some weeks later, the women were actually interviewed by a male experimental confederate. The women's appearance and behavior during this face-to-face interaction constituted the study's main dependent measures. The results provided dramatic confirmation for the hypothesis. Applicants expecting a traditional interviewer wore significantly more makeup and accessories and were judged to be significantly more attractive than applicants who assumed their interviewer was a feminist. During the interview, these applicants engaged in less direct eye contact with the interviewer when answering his questions and, in fact, talked less overall than applicants in the nontraditional interviewer condition. And when the interviewer asked them about plans for marriage and children, their answers consistently reflected traditional sex-role stereotypes.

If these women had been applying for a real job, with a real interviewer, would their conformity to his presumed expectations have been successful? The answer to this question may depend, in part, on the nature of the job. Various studies suggest that women trying for careers in fields traditionally occupied by men will be most successful if they opt for a self-presentational style which emphasizes the fit between their qualifications and the formal job requirements rather than the consistency between their style and the interviewer's personal prejudices. Popular literature advises female applicants for executive positions to behavior assertively [11] and to reinforce that message by wearing tailored clothes and minimum makeup and jewelry [12]. Research evidence tends to confirm the advisability of this approach. Attractiveness and perceived femininity seem to be positively correlated [13, 14] and Cash, Gillen and Burns found that attractive women applying for male-oriented jobs were judged to be less qualified and less likely to be hired than unattractive women [15]. Heilman and Saruwatari reported that attractive female applicants for management jobs were judged more negatively than unattractive ones [13]. Dipboye and Wiley asked professional interviewers to evaluate a male or female applicant on the basis of a videotaped interview for a research assistant position in which the applicant behaved in either a passive, stereotypically feminine or an assertive, stereotypically masculine manner [16]. The assertive woman was judged *more* favorably than the passive woman and *as* favorably as the assertive man.

Evidence for the advisability of adopting a feminine self-presentational style when applying for traditionally female-occupied jobs is less clearcut. Although Cash et al. [15] reported a tendency for attractive women to be rated more favorably than unattractive ones for female and neuter jobs, and Heilman and Saruwatari found that attractive applicants for a clerical position were rated more favorably than unattractive ones [16], Feldman-Summers and Kiesler could not find any work categories including traditional female occupations, in which women were expected to be more successful than men [17].

The second factor which must be considered is the fit between the interviewer's expectations and formal job requirements. If expectations and job requirements are consistent, the appropriate course of action is relatively straightforward. The female applicant interviewing with a liberated male for a male-dominated position would probably be wise to act in a nontraditional, stereotypically masculine way. Similarly, although perhaps not as surely, if the interviewer has traditional attitudes toward women and the job is typically classified as female, a stereotypically feminine self-presentational style may be the most viable option.

If the stereotypes associated with the position are *not* consistent with those held by the interviewer, however, the potential effect of a self-presentational style based on the interviewer's attitudes is not clearly discernible. It may be, for example, as von Baeyer et al. suggest, that if the position is seen as male-appropriate, "a highly feminine self-presentation might do more harm than good in the eyes of a male chauvinist interviewer." [10, p. 50] On the other hand, such a presentation might lead the interviewer to ignore any lack of fit between applicant qualifications and formal job requirements.

This chapter is a followup to von Baeyer et al., designed to explore these questions [10]. Given the salience and relatively greater legitimacy of position requirements as opposed to personal prejudices, we expected to find that female applicants whose self-presentational style was consistent with the sex-role linked stereotype of the job would be perceived as more suitable for the job than applicants whose behavior reflected the opposite stereotype.

Within these constraints, we expected males' own attitudes toward women to have an "amplifying" influence of some kind on their judgments. One possibility we considered was that men with relatively traditional attitudes toward women would predict greater success and satisfaction for stereotypically feminine women in traditionally female occupations and less success and satisfaction for assertive women in male-dominated occupations than their more liberated colleagues. Alternatively, traditional men could believe so strongly that a woman's place is in the home that they would predict less success and satisfaction for her than their nontraditional counterparts, regardless of the nature of the job.

METHOD

Subjects and Design

Subjects were forty-eight male undergraduates at the University of Waterloo who completed a scale assessing their attitudes toward women, watched a videotaped job interview in which a female confederate/applicant acted in a traditionally feminine or nontraditional manner and then predicted her success and satisfaction in a variety of traditionally male- or female-occupied jobs.

In order to control for possible actress effects, we used two actresses, each of whom made a traditional and a nontraditional videotape. The design was therefore a two (traditional or nontraditional self-presentational style) by two

(Actress X or Actress Y) by two (traditional or nontraditional attitudes toward women) factorial design.

Experimental Manipulation

Following the technique developed by Word et al. [6], the self-presentational style of the women posing as applicants in this study was patterned on the actual behavior of the subjects in the von Baeyer et al. study [10]. Half the male subjects saw a job applicant whose appearance and behavior conformed to traditional sex-role stereotypes. She wore a bracelet, hoop earrings and two rings, a scarf around her neck, eye makeup and lipstick. She looked at the interviewer when he was talking but lowered her eyes modestly when answering his questions. When asked about marriage and family plans, she replied that she was planning to get married soon and would interrupt her career, if necessary, in order to care for her children. For the other male subjects, the job applicant, although dressed identically to the traditionalist, wore no makeup, no jewelry and no scarf around her neck. She looked directly at the interviewer when listening to and answering his questions. When asked about marriage and children, she replied that if these events occurred, she would organize her time so that family commitments did not interfere with career advancement plans.

Dependent Measures

On the Attitudes Toward Women Scale, completed prior to the videotape evaluation, subjects used 4-point scales to indicate their agreement or disagreement with twenty-five statements reflecting either traditional or nontraditional attitudes about female gender-appropriate behavior [18]. Immediately after seeing the videotape, subjects completed the Videotape Appraisal form, rating various applicant characteristics on twelve 5-point scales. This measure served as a manipulation check.

Subjects then completed the success and satisfaction predictors which constituted the study's main dependent measures. On a series of 5-point scales, subjects rated the applicant on her probable success in each of four predominantly male-occupied and four predominantly female-occupied professions. On a second questionnaire, they then predicted her probable satisfaction with each of these professions.

The eight jobs evaluated in this study were chosen on the basis of a survey in which introductory psychology students gave their estimates of the percentage of men and women found in twenty occupations. According to this survey, 64 percent of personnel managers, 72 percent of department store managers, 78 percent of insurance agents and 79 percent of high school principals were judged to be male. The predominantly female professions, matched for status with the male occupations, included social workers (58% female), dieticians (72% female), librarians (73% female) and preschool teachers (86% female).

RESULTS

Overview

All dependent measures were subjected to three-way analyses of variance, with actress identity, self-presentational style and attitudes toward women as the independent variables. The significant actress identity main effects and interactions which occurred on five items did not affect the main pattern of results and will not be discussed.

Videotape Appraisal

Subject responses to the Videotape Appraisal items indicated that the experimental manipulation had been successful. Significant main effects for self-presentational style reflected subjects' perceptions that the traditionally feminine actresses wore more jewelry ($F(1,39) = 6.29, p < .05$) and maintained less direct eye contact with the interviewer ($F(1,40) = 44.03, p < .001$) than their less traditional counterparts. They were also judged to be more attractive ($F(1,40) = 9.92, p < .01$), less outgoing ($F(1,40) = 6.33, p < .05$), and less confident ($F(1,40) = 10.11, p < .01$) when presenting themselves in a traditionally feminine way. The one significant main effect for attitudes toward women reflected the fact that men with nontraditional attitudes perceived both actresses to be less outgoing, independent of self-presentational style, than did more traditional men ($F(1,40) = 4.40, p < .05$). Finally, both actresses in both style conditions were perceived to be equally well-groomed, feminine, likable and intelligent.

Success and Satisfaction Predictors

Male jobs (see Table 1)—As expected, self-presentational style was a highly significant determinant of predicted female success and satisfaction for three of the four predominantly male occupations: insurance agent ($F(1,40) = 9.48, p < .01$ and ($F(1,40) = 4.99, p < .05$, respectively), personnel manager ($F(1,40) = 7.70$, $p < .01$ and $F(1,40) = 6.38, p < .05$, respectively) and high school principal ($F(1,40) = 10.67$, $p < .01$ and $F(1,40) = 6.04$, $p < .05$, respectively). Presentational style was also significant for predicted department store manager satisfaction ($F(1,40) = 6.37, p < .05$) but not for success. Examination of the means indicates that in all cases, the nontraditional applicant was judged more likely to be successful and satisfied than the traditional applicant.

Subjects' attitudes toward women significantly influenced their responses only on the item dealing with the probability that the applicant would be successful as a personnel manager ($F(1,40) = 6.35, p < .05$). Examination of the means indicates that men with traditional attitudes toward women predicted less success for the female personnel manager ($M = 2.75$) than did their less traditional colleagues ($M = 3.39$). The significant negative correlation ($r(46) =$

Table 1. Mean Predicted Success and Satisfaction in Male-Dominated Occupations

	Self-Presentational Style [b]	
	Traditional	*Nontraditional*
Insurance Agent		
Success [a]	2.42[c]	3.29
Satisfaction [a]	2.33	2.96
Personnel Manager		
Success [a]	2.67	3.42
Satisfaction [a]	3.13	3.79
High School Principal		
Success [a]	2.46	3.29
Satisfaction [a]	2.88	3.58
Department Store Manager		
Success	3.17	3.50
Satisfaction [a]	3.08	3.71

[a] Significant difference between means.
[b] N per cell = 24.
[c] Definitely Unsuccessful/Dissatisfied = 1; Definitely Successful/Satisfied = 5.

$-.36$, $p < .01$) between attitudes toward women and perceived personnel manager success provides additional evidence for the reliability of this finding.

Female jobs (see Table 2)—Self-presentational style was a highly significant determinant of predicted satisfaction for three of the four predominantly female occupations: preschool teacher ($F(1,40) = 6.03$, $p < .05$), social worker ($F(1,40) = 11.66$, $p = .001$) and librarian ($F(1,40) = 6.07$, $p < .05$). In all cases, predictions were more positive for traditional than for nontraditional applicants. Regarding predictions for applicant's success, however, self-presentational style was only marginally significant for the occupation of social worker ($F(1,40) = 3.05$, $p < .10$) and non-significant for the other occupations.

Subjects' attitudes toward women marginally influenced their predictions regarding the applicant's probable success ($F(1,40) = 2.98$, $p < .10$) *and* satisfaction ($F(1,40) = 3.09$, $p < .10$) as a social worker. As compared to men with nontraditional attitudes toward women, men with traditional attitudes predicted less success ($M = 3.04$ versus $M = 3.48$) and less satisfaction ($M = 3.24$ versus $M = 3.61$) regardless of self-presentational style. The significant negative correlations between attitudes toward women, social worker success ($r(46) = -.24$, $p < .05$) and satisfaction ($r(46) = -.34$, $p < .01$) provides additional confirmation for the reliability of this finding.

Table 2. Mean Predicted Success and Satisfaction in Female-Dominated Occupations

	Self-Presentational Style [b]	
	Traditional	*Nontraditional*
Preschool Teacher		
Success	3.54 [c]	3.17
Satisfaction [a]	3.75	3.08
Social Worker		
Success	3.50	3.00
Satisfaction [a]	3.83	3.00
Librarian		
Success	3.46	3.21
Satisfaction [a]	3.13	2.33
Dietician		
Success	3.50	3.25
Satisfaction	3.04	2.92

[a] Significant difference between means.
[b] *N* per cell = 24.
[c] Definitely Unsuccessful/Dissatisfied = 1; Definitely Successful/Satisfied = 5.

DISCUSSION

As expected, self-presentational style was a highly significant determinant of predicted female success *and* satisfaction in both male and female-dominated professions. However, consistency of style with implicit position requirements rather than with the sex-role expectations held by the male subjects was the critical factor. Nontraditional female applicants were expected to be more successful than traditional applicants in all four male-dominated professions and more satisfied in three of them. Similarly, traditionally feminine applicants were expected to be more satisfied than the nontraditional applicants in three of the four traditionally female careers. Interestingly, subjects did *not* expect traditionally feminine applicants to be significantly more *successful* than less traditional applicants in traditionally female careers, although the means were in the expected direction.

Our general expectation that men's own attitudes toward women would influence their job-related judgments was confirmed, although not in either of the ways we had anticipated. Male subjects' own attitudes toward women influenced their predictions for success and satisfaction only for the two positions least clearly defined as male or female-dominated in the initial survey—personnel manager (64% male) and social worker (58% female). The more traditional the men's attitudes toward women, the less likely they were to predict her success as a personnel manager or her success and satisfaction as a social worker, regardless of her self-presentational style.

These results could reflect the traditional male's belief that women belong in the home and are not competent employees, regardless of their personal style or the nature of the job. But why would these beliefs influence male judgments only for the positions of personnel manager and social worker? Perhaps social work and personnel management are, in fact, "transitional" occupations, in which the percentage of the positions occupied by the formerly dominant gender is steadily decreasing. If this conceptualization is accurate, then the two occupations in this study on which men's *personal* attitudes influenced their judgments are precisely those two positions for which stereotypic sex-role *position* requirements are most ambiguous. When position requirements are clear, the intrusion of personal attitudes into the decision-making process may be relatively difficult to justify. When these requirements are ambiguous, however, due to the changing definition of the job itself, the interviewer may feel freer to allow his personal prejudices to influence his judgments.

It should be remembered, of course, that even for the positions of social worker and personnel manager, self-presentational style was a significant determinant of predicted success and satisfaction. On balance, therefore, these results indicate that women should opt for a self-presentational style consistent with position requirements, even if those requirements are changing.

What do these studies mean? What are their implications for female behavior? First, taken together, these studies suggest that sex-role stereotypes do share self-fulfilling prophecy characteristics with other behavioral expectations. Consciously or unconsciously, in social or business situations, we fulfill the sex-role stereotypes of the important others with whom we interact, those with the power to punish or reward us on the basis of our behavior.

These studies also confirm the interactive nature of self-fulfilling prophecies. As Zanna et al. point out, Pygmalion's Galatea was probably the only target of behavioral expectations with no expectations of her own [1]. They suggest that Henry Higgins and Liza Doolittle are more accurate exemplars of the self-fulfilling prophecy process, and the research cited here could be interpreted as supporting that contention. In the von Baeyer et al. work, the female job applicants interacted for approximately ten minutes with a male interviewer who was blind to condition and trained to conduct the interview in a neutral manner [10]. The interviewer's failure to emit verbal or behavioral cues consistent with his supposed attitudes toward women did not deter female applicants from behaving in ways consistent with their expectations of his expectations. In that study and in Zanna and Pack's [7] "blind date" study, half the women were induced to behave in nontraditional ways, based on their expectation that the male partner/interviewer was a feminist. In the real world, however, we would suggest that women are much more likely to assume, realistically, that the men with whom they interact have relatively traditional views regarding gender-appropriate behavior. Therefore, in the absence of clear, disconfirming evidence, women may choose to "play it safe," conforming, consciously or unconsciously, to traditional sex-role stereotypes.

Such behavior would seem to be dysfunctional for two reasons. First, the results of the present study indicate that conformity to traditional sex-role stereotypes in an occupational context has very limited utility. A traditionally feminine approach resulted in judgments of greater predicted satisfaction in traditionally female jobs but not necessarily greater success. In our society, the stereotypically masculine traits of ambition, rationality and decision-making ability are considered essential for work success [19], and these factors are probably considered important even in traditionally female positions.

Opting for traditionally feminine behavior in ambiguous situations is also dysfunctional in a broader context. Every time we conform to traditional sex-role stereotypes, we maintain and reinforce them. How many men and women in the process of "raising their consciousnesses" and changing their expectations remain unconvinced or "closet" feminists or revert to their original stance because they encounter only traditionally feminine women? And how many of the gender differences in behavior documented by psychologists over the years are at least partially attributable to the fact that males and females have been, and are, conforming to different sets of expectations, actual or presumed.

How can this circular behavioral confirmation process be short-circuited? One solution is to monitor one's own behavior very carefully so as not to confirm others' sex-role stereotypes or to elicit stereotypical behavior from them. Such a continual self-monitoring process would hopefully weaken gender-behavior links and eventually erode or eliminate sex-role stereotypes. Given the largely unconscious nature of much of our behavior, this advice is easier to give than to follow. One possibly helpful course of action, however, is to structure one's environment so as to make one's own unconscious conformity to traditional sex-role stereotypes less likely. An interesting possibility in this regard is that the effectiveness of the skirted suit as a business uniform may depend as much on its unrecognized effect on the wearer's actual beahvior as on its suppression of sex-role stereotypes held by male executives.

ACKNOWLEDGMENTS

The authors wish to thank Elizabeth Elliott, Adele Eyman, and Joel Goldberg for their assistance in conducting this research.

REFERENCES

1. M. P. Zanna, P. L. Sheras, J. Cooper, and C. Shaw, Pygmalion and Galatea: Interactive Effect of Teacher and Student Expectancies, *Journal of Experimental Social Psychology*, *11*, pp. 279-287, 1975.
2. R. Rosenthal and L. Jacobson, *Pygmalion in the Classroom*, Holt, Rinehart and Winston, New York, 1968.
3. W. D. Crano and P. M. Mellon, Causal Influence of Teachers' Expectations on Children's Academic Performance: A Cross-Lagged Panel Analysis, *Journal of Educational Psychology*, *70*, pp. 39-49, 1978.

4. C. Braun, Teacher Expectation: Sociopsychological Dynamics, *Review of Educational Research*, *46*, pp. 185-213, 1976.
5. M. Snyder, E. D. Tanke, and E. Berscheid, Social Perception and Interpersonal Behavior: On the Self-fulfilling Nature of Social Stereotypes, *Journal of Personality and Social Psychology*, *35*, pp. 656-666, 1977.
6. C. O. Word, M. P. Zanna, and J. Cooper, The Nonverbal Mediation of Self-fulfilling Prophecies in Interracial Interaction, *Journal of Experimental Social Psychology*, *10*, pp. 109-120, 1974.
7. M. P. Zanna and S. J. Pack, On the Self-fulfilling Nature of Apparent Sex Differences in Behavior, *Journal of Experimental Social Psychology*, *11*, pp. 583-591, 1975.
8. E. H. Raven, Social Influence and Power, in *Current Studies in Social Psychology*, I. D. Steiner and M. Fishbein (eds.), Holt, Rinehart and Winston, New York, 1965.
9. I. H. Frieze, J. E. Parsons, P. B. Johnson, D. N. Ruble, and G. L. Zellman, *Women and Sex Roles: A Social Psychological Perspective*, W. W. Norton and Company, New York, 1978.
10. C. L. von Baeyer, D. L. Sherk, and M. P. Zanna, Impression Management in the Job Interview: When the Female Applicant Meets the Male (Chauvinist) Interviewer, *Personality and Social Psychology Bulletin*, *7*, pp. 45-51, 1981.
11. J. Baer, *How to Be an Assertive(Not Aggressive) Woman in Life, in Love, and on the Job: A Total Guide to Self-assertiveness*, Rawson Associates, New York, 1976.
12. J. T. Molloy, *The Woman's Dress for Success Book*, Warner Books, New York, 1977.
13. M. B. Heilman and L. R. Saruwatari, When Beauty Is Beastly: The Effects of Appearance and Sex on Evaluations of Job Applicants for Managerial and Nonmanagerial Jobs, *Organizational Behavior and Human Performance*, *23*, pp. 360-372, 1979.
14. S. M. J. Towson and M. P. Zanna, *Do Clothes Make the Woman: Fashion and the Female Executive*, paper presented at the Canadian Psychological Association Conference, Winnipeg, Manitoba, June, 1983.
15. T. F. Cash, B. Gillen, and D. S Burns, Sexism and Beautyism in Personnel Consultant Decision-making, *Journal of Applied Psychology*, *62*, pp. 301-311, 1977.
16. R. Dipboye and J. W. Wiley, Reactions of College Recruiters to Interviewee Sex and Self-Presentational Style, *Journal of Vocational Behaviour*, *10*, pp. 1-12, 1977.
17. S. Feldman-Sumners and S. B. Kiesler, Those Who Are Number Two Try Harder: The Effect of Sex on Attributions of Causality, *Journal of Personality and Social Psychology*, *30*, pp. 846-855, 1974.
18. J. T. Spence, R. Helmreich, and J. Stapp, A Short Version of the Attitudes Toward Women Scale (AWS), *Bulletin of the Psychonomic Society*, *2*, pp. 219-220, 1973.
19. I. Broverman, S. Vogel, D. Broverman, F. Clarkson, and P. Rosenkrantz, Sex-Role Stereotypes: A Current Appraisal, *Journal of Social Issues*, *28*, pp. 59-78, 1972.

PART II

The Construction of Women (and Men)

The chapters in this section deal with the ways our culture as a whole defines sex and gender. Some of the chapters extend this kind of analysis to subcultures within the United States as well as cross-culturally. They raise important issues about how our assumptions determine the kind of questions we ask or do not ask. They also illustrate within a large range of content areas how the answers we find are determined by the questions we ask.

The study by Volentine and Brodsky supports the view that sex is personally constructed. Even with identical information about roles, individuals evaluate males and females differently. In the formation of stereotypes, sex of subject-sex of stimulus person interactions appear to be the rule. Males concentrate on expressive traits when characterizing individuals in roles that are important to them whereas females make more use of instrumental descriptors. Females in roles identical to male counterparts are described in more expressive terms than are males, especially by men. However, despite the popularity of the concept of androgyny, expressive and instrumental traits are rarely combined in descriptions of a particular person in a particular role.

Sedney's theoretical analysis of androgyny reveals that this concept is used by psychologists in a variety of ways. The way androgyny is conceived appears to be related to the theoretical framework in which the research is embedded. Unfortunately, researchers seldom consider alternative definitional possibilities and the once promising area of androgyny has become a morass of unreplicated studies, correlations between psychological measures with no theoretical justification for their connection, and disagreement about what, if anything, androgyny measures about gender roles. Sedney attempts to rescue the concept by a careful taxonomy that illustrates the way multiple methods produce multiple meanings.

The chapters by Marlowe and by Crawford look at humor to explore cultural constructions of women and men. Marlowe focuses on what and who is considered funny in our society. She points out that traditional humor is based on our assumptions about people as members of groups. Those who do not share sexist assumptions about women–feminists–may be said to have no sense of humor. Crawford looks at traditional methods for studying humor to explicate social constructs. She suggests that by focusing on humor appreciation rather than humor creation, we have neglected the social uses to which humor may be put. Women, in contrast to men, appear to use humor to create relationships. Their humor is more likely to be embedded in conversational context making it more difficult to study using conventional experimental methodology.

In a different way, Lykes also questions the assumptions behind traditional psychological research. She questions the implicit assumptions behind even such a well-intentioned procedure as informed consent. In the course of her research with Guatemalan Indian women, Lykes became aware that the use of written forms assumed the researcher's greater power vis-a-vis her subjects and subverted an honorable attempt at collaborative research. She raises questions about the meaning of traditional methodology in more oral and communal cultures than our own.

Even more serious questions about the relative power of researcher and subject are raised by Fine's account of an interview in a rape-crisis center. Ways of coping evaluated from a middle-class white perspective turn out to be inappropriate or harmful when seen from the life circumstances of a poor black woman without access to support systems or an alternative life style. Passivity may be the most adaptive response under her circumstances, but such behavior is defined as maladaptive by the mental health establishment. Both Lykes and Fine illustrate how attention to the phenomenology of women unlike ourselves reveals assumptions of which we had not previously been aware.

Some of the unresolved questions raised by articles in this section include: Do women and men have different realities? What accounts for the perceptual-cognitive differences found? Are there similarities between the realities of "the others" in our society; e.g., blacks, the poor, women, etc.? Are we eliminating differences between groups of women in order to maximize the similarities between them? What does androgyny as a psychological concept really imply? Is it a construct of psychologists rather than part of our consensual reality? What do "unimportant" aspects of our culture such as humor reveal about our cultural assumptions? How do the questions we do ask affect the people of whom we ask them in terms of psychological theory and practice? To what extent is what is known by psychology about sex and gender a product of the questions we have asked in the past?

FURTHER READINGS

Caplan, N. and S. D. Nelson. On Being Useful: The Nature and Consequences of Psychological Research on Social Problems, *American Psychologist*, *28*, pp. 199-211, 1973.

Datan, N. Corpses, Lepers, and Menstruating Women: Tradition, Transition, and the Sociology of Knowledge, *Sex Roles*, *14*, pp. 693-703, 1986.

Pleck, J. H. *The Myth of Masculinity*, MIT Press, Cambridge, 1981.

Spence, J. T. and L. L. Sawin. Images of Masculinity and Femininity: A Reconceptualization, in *Women, Gender, and Social Psychology*, V. E. O'Leary, R. K. Unger, and B. S. Wallston (eds.), Erlbaum, Hillsdale, New Jersey, 1985.

Unger, R. K. Looking Toward the Future by Looking at the Past: Social Activism and Social History, *Journal of Social Issues*, *42*, pp. 215-227, 1986.

Wallston, B. S. and V. E. O'Leary. Sex Makes a Difference: Differential Perceptions of Women and Men, in *Review of Personality and Social Psychology* (Volume 2), L. Wheeler (ed.), Sage, Beverly Hills, 1981.

CHAPTER 8

Personal Construct Theory and Stimulus Sex and Subject Sex Differences

SUSAN Z. VOLENTINE
STANLEY L. BRODSKY

The language used in the study of sex differences profoundly influences how the research problems are pursued. Grady pointed out two uses of "sex" as an independent variable [1, pp. 174-175]. First, she defined "*subject* sex differences" as assuming that "there are two types of people, females and males, who differ in terms of specific capabilities, abilities, or traits." The second use of the variable "sex" is as a *stimulus* variable where the sex differences are "in the eye of the beholder." These latter differences are inferred by individuals in their perceptions of men and women and are commonly labeled as "sex stereotypes."

It is important to be aware of this distinction between subject sex and stimulus sex variables as both types are often referred to by the same labels; that is, both subjects and stimuli are referred to as males and females or as men and women. It is important to recognize the type of variable to which the label refers.

In order to avoid erroneous conclusions, it is also important to determine if the obtained results are due to the subject or stimulus variables. For example, Horner concluded from her research on fear of success that females were afraid of achievement [2]. However, subsequent research determined that both male and female subjects projected unfortunate consequences to the female stimulus' achievement [3]. This result indicated that the correct locus of the effect was in the stimulus. This suggests that the results of Horner were due to the effects of sex stereotyping and were not due to the personality characteristics of females.

A second distinction important for the research on sex differences is that between the variables of sex and gender. Unger defined gender as the "nonphysiological components of sex that are culturally regarded as appropriate to males and females." [4, p. 1086] Unger further clarified her definitions as follows [5]:

> . . . sex refers either to the biological aspects of being male or female or to the stimulus aspects of being male or female. Gender refers to the psychological components assumed to be highly correlated to the sex and presumably accounts for many attributions made on the basis of sex.

As a result of this distinction between sex and gender, psychological differences found between the sexes (sex as a subject variable) would be considered as gender differences. In addition, psychological differences attributed to the sexes (sex as a stimulus variable) would also be a component of gender.

The application of cognitive theories to the area of sex and gender has been an important development to the conceptualization and integration of the research. For example, in the traditional sex stereotype research [6, 7], the usual results are simply a list of adjectives which differentiate the stimuli of men and women. In contrast, research which has applied implicit personality theory to the investigation of sex stereotypes [8-10] has utilized a more sophisticated methodology and has provided a theoretical framework in which to conceptualize the results.

In addition, the cognitive theory of gender schema theory has been applied to sex as a subject variable [11, 12]. Gender has also functioned as a subject variable in this research in that individual differences among subjects' self-concepts on gender related traits are evaluated. However, Bem described the schema concept as being ill-defined and as possibly not developed to the point where it can be properly labeled as a theory [11, pp. 355-356].

The concepts involved in the schema concept are contained within the cognitive theoretical approach of personal construct theory developed by Kelly [13]. This theory offers a well established theoretical framework and methodology which can examine both gender and sex as subject variables (as in gender schema theory) and as stimulus variables (as in implicit personality theory). The present research examined sex as a subject variable and as a stimulus variable using the framework of personal construct theory. First, this theory will be reviewed along with its applications to the variables of sex and gender.

PERSONAL CONSTRUCT THEORY

George Kelly constructed a personality theory which casts individuals in the role of scientists who develop theories in order to predict their world [13]. Kelly believed that the meaning an individual gives to events indicates important information about what kind of person he or she is. If we know an individual's constructs, we can then better understand the person. An important part of the theory is the process of anticipating events, for in personal construct theory anticipation is motivation; it is both the push and pull of existence.

The ways in which a person anticipates events are defined by the personal constructs he or she develops to subsume them. Only when the constructs are interrelated and organized into a hierarchical system of meanings can they become a useful tool for anticipation. Kelly presented two types of constructs which make up this hierarchical system. A higher order construct, called a superordinate construct, is one that contains other constructs within its range of meaning. The subordinate constructs are the building blocks of the theory and the individual combines them into higher order superordinate constructs. An example of superordinate construct is good/bad and serving as one of its subordinate constructs could be musical/nonmusical.

Personal construct theory can be used to evaluate sex as a stimulus variable by considering the construct of male/female as being a superordinate construct. Bannister and Mair suggested that in order to understand the meaning of the superordinate construct of male/female, one needs to determine the subordinate constructs which are subsumed by it [14]. The commonly used methodology to determine these subordinate constructs has been to locate constructs which are differentially applied to male and female stimulus persons personally known to the subjects. The results of such an analysis have bearing on how men and women are perceived in terms of sex stereotypes.

The Role Construct Repertory Test

Kelly's Role Construct Repertory Test (Rep Test) was orginally designed as a personality test using individuals' personal constructs to understand the meaning they placed on the world. Many modifications of the original test have been made to study the construing of experience [14, 15].

In order to elicit personal constructs, Kelly asked the subjects to respond to items that they were likely to face in building structure for their lives. To meet this goal, Kelly included people as items in his test because of their central position in individuals' experiences. The specific people are studied by a list of role title descriptions to which the subject supplies the names of people he or she knows personally. The method of triads is used; the subject is presented with three of the role titles and asked, "In what important way are two of them alike but different from the third?" The construct developed by the subject is recorded and the two alike role titles are indicated. Next, the person is asked to indicate how the third person is different and this response is recorded as the opposite. A new set of three role titles is selected and the process repeats for twenty to thirty such comparisons.

Kelly also presented a grid format analysis for the Rep Test [13]. In this analysis, the role titles stand as the column heads and the constructs as the row heads which then form a matrix of squares or a grid. In this grid analysis, the subject evaluates each of the role titles in terms of the applicability of the constructs. The subject indicates with a check mark those people who possess the construct and leaves blank those who possess its opposite. As a result, the pattern of check marks in the grid can be subjected to a nonparametric analysis as developed by Kelly, or it can be subjected to a factor analysis or cluster analysis as suggested by Fransella and Bannister [15, pp. 74-76]. These analyses of the grid provide information on the interrelationship of the constructs and on the hierarchical structure of the construct system.

Sex and Stimulus Variable

Kelly presented a method of assessing subjects' protocols in order to obtain differential perceptions of men and women [13, pp. 294-296]. A scanning procedure determined which constructs distinguished between the role titles identified as men and those identified as women. Kelly referred to these differentiated constructs as a masculine-feminine dimension. After determining which constructs were differentially attributed to men and women, the role titles were then evaluated in terms of consistency of the attribution of each of the two groups of constructs. For example, his analysis of one female's protocol revealed that she viewed her father as the most masculine person and her sister was seen as opposite to her father on this dimension. A second female's protocol revealed that she saw neither her mother nor herself as being feminine.

Differential perceptions of men and women also have been assessed through a cluster analysis technique from a free response method rather than from a Rep Test grid [16]. Rosenberg's research was conducted as part of his undergraduate seminar on personality research, and the members of his class developed and analyzed their own personal construct theories. Rosenberg presented an extensive cluster analysis of two of his students' protocols which revealed construct clusters that were related to the sex of the stimulus persons.

Rosenberg's analysis of a male subject's protocol revealed two clusters of positive characteristics that were seen as characterizing women. Cluster one consisted of *sweet, pretty, sexy,* and *nice smelling*, and cluster two consisted of physical characteristics such as *shapely, cute,* and *big breasts.* The same subject saw *stuck-up* and *small breasts* as representing a negative female pole. Also, this subject's protocol revealed a positive male pole which consisted of the characteristics of *individualistic, clever, optimistic, talkative, easy going, humorous,* and *made me laugh.*

An analysis of a female subject's protocol revealed two clusters of interrelated adjectives that positively described men. Cluster one consisted of *exciting, giddy, security, excited, romantic,* and *sexually arousing.* Cluster two consisted of *sexy, sensuous,* and *dramatic*.

Sex as a Subject Variable

Personal construct theory can also examine sex as a subject variable by evaluating the constructs developed by males and females. One related study used the Rep Test to examine subject differences between two gender-types of women (androgynous and feminine) [17]. Significant differences in construct systems were found; androgynous-typed women used more constructs which were judged to be masculine than did feminine-typed women. Also, in describing the self, the feminine-typed women used more constructs judged to be feminine than masculine. Although this study examined gender differences rather than sex differences, it offers a methodological format which can be applied to sex as a subject variable.

Sex as a Subject Variable and as a Stimulus Variable

The reviewed studies examined sex as a stimulus variable only through individual protocols. However, Ryle and Lunghi examined groups of protocols developed by males and by females in order to determine subject sex differences in the construing of the superordinate construct of male/female [18]. This study found no differences due to the sex of the subject but did find differences in perceptions due to the sex of the stimulus person. Fifty-three male and seventy female subjects evaluated instrumental and expressive qualities within the role titles. Instrumental qualities are stereotypically preferred for males and include independence, self-reliance, and other achievement oriented traits. Expressive qualities are stereotypically preferred for females and include nurturance, warmth, and other interpersonal traits. The subjects were supplied with eight constructs that referred to instrumental qualities and eight that referred to expressive qualities. The results demonstrated that the male role titles were construed by both male and female subjects as significantly more instrumental and less expressive than the female role titles.

This current research uses the methodology of personal construct theory in order to investigate the perceptions of actual men and women by male and female subjects. The purpose of this study is to investigate the commonalities which exist in the perceptions of men and the perceptions of women (sex as a stimulus variable) and to investigate the commonalities in the perceptions held by male subjects and held by female subjects (sex as a subject variable). This current research extends the methodology used by Ryle and Lunghi by broadening the scope of perceptions to encompass any possible trait which subjects chose to attribute to the two sexes [18]. Ryle and Lunghi examined only two possible dimensions of perceptions: expressiveness and instrumentality. Certainly many other dimensions of perception could be applied to the sexes. In the current study, rather than using supplied constructs related to a few dimensions, the subjects developed their own constructs; in order to clarify the distinction between sex as a subject variable and as a stimulus variable, subjects are referred to as either males or females and stimulus persons are referred to as either men or women.

METHOD

Subjects

Thirty-five female and thirty-three male introductory psychology students volunteered to participate in order to receive bonus course credit.

Materials

A modified version of the group form of the Rep Test was used to elicit the differential perceptions of the sexes. One form of this modified Rep Test referred specifically to men stimulus persons, and one referred specifically to women stimulus persons. The stimulus persons (role titles) are as follows: *mother* or *father, brother* or *sister, liked teacher, disliked teacher, closest friend, close associate who appears to dislike you, person whom you would like to get to know better, person for whom you feel sorry, a respected person,* and *an interesting person*. These ten role title descriptions were presented on a paper titled "Name List." On a separate piece of paper, a 10 × 10 matrix of squares matched a number within each row of squares to the number of a role title. Three squares selected by random in each column of the grid contained a circle.

Procedure

Each subject was given one of the name lists, either with descriptions of role titles that called specifically for a man or descriptions that called specifically for a woman. Sixteen males and sixteen females completed the grid using the women role titles, and seventeen males and nineteen females used the men role titles. The subjects aligned the name list with the grid so that three names were identified by the three circles in column one. The subjects then compared and contrasted the three persons and thought of a way in which two of them were alike and one of them was different. They were instructed to write this idea in a space labeled "Construct" at the top of the column. They also indicated what the opposite was of their construct in a space labeled "Opposite." Next, they put a check mark by all the people on their list who possessed that trait and left blank the space next to those people who lacked the trait. The above two steps, the formation of a construct and the evaluation of the role titles, were repeated for each column. This procedure resulted in ten comparisons being made for three different role titles so that ten constructs were developed by each subject.

Data Analysis

The data consisted of four sets of grids which differed on two variables, the sex of the subject and the sex of the stimulus person. Each set was factor analyzed using the principle components method with subsequent varimax rotation to an orthogonal solution provided by the BMD08M program from the

BMD, Biomedical Computer Programs [19]. The constructs provided by the subjects served as the variables; each subject provided ten variables. The ten role titles, or stimulus persons, served as the subjects, and the pattern of check marks served as the data points. The data matrix is presented in Table 1.

Each initial set of the resulting factors was subjected to a Scree Test [20] to determine a suitable factor size for the next rotation. The resulting factor loads were analyzed and the constructs that loaded greater than or equal to the absolute value of .3 on only one factor were considered as representing that factor. When the final number of factors was determined, additional constructs which loaded greater than the absolute value of .5 on only one factor and less than the absolute value of .4 on the others were included in the descriptions of the factor for additional interpretability.

Table 1. Data Matrix

			male subjects or female subjects			
men role titles	female role titles		S1	S2		S20
			1 . . . 10	11 . . . 20	. . . .	191 . . . 198
(father)	(mother)	1				
(brother)	(sister)	2				
		3				
		4				
		5				
		6				
		7				
		8				
		9				
		10				

A one or a zero is entered at every point.

RESULTS

The results of the four factor analyses are presented in Table 2.

Women Stimulus Persons

Male subjects – A four factor solution accounting for 71 percent of the total variance best represented the data. The four factors, listed with the percent of variance for which each accounted, were labeled as follows: Factor I (35%): Ideal companion, warm, caring, witty, intelligent; Factor II (15%): Open minded, bold, helpful listener; Factor III (11%): Responsible individual; Factor IV (10%): Lacking in helpfulness and warmth.

Table 2. Factor Analyses of Stimulus and Subject Sex Variables

	Women Stimulus Persons		*Men Stimulus Persons*	
	Male Subjects	*Female Subjects*	*Male Subjects*	*Female Subjects*
% total variance	*71%*	*69%*	*77%*	*74%*
Factors				
I	Ideal companion: warm, caring, witty, intelligent	Intelligent, disliked, lack of warmth	Wise, benevolent father figure	Ideal companion: easy going, sensitive
variance	35%	35%	33%	31%
II	Open minded, bold, helpful listener	Disliked, Uptight	Irresponsible youth	Obnoxious, outgoing, lacks positive traits
variance	15%	22%	14%	14%
III	Responsible individualist	Friendly, easy going, self-confident	Disliked, lacks interpersonal skills	Immature, lacks achievement oriented traits
variance	11%	11%	14%	12%
IV	Lacking in helpfulness and warmth	Intelligent, undependable	Daring, competitive gentleman	Religious, steadfast
variance	10%	9%	10%	9%
V			Intellectual	Aloof, gives bad first impression
variance			9%	9%

Traits with high loadings for each factor are as follows: Factor I: humorous, caring, encouraging, protective, true, fun to be with, and very understanding (all at .95). Factor II: open minded (.84), bold (.84), not likeable (−.79), open minded (.79), very considerate (.77), comforting (.71), helpful (.71), and thrifty (−.64). Factor III: outgoing (−.78), individualist (.76), teacher (.73), always in a good mood (.71), responsible (.64), looks out for #1 (.61), and vulnerable (−.57). Factor IV: false fronts (.86), loveable (−.83), helpful (−.71), nice and sweet (−.70), understandable (−.70), responsible (−.67), hard headed (.67), and hard to understand (.67).

Female subjects—A four factor solution accounting for 69 percent of the variance best represented the data. The four factors, listed with the percent of variance for which accounted, were labeled as follows: Factor I (35%): Intelligent, disliked, lack of warmth; Factor II (22%): Disliked, uptight; Factor III (11%): Friendly, easy going, self-confidence; Factor IV (9%): Intelligent, undependable.

Traits with high loadings for each factor are as follows: Factor I: outgoing (−.83), scholastic (.82), intelligent (.78), loving persons (−.78), easy to relate to (−.76), good personality (−.76), can act crazy (−.66), and offers constructive criticism (−.61). Factor II: easy to get along with (−.95), respectable (−.95), trustworthy and respectful (−.89), uptight (.66), would like to get to know better (−.66), intelligent (−.53), and outspoken (.52). Factor III: like a friend to me, friendly, ambitious, cheerful, considerate, optimistic (all at .93), responsible, and self-confident (both at .88). Factor IV: trustworthy (−.91), smart (.91), know me well (−.90), don't know well (.69), protective and motherly (−.64), and intellectual (.54).

Men Stimulus Persons

Male subjects—A five factor solution accounting for 77 percent of the total variance best represented the data. The five factors, listed with the percent of variance for which each accounted, were labeled as follows: Factor I (33%): Wise, benevolent father figure; Factor II (14%): Irresponsible youth; Factor III (14%): Disliked, lack of interpersonal skills; Factor IV (10%): Daring, competitive gentleman; Factor V (9%): Intellectual.

Traits with high loadings for each factor are as follows: Factor I: go out of their way for someone else (.88), offers guidance (.88), unable to communicate well (−.87), too particular (−.87), unfriendly (−.87), peaceful (.87), and happy (.87). Factor II: responsible (−.94), irresponsible (.94), athletic type (.94), girl crazy (.80), nasty talker (.79), outspoken (−.46), and young (.46). Factor III: untrustworthy (.87), unlikeable (.87), likeable (−.87), humorous (−.87), pleasant personality (−.85), easy going (−.85), funny (−.77), and leaders of people (−.75). Factor IV: a gentleman when it comes to ladies (.92), daring (.92), enjoys entertaining people (.77), open minded (−.73), competitive (.68), outgoing (−.57), outdoor type (.54), and serious (−.41). Factor V: enjoys learning through studying (.94), compassionate (−.82), easy going (−.80), different (.78), lacks responsibility (−.74), intellectual (.56), and well educated (.54).

Female subjects—A five factor solution accounting for 74 percent of the variance best represented the data. The five factors, listed with the percent of variance for which each accounted, were labeled as follows: Factor I (31%): Ideal companion, easy going, sensitive; Factor II (14%): Obnoxious, outgoing, lacking in positive traits; Factor III (12%): Immature, lacking in achievement oriented traits; Factor IV (9%): Religious, steadfast; Factor V (9%): Aloof, gives bad first impression.

Traits with high loadings for each factor are as follows: Factor I: sexy (.82), competitive (.82), easy going (.81), friendly (.81), fun to be with (.81), wealthy (.78), intelligent (.77), sensitive (.74). Factor II: witty (−.97), always trying (−.97), loveable (−.97), obnoxious (.86), outgoing (.84), sneaky (.84), and intelligent (−.81). Factor III: immature (.87), funny (−.87), responsible (−.84), friendly (−.84), responsible (−.84), independent (−.75), inspiring (−.70), and ambitious (−.57). Factor IV: friendly to everyone (.83), insecure (−.82), undependable (−.79), temperamental (−.77), religious minded (.69), good build (−.65), and religious (.33). Factor V: not loud or outspoken (−.90), easy to talk to (−.90), high morals (−.90), loveable (−.90), masculine (−.78), determination (−.76), unpredictable (−.75), and conservative (−.72).

DISCUSSION

The four factor analyses suggest that male and female subjects differentially perceive both men and women stimulus persons. Differences in perceptions appear to be due to the sex of the subject as well as due to the sex of the stimulus person. All four of the factor analyses accounted for at least 69 percent of the total variance, and the variables were combined into factors that were psychologically interpretable. Although each subject described a different person, the people chosen by each subject to fit each role title were similar in general characteristics. For example, the individual people occupying the role titles of mother, father, or teachers were similar across subjects in that they occupied positions of authority. Also, the people chosen for the role titles of close friend or liked teacher were similar in likeability. These similar characteristics contributed to the similarity of trait attributions made to the role titles.

The overall patterns of trait attributions revealed an emphasis on expressive, or interpersonal, traits. Indeed, expressive traits were central to all four of the first factors. These expressive characteristics involved concern for the needs of others present in traits such as nurturance and warmth. This concept of expressiveness was developed by Parsons and Bales in their sociological theory of sex role differences [21]. They argued that women fulflll an expressive role in society and men fulfill an instrumental role. This instrumental role involves attaining goals through traits such as independence, self-reliance, and assertiveness. This distinction between expressiveness and instrumentality has also been used in current concepts of sex differences [22-24] and in the previously reviewed study by Ryle and Lunghi [18].

Male subjects in particular tended to emphasize expressive traits. Four out of nine possible factors developed by the males contained clear expressive qualities (Factors I, II, and III for women stimulus persons and Factor I for men stimulus persons). In addition, male subjects discriminated between two types of expressiveness in women; that is, on Factors I and II they appeared to distinguish warmth from helpfulness. None of the factors developed by male subjects clearly emphasized instrumentality.

The preponderance of expressive traits was not as strong in the perceptions developed by female subjects; only 2 out of 9 factors pertained clearly to expressiveness (Factor I for women stimulus persons and Factor I for men stimulus persons), and one combined both instrumental traits and expressive traits (Factor III for women stimulus persons).

Another difference is in the attribution of negative traits. Here it is important to realize that a factor can contain negative traits in one of two ways; either by direct attribution of a negative trait or a failure to attribute a positive one. In their patterns of response, female subjects attributed negative traits and the absence of positive traits in a highly interrelated fashion; male subjects tended to attribute positive traits and the absence of negative traits in a similar pattern. Females, as a group, seemed to be more certain as to what types of people lacked positive traits or possessed negative traits than they were confident about the attribution of positive traits. This suggests that as a group females possess a more fully developed construct system underlying the "bad" pole of the superordinate construct of good/bad.

In examining sex as a stimulus variable, women stimulus persons as a whole had more expressive qualities attributed to them than did men stimulus persons. This outcome was particularly true in the attributions made by the male subjects to women stimulus persons (see Factors I, II, and III). Female subjects used expressive traits in two out of four factors when describing women stimulus persons (see Factors I and III). It is interesting to note that in their perceptions of stimulus women, female subjects were the only ones to combine expressive with instrumental characteristics (see Factor III). This suggests that to some degree, female subjects saw these characteristics as related. The factor content suggests an image of an achieving woman who also possesses valued interpersonal qualities, possibly representing an androgynous role model. Other than this one factor, expressive and instrumental traits were contained on separate factors.

Female subjects describing women stimulus persons showed an interesting connection of intelligence with negative traits. Intelligence was similarly associated with a lack of expressive characteristics on Factor I and with undependability on Factor IV. This connection between intelligence and negative traits was not found in any other combination of variables. In contrast, male subjects saw intelligence as connected with positive expressive traits in women (see Factor I).

It is interesting to note that females viewed instrumental women positively in Factor III but viewed intelligent women in a negative fashion in Factors I and IV. Possibly these results reveal the existence of two subtypes of female subjects—one type who sees women as capable of achievement and expressiveness, or androgyny, and a second type who sees intellectual pursuits as a downfall for women.

The analyses of attributions using the Rep Test provide insights into the ways in which traits are attributed to the two sexes by the two sexes. The overall results of this study suggest that our perceptions of others are complex phenomena which cannot be fully described in a dichotomous fashion such as expressive versus instrumental categories. Although expressive and instrumental traits were present in the results, these traits did not account for the range of perceptions, and their attribution was not dependent on the sex of the stimulus. However, expressive traits in particular are an important aspect of person perception, and women in particular seem to be evaluated on this dimension, particularly by males. Another provocative finding concerns the attribution of negative traits. Females seemed to be more confident as a group in the attribution of negative characteristics and were surprisingly negative toward intelligent women. Thus the myth that women cannot be both intelligent and attractive to others may still be alive among some women.

This study represents a new approach to the assessment of the perceptions of men and women and demonstrates how personal construct theory and its methodology can be applied to understanding the perceptions of men and women by males and females. Further research is needed to determine the generalizability of the specific perceptions found in this study to other population samples.

This study is unusual in its elicitation of perceptions of actual men and women. The typical approach to the perception of the sexes is found in the sex stereotype literature in which perceptions of sex labels are determined [6, 7]. The results from this current study have implications for the sex stereotype literature in that the perceptions of actual men and women were not based on an attribution of expressive traits to women and instrumental traits to men as it typically found with the labels of "men" and "women." Indeed, both actual men and women were described as possessing and lacking these traits on the different factors.

In addition to the methodology used in this current study, personal construct methodology can be adapted to study other aspects of sex and gender. For instance, the Rep Test could be used to determine those subjects who differentially ascribe constructs based on the sex of the role titles. In this way individual differences in reliance on the superordinate construct of male/female could be determined. Using the terminology of gender schema theory, subjects who use male/female to organize their construct system would be seen as utilizing a gender schema and those individuals who do not utilize male/female would be seen as functioning independent of a gender schema. It is our hope that the research presented in this study will generate interest in applying the methodology and theory of personal construct theory to research questions concerning sex and gender.

REFERENCES

1. K. Grady, Androgyny Reconsidered, in *Psychology of Women: Selected Readings*, J. H. Williams (ed.), Norton, New York, pp. 172-177, 1979.

2. M. A. Horner, Femininity and Successful Achievement: Basic Inconsistency, in *Roles Women Play*, M. H. Garskoff (ed.), Brooks/Cole, Belmont, California, 1971.
3. L. D. Monahan, D. Kuhn, and P. Shaver, Intra-psychic versus Cultural Explanations of the "Fear of Success" Motive, *Journal of Personality and Social Psychology*, *29*, pp. 60-64, 1974.
4. R. Unger, Toward a Redefinition of Sex and Gender, *American Psychologist*, *34*:11, pp. 1085-1094, 1979.
5. ———, Personal Communication, January 7, 1983.
6. J. P. McKee and A. C. Sherriffs, The Differential Evaluation of Males and Females, *Journal of Personality*, *25*, pp. 356-371, 1957.
7. P. S. Rosenkrantz, S. R. Vogel, H. Bee, I. K. Broverman, and D. M. Broverman, Sex-role Stereotypes and Self-concepts in College Students, *Journal of Consulting and Clinical Psychology*, *32*:3, pp. 287-295, 1968.
8. R. D. Ashmore and F. K. Del Boca, Sex Stereotypes and Implicit Personality Theory: Toward a Cognitive-Social Psychological Conception, *Sex Roles*, *5*:2, pp. 219-248, 1979.
9. R. D. Ashmore and M. L. Tumia, Sex Stereotypes and Implicit Personality Theory I: A Personality Description Approach to the Assessment of Sex Stereotypes, *Sex Roles*, *6*:4, pp. 501-518, 1980.
10. F. K. Del Boca and R. D. Ashmore, Sex Stereotypes and Implicit Personality Theory II: A Trait-inference Approach to the Assessment of Sex Stereotypes, *Sex Roles*, *6*:4, pp. 519-535, 1980.
11. S. L. Bem, Gender Schema Theory: A Cognitive Account of Sex Typing, *Psychological Review*, *88*:4, pp. 354-364, 1981.
12. H. Markus, M. Crane, S. Bernstein, and M. Siladi, Self-Schemas and Gender, *Journal of Personality and Social Psychology*, *42*:1, pp. 38-50, 1982.
13. G. A. Kelly, *The Psychology of Personal Constructs* (2 vols.), Norton, New York, 1955.
14. D. Bannister and J. M. M. Mair, *The Evaluation of Personal Constructs*, Academic Press, London, 1968.
15. F. Fransella and D. Bannister, *A Manual for Repertory Grid Technique*, Academic Press, London, 1977.
16. S. Rosenberg, New Approaches to the Analysis of Personal Constructs in Person Perception, *Nebraska Symposium on Motivation* (Vol. 24), University of Nebraska Press, Lincoln, Nebraska, pp. 179-242, 1976.
17. G. Tunnell, Sex Role and Cognitive Schemata: Person Perception in Feminine and Androgynous Women, *Journal of Personality and Social Psychology*, *40*:6, pp. 1126-1136, 1981.
18. A. Ryle and M. Lunghi, Parental and Sex-role Identification of Students Measured with a Repertory Grid Technique, *British Journal of Social and Clinical Psychology*, *11*, pp. 149-161, 1972.
19. W. J. Dixon (ed.), *BMD: Biomedical Computer Programs*, University of California Press, Berkeley and Los Angeles, California, pp. 255-268, 1977.
20. R. B. Cattell, the Scree Test for the Number of Factors, *Multivariate Behavioral Research*, *1*, pp. 245-276, 1966.

21. T. Parsons and R. F. Bales, *Family Socialization and Interaction Process*, Free Press, Glencoe, Illinois, 1955.
22. J. T. Spence and R. L. Helmreich, *Masculinity and Femininity: Their Psychological Dimensions, Correlates, and Antecedents*, University of Texas Press, Austin, Texas, 1978.
23. ———, The Many Faces of Androgyny: A Reply to Locksley and Colten, *Journal of Personality and Social Psychology*, *37*:6, pp. 1032-1046, 1979.
24. ———, Androgyny versus Gender Schema Theory: A Comment on Bem's Gender Schema Theory, *Psychological Review*, *88*:4, pp. 365-368, 1981.

CHAPTER 9

Conceptual and Methodological Sources of Controversies about Androgyny

MARY ANNE SEDNEY

From the time Sandra Bem introduced the concept of androgyny to psychologists [1], the construct has been hailed by researchers and critics alike. Researchers have found the concept and its associated scales (e.g., Bem Sex Role Inventory, BSRI [1]; Personal Attributes Questionnaire, PAQ [2]) a rich source of hypotheses about the relationship of combinations of femininity and masculinity with behaviors ranging from coital position [3] to vocational status [4]. While displaying less overt enthusiasm, critics, too, have found androgyny a productive stimulus for thinking and writing, as they have found fault with its philosophical foundations [5], measurement [6], and perceived threats to feminism [7].

As is often the case with new constructs, the initial period of productivity has been followed by a stage of disagreement and confusion. Androgyny researchers appear to be caught up in disagreements about the "correct" way to measure androgyny [8-11], the "right" age at which to find it [12-17], the "right" way to score available measures [2, 18-20], as well as the general validity of predictions derived from the concept of androgyny [21-27]. The present chapter introduces a taxonomic framework designed to clarify sources of some of these disagreements. Discussion of the proposed framework will show that many disagreements are based in fundamental conflicts about how to conceptualize androgyny and how to understand personality processes, rather than simply in conflicting data.

A major premise of the present discussion is that much of the "crisis" in the androgyny literature can be laid to sloppy thinking about the nature of androgyny. The term androgyny has been used, variously, to cover a balance of socially-defined traits, a lack of adherence to stereotyped norms, and endorsement of feminine and masculine identity.

This careless use of the term androgyny is part of a larger problem of an overgeneral use of the term "sex" to refer to biological, psychological, behavioral, social, and political processes. Likewise, "sex role" variously refers to ascribed role, occupation, attitudes, expectations, traits, identity, behaviors, and sexual preference. Several authors have pointed out that the variable sex can function in various ways: it refers to genetic, physiological, psychological, behavioral, and social variables that do not coincide [28, 29]. In short, sex is a multidimensional variable, with genetic, physiological, psychological, behavioral, and social dimensions.

Some attempts have been made to deal with the multidimensionality of sex, such as using the word "gender" for socially-rooted dimensions and "sex" for biologically-rooted dimensions. However, none of the solutions offered have isolated the psychological processes involved, either as subjective states or as immediate causes of behavior.

An additional framework is needed to delineate the psychological aspects of sex and gender. To do so for all sex and gender-related variables is beyond the scope of the present chapter. The recent attention to psychological androgyny among researchers makes androgyny an appropriate analogue for the development of such a framework.

The taxonomic framework proposed in this chapter is designed to assist the understanding of androgyny by specifying the variations in conceptions of androgyny and personality processes that underlay research in the field. By making clear these distinctions, more precise thinking about the psychological processes and causes at work within the variable of androgyny, and more precise measurement will be encouraged.

CONCEPTIONS OF ANDROGYNY

A review of major definitions of androgyny reveals a consensus on two major aspects of androgyny: androgyny includes both positive feminine and masculine[1] characteristics; and these characteristics are socially-defined rather than necessarily biologically-linked [1, 4, 13, 30]. "Feminine" is what people think is or should be associated with females; "masculine" is what people think is or should be associated with males.

However, the status of the relationship of these feminine and masculine characteristics is less clear-cut, as described below and depicted in the horizontal dimension of Table 1. Different authors (and sometimes the same author at

[1] Spence and Helmreich eschew the "feminine" and "masculine" labels in favor of "expressive" and "instrumental" [31]. Nevertheless, the origin of this area of research was concerned with expected and/or real differences between females and males; thus the labels feminine and masculine.

Table 1. Androgyny Research as a Function of Conception of Androgyny and Methodological Perspectives on Personality Processes

	Methodological Perspectives on Personality Processes			
Conceptions of Androgyny	*Traitist*	*Situationist*	*Attitude/Belief System*	*Cognitive Organizing Principle*
Co-presence of femininty and masculinity	[17, 21, 22, 39-46]	[50, 52, 53]	[56 (AWS)]	[58, 59 (high A)]
Integration of femininity and masculinity	describe hybrid traits, [49]	[50]	agree with statements favoring integration of feminine and masculine roles	consistent responses to hybrid terms
Transcendence of femininity and masculinity	non-existent? subgroup of undifferentiated?	[55]	agree with statements reflecting neither masculine nor feminine roles	[59 (low A), 57, 60-62]

different times) have based their thinking about androgyny on at least three notions of how femininity and masculinity are related in the androgynous person. To some authors, these characteristics are potentially independent and, hence, their mere *co-presence* in a person constitutes androgyny. From this "dualistic" perspective [23], an androgynous person is one who is sometimes feminine and sometimes masculine, sometimes warm and sometimes assertive, sometimes compassionate and sometimes independent, sometimes supportive and sometimes confrontative, depending on what is most appropriate in the situation. Elements of the traditional stereotypes are preserved intact as the androgynous person takes on both feminine and masculine stereotypes. According to such a definition, an androgynous person could behave in very traditional ways.

To other authors, however, the mere co-presence of traditional femininity and masculinity is insufficient for androgyny. From this "hybrid" perspective [23], androgyny is the *integration* of femininity and masculinity. The individual moves beyond stereotypic masculine and stereotypic feminine behavior in separate situations to a blending of masculinity and femininity in a single action. Assertiveness is tempered with warmth, independence with compassion, confrontation with supportiveness, not only in the long run but also in a single situation. As Kaplan pointed out, our language does not have many words that encompass these androgynous hybrids [32]. She proposed hyphenated terms. For example, "assertive-dependency" would "signify the recognition and acceptance of one's legitimate dependency needs, and the active pursuit of ways in which to fulfill these" [32, p. 227]. Such phrasing represents the integration perspective, while the co-presence perspective requires only that the individual be sometimes assertive and sometimes dependent without necessarily blending these components.

A third approach to conceptions of androgyny, the *transcendence* perspective, moves still further beyond stereotypic femininity and masculinity. As its name implies, transcendence involves a transcendence of traditional sex-roles, rather than a combination of these roles. For the transcendent individual, "assigned gender is irrelevant to decision-making" [33, p. 205]. Within this conception, androgyny is a movement beyond traditional femininity and masculinity; a mature "none of the above" in response to the question, "Are you masculine or feminine?' Rather than incorporating some parts of traditional femininity and masculinity, the transcendent person is neither feminine nor masculine. Masculinity and femininity, alone or in combination, are simply not part of the transcendent person's world.

While theorists might argue that any one of these three conceptions of androgyny constitutes the "correct" one, and researchers might try to present data demonstrating the accuracy of a conception, such claims are unresolvable, for there is no basis for establishing the validity of any one conception of a construct such as androgyny.

PERSONALITY PROCESSES: PERSPECTIVES AND METHODS

Variations in work on androgyny reflect not only the differences in conceptions of androgyny noted above, but also differences in researchers' understanding of personality processes in general. Androgyny research is a subset of research on personality and each androgyny researcher approaches the topic with certain paradigmatic preconceptions about personality processes arising out of background, training, and personal philosophy.

Descriptions of the major psychological approaches that appear to have served as a basis for androgyny researchers follow (and are depicted on the vertical dimension of Table 1), along with a discussion of methodological approaches to which they give rise.

The personality *trait* approach has a long history in psychology. Traitists look for personal consistencies across situations. The typical measurement device is the personality inventory, although interviews or questionnaires for self-reports of behaviors across situations are sometimes used.

Partly in response to calls from critics of the trait approach, a large group of psychologists concentrate their research efforts on looking for variations in an individual's behavior within situations. Since the term behaviorist has additional connotations not appropriate here, I will use the term *situationist* to designate this approach. The emphasis is on the situational, contextual, interpersonal, external elements of behavior, rather than the internal, individual consistency, transituational elements focused on in the trait approach. Frequent measurement devices include direct observations and self-reports of behavior in particular situations. Specific behaviors in specific situations rather than generalized tendencies are the focus of interest.

Shifting to a more social psychological approach, one finds researchers who concentrate on the attitudinal foundations of behavior. They explain behavior as a function of a person's *belief system*. Whereas traitists ask their subjects, "What are you like?" and situationists ask, "What do you do?" attitudinalists ask, "What *should* you (or other people) do or be like?" Attitude surveys, in which respondents report the extent of their agreement or disagreement with relevant statements, are the measure of choice. In sex role research, the attitude questionnaires commonly concern stereotypes, and focus on the degree of acceptance of conventional standards of behavior for women and men.

As psychology moves through its "cognitive revolution" [34], an increasingly large number of psychologists conceptualize behavior in terms of cognitive principles. They look at differences in individuals' ways of *cognitively organizing* their worlds. A person's self-schema [35] or personal construct system [36] is the basis of her or his perceptions of self, others, and events. Measurement of constructs are indirect and not well-developed. They include devices such as George Kelly's Role Construct Repertory Test and a variety of indicators used by Markus (specific response latency, retrieval of behavioral evidence, etc.), and focus on individual differences in information processes and uses of categories.

RESEARCH IN ANDROGYNY: CONCEPTIONS OF ANDROGYNY AND METHODOLOGICAL PERSPECTIVES ON PERSONALITY PROCESSES

Consideration of these three conceptions of androgyny and four methodological perspectives on personality processes yields a 12-cell matrix (Table 1) that can serve as a taxonomic framework for androgyny research. Each cell represents an approach to androgyny research, and, for each one, indicators of androgyny corresponding to that conception of androgyny and that perspective on personality will be discussed. Examples of research on androgyny consistent with a particular cell will be pointed out when possible.

Traitist

Co-presence of femininity and masculinity – The most well-developed cell in the matrix is the first one. All of the commonly-used measures of Androgyny–BSRI [1] [2], PAQ [2], PRF ANDRO [4], and rescoring of the *F* scale of the Adjective Check List [38]–incorporate a trait perspective on personality processes and a femininity-masculinity co-presence conception of androgyny. Despite differences in scale development, these instruments reflect a view that there are separate masculine and feminine traits that can potentially sum to androgyny.

Research representative of the trait/co-presence view of androgyny is cited in the first cell of Table 1 [17, 21, 22, 39-46]; this is not an exhaustive list. The most common approach among these researchers is to hypothesize a relationship of combined femininity and masculinity, with other aspects of personality, such as behaviors, attitudes, developmental level, or developmental experience.

Availability of these trait/co-presence measures makes their use appealing to researchers, even when the researchers' thinking is not consistent with a trait or co-presence approach. For example, Brewer and Blum apparently view androgyny as a rejection of traditional stereotypes [40], a view consistent with the attitudinal perspective on personality. Yet they used the BSRI as the indicator of androgyny when testing their ideas. Spence and her colleagues have warned repeatedly against such equation of sex-role-related traits and attitudes [47, 48], yet the practice persists.

[2] While it is true that statements by Bem in her original paper [37] allied her with an anti-trait position, the BSRI is clearly a trait measure in that it asks respondents to indicate their behavior in general, across situations.

Integration of femininity and masculinity – Moving vertically to the second cell in the matrix, one considers a traitist approach to the integration of femininity and masculinity. The focus is on single traits that encompass both femininity and masculinity. An inventory for such traits is not currently available but could be devised by asking respondents how characteristic various hybrid traits are of them. For example, they could be given a description of "assertive-dependency' or "supportive-confrontation" and asked to indicate how characteristic that description is of them.

An alternative possibility for combining the traitist and integration approaches involves examination of the statistical interaction of femininity and masculinity [49]. One problem with this approach is that it precludes the possibility of examining individual differences, the frequent focus of personality research. Due to the nature of the statistical procedures used, only group effects can be used. One of Bem's original postulates was that there are individual differences in the relationship of masculinity and femininity; that is why any measuring device should allow them to vary independently. One would expect that this individual variation would diminish the size of any group F × M interaction effect.

Transcendence of femininity and masculinity – It is difficult to envision a trait-transcendence approach, for the notion of transcendence focuses on process and contradicts the existence of discrete traits. Since these elements are antithetical to one another, the cell corresponding to their interaction might be non-existent.

However, alternatively, subjects who score as "undifferentiated" on trait measures of androgyny may include those who transcend traditional femininity and masculinity. Scoring low on both the femininity and masculinity scales, the undifferentiated may be viewed as rejecting the extremes of traditional feminine and masculine traits. Although some among this group may be scoring relatively low for other reasons such as low self-esteem, the group may include individuals who display a disregard for the extremes traditionally assigned differentially to females and males–a description consistent with a transcendence conception of androgyny.

Situationist

The second column in Table 1 represents the psychological perspective I have labeled situationist. Despite initial attention in the androgyny literature to the importance of situational appropriateness of feminine and/or masculine responses, surprisingly little androgyny research is directed to specific behaviors in specific situations. The notable exception is Bem's original laboratory research [50-52]. Although her purpose was validation of her trait test, the BSRI, her work does suggest situationist alternatives to trait perspectives on androgyny.

Co-presence of femininity and masculinity – For one who uses the co-presence conception of androgyny, the behaviors of interest would be those labeled feminine or masculine, and the androgynous person would engage competently in both. In Bem's early laboratory studies separate situations were contrived so that subjects' resistance to group pressure, nurturance responses to an infant, and comforting of a lonely peer could be observed [50, 52].

Although these studies were designed to examine evidence for trait-like consistency, one could develop a similar situational measure of the co-presence conception of androgyny without accepting those implications. Subjects could report their specific behaviors in specific situations, or be observed in field or laboratory situations. The situations of interest would be those demanding either masculine or feminine responses, and androgynous subjects would be the ones who performed competently in both types of situations.

LaFrance and Carmen assessed specific behaviors at the micro level by examining use of both feminine-typed (gazing and smiling while not speaking) and masculine-typed (interrupting and filling pauses with non-semantic vocalizations such as "uh" and "um") nonverbal behavior [53]. Their procedure is consistent with a co-presence conception of androgyny for they studied feminine and masculine responses separately, and did not look at their integration (a difficult task at the micro level).

Integration of femininity and masculinity – Viewing androgyny from the integration and situational perspectives results in the examination of the hybrid concepts, discussed above, at the behavioral level. Although not labeled as such, one of Bem's laboratory situations [50] is consistent with the integration/situational approach. Subjects' responses to a kitten were coded. Although the situation was designed to elicit feminine "nurturance," the sex-typed feminine women were the least nurturant in their responses. One interpretation of these findings is that the situation actually called for an integration of feminine nurturance and masculine assertiveness. Unlike Bem's infant and lonely peer situations in which the one-in-need-of-nurturance was put in direct contact with the subject, the kitten situation required more "reaching out" in the expression of warmth [54]. It is a situation requiring "assertive-warmth."

A researcher could contrive other situations requiring hybrid behaviors, and observe subjects' responses in those situations. Alternatively, self-reports of specific hybrid behaviors in naturally-occurring situations could be recorded.

Transcendence of femininity and masculinity – Moving to the cell that represents the intersection of the situationist perspective and the transcendence conception of androgyny involves consideration of specific behavioral signs that the subject has transcended traditional sex-roles. One approach would involve the researcher looking for indicators that the subject is not at the extremes in either feminine or masculine behaviors. The rationale for this approach is similar to that outlined in the transcendence-traitist cell.

An alternative approach would be to examine the extent to which subjects vary their behavior according to traditional gender-contingent demands of the situation. Subjects who vary their behavior as situational demands for traditional gender-related responses change would be regarded as not having transcended traditional sex-roles. Subjects who remain consistent (yet appropriate, in the broadest sense) in their behavior as these situational pulls change would be viewed as having transcended traditional sex-roles.

Andersen and Bem provide an example consistent with this approach as they rated subjects' differential responsiveness to attractive and unattractive members of the other sex [55]. One could think of equivalent responsiveness to such partners as evidence of sex-role transcendence.

Attitude/Belief System

Attitudes are included in the taxonomic framework for the sake of completeness. Beliefs about appropriate behaviors for the sexes are likely to be related to other dimensions of gender-related behavior and, therefore, potentially part of the process of the expression of androgyny.

Co-presence of femininity and masculinity – From the perspective of this conception of androgyny, the androgynous person is one who does not link sex to roles. While still aware of the norms for the sexes, this person believes these norms can and should be violated. The androgynous person would be one who has positive attitudes about women's employment opportunities and men's parenting opportunities; women's capacity for leadership positions and men's capacity for intimate relationships.

Questions asked from this perspective would be similar to ones asked on a traditional sex-role attitude questionnaire such as the Attitudes Toward Women Scale [56], with a distinction made between questions that describe "good things" for women and "good things" for men. The androgynous person would be one who agrees with both types of statements; who believes in access to the traditional female role for both sexes, and access to the traditional male role for both sexes. No consideration would be given to how these beliefs would be integrated in an individual's or family's life.

Integration of femininity and masculinity – Attitude evaluators who accept an integration conception of androgyny would look for subjects' agreement with statements describing an integration of traditional female and male roles. Consistent with others who endorse the integration conception, they would elaborate new possibilities that go beyond traditional roles. Attention would be given to what is good for the sexes together, while the potential conflicts would be recognized and remedies offered. Research would focus on subjects' attitudes toward the social change that would be required for a blending of feminine and masculine roles. For example, in assessing attitudes toward roles at work, they would move beyond questions focused on equal rights for the sexes to inquiries about the structural changes, such as free day care, flex time and good part-time jobs, that would support greater ease in participation in both work and family life.

Transcendence of femininity and masculinity – The researcher who wishes to translate the transcendence conception of androgyny into attitudinal terms would assess subjects' agreement with statements indicating no roles, neither female nor male. The emphasis would be on what is good for people, with no regard for their sex or role. In presenting statements with which subjects could agree or disagree, the researcher might include statements about what is good for the survival of humanity, such as non-violence, peace or creativity. While there is attitude research in these areas, it usually is not thought of as gender research.

Cognitive Organizing Principles

The fourth column in Table 1 represents the perspective I have labeled Cognitive Organizing Principle. From this perspective, femininity, masculinity and androgyny are viewed as cognitive structures that come into play as the person organizes her or his experience. The focus is on processes involved in information processing, such as perception, attention, categorization, memory, etc.

Co-presence of femininity and masculinity – This cell includes work that considers androgyny as the co-presence of feminine and masculine dimensions in the construction of experience. Androgynous people would be seen as differing from sex-typed people in that the sex-typed people organize experience around either (but not both) the feminine or masculine dimension more strongly than the other.

Methodologically, the search is for ways to ascertain the dimensions used to structure experience. In the context of a discussion of sex-role transcendence (discussed below) Garnets and Pleck suggested a strategy that could be modified to serve as an indicator of the co-presence of feminine and masculine dimensions in a construct system [57]. They suggested that items to which one responds consistently constitute a single dimension. Thus, one could examine a subject's rating of the self (or another person, an object, or an experience) on the BSRI, looking for high consistency (low variance) in responses to items on the femininity scale as an indicator of a feminine dimension, and high consistency (low variance) in responses to items on the masculinity scale as an indicator of a masculine dimension. The presence of both dimensions in the person's framework would constitute androgyny.

Awareness of conventional gender-attributed characteristics has been considered an indicator of a person's cognitive organizing framework [58]. Wolff and Taylor reasoned that sex-typed people would be more aware of their own group's stereotypes, while androgynous people would be very aware of both feminine and masculine stereotypes. They looked at how many female and male stereotypes a person could list in a limited time period.[3]

Markus and her colleagues looked for evidence of self-schemas about gender in various indicators of information processing, such as differential recall for feminine and masculine items, and latency of response to feminine and masculine items [59]. For Markus, the highly androgynous person is one who reveals a well-articulated knowledge structure for both dimensions by using both femininity and masculinity schemas.

Integration of femininity and masculinity – In order to assess the integration conception of androgyny from the perspective of cognitive organizing perspective, one would look for evidence of a single androgyny dimension, rather than separate femininity and masculinity dimensions, in perceptions, schemas, or constructs. To date, no such efforts seem to have been made but some of the methods outlined in the co-presence discussion could be extended to an integration conception. For example, rather than looking for evidence of consistent responses to feminine or masculine terms, one could look for consistent responses to androgyny terms (modeled after the hybrid traits discussed above) in rating self, other or experience. Speed and latency of responses to such androgyny terms could be another indicator, or one could look for subjects' abilities to provide behavioral examples of those androgyny terms.

Transcendence of femininity and masculinity – The search here focuses on subjects who use neither the femininity nor the masculinity dimensions in organizing their experience. Markus refers to these subjects as "aschematic" about gender [59]. Another way of expressing the idea is to say that, for this version of the androgynous person, gender has low salience.

Garnets and Pleck labeled as sex-role transcendent those subjects who respond with low consistency (high variance) to feminine and masculine terms [57]. It is as if, for these subjects, the terms usually seen as constituting femininity (or, likewise, masculinity) do not constitute a single organized factor. Garnets and Pleck used BSRI ratings of same-sex ideal for their data base but one could examine ratings of real self, other people, or any experience or object.

Several researchers have examined the degree to which subjects distinguish between maleness and femaleness. In general, they infer that, while sex-typed subjects organize their experience along gender-related lines and thus make such distinctions, androgynous subjects do not. Whether marking off units for videotaped behaviors of females and males [60] or rating the masculinity-femininity of handwriting samples [61], subjects who are less likely to draw distinctions between the sexes would be seen as androgynous. Memory tasks

[3] However, their conclusion that BSRI androgynous subjects were more aware of both stereotypes than sex-typed subjects is not consistent with the data they presented. There was no direct statistical comparison of sex-typed and androgynous subjects' responses.

such as those using pictures of people engaged in gender-traditional and nontraditional activities [62] could be used to find whether gender is a salient dimension. Subjects who recall both types of pictures equally well may not be aware of the gender dimension while perceiving the pictures.

While using signs of both a feminine and masculine schema as evidence for androgyny (see above), Markus also examined a group of people she called "aschematic" [59]. While those with both schemas would correspond to the co-presence conception of androgyny, those without a schema for gender would correspond to the transcendence conception of androgyny. Their lack of a schema for gender was indicated by recall of fewer words and behavioral examples, lower levels of confidence, lower consistency in latency and confidence in ratings of terms usually associated with gender.

Bem's most recent research on gender schema theory [63, 64] cannot be classified in a particular cell of this column. While she is using a cognitive organizing principle approach, the nature of the indicators she uses precludes a judgment about the conception of androgyny at the basis of her work. Part of the difficulty stems from the fact that her recent discussions focus more heavily on sex-typed than non-sex-typed subjects. But the major difficulty is that she seems to treat gender schema as a single bipolar dimension, feminine-masculine, rather than as two independent dimensions, feminine and/or masculine. Her non-sex-typed subjects may include those who use both a feminine and a masculine schema, neither schema, or a weak feminine-masculine schema.

DISCUSSION

One may be left asking, "Will the 'real' androgynous person please stand up?" This is precisely the issue that cannot be resolved. As an analogy, consider intelligence. Psychologists have argued for decades about how to detect the "real" intelligent person. Yet it has been more fruitful, in terms of understanding the processes involved, to conceptualize intelligence as a composite of several functions rather than as a unitary phenomena [65, p. 348]. At different times intelligent, adaptive functioning requires mathematical skills, creative use of mechanical devices, clear understanding of written material, or quick learning. All these spheres constitute components of intelligence, overlapping but not necessarily the same, developed by different routes at different times. No single sphere can account for or represent the totality of intelligence.

So it is with androgyny. At the present state of knowledge, no single cell in the matrix nor its accompanying measure can profess to explain non-sex-typed behavior. Androgyny can be thought of as a summary term for a number of processes that each must be explored to provide a full understanding of the construct.

Only if people were completely consistent in the various dimensions of personality would one expect to find perfect agreement in findings derived from the different cells in the matrix. Fairly common findings of positive relationships between variables consistent with different cells [e.g., 25, 46, 50, 52, 53, 55, 60, 61, 63, 66-68] suggest that the various aspects of androgyny do share some variance. However, failures to find significant relationships [e.g., 2, 39, 43, 47, 69-71] remind us that there is also a certain degree of independence among cells.

Implication of Taxonomic Framework

The major issue for androgyny research is construct validation and the proposed taxonomic framework serves as one organizing schema for that process. Androgyny is a rich, complex concept with many dimensions and possible implications. A first requirement for testing the variety of relationships suggested by the androgyny construct is appropriate multiple methods for indicating androgyny. As the taxonomic framework makes clear, there are a variety of possible personality processes involved in the development and expression of androgyny.

At a minimum, the taxonomic framework points to the need for researchers to be clear in their thinking and writing about why they expect certain relationships with androgyny. Detailing conceptual and methodological differences within the androgyny literature serves to highlight theoretical and measurement inconsistencies in some studies. Perhaps one reason that obtained results do not agree with proposed hypotheses in some cases is that the theory and the measurement of a particular researcher are not rooted in the same cell. Spence and Helmreich frequently have pointed out the problem of researchers who assume traits, roles, and attitudes invariably coincide [cf., 31, 47, 48, 72]. Nevertheless, researchers continue to use the trait-based BSRI or PAQ while conceptualizing androgyny in attitudinal terms [e.g., 39-41, 43].

The inconsistencies of theory and measurement that sometimes appear in the literature reflect the limited nature of most researchers' choice of an androgyny measure. The matrix highlights the fact that, to date, most androgyny research has used trait scales based on a co-presence definition of androgyny. Messick cautions against overreliance on one measure [71, p. 583]:

> One serious but common confusion occurs when a single test is used to represent the construct in studies intended to elaborate the construct's nomological network. Since no such test is a pure exemplar of the construct but contains variance due to other constructs and method contaminants, there is no solid basis for concluding that an observed relationship stems from the part of the test variance reflective of the construct or from other parts.

He goes on to recommend that, "the best way to reduce this nomological noise is to use multiple measures of constructs routinely in network explanations" [71, p. 584].

Research Context

A full understanding of research on androgyny requires attention to the context in which that research is conducted. Clearly, the bipolar and dichotomous traditional measures of masculinity-femininity that thrived for so long among psychologists [73] reflected a cultural assumption that males and females are and should be opposites. One explanation for the explosion of interest when Bem introduced the alternative notion of androgyny in the early 1970s is that this concept coincided with a broader interest in alternatives to traditional sex-roles.

The research context for androgyny includes both a pragmatically-oriented American psychology that has a tradition of studying personality via traits, and a sex-typed culture. American psychology historically has been more practical in its orientation than the more philosophically-oriented European psychology. One expression of this pragmatism is American psychology's enthusiasm for research topics that have a scale available for measurement. Witness the upsurge of research that followed scales developed for intelligence, locus of control, and need for achievement, to name a few. The initial enthusiasm is often accompanied by sometimes atheoretical efforts to examine the relationship of the new scale with a wide variety of variables. There also is a tendency to reify a construct once a test for it is available. Androgyny research has followed this pattern.

There is a long tradition within American psychology of studying personality in terms of traits, at the expense of explorations of more process-based notions. This tradition may reflect the pragmatism noted above, for traits are relatively easy to study via personality inventories that can be administered to the large groups of subjects favored by American psychology journals. It should not be surprising then that most research on androgyny is clustered in the first cell of the matrix, corresponding to a trait conception of androgyny.

An additional element in the research context is our sex-typed culture that accepts many non-biological gender differences such as economic, political, and social disparities between the sexes. This context may help explain the difficulty we have in envisoning a sex-role transcendent concept of androgyny, and the paucity of research in cells corresponding to this concept. In a culture that implicitly accepts gender as a basis for decision-making, finding either researchers or research subjects who can think of the possibility that assigned gender is irrelevant to decision-making is uncommon. Researchers seem to have a much easier time thinking about people who combine rather than transcend masculinity and femininity.

Our sex-typed culture may also help explain the ready acceptance of "findings" of masculinity and psychological well-being relationships that contrast with the androgyny-well-being relationship that was originally hypothesized. Most of these "findings" are based on research that is flawed by method contamination and overlap of items [65, p. 190]. Yet, methodological errors that should have been apparent to beginning students in research methods apparently have been overlooked by editors of even the top journals in the field. In a culture that values masculinity more than femininity, findings of masculine "superiority" have not been subjected to very critical review. Researchers themselves reflect this cultural context, as they have neglected examination of the more "feminine" interpersonal domains in their search for the ways that both femininity and masculinity may contribute to well-being.

Thus, ironically, while androgyny was originally offered as a way of envisioning alternatives to traditional sex-typing, much of androgyny research seems to have been constrained by existing professional and social biases. What was designed to be a "new" model has generated primarily "more of the same" methods using fairly traditional scales that lead to results that often confirm old biases. Recognition of the traditional context that envelops androgyny is a necessary precursor to fuller exploration of its new possibilities for both understanding and envisioning behavior.

REFERENCES

1. S. L. Bem, The Measurement of Psychological Androgyny, *Journal of Consulting and Clinical Psychology*, *42*, pp. 155-162, 1974.
2. J. T. Spence, R. L. Helmreich, and J. Stapp, Ratings of Self and Peers on Sex-role Attributes and Their Relation to Self-esteem and Conceptions of Masculinity and Femininity, *Journal of Personality and Social Psychology*, *32*, pp. 29-39, 1975.
3. E. R. Allgeier and A. F. Fogel, Coital Position and Sex Roles: Responses to Cross-sex Behavior in Bed, *Journal of Consulting and Clinical Psychology*, *46*, pp. 588-589, 1978.
4. J. I. Berzins, M. A. Welling, and R. E. Wetter, A New Measure of Psychological Androgyny Based on the Personality Research Form, *Journal of Consulting and Clinical Psychology*, *46*, pp. 126-138, 1978.
5. E. E. Sampson, Psychology and the American Ideal, *Journal of Personality and Social Psychology*, *35*, pp. 767-782, 1977.
6. R. F. Strahan, Remarks on Bem's Measurement of Psychological Androgyny: Alternative Methods and a Supplementary Analysis, *Journal of Consulting and Clinical Psychology*, *43*, pp. 568-571, 1975.
7. J. G. Raymond, *The Transsexual Empire*, Beacon Press, Boston, 1977.
8. S. Bem, Theory and Measurement of Androgyny: A Reply to the Pedhazur-Tetenbaum and Locksley-Colten Critiques, *Journal of Personality and Social Psychology*, *37*, pp. 1047-1054, 1979.
9. N. E. Downing, Theoretical and Operational Conceptualizations of Psychological Androgyny: Implications for Measurement, *Psychology of Women Quarterly*, *3*, pp. 284-292, 1979.
10. E. J. Pedhazur and T. J. Tetenbaum, Bem Sex Role Inventory: A Theoretical and Methodological Critique, *Journal of Personality and Social Psychology*, *37*, pp. 996-1016, 1979.

11. J. Worell, Sex Roles and Psychological Well-being: Perspectives on Methodology, *Journal of Consulting and Clinical Psychology*, *46*, pp. 777-791, 1978.
12. B. Abrahams, S. S. Feldman, and S. C. Nash, Sex Role Self-concept and Sex Role Attitudes: Enduring Personality Characteristics or Adaptations to Changing Life Situations? *Developmental Psychology*, *14*, pp. 393-400, 1978.
13. J. H. Block, Conceptions of Sex Role: Some Cross-cultural and Longitudinal Perspectives, *American Psychologist*, *28*, pp. 512-526, 1973.
14. J. S. Hyde and D. E. Phillis, Androgyny Across the Lifespan, *Developmental Psychology*, *15*, pp. 334-336, 1979.
15. M. A. Sedney, Growing More Complex: Conceptions of Sex Roles Across Adulthood, *International Journal of Aging and Human Development*, *22*, pp. 15-29, 1985.
16. K. A. Urberg and G. Labouvie-Vief, Conceptualizations of Sex Roles: A Life Span Developmental Study, *Developmental Psychology*, *12*, pp. 15-23, 1976.
17. M. S. White, Measuring Androgyny in Adulthood, *Psychology of Women Quarterly*, *3*, pp. 293-307, 1979.
18. S. L. Bem, On the Utility of Alternate Procedures for Assessing Psychological Androgyny, *Journal of Consulting and Clinical Psychology*, *45*, pp. 196-205, 1977.
19. J. L. Orlofsky, A. L. Aslin, and S. A. Ginsburg, Differential Effectiveness of Two Classification Procedures on the Bem Sex Role Inventory, *Journal of Personality Assessment*, *41*, pp. 414-416, 1977.
20. M. A. Sedney, Comments on Median Split Procedures for Scoring Androgyny Measures, *Sex Roles*, *7*, pp. 217-222, 1981.
21. L. C. Bernard, Multivariate Analysis of New Sex Role Formulations and Personality, *Journal of Personality and Social Psychology*, *38*, pp. 323-336, 1980.
22. W. H. Jones, M. E. O'C. Chernovetz, and R. D. Hansson, The Enigma of Androgyny: Differential Implications for Males and Females? *Journal of Consulting and Clinical Psychology*, *46*, pp. 298-313, 1978.
23. A. G. Kaplan and M. A. Sedney, *Psychology and Sex Roles: An Androgynous Perspective*, Little, Brown, Boston, 1980.
24. J. A. Kelly and J. Worell, New Formulations of Sex Roles and Androgyny: A Critical Review, *Journal of Consulting and Clinical Psychology*, *45*, pp. 1101-1115, 1977.
25. H. M. Klein and L. Willerman, Psychological Masculinity and Femininity and Typical and Maximal Dominance Expression in Women, *Journal of Personality and Social Psychology*, *37*, pp. 2059-2070, 1979.
26. A. Locksley and M. E. Colten, Psychological Androgyny: A Case of Mistaken Identity? *Journal of Personality and Social Psychology*, *37*, pp. 1017-1031, 1979.
27. J. S. Wiggins and A. Holzmuller, Psychological Androgyny and Interpersonal Behavior, *Journal of Consulting and Clinical Psychology*, *46*, pp. 40-52, 1978.

28. A. C. Rosen and G. A. Rekers, Toward a Taxonomic Framework for Variables of Sex and Gender, *Genetic Psychology Monographs, 102*, pp. 191-218, 1980.
29. R. K. Unger, Toward a Redefinition of Sex and Gender, *American Psychologist, 34*, pp. 1085-1094, 1979.
30. J. T. Spence and R. L. Helmreich, *Masculinity and Femininity: Their Psychological Dimensions, Correlates and Antecedents*, University of Texas Press, Austin, 1978.
31. ——, Masculine Instrumentality and Feminine Expressiveness: Their Relationships with Sex Role Attitudes and Behaviors, *Psychology of Women Quarterly, 5*, pp. 147-163, 1980.
32. A. G. Kaplan, Clarifying the Concept of Androgyny: Implications for Therapy, *Psychology of Women Quarterly, 3*, pp. 223-230, 1979.
33. M. Rebecca, R. Hefner, and B. Oleshansky, A Model of Sex Role Transcendence, *Journal of Social Issues, 104*, pp. 192-233, 1976.
34. W. Dember, Motivation and the Cognitive Revolution, *American Psychologist, 29*, pp. 161-168, 1974.
35. H. Markus, Self-schemata and Processing Information About the Self, *Journal of Personality and Social Psychology, 35*, pp. 63-78, 1977.
36. G. A. Kelly, *The Psychology of Personal Constructs*, Norton, New York, 1955.
37. S. L. Bem, Psychology Looks at Sex Roles: Where Have All the Androgynous People Gone? paper presented at the UCLA Symposium on Women, Los Angeles, May 1972.
38. A. B. Heilbrun, Measurement of Masculine and Feminine Sex Roles as Independent Dimensions, *Journal of Consulting and Clinical Psychology, 44*, pp. 183-190, 1976.
39. E. R. Allgeier, The Influence of Androgynous Identification on Heterosexual Relations, *Sex Roles, 7*, pp. 321-330, 1981.
40. M. B. Brewer and M. W. Blum, Sex-role Androgyny and Patterns of Causal Attribution for Academic Achievement, *Sex Roles, 5*, pp. 783-796, 1979.
41. M. E. Chernovetz, W. H. Jones, and R. O. Hansson, Predictability, Attentional Focus, Sex Role Orientation, and Menstrual-related Stress, *Psychosomatic Medicine, 41*, pp. 383-391, 1979.
42. J. F. Flaherty and J. B. Dusek, An Investigation of the Relationship Between Psychological Androgyny and Components of Self-concept, *Journal of Personality and Social Psychology, 38*, pp. 984-992, 1980.
43. R. O. Hansson, W. H. Jones, and M. E. Chernovetz, Contraceptive Knowledge: Antecedents and Implications, *The Family Coordinator, 28*, pp. 29-34, 1979.
44. D. M. Hoffman and L. S. Fidell, Characteristics of Androgynous, Undifferentiated, Masculine, and Feminine Middle-class Women, *Sex Roles, 5*, pp. 765-781, 1979.
45. J. A. Kelly and L. Worell, Parent Behaviors Related to Masculine, Feminine, and Androgynous Sex Role Orientations, *Journal of Consulting and Clinical Psychology, 44*, pp. 843-851, 1976.

46. D. T. Kenrick, D. O. Stringfield, W. L. Wagenhals, R. H. Dahl, and H. J. Ransdell, Sex Differences, Androgyny, and Approach Responses to Erotica: A New Variation on the Old Volunteer Problem, *Journal of Personality and Social Psychology*, *38*, pp. 517-524, 1980.
47. R. L. Helmreich, J. T. Spence, and C. K. Holahan, Psychological Androgyny and Sex Role Flexibility: A Test of Two Hypotheses, *Journal of Personality and Social Psychology*, *37*, pp. 1631-1644, 1979.
48. J. T. Spence, Traits, Roles, and the Concept of Androgyny, in *Psychology and Women: In Transition*, J. Gullahorn (ed.), Winston and Sons, Washington, D.C., 1979.
49. D. Lubinski, A. Tellegen, and J. N. Butcher, The Relationship Between Androgyny and Subjective Indicators of Emotional Well-being, *Journal of Personality and Social Psychology*, *40*, pp. 722-730, 1981.
50. S. L. Bem, Sex Role Adaptability: One Consequence of Psychological Androgyny, *Journal of Personality and Social Psychology*, *31*, pp. 634-643, 1975.
51. S. L. Bem and E. Lenney, Sex Typing and the Avoidance of Cross-sex Behavior, *Journal of Personality and Social Psychology*, *33*, pp. 48-54, 1976.
52. S. L. Bem, W. Martyna, and C. Watson, Sex Typing and Androgyny: Further Explorations of the Expressive Domain, *Journal of Personality and Social Psychology*, *34*, pp. 1016-1023, 1976.
53. M. LaFrance and B. Carmen, The Nonverbal Display of Psychological Androgyny, *Journal of Personality and Social Psychology*, *38*, pp. 36-49, 1980.
54. S. L. Bem, Probing the Promise of Androgyny, in *Beyond Sex Role Stereotypes: Readings Toward a Psychology of Androgyny*, A. G. Kaplan and J. P. Bean (eds.), Little, Brown, Boston, 1976.
55. S. M. Andersen and S. L. Bem, Sex Typing and Androgyny in Dyadic Interaction: Individual Differences in Responsiveness to Physical Attractiveness, *Journal of Personality and Social Psychology*, *4*, pp. 74-86, 1981.
56. J. T. Spence and R. Helmreich, The Attitudes Toward Women Scale: An Objective Instrument to Measure Attitudes Toward the Rights and Roles of Women in Contemporary Society, *Journal Supplement Abstract Service Catalog of Selected Documents in Psychology*, *2*, pp. 66-67 (ms. no. 153), 1972.
57. L. Garnets and J. H. Pleck, Sex Role Identity, Androgyny, and Sex Role Transcendence: A Sex Role Strain Analysis, *Psychology of Women Quarterly*, *3*, pp. 270-283, 1979.
58. L. Wolff and S. E. Taylor, Sex, Sex-role Identification, and Awareness of Sex-role Stereotypes, *Journal of Personality*, *46*, pp. 177-184, 1978.
59. H. Markus, M. Crane, S. Bernstein, and M. Siladi, Self-schemas and Gender, *Journal of Personality and Social Psychology*, *42*, pp. 38-50, 1982.
60. K. Deaux and B. Major, Sex-related Patterns in the Unit of Perception, *Personality and Social Psychology Bulletin*, *3*, pp. 297-300, 1977.

61. R. Lippa, Androgyny, Sex-typing, and the Perception of Masculinity-Femininity in Handwritings, *Journal of Research in Personality, 11*, pp. 21-37, 1977.
62. L. S. Liben and M. L. Signorella, Gender-related Schemata and Constructive Memory in Children, *Child Development, 51*, pp. 11-18, 1980.
63. S. L. Bem, Gender Schema Theory: A Cognitive Account of Sex Typing, *Psychological Review, 88*, pp. 354-364, 1981.
64. ____, Androgyny and Gender Schema Theory: A Conceptual and Empirical Integration, in *Nebraska Symposium on Motivation*, Vol. 32, T. B. Sonderegger (ed.), University of Nebraska Press, Lincoln, 1985.
65. A. Anastasi, *Psychological Testing*, 5th edition, Macmillan, New York, 1982.
66. R. L. Leahy and M. Eiter, Moral Judgment and the Development of Real and Ideal Androgynous Self-image During Adolescence and Young Adulthood, *Developmental Psychology, 16*, pp. 362-370, 1980.
67. J. L. Orlofsky, Sex-role Orientation, Identity Formation, and Self-esteem in College Men and Women, *Sex Roles, 3*, pp. 561-575, 1977.
68. G. Tunnell, Sex Role and Cognitive Schemata: Person Perception in Feminine and Androgynous Women, *Journal of Personality and Social Psychology, 40*, pp. 1126-1136, 1981.
69. A. H. Eagly, W. Wood, and L. Fishbaugh, Sex Differences in Conformity: Surveillance by the Group as a Determinant of Male Nonconformity, *Journal of Personality and Social Psychology, 40*, pp. 384-394, 1981.
70. J. L. Orlofsky, Relationship Between Sex Role Attitudes and Personality Traits and the Sex Role Behaviors Scale – 1: A New Measure of Masculine and Feminine Role Behaviors and Interests, *Journal of Personality and Social Psychology, 40,* pp. 927-940, 1981.
71. P. B. Zeldow, Psychological Androgyny and Attitudes Toward Feminism, *Journal of Consulting and Clinical Psychology, 44*, p. 150, 1976.
72. J. T. Spence, Gender Identity and Its Implications for the Concepts of Masculinity and Femininity, in *Nebraska Symposium on Motivation*, Vol. 32, T. B. Sonderegger (ed.), University of Nebraska Press, Lincoln, 1985.
73. A. Constantinople, Masculinity-Femininity: An Exception to the Famous Dictum? *Psychological Bulletin, 80*, pp. 389-407, 1973.

CHAPTER 10

A Sense of Humor

LEIGH MARLOWE

RESEARCHING HUMOR

Humor includes word play and graphics in all their forms, accidental and intentional actions, and various presentations of them that make us smile or laugh. The situational context and chronological sequence of humorous events are also important. Despite currently irreconcilable theoretical approaches and perspectives, general agreement exists that humor is a human capacity, like walking and talking, developmentally programmed for the species.

Since individual behavior is embedded in sociocultural frameworks, it seems most productive to examine humor social-psychologically. A social psychological account of humor should address differential socialization of verbal behavior by gender (with its kinesic and paralinguistic accompaniments), and, how humor is used to maintain boundaries between gender groups.

Psychological research typically goes the intra/interpersonal route, studying response preferences (often by sex) to humorous stimuli. The behavior studied is humor appreciation, not production – a passive rather than active function. Sociology frequently focuses on institutional structures where humor occurs, by observing events in them. The sociological orientation is circumstantial rather than individual. Since ethnological studies of humor require difficult, deep understanding [1], anthropologists tend to examine ceremonial mimicry and ritual clowning. From anthropology, some psychologists and sociologists picked up the "joking relationship," but this highly formalized scenario has limited value beyond sensitizing us to possibilities of its occurrence.

Historically, women have been written out of humor. For example, nineteenth-century American women, famous and well-off in their times from their humorous productions [2], are totally omitted from *American Humor* [3], even though this work concentrates on the nineteenth century, and was touted by novelist-critic Bernard DeVoto as "by far the most important book written in the field." Throughout Rourke's array, maleness measures all laughable cognitions, so that only men's views of humor prevail.

Mirth and laughter help our bodies deal with stress. Feminists who seek social, economic, and political equity for women in society are constantly put in adversary situations. Feminist psychology, devoting much research effort to the heavier aspects of women's oppression (such as patriarchally alleged incapacitating effects of reproductive functions on cognitive as well as occupational activities), needs to practice humor to survive [4]. Physiologically, laughter has therapeutic effects, through its induction of relaxation and amusement, activating immune enhancement of the parasympathetic nervous system [5]. Additionally, laughter has unique cardio-respiratory effects which mitigate the impact of stress [6]. Correlatively, anxiety, stress, and unhappiness activate opposite effects of the sympathetic nervous system: these effects also contribute to aging.

PSYCHOLOGICAL CONTRIBUTIONS

Most psychological research has been on reactive, rather than creative humor, whereas theory (even though in disagreement and disarray), tends to include the act of producing the stimulus as well as the response [7]. Psychological studies show that relatively little production, expression and appreciation of humor involve formal jokes. Humor often depends on a temporal/situational gestalt: an incongruous juxtaposition of elements violates socially learned expectations. Consequently, laboratory techniques using preselected stimuli (cartoons, films, recordings, written materials, etc.) may be inappropriate discovery tools. Demand characteristics of an experiment or even of a standardized observational schedule obliterate the imaginative spontaneity essential to humor.

Investigations comparing boys and girls, women and men, suggest differences in humor. Males prefer sexual and aggressive humor, and (with less empirical support), females prefer absurd nonsense [8, 9]. Women laugh less (and feminists least) at sexual jokes, and at jokes directed against women. Piagetan studies of cognitive development seem in the main to overlook humor behavior, although increasing verbal and social competence are involved in imaginative play.

Behavior scientists need to examine the kinds of verbal and social competence expected in girls and boys, how they affect imagination, and, in the present instance, the appreciation and production of humor. Explanations of sex differences in social behaviors generally invoke biological properties or socialization effects. Undoubtedly both kinds of explanations have merit, and with regard to humor, neither neurophysiology nor gender stereotyping has yet been fully explored. Sexual bimaturation – the differential rates of female and male development – and its sequelae, such as earlier cerebral lateralization and language acquisition in females, together with possible differences in hemispheric responsiveness [10] and differences in activity level may all be related to humor behavior.

Verbal Socialization

Acquired by the time language effectively begins, at approximately two years of age, gender identity forms the base for culturally approved verbal style and usage. Because child care is still primarily a female enterprise, both girls and boys first learn the mother tongue, a circumspect version of the vernacular, excluding vulgarisms, argot, and obscenities. Boys, encouraged to engage the male environment, soon learn male language with its ruder lexicon and syntax. By acquiring appropriate male verbal behavior with its accompanying kinesic and paralinguistic enhancements, boys become initiates of male culture, which perceives, defines, and excludes females and femininity as deviant.

Observed gender differences in speech have been extensively documented [11]. For example, individually, female pronounciation and intonation are different from male; interactionally, female deference to males appears in conversation as briefer turns, overlapped by male interruptions and male lapses in attention. Femininity requires retaining elements of paralinguistic childishness, such as low volume and high pitch, in laughter as well as voice. Kinesically, feminine females should smile (but not too broadly) and inhibit emphatic gesticulations (frowns, sneers, pointing). Obviously, gender-based socialization of language prevents females from freely appreciating humor – and, incidentally, physiologically benefitting from the mirth response.

Women's roles generally require discretion in the use of vigorous response, monitoring one's own behavior to the point of self-consciousness so that one's actions do not provoke others. These norms limit women's production of humor. Inhibition is associated with humorlessness [12], and, by blocking spontaneity, self-consciousness is incompatible with humor behavior [13]. For example, Goldstein found that women controlled their joking in the presence of men (but not vice versa) [14].

All forms of cultural expression embody social values and are culturally defined by those possessing social power. Departures from established forms have difficulty getting past institutional gatekeepers and may be evaluated by those gatekeepers as peculiar, especially those expressions upsetting to institutionalized arrangements between social groups.

Spradley and Mann describe how bartenders keep the sexual humor of cocktail waitresses in check by a one-upmanship of male sexual domination that puts the waitress down, i.e., in her proper place in the structure of gender arrangements in the bar milieu [15]. Bartenders control who is permitted a greater latitude of expression in sexuality (even when expression is only what anthropologists refer to as a "joking relationship").

The media ignore, trivialize or rename women's efforts towards equity by referring to women as "libbers" (irrespective of their own self-definitions). Newspapers frequently put news about women in their "style" or "family living" sections even when the news content has nothing to do with either. These examples illustrate the control function of verbal labeling and categorizing.

Bernard asserts that American English fails to express female experience, and that socially prescribed female language usage disadvantages women in social interaction, holding "the female world . . . in a state of cultural siege." [16] For example, action descriptors favor males, who, when excited, snort, guffaw, bellow, and roar, whereas women sniff, giggle, and become strident or shrill. Likewise, men set standards for what is and isn't funny, who can joke, and how.

In performance, women comedians usually do not use dialect as a humor form except when self-referenced as for example, a Puerto Rican comic artist using Hispanicisms. More often, women use exaggerated feminine genderlect (sexually defined dialect). Women imitating male genderlect, especially using "strong" language (swear words, smut) threaten current power relations. Male gatekeepers define such behavior as pornographic: performed by men, it would be simple sexual humor.

Impressionists imitate real living or well-known recently deceased people; impersonators make up characters, often social stereotypes. The younger women comic artists who do impressions, tend to avoid including real living male figures, though men impressionists cross the sexual border with impunity. Male comics cross-talking and cross-dressing are considered screamingly funny. Impersonations of men by women are rare, too, and may be tempered by the woman comic artists' choice of a disliked or outcaste character (e.g., mogul-type or transsexual). Norms of female verbal socialization invalidate our cognitions of the adjacent sex and squelch our imaginative play caricaturing them.

Intergroup Functions of Humor

Male sexual humor and demeaning characterizations of women maintain boundaries between women and men: men may laugh at women; women must laugh at themselves. Such boundaries sustain the social fabric by controlling action and affect toward culturally defined elements and events of the social environment. Though sometimes the interaction of particular women and men, as in a marriage, may be analyzed as interpersonal behavior, in general, female-male relations are better understood in terms of role relations. Even complementary roles, again as in marriage, refer to traditionally unequal groups (husbands and wives). Thus, group relations encompass explicit and implicit understandings of power, hierarchy, dominance, control, behavioral latitude, and access to culturally valued space, time, objects, and events [17].

As with other forms of power, humor flows down social hierarchies. Differential status of the sexes structures interpersonal relations between the sexes in terms of a game. Formal rules govern games, whereas humor depends on imaginative spontaneity and cognitive restructuring. Hence, interpersonal relations between the sexes tend to be humorless.

An intergroup approach suggests that analysis of gender socialization lacks political clout because its focus on roles ignores the institutional structures within which roles exist. Institutional structures regulate relations within and between sex groups, in effect, treating them as castes. These structures socially elevate men and derogate women, thereby psychologically weakening women's group identity.

In addition to an absence of collective consciousness [18], a difference between women and other minority groups is that women are supposed to acquiesce with good grace to charades enacted at their expense. Women's failure to do so is considered a breach of social etiquette by men, who may allege that this illustrates women's lack of a sense of humor [19]. For example, "the new man" is supposed to be sensitive, warm, tender, and caring. If a woman comic artist concludes, in her performance that "the new man" is a woman, women laugh – but men withhold approval by not laughing.

Acceptable arrangements between the sexes are strictly formalized ("hyper-ritualized") by scenes of social ceremonies represented in print advertisements [20]. Ads display nonverbal signals detailing female-male relations in terms of gesture, posture, expression, relative size, and placement of figures in foreground or background. Though people recognize the artificiality of ads, nevertheless people accept ads' cues as legitimate representations of immutable reality. In ads, as in cartoons, women speak less and are restricted from using male gestures unless an ad deliberately portrays role-reversal. Otherwise, gender advertisements reinforce women's lower status.

Two examples – Sexual humor illustrates intergroup functions as described in the preceding paragraphs [21-23]. Tacitly outlined in male terms, male sexual humor uses the symbolism of domination and power, not seduction and sensuality. Exaggerations of male sexual prowess and/or lack of same, abound, with women almost invariably victims or butts of male sexuality. The obvious conclusion is that sexual joking is a male privilege, emphasizing a sense of male community and male norms among the jokers. But deviations exist.

Created by prostitutes and studied by folklorists, whorehouse humor is not in the main trickle of humor research [24]. Whorehouse humor deals with how, despite their socially (defined) inferior status, prostitutes control their clients by poking fun at them. For example, a sailor asks a belle du jour how he's doing, to which she replies, "About three nots." He queries, "Three knots?" Her answer: "You're not hard, you're not in, and you're not getting your money back."

Likewise conspicuous by omission is the Hispanic custom of dirty showers, which give some recognition to female involvement in sexuality. At a dirty shower, the prospective bride views pornographic photos, listens to obscene versions of the rosary, and otherwise carries on in an outrageously lewd and lascivious fashion with her peers. Dirty showers do not strengthen bonds among women because their purpose is to get the bride to accept her subordinate position in macho Latin society. Dirty showers convince women of their powerlessness, thereby contributing to the strength of male bonds.

Perhaps dirty showers have not made a splash in social science journals as models of anticipatory socialization because they prove that women can do "it" (burlesque human sexuality), and poking fun at sexual functions threatens male sexual hegemony by suggesting that the intergroup boundaries between the sexes in this area may not be as impermeable as men would prefer.

HUMOR AND COMEDY AS NON-TRADITIONAL OCCUPATIONS

Most of us are adequately socialized to cultural conventions. Humor, except as defined in male terms is beyond the perimeter of acceptable female behavior. Verbalizing about the unacceptable opens the possibility of having opinions about it and doing it. When women produce and present humor they reverse conventional social situations by putting themselves in the foreground, threatening the most basic social gender arrangements.

"Dumb broads" are funny, but a *witty woman* irrevocably offends the status quo, for wit demonstrates "intellectual self-assurance." [25] Etymologically, "to wit," meant, "to know"; a witch was a knowledgeable woman. Negative connotations accrued to this word while its masculine counterpart, "wizard," remained benign.

Written and drawn humor by women has been more acceptable than comedy. The reader/viewer need not be constantly aware of the sex of who deliberately causes amusement. The boundary-breaching woman humorist writes or sketches scenes whose outlines are familiar, but the details of which are at variance with conventions, viewing both sexes as amusing in non-sterotypical ways. Traditional analysis in social science holds that men bond with men, while women bond with kin, therefore, women are more psychologically involved with the adjacent sex than *vice versa.* Hence, women's humor is less hostile to men than men's is towards women – a logical concomitant of women's aversion to aggressive humor.

To the extent that some forms of humor are incompatible with aggression [26], those forms may serve as vehicle to reduce intersexual hostility. A contemporary experiment demonstrated that previously angered subjects interrupted by non-aggressive cartoons, directed less aggression against their provocateur than control subjects who had not been angered at all. (All the subjects were males.)

Historically, the forgotten women humorists of nineteenth century America, knowingly or not, acted as equalizers in the first wave of American feminism. (In [2], see: Mary Abigail Dodge, Rose Terry Cooke, Marietta Holley, Sarah P. W. Parton, and Frances M. B. Whitcher.) Like the male humorists of their time, their humor was meant to be read, though Whitcher was also dramatized [2]. Time and topical constraints prevent me from exploring whether women who entertained in nineteenth century music halls or vaudeville were comic artists.

Comedy performed by women in various formats; standup, skits, screwball–

even self-deprecating comedy–shatters the shackles of constrained action and verbal behavior prescribed by socially defined femininity. The comedian's conversational dominance commands attention and if successful, produces involuntary convulsions of laughter in the audience. The comic artist legitimately and deliberately provokes response ("she asks for it") and when the audience gets it (as she delivers her punch lines), she gets what she deserves (their laughter). All these actions violate norms of gender-based verbal socialization prescribed for females: passive self presentation; hesitant, tentative speech; eye-contact avoidance, and, closed body postures. By modeling risk-taking, the comedy act suggests new role performance for women.

Contemporary Comic Artists

Sponsored by The Association of Comedy Artists and the Young Women's Christian Association of the City of New York, the First Conference on Women in Humor took place in 1983. An all-women comic arts evening highlighted the standard conference format: panel followed by workshops. The consensus was that comedy is a serious art form requiring creative brilliance, and that it is difficult to be humorous on purpose. Deliberate humor can be socially relevant and politically powerful. To be a performer in this milieu requires the ability to experience rejection and continue to compete because the need to achieve predominates. Few women are yet socialized to such singlemindedness of purpose and behaviors to support it, especially a purpose that involves exposing one's self to critical audiences of strangers as if they were close associates.

The comic arts have been a masculine territory, but a determined group of entertaining young women intend to invade this potentially lucrative field, as headlining standup comics, not just as tokens. Comedy shows and comedy clubs are controlled by men. Indeed, most of the patrons are men, perhaps because such a large part of what passes as humor is misogynism. Like all women breaking into NTOs, women comic artists initially receive much negative attention. The audience's first response is to examine her as a woman, before they listen to her comedy. It is particularly hard to go on stage as a standup following a man who has done a line of anti-woman material. The audience is primed to see if she *looks* funny, i.e., departs from current standards of feminine attractiveness, and only grudgingly ready to admit she *is* funny – for a woman. When a woman's act flops, she is often made fun of, while a mediocre performance by a male will be tolerated.

Women standups admit to holding in check certain comic aspects of life, such as vigorous slapstick (involving touching) and references to their own promiscuity (e.g., "I've gone to bed with men, who, if they were women, I wouldn't have lunch with" – is not acceptable). Unlike men standup comics, women can't afford to get angry at and verbally spar with an unruly or heckling audience. Not only does dueling easily divert attention from their performance, it looks bad, i.e., too obviously aggressive. Nevertheless, this bold group does not make gender substitutions in, or neuter their material; e.g., on how to attract the adjacent sex – a common comic theme: "I never wear floral perfume – most men don't like flowers. I have a scent like the interior of a new car."

Even people who shun the performing comic arts as vulgar may be able to remember male comedy teams, and perhaps some comic couples – but not women's ensembles. This, too, is changing. Several groups of women comic artists now perform in the most chic of the cosmopolitan clubs. By no means is this feminist comedy, but it is not the anti-woman, self-deprecating humor that we tend to associate with more "established" women in the field, a generation older than these newcomers. For example, a performance of Shakespeare in the Slums (a take-off on New York City's Shakespeare in the Park) presents a hilarious Black Juliet explaining it all to the street people. And, it is ideologically gratifying to see women relying so much on each other, as individuals and as a group, in the intimate interchange with the audience that is at the heart of on stage humor.

Ladies Against Women improvises politically powerful and socially relevant humor in guerilla theater. Ladies Against Women sponsors various spoof campaigns (e.g., Crusade to Protect the Unconceived) and demonstrates (e.g., as Moral Monopolists) at diverse events, such as speeches by Schlafly or Falwell (always appropriately dressed and postered for the occasion). Media coverage of Ladies Against Women has "far exceeded their expectations." Indeed, their ridiculous antics effectively attract attention away from the targets of their humor. The roots of Ladies Against Women reach to anti-nuclear politics more than to the women's movement [27-29]. Interestingly, very little humor derives from right-of-center political positions [30] – or from the extreme left. Perhaps humor is as incompatible with dogmatic thought as it is with some forms of aggression.

The women comic artists discussed in the preceding paragraphs illustrate the timeliness integral to humor [31]. Reflective of social changes in women's aspirations and women's concerns, their comedy may contribute to the acceleration of such diversification. At least, they sensitize the wide audience towards which they direct their performing ambitions to the existence of imaginative alternatives, as well as to comedic perspectives on reality.

FUTURE DIRECTIONS

Our socialization as females inclines women to want to be acceptable, to achieve a revolution without exposing reality or hurting anyone's feelings. Obviously, this is quite impossible, for the content of feminist humor aims at changing women's behavior, and aims at changing women's relations with men. Feminist humor should also give women opportunities to laugh at some shapes their new selves assume, extremes permitted by fads tolerated within the women's movement. Examples of these include goddess religion, alternative health practices, martial arts training, etc. Humor is a survival mechanism: feminists need it as much as women need political techniques.

Feminist humor uses women's oppression by the patriarchy as a central theme [19]. It is not the obverse of conventional patriarchic humor, but men take offense because they expect misandry, anticipating themselves as targets of the punchline, anticipating having their selves bruised. Feminists want to "pick up" women, not "put down" men. Since women are not supposed to be impolite or upsetting, some feminist humor is edgy, because the territory is socially dangerous. Sometimes, it's hard to "get," (for an audience to respond to feminist humor), because it is quick: one can take one's time only if one has established privilege.

Through humor, women can recognize what's laughable, and point the route away from what *is* to what is *imaginable.* Humor can be a liberating and humanizing venture for everyone. It's a positive personal experience to be able to laugh at ourselves, but a negative one to be the object of hostile humor. Opening comic artistry to women breaks the barriers of gender stereotyping. When women practice the comic arts on a par with men, the outcomes – mirth and laughter – will be accessible to a wider audience. If we move toward a more equalitarian society, psychosocially healthier for all of us, we can expect to see more humor, and more feminist humor, from women.

ACKNOWLEDGMENT

Many thanks to Alice Sheppard for her generosity in sharing materials that would not have been available otherwise.

REFERENCES

1. O. Klineberg, *Social Psychology,* Holt, New York, pp. 190-193, 1954.
2. E. T. James, J. W. James, and P. S. Boyer (eds.), *Notable American Women: 1607-1950,* Belknap Press, Cambridge, Massachusetts, 1971.
3. C. Rourke, *American Humor: A Study of National Character,* Doubleday Anchor, Garden City, New York, 1955.
4. L. Marlowe, *Getting Down to Mirth,* paper presented at the Seventh National Conference on Feminist Psychology of the Association for Women in Psychology, Santa Monica, California, 1980.
5. J. H. Abeles, Humoral Humor (Letters), *The Sciences, 22:*9, p. 3, 1982.
6. L. Peter, Laughter, *Ms Magazine, 11:*11, p. 88, 1983.
7. D. R. Ferris, Humor and Creativity: Research and Theory, *Journal of Creative Behavior, 6:*2, pp. 75-79, 1972.
8. H. M. Lips, *Women, Men and the Psychology of Power,* Prentice-Hall, Englewood Cliffs, New Jersey, pp. 119-120, 1981.
9. A. S. Groch, Generality of Response to Humor and Wit in Cartoons, Jokes, Stories and Photographs, *Psychological Reports, 35,* pp. 835-838, 1974.

10. H. Leventhal and G. Cupchik, A Process Model of Humor Judgment, *Journal of Communication, 3,* pp. 190-204, 1976.
11. N. Henley and B. Thorne (eds.), *Language and Sex,* Newbury House, Rowley, Massachusetts, *(passim),* 1975.
12. J. Levine, *Motivation in Humor,* Atherton, New York, *(passim),* 1969.
13. W. F. Fry, Jr., *Sweet Madness,* Pacific Books, Palo Alto, California, *(passim),* 1963.
14. J. H. Goldstein, *Social Psychology,* Academic Press, New York, pp. 453-456, 1980.
15. J. P. Spradley and B. J. Mann, *The Cocktail Waitress,* Wiley, New York, pp. 87-100, 1975.
16. J. Bernard, *The Female World,* Free Press, New York, Part V *(passim),* p. 459, 1981.
17. S. Tortu, *Women and Men: An Intergroup Analysis,* paper presented at the annual conference of the Association for Women in Psychology, Boston, Massachusetts, 1981.
18. H. Hacker, Women as a Minority Group, *Social Forces, 30,* pp. 60-69, 1951.
19. G. Kaufman and M. K. Blakely, *Pulling Our Own Strings,* Indiana University Press, Bloomington, Indiana, Dear Gloria and Introduction, 1980.
20. E. Goffman, *Gender Advertisements,* Harper Colophon, New York, 1979.
21. J. R. Cantor, What Is Funny to Whom?, *Journal of Communication, 26:*3, pp. 164-172, 1976.
22. G. A. Fine, Obscene Joking Across Cultures, *Journal of Communication, 26:*3, pp. 134-140, 1976.
23. A. J. Chapman and N. J. Gadfield, Is Sexual Humor Sexist?, *Journal of Communication, 26:*3, pp. 141-153, 1976.
24. C. E. Schutz, *The Phallic Fallacy – Political Potency in Feminist Humor,* paper presented at The Second International Conference on Humor, Los Angeles, California, 1979.
25. N. Walker, Wit, Sentimentality and the Image of Women in the Nineteenth Century, *American Studies, 22:*2, pp. 5-22, Fall 1981.
26. R. A. Baron and D. Byrne, *Exploring Social Psychology,* Allyn and Bacon, Boston, Massachusetts, pp. 230-232, 1979.
27. *Ms Magazine,* p. 24, April 1982.
28. D. Van Kleef, Further Antics of Ladies Against Women, *Ms Magazine,* p. 47, August 1982.
29. *Ms Magazine,* p. 12, February 1983.
30. S. Allen, The Uses of Comedy, *Journal of Creative Behavior, 6:*2, pp. 83-85, 1972.
31. C. Fadiman, Humor as a Weapon, *Journal of Creative Behavior, 6:*2, pp. 87-92, 1972.

CHAPTER 11

Humor in Conversational Context: Beyond Biases in the Study of Gender and Humor

MARY CRAWFORD

> HUMOR: a verbal weapon in the social arsenal constructed to maintain caste, class, race and sex inequalities (Naomi Weisstein)
>
> HUMOR, WOMEN'S: often ironic art form, developed as a coping mechanism, openly shared with women but seldom around men (P. R. Mecking)
>
> HUMORLESS: (when applied to women, the word is) insidious . . . boring and predictable if seen through, devastating if believed (Mary Daly)
>
> from *A Feminist Dictionary* [1]

What does psychological research reveal about women's humor? This deceptively simple question started me on a long path of inquiry. The research literature is vast—humor has been examined from motivational, cognitive, physiological, and social psychological perspectives—and I began by trying to find studies that focused on women. The path twisted and turned as I began to critically examine the empirical literature for gender bias. It broadened as I encountered aspects of humor that had not been studied and began to use alternative research methods. My travels in search of women's humor are instructive not only for what I learned about gender and humor *per se*, but because the ways in which my questions changed at each new phase exemplify phases in the feminist critique of social psychology [4]. In this chapter I will recapitulate that journey by analyzing sources of gender bias in psychological research on humor, suggesting alternatives to the most widely used method for studying humor, describing research that uses these alternative methods to focus specifically on women, and connecting problems in humor research to wider methodological problems in psychology.

PSYCHOLOGICAL RESEARCH ON HUMOR

Empirical research on humor has frequently involved the experimental manipulation of humorous stimuli in attempts to specify the characteristics of stimuli or subjects that affect appreciation of humor. In the prototypical experiment, subjects rate the funniness of jokes or cartoons that vary on a dimension such as hostility; ratings may also be correlated with subjects' scores on personality measures. The creation of humor has been studied only infrequently, as Marlowe points out [5]. The social functions of humor have been examined primarily by comparing members of various "reference groups" such as Blacks versus Whites or liberals versus conservatives.

Gender has not been ignored in this literature. Indeed, it is the most frequently analyzed "group" variable. There are many reports of significant gender differences but little consistency across studies, perhaps because gender has rarely been a central research question. Rather, male and female subjects have been included in experimental designs routinely and differences have been documented when they occurred [6].

SOURCES OF GENDER BIAS IN EXPERIMENTAL DESIGN

Critics of psychological methods have identified potential sources of gender bias at each stage of the research process [4, 7]. For example, bias can occur in the researcher's choice of topic. In humor research, the humor studied tends to be public rather than private—the routines or jokes of professional comedians rather than spontaneous humor among friends. Further, humor research has focused on the appreciation of humor rather than on the ability to create humor or use it in socially skilled ways. The emphasis on public humor ignores male authorship and control of such humor [5] and, like the emphasis on appreciation, results in the neglect of spontaneous, socially situated humor, which constitutes a much greater proportion of humorous events in the lives of both women and men [8].

Researchers may also incorporate bias in their choice of subjects. As noted earlier, humor researchers have not neglected to include women as subjects, but have frequently tested for gender differences in the absence of either clear theoretical reasons or systematic observation that would predict a particular pattern of differences. Thus, the literature reflects many of the weaknesses associated with the "sex differences" approach to gender [9, 10] and few of the insights that result from viewing gender as a cognitive variable [11] or social category [9].

The operationalization of variables is another potential source of bias in research design. In experimental research on humor, the stimuli are usually set-piece jokes. Joke-telling is both more characteristic of and more normatively acceptable for males in American culture [12, 13], suggesting that stimuli may have different meaning for female and male subjects. Studies of hostile and sexual humor have frequently failed to systematically control for such variables as gender of the initiator/recipient of aggression or the butt of sexual humor [14]. One critic has noted [15]:

> It is rare to find the image of a woman in a mainstream joke used to symbolize universal human attributes. The reason for this could be that our society does not find images of women to be neutral. Mentioning a woman in a joke is frequently done so as to make some kind of statement about the nature and motivations of women. And the most effective way to make this statement is to have women function as the butts of jokes rather than as the subjects or heroes.

A final source of gender bias in experimental research is in the interpretation of gender differences. Women's lower ratings of sexual and hostile jokes have been taken as evidence of greater sexual inhibition or conventionality. The possibilities that women may appreciate (or create) uninhibited or unconventional humor of a different sort, or that women's humor may have social functions other than the release of hostility or sexual tension, have rarely been addressed.

Researchers have tried to remedy gender bias in humor experiments by systematically varying the gender of the recipient of hostility [16] or the butt of sexual innuendo [17] and by including the humor of female comedians in stimulus materials [18]. But, in spite of these corrective measures, the validity of studying humor primarily by systematically manipulating variables in laboratory settings is open to question. If the problem with humor research were simply that it has incorporated the sorts of gender bias described here, it could be remedied relatively easily through better use of experimental methods. But, although better experimental design is necessary and important, it must be accompanied by a broadening of methods and by "triangulation"—converging on related questions with a variety of methods [4]. Researchers have relied too heavily on strictly experimental, rather than broadly empirical, methods. They have also studied behavior out of context, and the consequence has been a limited understanding of the ordinary social functions of humor.

Because researchers have not analyzed women's humor at the descriptive level, the variables chosen for manipulation in the laboratory reflect a lack of understanding of its characteristics and functions. The focus on appreciation of "canned" commercial humor has probably occurred because appreciation (typically operationalized as Likert-scale ratings of funniness) is easier to measure than humor production and commercial humor is easier to define and manipulate than spontaneous humor. The relationship of the research to the ordinary meanings and functions of humor in women's (and men's) lives remains unexamined.

Over-reliance on the experimental method may also lead to treating interactional phenomena as though they were properties of individuals. Attempts to study humor in terms of individual traits or isolated responses neglect to recognize that humor emerges in a complex social context and may serve many different social functions. Ultimately a field theory of humor is required:

> There is an old saying often used when a joke or comic story falls flat: "you had to be there. . . ." But what does it mean to say "You had to be there?" First of all, it suggests that humor is a fragile phenomenon quite dependent on social and interpersonal conditions present in a particular situation. It also suggests that over and above the immediate situation are a great many societal institutions and traditions serving to define what is taboo and what is acceptable and that these larger social concerns function as distant, but significant, contexts for the present one. It also suggests that "being there" requires not only a mental commitment but the embodied participation of an engaged person. In short, "being there" implies a field theory of humor that pays full attention to the laughing/smiling person in the full, rich context of his or her contemporary first-person world [19, p. 228].

ALTERNATIVE METHODS

How can researchers find the "lost" aspects of humor creation and women's humor? The use of empirical alternatives to the experimental method has led to a consistent, though as yet incomplete, description of women's humor and has potential for the study of creative, spontaneous humor in general. These methods include structured and unstructured self-report [20] and naturalistic and participant observation [21, 22].

I began my own research on humor [20] by asking for women's and men's perceptions of their sense of humor rather than by imposing an experimenter-defined "humor stimulus" on them. My students and I developed a lengthy exploratory questionnaire covering many aspects of humor creation and appreciation. A deliberately heterogeneous sample of over 200 people varying widely in age, education, and occupation was asked to complete the questionnaire after describing in a paragraph "the person who has the best sense of humor of anyone you know."

The results of this foray into "real" humor were enlightening. A factor analysis of questionnaire results revealed ten important dimensions of humor. Women and men were more alike than different in their perceptions, responding similarly on factors that tapped creative spontaneity, ability to tolerate being the butt of humor, and enjoyment of cartoon and sexual humor. Gender differences emerged on only four factors: Men were higher in the production and enjoyment of hostile humor, jokes, and slapstick comedy. Women were higher in the production and appreciation of anecdotal humor. Although men and women agreed that the two genders do not differ in their sense of humor "on the average," men rated themselves as having a better sense of humor than women rated themselves.

The questionnaire data were subject to the obvious limitation that respondents could provide information only about preselected humor varieties. Also, the desire to present oneself in a positive light can affect questionnaire results. The open-ended question, in which respondents were free to articulate definitions of "having a sense of humor," by describing someone else, was used for its potential to uncover unanticipated aspects of women's and men's understanding of humor.

The open-ended question allowed an unobtrusive measure of bias in perceiving an individual's sense of humor as outstanding. Most respondents wrote about a specific person whose gender was identifiable from pronouns. Respondents were far more likely to nominate a male as having an outstanding sense of humor, women by about a 2:1 ratio and men by about a 5:1 ratio.

Content analysis of responses to the open-ended request showed that they were consistent with the questionnaire factor structure and also revealed other aspects of the meaning and functions of humor. Creative spontaneity and the ability to laugh at oneself were valued highly in both men and women by both men and women. The most striking gender difference, and one not tapped by the questionnaire, was that women defined an outstanding sense of humor as one that breaks social tension, eases another's unhappiness, and cheers rather than wounds—humor as an expression of compassion rather than hostility.

These results show, then, that women and men both believe, to varying degrees, that women are less likely to possess an outstanding sense of humor. They agree in valuing some qualities comprising a sense of humor, and they see themselves as creating and appreciating several types of humor similarly. They differ in their valuing of compassionate aspects of humor and in the extent to which they create and enjoy hostile humor, jokes, and anecdotal humor.

This preliminary research was the basis for the construction of a Short Humor Questionnaire for use in further research [23]. It also provided a beginning for a re-visioning of gender and humor. How and when do men and women use humor similarly and differently in their daily lives? My respondents' self-reports gave clues about the sorts of situations in which gender differences will emerge. Even though men describe creative spontaneity and (to a lesser extent) compassion as important when writing about another individual who has an excellent sense of humor, the humor they attribute to themselves is both hostile and non-spontaneous. It is also highly "portable." Set-piece jokes can be carried about and inserted into various situations. For example, male college professors tend to rely on joke and storytelling formats for classroom humor [22]; they are also perceived by students as more likely than female professors to use hostile, belittling classroom humor [24]. (That humor content may be hostile, racist or sexist is perhaps justified to the teller by its context-independent presentation—it is "not intended to be taken personally" by the hearer.) In contrast, female college professors use a greater proportion of spontaneous humor in the classroom, and their humor is more closely related to their educational message [22].

The humor that women differentially attribute to themselves, the relating of anecdotes about one's own and one's friends' personal experiences, is consistent with the humor they value in others. It involves not only creative spontaneity but connectedness and compassion; it invites self-disclosure and reciprocal sharing of perspectives; it is dependent on the immediate social context. Indeed, it is likely to be found in its purest form in a context of conversation among friends. To understand gender and humor we must compare the conversational styles of women and men, and to understand women's humor we must examine women's conversations with friends.

WOMEN AND MEN IN CONVERSATION

A great deal of communication research suggests that males and females tend to use different conversational strategies [25] stemming from learned differences in conversational goals. For women, the primary goal of conversation is intimacy and for men the goal is positive self-presentation [26, 27].

Gender-linked conversational goals may result in very different interaction climates in all-female and all-male groups. As Jenkins speculates,

> Women and men in same-sex groups experience a different kind of "likeness" due to their status in society and their roles and relationships. Men in their groups seem to be saying, "I'm great. *I'm great, too*. Gee we're a great bunch of guys." In contrast, women seem to be saying, "Did this ever happen to you? *Yeah*. Oh, good, I'm not crazy. . . [21].

Research on gender and communication provides a useful framework for the study of women's conversational humor, especially when it is extended to include the communicative experiences of diverse groups of women. The neglect of social class and ethnic group in the women-and-language literature and the neglect of women in the black communication literature preclude a good understanding of class and minority group diversity in women's conversational style. But recent research is addressing relevant issues. Stanback has proposed that the communicative style of middle-class black women is characterized by a tendency toward equality with males stemming from the black women's tradition of work outside the home and the acceptability of self-reliance, strength, and autonomy for women within the black community [28]. At the same time, there is pressure toward more gender-differentiated styles due to blacks' recognition that such differentiation is the norm in white middle-class culture. The juxtaposition of a tradition of female outspokenness and an ideal of femininity based on white norms may create a unique set of contradictions for black female speakers.

WOMEN'S AND MEN'S CONVERSATIONAL HUMOR

With respect to white middle-class speakers, Jenkins proposes that, given the differences in women and men's goals for friendly conversation, their humor can reasonably be expected to serve different functions [21]. Women's humor supports a goal of greater intimacy by being supportive and healing, while men's humor reinforces "performance" goals of competition, the establishment of hierarchical relationships, and self-aggrandizement.

Jenkins' view of gender differences in humor style, derived from direct observation and conversational analysis, is strikingly congruent with my respondents' self-reports. The males in my sample reported greater production and appreciation of hostile (racist, sexist, and aggressive) humor and greater enjoyment of set-piece jokes. Jenkins comments:

> Men's humor is characterized as self-aggrandizing one-upmanship. There is a greater use of formulaic jokes . . . which are clearly separate from the ongoing conversation and which involve "performance." Joking for men establishes them as credible performers and affords them an audience for whom they demonstrate their prowess. Their jokes are less personal, like their social groups, and they can be told in a variety of settings. Men can develop a repertoire of jokes which they can use to compete with other men for audience attention and honors. Their jokes are exclusive in that they more often put down others or are told at the expense of others. The teller rarely identifies with the butt of the joke. . . .

The women in my sample reported a greater use of anecdotal humor, "telling funny stories about things that happen to you and your acquaintances." Furthermore, they valued in others humor that eased difficult moments in interaction and expressed compassion or empathy. Jenkins characterizes women's humor as follows:

> . . . much more context-bound. It is more often created out of the ongoing talk to satisfy the needs of [a] particular group of women. Since the goal of interaction is intimacy, there is not the same need to compete for performance points. . . . [women's] humor includes and supports group members by demonstrating what they have in common [21, p. 6].

SELF-DEPRECATION IN WOMEN'S HUMOR

Much has been made over women's tendency to rely on self-deprecation in humor [29]. Experimental studies have drawn conclusions about women's preference for self-deprecation from a narrow set of situations. In one study, women rated self-deprecating comedy routines funnier than did men. In another, both males and females preferred jokes with a female as butt to those with a male. Drawing general conclusions from these data is clearly unwise. Rating self-deprecating jokes as funny is not the same as being self-deprecating. In addition, defining women's humor as characteristically self-deprecating based on joke-rating tasks involves making judgments about subjects' intentions. But the experimental methods that form the basis for this judgment do not directly address the intentions of subjects. Judging from my own research and Jenkins' analysis, I believe that the characterization of women's humor as self-deprecating may be inaccurate. In this section I will speculate on the reasons why this characterization has persisted and on possible meanings of apparent self-deprecation in women's humor.

In evaluating women's humor self-deprecation has perhaps been confused with self-disclosure. A common type of women's humor involves describing one's mistakes or human frailties. As Jenkins points out, this type of humor is problematic only from the male-as-norm perspective, where the humorist's intent should be to show himself off to best advantage. Among women, self-disclosure can contribute to the goal of conversational intimacy, implying "... that we are close enough to share our less than ideal selves" [21, p. 7]. Among my respondents, women reported that they value women and men who have the ability to laugh at themselves, but the examples they provided did not reveal self-hatred. One woman described her choice as follows: "His humour pokes fun at human weakness in general and his own in particular. The essence of his humour (and why I found it admirable) is truth . . . [but his] remarks never injure."

Women's humor may also be typed as self-deprecating because professional women comedians have traditionally adopted such a stance. Lucille Ball, Imogene Coca, Phyllis Diller, and Goldie Hawn are a few examples among white performers, Beulah and "Moms" Mabley among blacks. A content analysis of comic monologues recorded by both black and white performers found that 63 percent of women comedians'– and 12 percent of men comedians'–punchlines were self-deprecating [18]. It was suggested that women comedians must reflect mass values in order to keep a mass audience. It should be obvious that women's access to and acceptance in broadcast media have depended on the acceptability of their stance to the men who control those media. There is no research that connects professionally produced humor with conversational humor but it should not be assumed that one closely reflects the other.

Third, humor that involves recounting stories about one's negative experiences can be a form of "getting even" [21] or satirizing the dominant group's expectations. (A woman responds to the sexist comment of a male colleague about the alleged incapacitating effects of PMS on women's job performance by relating it to a group of women friends who not only laugh at his foolishness but go on to list all the tasks for which they personally are totally incapacitated for many days each month by PMS: balancing the checkbook, attending PTA meetings, listening to sexist remarks. . . . And the cures for PMS: equal pay, state-supported child care, French food. . . .) Thus, the apparent self-deprecation involved in recounting one's experience of being angered and humiliated by a sexist remark becomes an act of satirizing the dominant group's view and affirming one's own, subversive view of reality.

Lesbian humor may prove a particularly rich source of this self-affirming and bonding humor [21]. It affirms the validity of lesbian identity by laughing at both the folly of those who assume heterosexuality and at the shared experiences of coping in a "straight" world. Although lesbian humor has been little studied, context-sensitive methods could be used to analyze the humor of lesbian friends. In addition, analyzing professionally produced lesbian humor may be less problematic than analyzing "mainstream" commercial humor simply because lesbian humor is "marginal"–less subject to mass market pressure and more likely to be supported directly by women. Kate Clinton's routine on "de-dyking the apartment" before a visit from parents exemplifies humor coming from the everyday experience of lesbian women.

The stereotype that women's humor is self-deprecating appears to result at least partly from misuse of the experimental method. External variables have been manipulated, controlled, and measured, and relationships among these variables have been used to infer subjects' intentions. But if knowledge of subjects' intentions is a research goal, methods that permit subjects to articulate their intentions should be used, and their subjective accounts should be taken seriously as data. I have suggested intentional orientations that may explain apparent self-deprecation in women's humor. These include a desire to increase group intimacy through self-disclosure and a goal of satirizing the negative and contradictory role messages directed at women. But these orientations are not amenable to study if the researcher objectifies her subjects and distances herself from their subjective interpretation of their own experience. They require research methods that are not only sensitive to the social context of behavior but that allow the experimenter's perceptions to be validated against those of the subject.

CONCLUSION

Experimental research on humor has been compromised by the sorts of gender biases found in other areas of psychological research, such as bias in choice of stimuli and interpretation of gender differences. There are many studies of how females and males rate the funniness of hostile, sexist, and/or male-selected humor; these studies, not incidentally, sometimes find women to be "deficient" in humor appreciation. To the extent that women's and men's humor modes and preferences differ (and there are distinct differences within a general pattern of similarity), research has favored the humor of males. Men's preferred humor is more adaptable to laboratory study since it relies more on non-spontaneous jokes than on material from its immediate social context.

Further, over-reliance on experimental, rather than broadly empirical, methods has produced a body of knowledge that focuses on relatively trivial aspects of humor appreciation while ignoring creativity, conversational humor, and the intentions underlying the social use of humor. There are comparatively few naturalistic studies of conversational humor, no studies that recognize the effects of women's (or men's) differences in class, race, and sexual orientation, and few studies that examine participants' reasons for their behavior, and thus there is no ecologically valid psychology of humor. This situation results from inherent limitations of the experimental method and can be redressed by converging on related questions with a variety of methods.

Experimental research on humor has served neither women nor men well, but it has been particularly unsuited to the humor of women. If we study women with a variety of empirical methods we will be able to fill in the picture of women's humor I have sketched, account for racial and ethnic diversity, and show how women use humor to create intimacy, solidarity, and support as well as to express hostility and acknowledge conflict. An ecologically valid account of women's humor must consider its participants' intentions, its immediate context, and its wider social context. Without this understanding, the magic that is women's humor evaporates.

ACKNOWLEDGMENTS

I gratefully acknowledge the contributions of Roger Chaffin, Margaret Gentry, Amy Gervasio, and Jeanne Marecek, who read earlier drafts of this chapter and participated in discussions of related issues, and the Jane Watson Irwin Endowment, which enabled me to work with a stimulating group of colleagues and students in psychology and women's studies at Hamilton College.

REFERENCES

1. C. Kramarae and P. Treichler, *A Feminist Dictionary*, Pandora Press, Boston, Massachusetts, 1985.
2. J. H. Goldstein, P. E. McGhee, J. R. Smith, A. J. Chapman, and H. C. Foot, Humour, Laughter and Comedy: A Bibliography of Empirical and Nonempirical Analyses in the English Language, in *It's a Funny Thing Humour*, A. J. Chapman and H. C. Foot (eds.), Pergamon Press, Oxford, England, 1977.
3. P. E. McGhee and J. H. Goldstein, *Handbook of Humor Research, Volumes 1 and 2*, Springer-Verlag, New York, 1983.
4. B. S. Wallston and K. E. Grady, Integrating the Feminist Critique and the Crisis in Social Psychology: Another Look at Research Methods, in *Women, Gender and Social Psychology*, V. E. O'Leary, R. K. Unger, and B. S. Wallston (eds.), Erlbaum, Hillsdale, New Jersey, pp. 7-33, 1985.

5. L. Marlowe, A Sense of Humor, in *Representations: Social Constructions of Gender*, R. K. Unger (ed.), Baywood Publishing Company, Amityville, New York, 1988.
6. P. McGhee, Humor Development: Toward a Life-Span Approach, in *Handbook of Humor Research, Volume 1*, P. H. MCGhee and J. H. Goldstein (eds.), Springer-Verlag, New York, 1983.
7. K. E. Grady, Sex Bias in Research Design, *Psychology of Women Quarterly*, *5*, pp. 628-636, 1981.
8. D. B. Graever and S. J. Morris, College Humor in 1930 and 1972: An Investigation Using the Humor Diary, *Sociology and Social Research*, *59*, pp. 406-410, 1975.
9. K. Deaux, From Individual Differences to Social Categories: Analysis of a Decade's Research on Gender, *American Psychologist*, *39*:2, pp. 105-116, 1984.
10. R. K. Unger, Toward a Redefinition of Sex and Gender, *American Psychologist*, *34*:11, pp. 1085-1094, 1979.
11. ——, Psychological, Feminist, and Personal Epistemology: Transcending Contradiction, in *Feminist Epistemology*, M. Gergen (ed.), New York University Press, New York, in press.
12. R. Middleton and J. Moland, Humor in Negro and White Subcultures: A Study of Jokes Among University Students, *American Sociological Review*, *22*, pp. 61-69, 1959.
13. E. E. Smith and J. D. Goodchilds, Characteristics of the Witty Group Member: The Wit as a Leader, *American Psychologist*, *14*, pp. 375-376, 1959.
14. P. E. McGhee, The Role of Laughter and Humor in Growing Up Female, in *Becoming Female: Perspectives on Development*, C. B. Kopp (ed.), Plenum, New York, pp. 183-206, 1979.
15. S. LeBell, Properties of the Feminist Joke, unpublished B.A. Thesis, University of California at Berkeley, 1981. Cited in N. Levidow, When Women are People, Too: A Look at the New Feminist Comedians, in *The Language of Humor and The Humor of Language: Proceedings of the 1982 WHIM Conference*, Nilsen, Tempe, Arizona, 1983.
16. J. Losco and S. Epstein, Humor Preferences as a Subtle Measure of Attitudes Toward the Same and Opposite Sex, *Journal of Personality*, *43*:2, pp. 321-334, 1975.
17. A. J. Chapman and N. J. Gadfield, Is Sexual Humor Sexist? *Journal of Communication*, *26*:3, pp. 141-153, 1976.
18. J. B. Levine, The Feminine Routine, *Journal of Communication*, *26*:3, pp. 173-175, 1976.
19. H. R. Pollio, Notes Toward a Field Theory of Humor, in McGhee and Goldstein, pp. 213-230 (p. 228).
20. M. Crawford, Gender Differences in Humor Preferences, paper presented at Eastern Psychological Association, Boston, Massachusetts, April, 1985.
21. M. Jenkins, What's So Funny? Joking Among Women, in *Proceedings of the First Berkeley Women and Language Conference*, S. Bremner, N. Caskey, and B. Moonwomon (eds.), Berkeley Women and Language Group, University of California at Berkeley, 1985.

22. J. Bryant, P. Cominsky, and D. Zillman, Teachers' Humor in the College Classroom, *Communication Education*, *28*, pp. 110-118, 1979.
23. M. Crawford, *The Short Humor Questionnaire*, copyright 1987.
24. ____, *Classroom Climate at West Chester University: A Report to the University Community*, West Chester University of Pennsylvania, West Chester, Pennsylvania, 1986.
25. P. A. Treichler and C. Kramarae, Women's Talk in the Ivory Tower, *Communication Quarterly*, *31*, pp. 118-132, 1983.
26. D. Maltz and R. A. Borker, A Cultural Approach to Male/Female Miscommunication, in *Languages and Social Identity: Studies in International Sociolinguistics*, J. J. Gumperz (ed.), Cambridge University Press, Cambridge, England, 1982.
27. F. L. Johnson and E. J. Aries, The Talk of Women Friends, *Women's Studies International Forum*, *6*, pp. 353-361, 1983.
28. M. Stanback, Language and Black Women's Place: Evidence from the Black Middle Class, in *For Alma Mater: Theory and Practice in Feminist Scholarship*, P. A. Treichler, C. Kramarae, and B. Stafford (eds.), University of Illinois Press, Urbana, Illinois, pp. 177-191, 1985.
29. D. Zillman and S. H. Stocking, Putdown Humor, *Journal of Communication*, *26*:3, pp. 154-163, 1976.

CHAPTER 12

Dialogue with Guatemalan Indian Women: Critical Perspectives on Constructing Collaborative Research

M. BRINTON LYKES

Between 1979 and 1983 50,000 to 100,000 Guatemalans were killed, thousands more were disappeared, over 400 rural villages were destroyed and between 100,000 and 200,000 Guatemalan children were orphaned [1, 2]. Although I have seen these figures many times since 1983 and listened to or read many personal testimonies of survivors of the military's violent counterinsurgency program in January of 1983 I knew very little either about the Guatemalan people's most recent struggle to redress gross economic, political and cultural repression or of the military's strategies for combatting their resistance. At the time I was completing the data collection stage of a study of alternative conceptualizations of the self [3, 4]. I was interviewing women in the United States who had been working in community- or work-based projects for social change in an effort to better understand the ways in which their notions of themselves as women were related to these activities. I was also working with a number of community-based women's projects for social change, and in the Latin American solidarity network. Through this work I traveled to Central America where I met several Guatemalans who spoke of their experiences, the need to flee their country, and their desire to develop stronger solidarity ties with women in the United States. At their initiative I agreed to join two friends

* The study reported in this paper was partially funded by grants from a Rhode Island College Faculty Scholars Award and from the Rhode Island College Research Fund. I would also like to thank members of my Feminist Methodology Research Group, Abigail J. Stewart and G. Ramsay Liem for their continuing support of this work. Finally, I would like to thank G. Ramsay Liem, Abigail J. Stewart and Rhoda Unger for their comments on earlier drafts of this work.

to work on developing a national U.S. tour through which Guatemalan women could share their stories with mainstream women's groups. We networked with groups already working in the U.S. and designed a tour to both educate a new sector of the U.S. public about the situation of women and children in Guatemala and to raise funds to support refugees in Guatemala and in Mexico. Although my involvement in planning this tour grew out of political work in the feminist and Latin American struggles, because of my training and research interests I was also eager to learn more about how the Guatemalan women who came to the United States understood their experiences, about how they thought about and talked about their struggles and about how they understood themselves as Indian women. I was able initially to explore this last concern in a conversation with Juanita, one of the women on the tour.

INITIAL CONVERSATIONS: DECIDING TO COLLABORATE ON A RESEARCH PROJECT

In discussing her first experiences in the United States Juanita expressed concern over the orientation program that we had organized, and more particularly, over the response of one of the resource people we had invited to give her feedback on a "trial run" of her presentation. Upon completing her story Juanita was told by one of the listeners that it had been very moving but that it would not do for a U.S. audience because it was not clearly her "own" story. The critic suggested that Juanita's presentation had been a story of a family, of a community, not of an individual, and that in order to reach U.S. audiences Juanita had to be more personal, to describe her individual reality and how the events she recounted had affected her personally. Juanita told me how surprised and confused she had been by these comments, how she had been unsuccessful in her efforts to convince her critic that she had told *her* story, and that she remained confused about what women in the United States meant by telling one's story. For her, her story and the story of her people were synonymous (personal communication, 1983).

I returned frequently to this conversation and to my own growing concern about how the descriptions I was documenting in conversations with women in the United States might converge with or be distinguished from the reflections of women in or from a less individualistic, more community-based, society. Some of the Guatemalan Indian women with whom I had begun to work, and others whose stories I was reading in testimonies, came from rural communities steeped in rich traditions and ritual practices that affirmed community life but, simultaneously, rigid, yet complementary, gender roles that maintained women's place within the home and community [5]. In addition, these women had actively engaged in community-based projects to improve their own and others' lives. From this perspective they shared certain experiences with the women I had been interviewing. Yet the social, political, economic and cultural contexts for this work differed dramatically. I was increasingly interested in how these women understood themselves as Indian women as they were forced to journey from the Guatemalan Highlands to life in exile in Mexico or the United States. I was also challenged to respond to that "reality," to the violent repression that had necessitated their flight, that was requiring new struggles of them as exiles.

BACKGROUND ON THE SITUATION IN GUATEMALA

Before the project could move forward I felt I needed to know more about the history of the Guatemalan people with whom I had begun to work. I read about the beauty and natural wealth of the country and about the ancient Mayan civilization [6]. This story describes four and a half centuries of oppression and exploitation, from the destruction of life and community at the time of the Conquest through the violent repression of the recent counterinsurgency. Yet this story is also one of continual resistance. Evidence of major recent resistance efforts involving Indians and Ladinos include the development of a variety of organizations (e.g., unions, cooperatives, community development projects, student associations, Christian base communities and guerrilla organizations). Most of these developed during the past twenty-five years as part of an overall effort to break the minority's hold on power, particularly the ownership of over 80 percent of the land by less than 4 percent of the farmers. These efforts are grounded in a struggle to establish a new power base rooted in the economic, political, social and cultural concerns of the majority of the population.

This most recent phase of the struggle for self-determination was met by violent military action (especially between 1979 and 1983), action within the context of a counterinsurgency strategy that led to the deaths of over 50,000 Guatemalans [1]. The worst of the systematic and brutal attacks against the Guatemalan people were felt by the Indians of the Guatemalan Highlands where over 400 rural villages have been destroyed [2]. Approximately one million people are internal refugees within their country; another 150,000 have sought refuge in Mexico and between 100,000 and 200,000 Guatemalan children have been orphaned [1, 2, 7]. The extermination of entire villages and the massacre of children and the elderly suggest strongly that the military project was intended not only to control revolutionary activity but to strike at and weaken or destroy key elements in Indian life, elements that give culture its coherence, elements that act as axes of community life and identity [8].

CONTINUING THE CONVERSATION

This violence, brutality and destruction was inflicted on particular individuals, each with his or her story, each a part of a community of friends and family that mourn her or his death or disappearance, each loss a statement about the military's strategies for controlling the population. The worst of these violent abuses of human rights and the army's penetration of all levels of civilian life have been documented, for example, in testimony before the Permanent People's Tribunal [9] from January 27 through 31, 1983 and in numerous publications by Americas Watch and other human rights groups. I confronted these facts in the stories of the women who toured the United States and in the testimonies I was reading.

I was able also to travel to Guatemala and Mexico several times in 1985 and 1986 and experienced more directly the beauty of the land, the richness of the Mayan traditions, and simultaneously, in stark contrast, the population's fear, and despite massive repression, continuing resistance to efforts to silence the majority of the people. I was disturbed to realize how little I had known about the situation here, and found myself confronting not only the Guatemalan reality surrounding me but also the reality of the United States, of my professional development, of my community and of my personal relations. I also confronted a wall of silence about Guatemala from the mainstream press to the solidarity movement. As I began to penetrate that silence, to listen to personal testimonies and read human rights reports, I returned repeatedly to Falla's description of the counterinsurgency as a "partial genocide" [8].

This silence, constructed within the country, but sustained by the international community is an element in the strategy of counterinsurgency. The violent death or disappearance of a loved one is rarely publically recorded. When stories do appear in newspapers or on television events are frequently mystified, with the violent murder of women and children described as successful efforts to stop terrorism or to quiet communists who are described as disrupting community life. I remembered stories of the silence surrounding the Holocaust and asked myself repeatedly when and where I would speak.

Conversations with friends and colleagues when I returned from travels to the region furthered the process of breaking the silence about what I had seen, heard, and read. I next began a series of educational presentations and fundraising efforts on behalf of Guatemalan refugees, engaging my teaching and fundraising skills in efforts to speak to wider audiences. Through this I was able to follow through on the work begun in our "Woman to Woman" tour. But that was not enough. These felt like extra-curricular activities and I wanted to engage my skills as a psychologist in contributing to efforts to break the public silence surrounding this genocide. I wanted to contribute more directly to a process whereby the meaning of the events of the late 1970s and early 1980s from the point of view of those who had suffered most could be further developed and articulated.

I shared my concerns and hopes with a friend in Mexico. Although we agreed that human rights groups were publicizing the testimonies of victims of torture and abuse we felt that the meaning of these experiences to those who had suffered them and their broader social and political context was of necessity less well developed in the human rights reports. Much less well known, for example, were the detailed stories of the women and men who actively participated in struggles for change in their communities, who resisted military repression, who may not have been physically abused, but who were forced to flee their country during the early 1980s. A number of Guatemalans living in exile had shared with my friend their sense of the importance of recording these stories, both as a record for the communities in exile and for those who have remained inside the country or have chosen to return as they continue the process of rebuilding their resistance movements. Specifically, the Center for Guatemala Studies, an interdisciplinary research center in Mexico City with whom my friend was affiliated, was interested in collecting the stories of Indian leaders and making these available to the communities in exile as resources in educational and community training programs. In addition to documenting earlier work in Guatemala they hoped to develop a record of the continuing work among Indian communities living in exile.

As we spoke my friend and I found that we also shared an interest in better understanding the conditions under which people come to understand themselves as actors constructing their future, as active participants in the social and political development of their people. We agreed that a project that documented the processes by which women, beginning with their immediate concerns, develop a political consciousness that is accompanied by action and gives social meaning to their activity, would contribute both to a better understanding of Guatemalan women's resistance efforts and, more generally, to our knowledge about the development of political self-consciousness among women. The project was conceived thus as a concrete resource for existing Guatemalan communities, as a vehicle for exploring a more theoretical problem of interest to self theorists and to psychologists more generally, and as making a contribution to the collective task of breaking the silence surrounding Guatemala's recent history. We sought to document through oral history interviews some of the processes by which some representatives of the Guatemalan refugee communities in Mexico understand themselves and how their sense of who they are as Guatemalan Indian women is sustained and transformed in the experiences of being in exile.

In this chapter I describe aspects of the ongoing collaboration between North American women and Guatemalan Indian women from my perspective as one of the North American women participants. What follows is a description and analysis of how the research itself developed. It includes a discussion of how we resolved some of the methodological challenges we confronted and provides a base from which to reflect on some of the ways we as women from different economic, cultural and racial groups are working together and independently to find our individual and collective voices to break the silence surrounding Guatemalan women's experiences, and thereby to contribute to an ongoing process of naming the meaning of these events.

DEVELOPING THE RESEARCH PROJECT

Although my colleague and I had identified several research questions and agreed that we would collaborate we did not have a strategy for proceeding. Our challenge as North American researchers was to clarify a strategy for addressing our interests in 1) theory-building about women's development of political self-consciousness and self-understanding; 2) speaking out about the realities of life for Indians in Guatemala and contributing to or supporting the Guatemalan struggle; and 3) documenting Guatemalan exiles' experiences for the Center's educational programming.

Research strategies I had learned in methods courses or through previous work fell far short of this challenge. My understanding of our field had been shaped in part by my resonance to McGuire's [10], Gergen's [11, 12] and Sampson's [13] criticisms of the experimentalist's claims to "objectivity" or scientific distance and this analysis was, broadly speaking, reflected in my earlier work. Yet despite general agreement among social psychologists that the "crisis literature" and its critical discussion of experimental social psychology (of its ahistoricity [14, 15], its failure to take seriously the social context in which activity is embedded in describing social behavior [16-18] and its narrow data base [18]) had accurately captured the limitations of research in the field, mainstream journals continued to be dominated by studies using these methods [19]. The field's incorporation of this self-critical posture has not changed significantly its practice (see [20] for a similar argument concerning feminist criticisms). Although ideologically convinced that these critics were correct, it was the concrete problems I confronted in undertaking research with Guatemalan women that enabled me to depart more significantly from the quantitative methods of my training towards a more qualitative participatory model of research that would enable me both to better address the questions I was asking and to engage in research that is consistent with my social goals and commitments [19, 20-22].

Oral history interviews were selected as the appropriate method for this study because they are both sensitive to the single individual's experiences, enabling us to look at a woman's understanding of herself and her elaboration of the social meaning of her life, and to the Guatemalan community's long tradition of oral communication. Further, these stories are a rich record of the lives of a select number of Guatemalan women and can be examined not only for what is said but for how it is said [23, 24]. In addition, recording mlutiple stories facilitates better understanding of how individuals have responded to their experiences and enables the reconstruction of the collective experiences of a people as a basis for understanding what binds them together and creates an effective community. Finally, the open-ended interview that encourages the participant to tell her own story is sensitive to the developing collaborative relationship between ourselves and the participants, one that would both reflect and foster trust and sharing and complement our ongoing work and personal ties to Guatemalan Indian communities in Mexico.

Informed by a number of diverse strategies for developing our oral history method of collaborative research (see e.g., Langness and Frank's work on life stories [25], Frisch's historical approach [26] and Bertaux's [27] or Reinharz's [28] sociological perspectives) we began the more formal research project. Despite important theoretical differences in these distinctly disciplinary approaches to oral history (a discussion of which is beyond the scope of my chapter), we found that there were certain strategic issues that all researchers confront in collecting data that importantly shaped our work and provide an important lens through which to analyze and evaluate multicultural collaborative research. The remainder of this chapter will briefly discuss two of these issues, the identification of participants and the selection of a method, and discuss in some detail our process of "obtaining" informed consent. All three of these issues deal in some way with the question of control over the research process. Our experience suggests that assumptions of researcher control and participant powerlessness are implicit in these methods and that they contribute to and are shaped by the competing interests of researcher and participant that are part of and are played out in the research process.

Who Would We Talk With

The voices of this project are those of two North American women and a number of Guatemalan Indian women. Together the North American "researchers" have had ongoing involvement in and engagement with Guatemalans in the United States, Mexico and Guatemala for over ten years. The identification of Guatemalans who might have been interested in collaborating in this project was possible because of this previous work. This previous contact was particularly important given the political and social reality in Guatemala and the caution Guatemalans must exercise in speaking to anyone about their experiences. The need for such caution was expressed repeatedly by the women with whom we spoke. One woman turned off the tape recorder when she spoke of her husband's current work, fearing that he was such a well known leader that no precautions we would take could guarantee his anonymity. Because we were trusted friends we were allowed to record past activities. But the political realities for Guatemalans in exile and the public nature of our work are such that current activities were not recorded. These political realities framed and set limits on our collaboration as it developed.

"Subject selection" involved a process of articulating our interests to a number of different groups of Guatemalan women and continuing dialogue with those individuals or groups who expressed interest in the work and wanted to know more. The initial selection of which groups we would contact was shaped by our ongoing work with Guatemalans, the social, political and geographic realities within their communities, and a desire to focus the current study on the experiences of Quiché Indian women from the Guatemalan Highlands. This latter priority developed due to the particular impact that the violence of recent years has had on this group, the initial interest of a number of Quiché Indian women in the project and our knowledge that Guatemalan life differs significantly from group to group (e.g., there are 23 different linguistic groups, [5]) and from region to region. If our interviews were to give us a sense of the experiences of anyone beyond the individual woman with whom we spoke we felt that we needed to begin with women from only one of the twenty-three groups in one of the regions.

The decisions about which particular women would be interviewed emerged out of continuing conversations among ourselves as researchers, our contact people (who work with or are members of the communities described above) and individual women in these communities. Participation in the project reflects therefore both an individual's decision to tell her story and a decision about how her participation contributes to and is shaped by her own and her community's current experiences. Hence, although the decisions were made by individual researchers and participants, they also quite clearly reflect the individual's and her community's and/or organization's interests. Despite the fact that this research would be impossible without considerable overlap in interests among researchers and participants there are clear differences and potential, if not actual, competing interests among all participants.

For example, one group of women we approached expressed initial interest in the project and two members agreed to be interviewed. Serious health complications prevented both women from participating in their scheduled interviews. Although both interviews have been rescheduled subsequent conversations with others who work with this group suggest that the group's own more group-focused project (in contrast to our work of telling individual stories) may take precedence over participation in other activities, that is, for example, in our research. Although one could view both the initial reason for cancelling the appointments and the current hesitancy as individual excuses or changes in mind they are also reflective of broader group and community concerns. The health complications reflect symptoms that have developed in efforts to cope with the severe stressors of violence and exile and the lack of effective medical resources for the refugee community. The shift in focus towards putting more energy into their own group's project reflects, in part, an important tension between participating exclusively or primarily in activities with one's own organization and engaging with others in work that broadens the base of one's effort. It may also, in part, reflect renewed questions about our project, its goals, and its consequences for their work. Despite our contacts and ongoing work with Guatemalans we are outsiders and as such any collaboration must both bridge that difference and recognize the limits that it imposes.

Our response to the cancellation of these two interviews has been to reschedule conversations about the project before proceeding to conduct additional interviews. As a researcher this experience has been, on the one hand, frustrating and has "reduced my sample." As a collaborator, an activist, a seeker of knowledge and understanding of Guatemalan Indian women it has broadened my view of Indian women's experiences and provided an opportunity for elaborating and reflecting on my "agenda" in the project.

How Would We Proceed

Having identified some participants and agreed on an oral history method we needed to clarify the types of information we hoped to elicit, both in terms of developing an historical record and in terms of our more theoretical concerns. We developed a series of guiding questions that would provide a structure for our open-ended, in depth interviews and enable us to gather similar types of information from each participant. We conducted our first interview with these questions (see Appendix A). Not surprisingly, the interview strategy has been modified in collaboration with the Guatemalan participants to include a range of interactions and conversations that are broader in scope than the original questions.

Thus far, we have done intensive interviews with three Guatemalan Indian women and had lengthy conversations with several others. We have also spent a day with one of the women and her family and engaged in a focus group interview with four Guatemalan Indian women, including two who had been interviewed. All participants in the focus group had read the transcripts of the interviews we had conducted, and together we discussed them. Whenever possible these conversations have been recorded. These different types of interactions have developed from the demands of the situation and from initiatives taken by some of the participants as they continue to identify ways in which this work intersects with and can be of service to their continuing activities. For example, the focus group interview was an opportunity to discuss divergent perspectives on the meaning of being an Indian woman and to reflect on some of the ways in which being in exile contributed to changing understandings of oneself. The views expressed in this discussion were later used as a basis from which to plan for conversations with other Indian women in an educational program women in the focus group had designed to help other compañeras better understand their history and their current experiences.

As researchers our concern for the comparability of data from the different participants has dictated a continuing commitment to conduct an oral history interview with each of the "formal participants." However our additional conversations are key to the deepening of our understanding of Indian refugee women's reality and have made of this work a more truly collaborative project. The decision to incorporate multiple forms of interaction was a natural development of our process and has been one of the strengths of the method we are developing. Yet the amount of time I have been able to spend with these women (a total of five weeks in Mexico at two different time periods) has limited the number of interactions that we can have and suggests the role that material constraints (i.e., time) play in shaping research methods. The method described here derives from the different interests of the collaborators and our effort as researchers to develop a strategy that is responsive to these interests in the context of real material constraints of time and resources.

Informed Consent

Having seen the necessity for flexibility in the selection of participants and of a method, I was somewhat surprised by my own reaction to another convention of the research process that required similar flexibility, that is, the informed consent form. Before beginning this research I had carefully studied a number of informed consent forms from other oral history projects conducted in the United States. I had developed what I felt was a form that provided optimal protection of the identity of the participants and gave them a range of options concerning their continuing control over how the oral histories would be used. The Committee for the Protection of Human Subjects at my university provided useful comments and I felt satisfied with the final document. My sense was confirmed by a colleague with whom I shared my form who found it to be so thorough that she adopted it for her own field research and described it as an "empowering instrument." Nevertheless, in subsequent experience with the form I recognized assumptions that I had brought to the research project that belied my own articulated goals of collaboration.

Concretely, the form (see Appendix B) has been a major obstacle at the beginning of each interview. Intended to "protect the subjects of the research," the women with whom I spoke experienced it as a barrier or hurdle. My conversation with one of the women is illustrative. When I presented the form she suggested that she had already agreed to talk to me (otherwise she would not be there) and that by agreeing to tell her story she had indicated her consent. Her consent meant that whatever she would tell me was a part of our public record, to be used in support of the Guatemalan struggle as I understood that task. She found my choices concerning future use of the material as described on the form confusing and suggested that her signature was unnecessary, that we had already settled the question of the use of the material. When we had finally seemed to agree that she had *de facto* chosen Form A or unrestricted use and she checked this line she again refused to sign her name, indicating that she did not see why it was necessary.

My initial response to her hesitancy to sign was to interpret this as my failure to adequately communicate the purposes of the form or my faulty Spanish. I knew that the form *per se* was very much outside of her experiences and felt that I needed to "educate" her to its usefulness. I worried further that her reluctance to sign was an indication that she might have agreed to participate as a favor or without fully understanding the project and I became increasingly invested in trying to clarify the form and why it was an important document that protected her interests. The traditionally trained social psychologist in me reacted almost mechanically and upon reflection I realize that *I* was shifting the context of our relationship, one that had been collaboratively constructed to that point. My own somewhat automatic response as social scientist took on a life of its own and prevented me from responding to the experience itself.

By the third interview I began to discern that I was in fact misinterpreting the participants reality *and* our relationship. I had come to this project with a clear analysis of my power as Other, with my role as a university professor with a Ph.D. and as a white North American. Yet I was also a concerned researcher who was acutely aware of the ways in which researchers have taken advantage of subjects, misinterpreted their reality, and given them inadequate access to their own labor. I recognized the many ways in which the participant both makes her/himself vulnerable in sharing his/her story and has no real control over how the researcher reconstructs that story [29, 30]. I had therefore designed a form that I thought would address this imbalance of power, providing a base from which the participants could assert their agenda. I would, thereby, "empower" the participants.

My resocialization as a concerned researcher masked both my knowledge of the history of informed consent and its roots in the doctor-patient relationship and my knowledge base as an activist and political participant in the ongoing struggle of the Guatemalan people. On the one hand, I had failed to recognize that my form was constructed on the same foundation underlying all informed consent in social science research. The form both releases the sponsoring university or funding agency from any liability while enabling it to maintain a certain control over the researcher. Further, it gives control or license to the interviewer. As long as consent is given neither the sponsoring organization nor the researcher have responsibility for or to the participant. The former is not legally libel and the latter can now use the data in any way she or he, as scientist, determines. In sharp contrast to an ideology that recognizes the participant as subject with particular interests that I was communicating verbally and in our developing relationship, the form itself reflects an elaborate variation on more traditional documents. Although the elaboration places some limits on the license I as researcher can take with the participant's story, control remains in my hands. In addition, through introducing the form when I did I asserted my role as researcher, changing the terms of the previously established grounds for our interview. Reflecting on my experiences with the form revealed the complexity of both my role as researcher/activist and the constraints on developing collaboration between subjects in a context of real power imbalances. More importantly, I began to understand more clearly how previous analyses of the researcher-participant relationship, including my own, that described this power imbalance were still written from the perspective of the person in power, now the concerned researcher, and failed to understand the power of the participant. As the examples described above suggest the participants are not only aware of their power, they use it. Turning off the tape recorder, using the time of the interview to ask questions about the pre-Conquest history of Mayan Indians, and deciding what experiences to include in the telling of a story are three additional examples of the participants' role in constructing the collaboration, indices of her subjectivity. From this perspective the language of my form (for example, "this project is being undertaken by trained personnel for a serious scientific purpose and . . . careful attention to my [i.e., the participant's] general welfare will be provided throughout") is particularly paternalistic and gratuitous.

The basis for our (i.e., North American and Guatemalan) collaboration has been established long before we undertook this particular research project. The Guatemalan women evaluated our invitation to participate in the oral history project within the context of their community's ongoing struggle and a decision to develop ties with North American women was made in the context of ongoing systems that they have developed for decision making. In my decision to become involved in their lives and in their decision to include this project in their ongoing work we had, in a small and limited way, initiated a joint effort. Making these decisions, that is to interview and be interviewed, represented a concrete affirmation of mutual trust. The issue of consent had been settled. In some limited ways I had entered into their systems of social and political organizing, into their ongoing community dynamics with its many contradictions and conflicts. In other, also limited, ways their decision to be interviewed constituted their entry into my community. We have also, through the collaboration, begun a process of constructing a different reality, one that reflects the conversations that we are building together.

The informed consent form, which I introduced as a mechanism for "protecting the subjects" of the research project, was instead a barrier and forced me to confront the chasm between the needs and demands of research conducted within the boundaries of the university and the systems of trust and mistrust and of sharing and withholding that were already a part of this collaboration. In introducing a strategy that I thought I had constructed in a way to guarantee that the subjects or participants in the research maintained control over their words I was rather assuming that either I had control or needed to gain control over the process. I was, on the one hand, seeking to protect myself while, on the other hand, implicitly asserting that I needed to protect them from abuses of my control. The introduction of the form threatened to undermine our previously negotiated contractual arrangement of trust. Upon reflection I have come to see their resistance as a reaffirmation of that relationship, as an assertion of the control they know is theirs, and, finally, as a refusal to allow me to shift the grounds of my control. Their resistance to signing the informed consent form became an opportunity to more fully clarify both the meaning of the form and the developing meaning of our relationship.

I have not jettisoned the form. Rather my current understanding of its meaning-in-context provides an alternative perspective from which to introduce a discussion of informed consent in our next oral history interview and increased clarification of the nature of the relationships developing in this project and how they shape the outcomes of our collaboration.

DISCUSSION

All research involves the selection of a method, identification of participants and development of an informed consent form. These are sometimes viewed as neutral, value free strategies for accomplishing the goal of testing a hypothesis or answering a research question. Concerned social scientists have identified some of the biases within research methods and sought to develop strategies that protect participants. As a first world North American woman and a concerned social scientist I was aware of the power and resources I brought to this collaboration when I began my work. (I was also aware of my weaknesses, for example, limited proficiency in Spanish and no proficiency in Quiché.) Minimally, I brought the power of my education, the power of being from the "first world," the power of access to methods of communication beyond the local community and the power of financial and professional resources to make these stories available. My recognition of my position enhanced my sensitivity to the power differential between researcher and participant and led to my efforts to develop strategies for empowering participants to redress this imbalance. By choosing to undertake a process of participatory, collaborative research I entered a process of negotiation with a number of Guatemalan women that revealed and challenged unexamined assumptions of power and control implicit in my research strategies. The negotiated relationship of trust, based in earlier conversation and shared solidarity in a broader political process, provided a context for re-examining some of my research strategies and clarifying the ways in which they functioned to maintain rather than reduce the power imbalance between participant and investigator.

Rather than negate other considerations or analyses of the research process this analysis contributes to a developing understanding of collaborative research by documenting other dimensions underlying the power relations in the research process. In a process where there were a relatively high number of shared interests between researchers and participants the examples discussed here provide evidence of competing interests between these parties and indicate how some of them are being confronted. The decision to engage in collaborative research does not *de facto* resolve competing interests. Nor does it minimize the importance of developing strategies for ensuring, for example, the anonymity of our informants, concerns that are even more critical in research with members of oppressed groups than in university based work with college sophomores. Rather it affirms a commitment on the part of both researcher and participant to engage the research process as subjects, as constructors of our own reality. The commitment to collaborative research and the ongoing negotiation of the trusting relationship required by all collaboration provides a context or framework for the work, and a baseline for understanding when one or another fails to treat the other as subject.

As suggested in this discussion I both underestimated the power of the participants at some points in our process and underestimated the power of the research strategies I was using (e.g., informed consent). Collaboration and trust do not negate power differentials; rather they create a bond between two active subjects who must then negotiate the power differential between them as they encounter it. This chapter describes several examples of these negotiations.

Recognition of the dynamics of power and control implicit in our research tools and of the differing forms of power and control the participants bring to the research situation suggest the importance that the research process itself plays in constructing the data that is being gathered. Although further elaboration of this point is beyond the scope of this chapter it is evident in the stories that are being recorded and more obviously in the group conversations and reflections on the interviews that have been recorded that new meanings are constructed in and through this engaged collaboration. What is recorded are the stories of a person or of groups of persons that are constrained or facilitated by the negotiated relationships between specific North American and Guatemalan compañeras.

The understanding of Guatemalan Indian women's experiences that emerges from this project is and will always be provisional. It draws its energy and forcefulness from the collaboration of a small number of Guatemalan Indian women who are refugees in Mexico and an even smaller number of North American researchers who are committed to continuing involvement in solidarity with the people of Guatemala. The perspectives that emerge are particularly rich because they benefit from a self-consciously collaborative effort to understand the self-understanding of Guatemalan Indian women and their continuing participation in the struggles of their people. The text that emerges is a document built from the interactive process of reflection, of sharing, and of criticism. It documents one phase of a developing solidarity among women from different cultural, racial, class and national backgrounds who have engaged the common question of understanding Guatemalan women's experiences. It tells the stories of some Indian women and, by speaking to a community of psychologists and researchers, contributes to a broader collective process of breaking the silence surrounding Guatemala.

My personal decision to draw more fully on my professional expertise in my work with Guatemalans also reflects a turning point in my development as a psychologist. The work described here reflects collaborative research that is grounded in and derives from social and political commitment of solidarity with the people of Guatemala [31]. Although that commitment has been part of my work for a number of years it has been through participation in this research that I have been able to find more fully my voice as a North American feminist psychologist and the meaning of this experience is being mutually constructed in this collaboration.

APPENDIX A
GUIDELINE QUESTIONS FOR INTERVIEWS WITH GUATEMALAN INDIAN WOMEN
(English Version)

1. Experiences in family and community: Can you tell us about your experiences in childhood? in adolescence? in adulthood?
   (a) in your family, and
   (b) in your community.
2. What kinds of political involvements/experiences have you had? What have those experiences meant to you?
3. Did you participate in other groups or organizations in your community? What were those experiences like?
4. How has your participation changed you?
5. What people are most important in your life, what people have made the most differences in your life?
6. What has it meant to you to be an Indian?
7. What has it meant to you to be a woman?
8. Was religion or the church important in your life? Can you tell us about your experiences in the church or with religion?
9. Tell us about the situation before you came to Mexico.
10. Tell us about what you have done in the time you have been in Mexico.
11. What do you feel that you have accomplished in your life?
12. What do you want for your children?
13. Background information that did not come out in the conversation, including education (formal and informal; parents, self and children); size of family of origin and of current family; occupation (of self, spouse, parents).
14. Is there anything else you would like to tell us about; are there any questions you would like to ask of us; what has this experience been like for you?

APPENDIX A
(Spanish Version)

1. Experiencias en la familia y la communidad: Cuentos de tu niñez, juventud y ahora como adulta en relación a tu familia y tu comunidad.
2. ¿Qué tipo de participación o experiencia política hastenido tú? ¿Qué has ha significado en tu vida?
3. ¿Participabasen otros grupos u organizaciones en tu comunidad? ¿Cómo eran esas experiencias?
4. ¿Cómo te cambió tu participación?
5. ¿Quién(es) ha(n) sido las personas que más te han influenciado en to vida?

6. ¿Qué te ha significado ser indígena?
7. ¿Qué te ha significado ser mujer?
8. ¿Han tenido importancia en tu vida la religión o la iglesia?
9. Cuéntanos sobre tu situación immediatamente antes de venir a México.
10. Cuéntanos sobre lo que tú has hecho desde la llegada a México (en tu familia, a qué te dedicas. . .)
11. Hasta ahora, ¿qué has logrado en tu vida?
12. ¿Qué quieres para tus hijos?
13. Información generale: educación (formal y no formal) propia, de los padres e hijos; tamaño de su familia, de niñez y actual; a qué se dedica, en Guatemala, en Mexico—su esposo, los padres. ¿Había viajado fuera de su comunidad antes de venir a Mexico?
14. Al fin: ¿Tienes otras cosas que quieres contar? ¿Otras experiencias? ¿Otras preguntas? ¿Qué te pareció esta experiencia de hablar de tu vida?

APPENDIX B
INFORMED CONSENT AGREEMENT
(English Version)

I agree to participate voluntarily in this study of Guatemalan women's experiences in family and community. My participation involves an oral history interview in which I will discuss my experiences in my family and community in Guatemala and in Mexico. I understand that the interview will take between 3 and 6 hours.

The material to be gathered will be recorded and will be transcribed. I will have the right to edit and correct the transcript of the interview during a period of 3 months after it is returned to me. The material will be kept strictly confidential until I have edited the transcript.

FORM A: After this time the tapes and transcripts will be available for use by students, scholars and others. The researcher may publish this material for the purposes of the project described here and may authorize publication of the transcripts or quotations from the transcripts in appropriate cases. (Unrestricted use.)

FORM B: After this time the tapes and transcripts will be available for use by students, scholars and others. The researcher will neither publish this material herself nor authorize publication of the transcripts or quotations from the transcripts during the interviewee's lifetime except with my written permission. (Restricted publication.)

FORM C: The tapes and transcripts will only be available for use by students, scholars and others for a period of years (specified by the interviewee) to those who obtain my written permission. The researcher will neither publish this material herself nor authorize publication of the transcripts or quotations from the transcripts during the interviewee's lifetime except with my written permission. (Restricted as to use and publication.)

I understand that this project is being undertaken by trained personnel for a serious scientific purpose and that careful attention to my general welfare will be provided throughout. Any questions I have about the project will be answered by the interviewer to the best of her ability. I understand that I am free not to answer any questions at any time.

I have read the above agreement. I understand what is being asked of me and am willing to participate in this project and to have the materials used in the ways described above.

____
Interviewee's Signature

____
Interviewer's Signature

____
Date

APPENDIX B
(Spanish Version)

Voluntariamente doy mi acuerdó de participar en este estudio de las experiencias familiares y de sus comunidades vividas por mujeres guatemaltecas. Mi participación implica una entrevista de historia oral en la cual hablaré de mis experiencias en la familia y la comunidad, tanto en Guatemala como en Mexico. Entiendo que la entrevista llevará de 3 a 6 horas.

Las entrevistas serán grabadas y transcritas. Reservo el derecho de revisar, editar y corregir la transcripcion de la entrevista durante un período de 3 meses después de que me la entreguen. Los contenidos no se publicarán hasta que yo los revise.

Marque una de las siguientes opciones:

Después de la revisión, los cassettes y sus transcripciones estarán disponibles para el uso de académicos, estudiantes y otros. La investigadora puede publicar los contenidos para los fines del proyecto aquí descritos y puede autorizar la publicación de dichas transcripciones o citas de las mismas en casos apropriados. (Uso ilimitado).

Después de la revisión, los cassettes y sus transcripciones estarán desponibles para el uso de académicas, estudinates y otros. La investigadora ni publicará las transcripciones o citas de las mismas, ni autorizará su publicación durante la vida de la entrevistada sin pedir su permiso por escrito. (Publicación restringida).

Los cassettes y las transcripciones estarán disponibles únicamente para el usos de académicos, estudiantes y otros a los que concedo mi permiso por escrito, durante un período de tiempo que yo defino. La investigadora ni publicará, ni autorizará su publicacion por otros, de los contenidos de las entrevistas durante la vida de la entrevistada, a menos que le dé mi permiso por escrito. (Uso y publicacion restringidos.)

Entiendo que este proyecto se está llevando a cabo por personas capacitadas con fines científicos y que pondrán atención a la cuestión de mi seguridad.

Cualquier pregunta que yo peuda tener será respondida por la entrevistadora. Entiendo que no tengo que contestar todas las preguntas que me hagan y que la decisión de no responder no implicará ninguna consecuencia negativa para mí.

Yo he leido este acuerdo; entiendo los puntos y lo que se me estan pidiendo. Estoy dispuesta a participar en este proyecto y a que los contenidos pueden usarse de la manera marcada arriba.

____

Firma entrevistada

____

Firma entrevistadora

____

Fecha

REFERENCES

1. C. Kruger and K. Enge, *Security and Development in the Guatemalan Highlands*, Washington Office on Latin America, Washington, D.C., 1985.
2. Amnesty International Publication, *Guatemala: The Human Rights Record*, London, United Kingdom, 1987.
3. M. B. Lykes, *Autonomous Individualism versus Social Individuality: Towards an Alternative Understanding of the Self*, University Microfilms International, #8416004, Ann Arbor, Michigan, 1984.
4. ——, Gender and Individualistic versus Collectivist Bases for Notions about the Self, *Journal of Personality*, *53*, pp. 356-383, 1985.
5. R. Menchu, *I, Rigoberta Menchu: An Indian Woman in Guatemala*, with E. Burgos-Debray (ed. and intro.), translated by A. Wright, Verso Editions, London, 1984.
6. L. Frank and P. Wheaton, *Indian Guatemala; Path to Liberation: The Role of Christians in the Indian Process*, EPICA Task Force, Washington, D.C., 1984.
7. America's Watch and British Parliamentary Human Rights Group, *Human Rights in Guatemala: During President Cerenzo's First Year*, New York, 1987.
8. R. Falla, Vision de Pueblo Indígena del Genocidio que Sufre, (Sequnda Parte), Tribunal Permanente de los Pueblos. Excerpted in English in S. Jonas, E. McCaughan, and E. S. Martinez (eds. and trans.), *Guatemala: Tyranny on Trial*, Synthesis Publications, San Francisco, 1984.
9. S. Jonas, E. McCaughan, and E. S. Martinez (eds. and trans.), *Guatemala: Tyranny on Trial: Testimony of the Permanent People's Tribunal*, Synthesis Publications, San Francisco, 1984.
10. W. J. McGuire, The Yin and Yang of Progress in Social Psychology, *Journal of Personality and Social Psychology*, *26*, pp. 446-456, 1973.
11. K. Gergen, Experimentation in Social Psychology: A Reappraisal, *European Journal of Social Psychology*, *36*, pp. 1344-1360, 1978.

12. K. Gergen, The Positivist Image in Social Psychological Theory, in *Psychology in Social Context*, A. R. Buss (ed.), Irvington, New York, 1979.
13. E. E. Sampson, Scientific Paradigms and Social Values: Wanted–A Scientific Revolution, *Journal of Personality and Social Psychology, 36*, pp. 1332-1343, 1978.
14. L. Finison, *Social Action in Historical Perspective*, discussion-workshop at the meeting of the New England Social Psychological Association, Boston, April, 1980.
15. K. Gergen, Social Psychology as History, *Journal of Personality and Social Psychology*, *26*, pp. 309-320, 1973.
16. A. R. Buss, The Emerging Field of the Sociology of Psychological Knowledge, *American Psychologist*, *30*, pp. 988-1002, 1975.
17. E. G. Mishler, Meaning in Context: Is There Any Other Kind? *Harvard Educational Review*, *49*, pp. 1-19, 1979.
18. E. G. Mishler, L. R. Amarasingham, S. T. Hauser, R. Liem, S. D. Osherson, and N. E. Waxler, *Social Contexts of Health, Illness, and Patient Care*, Cambridge University Press, Cambridge, 1981.
19. D. O. Sears, College Sophomores in the Laboratory: Influences of a Narrow Data Base on Social Psychology's View of Human Nature, *Journal of Personality and Social Psychology*, *51*, pp. 515-530, 1986.
20. M. B. Lykes and A. J. Stewart, Evaluating the Feminist Challenge to Research in Personality and Social Psychology: 1963–1983, *Psychology of Women Quarterly*, *10*, pp. 393-411, 1986.
21. F. D. Miller and B. Zeitz, A Woman's Place is in the Footnotes, *Personality and Social Psychology Bulletin*, *4*, pp. 511-514, 1978.
22. D. Spender, The Gatekeepers: A Feminist Critique of Academic Publishing, in *Doing Feminist Research*, H. Roberts (ed.), Routledge and Kegan Paul, Boston, 1981.
23. E. G. Mishler, The Analysis of Interview Narratives, *Narratology and Psychology*, Praeger Publishers, New York, 1985.
24. M. A. Paget, Experience and Knowledge, *Human Studies*, *6*, pp. 67-90, 1983.
25. L. L. Langness and G. Frank, *Lives: An Anthropological Approach to Biography*, Chandler and Sharp, Novato, California, 1986.
26. M. Frish, Oral History and HARD TIMES: A Review Essay, *Oral History Review*, pp. 70-80, 1979.
27. D. Bertaux (ed.), *Biography and Society: The Life History Approach in the Social Sciences*, Sage, Beverly Hills, 1981.
28. S. Reinharz, *On Becoming a Social Scientist: From Survey Research and Participant Observation to Experiential Analysis*, Transaction Books, New Brunswick, New Jersey, 1984.
29. L. Stanley and S. Wise, *Breaking Out: Feminist Consciousness and Feminist Research*, Routledge and Kegan Paul, Boston, 1983.
30. A. Oakley, Interviewing Women: A Contradiction in Terms, in *Doing Feminist Research*, H. Roberts (ed.), Routledge and Kegan Paul, Boston, 1981.
31. B. DuBois, Passionate Scholarship: Notes on Values, Knowing and Method in Feminist Social Science, in *Theories of Women's Studies*, G. Bowles and R. D. Klein (eds.), Routledge and Kegan Paul, Boston, 1983.

CHAPTER 13

Coping with Rape: Critical Perspectives on Consciousness

MICHELLE FINE

> Prosecute? No, I just want to get home. While I'm pickin' some guy out of some line, who knows who's messin' around with my momma and my baby.
>
> Altamese Thomas,
> 24-year-old rape survivor
> October 1981, Hospital Emergency Room

At 2:00 a.m. one October morning, Altamese Thomas was led out of a police car, entered the hospital in pain, smelling of alcohol. Altamese had been drinking with some women friends in a poor, high crime, largely Black neighborhood in Philadelphia. She found herself in an alley, intoxicated, with pants down. She reports being gang-raped. The story unfolds, from intake nurse, the police and from Altamese herself.

I was awakened, in the small office for volunteer rape counselors, when the emergency room nurse telephoned me: "A Code-R just arrived." "Code-R" is the euphemism used to describe a woman who has been raped. I spent the remainder of the evening and some of the morning with Altamese. A twenty-four-year-old Black mother of three, two of her children have been placed by the state in foster care. From 2:00 a.m. until 7:00 a.m. we held hands as she smarted through two painful injections to ward off infection; traveled through the hospital in search of X-rays for a leg that felt (but wasn't) broken; waited for the Sex Offender Officers to arrive; watched Altamese refuse to speak with them; and returned to the X-ray room for a repeat performance–and we talked.

I introduced myself and explained my role. Interested primarily and impatiently in washing "the dirt off" and receiving necessary medical care, Altamese was unambivalent about her priorities. She did not want to prosecute, nor talk with social workers or counselors. She couldn't call upon her social supports. She just wanted to get home. For five hours, we talked. Our conversation systematically disrupted my belief that I understood anything much about the psychology of taking control in the face of injustice. Through my dialogue with Altamese, this chapter provides a critical analysis of the class, race and gender biases woven into the social psychological literature on coping with injustice.

THE PSYCHOLOGY OF TAKING CONTROL

When confronting life crises, injustices or tragedies, psychologists argue, people fare best by assuming control over their circumstances. Accepting responsibility for one's problems and/or solutions correlates with psychological and physical well being [1], across populations as diverse as rape survivors [2, 3], disabled adults [4], the institutionalized elderly [5, 6], unemployed men and women [7], school children with academic problems [8], even high school drop outs [9]. This article examines the assumptions which underlie present formulations of Taking-Control-Yields-Coping. Weaving relevant theory and research with excerpts from the dialogue between this rape survivor and the author, it will be argued that the prevailing coping-through-control ideologies are often limited by class, race and gender biases. Further, these models are disproportionately effective for only a small and privileged sector of society.

Psychologists have demonstrated that individuals cope most effectively with unjust or difficult circumstances by controlling their environments [10, 11]. This may involve attributing behavioral blame for the onset of bad events [12], or personal responsibility for initiating change [1]. Taking control may require participating in social programs and "getting help" [13, 14], and relying upon one's social supports [15-17].

The current Taking-Control arguments often assume that people *can* control the forces which victimize them, *should* utilize available social programs, and *will* benefit if they rely on social supports. What is not explicit is that these prescribed means of coping are likely to be ineffectual for most people [18, 19]. Persons of relatively low ascribed social power–by virtue of social class position, ethnicity, race, gender, disability or sexual preference–cannot control those forces which limit their opportunities [20]. But while it has been proposed that many then learn to be helpless [21], I maintain instead that they do assert control in ways ignored by psychologists. For many, taking control involves ignoring advice to solve one's problems individually and recognizing instead the need for collective, structural change [22]. Taking control may mean rejecting available social programs as inappropriate to one's needs [8, 23], or recognizing that one's social supports are too vulnerable to be relied upon [24]. Such acts of taking control have long been misclassified by psychologists as acts of relinquishing control.

ACCESS TO MEANS OF TAKING CONTROL: A FUNCTION OF SOCIAL POWER

The control-yields-well-being proposition is empirically robust and admittedly compelling. As a psychologist interested in the social psychology of injustice, I study and support efforts which encourage people to take control of their lives. A review of this literature reveals, however, *individualistic* coping strategies, effective for persons of relatively high social power, promoted *as if* they were optimal and universal ways to cope. By establishing a hierarchy of appropriate ways to take control, this literature often 1) denies the complex circumstances many people confront, 2) *de facto* delegitimates those strategies for taking control employed by persons of relatively low social power, 3) encourages psychological and individualistic responses to injustice, which often reinforce existing power inequities [25], and 4) justifies prevailing social structures.

Advancing the position that people need to exert individual control over their lives presumes that all people are able to do so, that all people want to do so, and that to improve their life circumstances, people need to change themselves rather than social structures. Three fundamental problems with this formulation emerge.

First, if asserting individual control promotes psychological health it may be because individualism is socially reinforced in our society [26]. Positive reinforcement follows individualistic acts (e.g., "Pulling oneself up by the boot-straps") [22, 27] with social disapproval displayed for collective acts (e.g., in school these collective acts may be considered cheating; at work trouble making). The health that is associated with acts of individualistic control may therefore derive from social and ideological supports in our culture, not because individual control is inherently healthy.

Given that psychological well being stems in part from social rewards for individualism and internality, a second problem emerges with this model of coping. If unfair treatment occurs and control of that treatment is unlikely, a presumption of internality may be delusional! Externality may benefit persons whose life conditions are indeed beyond their control [28]. To nurture the much-encouraged illusion of internality in many circumstances would be unreasonable. In situations of low probability of success for redressing an injustice, attempts to redress injustice personally can breed helplessness.

It may be true that when persons of relatively high social power assert a single act of "taking control" (e.g., voice a grievance or file a complaint) they are likely to succeed. In contrast, the undocumented worker who is sexually harassed by her factory foreman might be foolish to file a grievance. "Bearing it" does not mean she has given up, but rather that she determined a solution by which she can be in control and employed. Establishing strategies to survive, when change is unlikely, needs to be recognized as acts of control.

A third problem with current control formulations is that they often decontextualize coping [29]. The presumption that psychologists can extract optimal ways to assume control over failure or adversity *across situations* reduces the complexities of the situations *ad absurdum* [18].

The strategies popular in the literature and undoubtedly effective in many cases, may benefit persons of relatively high social power (e.g., by attributing successes to stable internal factors and failures to unstable factors; taking responsibility for solutions; relying on social supports, or utilizing available social programs). As psychologists, however, we lack an understanding of how people who are systematically discriminated against and restricted to low power positions take control. We fail to understand how they determine what is controllable and what is not [30]. We dismiss control strategies that look like "giving up" but are in fact ways to survive. Even more serious, we avoid the study of those ways of taking control which systematically disrupt traditional power relations [31, 32]. Our literature legitimates existing power asymmetries.

There are two major consequences to these theoretical problems. First, control efforts enacted by low power persons are often misdiagnosed as giving up. Such attempts to take control tend to be misread as counter productive ("Why don't they do something about their work conditions if they are dissatisfied, rather than slowing down on productivity?"); distorted as self-effacing ("Even she blames herself for the rape."); diagnosed as masochistic ("She must enjoy the abuse, why else would she stay?"); classified as learned helplessness ("She always says–'I can't do anything about it.'"); or denigrated as psychological resistance ("I tried to offer help but he won't listen!") by laypersons and psychologists alike. These behaviors may indeed function as strategies of asserting control; if not resistance.

Second, the existing body of research on allegedly healthy ways of coping reproduces existing power inequities by prescribing *as optimal* those ways of coping which are effective for high power persons [33]. Social programs designed for low power persons are often organized toward coping strategies (such as individualism and reliance on social institutions), effective for high power persons. The models are deceptive for persons of low social power who depend on higher power persons, economically, socially, and/or psychologically, and have other low power persons (e.g., kin) highly dependent upon them. This precarious web of interdependencies creates conditions in which social institutions are likely to be unresponsive and individualism to be inappropriate. Many low power persons will not improve their own circumstances at expense to others, and most are unlikely to have access to standard tools of control (e.g., grievance procedures, money, or leverage with Congressional representatives). If they do, these tools are unlikely to promote the kinds of changes they need [34]. Consequently, when low power persons decide *not* to use the resources or programs offered them (e.g., "Because my mother is sick, and I have to take care of my children.") their disadvantaged circumstances may come to be viewed as deserved. The perception that they are *unwilling* to act on their own behalf provides evidence of helplessness, if not laziness. Their need to rely on high power persons is then confirmed. The power asymmetries built into these relationships are systematically justified [35].

Below, through a dialogue between the author and a woman who survived a rape, a dialogue situated in a hospital emergency room the evening of the rape, we analyze how persons of relatively low social power do assert control, and how easily a psychologist can misread these as efforts to give up.

* * *

Altamese Thomas	*Michelle Fine*
	3:00 AM Altamese, the police will be here to speak with you. Are you interested in prosecuting? Do you want to take these guys to court?
No, I don't want to do nothin' but get over this . . . When I'm pickin' the guy out of some line, who knows who's messin' around with my momma, or my baby. Anyway nobody would believe me. [Can I wash now?]	
	3:30 AM [Once the exam is over you can wash and brush your teeth. First we need to wait for the doctor for your exam.] Wouldn't your friends testify as witnesses?
Where I live, nobody's gonna testify. Not to the police. Anyway, I'm a Baptist and I know God is punishing him right now. He done bad enough and he's suffering.	
	4:00 AM Maybe if we talked about the rape you would feel better.
You know, I don't remember things. When I was little lots of bad things happened to me, and I forget them. My memory's bad, I don't like to remember bad stuff. I just forget. When I was a young child, my momma told me about rape and robberies. I told her she was wrong. Those things happen in the movies, not here. When I saw such things on the streets I thought they was	

Altamese Thomas	*Michelle Fine*
making a movie. Then one day a lady started bleeding, and I knew it was no movie.	
	4:30 AM . . . Do you think maybe you would like to talk with a counselor, in a few days, about some of your feelings?
I've been to one of them. It just made it worse. I just kept thinking about my problems too much. You feel better when you're talking, but then you got to go back home and they're still there. No good just talking when things ain't no better.	
	Is there anyone you can talk to about this?
Not really. I can't tell my mother, not my brothers either. They would go out and kill the guys. My mother's boyfriend too. I don't want them going to jail 'cause of me.	
	You said you sometimes meet with a social worker. Can you talk with your social worker?
She's the one who took away my kids. If they take my baby, I would kill myself. I ain't gonna get myself in trouble, all I got is my baby and she already thinks I'm a bad mother. But I love my babies and I try hard to take care of them. [I just don't understand why men have to rape. Why do they have to take when they could just ask?]	
	How about one of your teachers at ____________ college? Can you talk to them?
Those teachers think I'm stupid. Sometimes they call on me and I don't answer. When you got problems, your mind is on the moon. He calls on you and you don't know what he's saying.	

Altamese Thomas	*Michelle Fine*
They treat you like a dog and you act like a dog.	
	5:30 AM Soon you will get to leave here and go home, where you'll feel safe.
It ain't safe there. I live in the projects with my baby. I can't go back there now. It feels safer here . . . I hurt so much.	
	7:00 AM Can I call you next week just to see how you're doing?
Sure. . . .	

ASSERTING RELATIONAL CONTROL

At first glance, one might say that Altamese abdicated control: She "gave up." Unwilling to prosecute, uninterested in utilizing her social supports, she relied on God for justice. Resistant to mental health, social service, educational and criminal justice assistance, she rejected available options. Her coping mechanisms might be said to include denial, repression, and paranoia. She doesn't trust her friends to testify, her family to listen, her social worker to be supportive, her teachers to understand or the police to assist. She has refused available mechanisms of control.

And yet through our dialogue it was obvious that each of her decisions embodies a significant assertion of control. Likely to be misclassified as helpless or paranoid, she asserted strategies for taking control which insure both her well-being and that of her kin. Altamese organized coping around relational concerns [24]. Worried about her mother, child and siblings, she rejected options offered to help her cope. She viewed my trust in the justice system as somewhat absurd; my commitment to talking about the rape to friends, social workers, teachers or family somewhat impulsive; my expectations of witnessess coming forth almost naive, and even my role as volunteer counselor somewhat unusual.

* * *

Altamese	*Michelle*
So, you're a nurse?	7:00 AM Actually I volunteer here, talking with women who have been raped.
You mean you do this for fun?	
	I do it because I think it's important. Do you?
. . . I don't know how you can do it all the time.	

Most people are denied the means to assume control over fundamentally changing their lives. Although prevailing ideology argues otherwise [36],

Altamese and the millions of women who are unemployed, poor, minority and/or disabled and responsible for a network of kin, have limited options [37]. Although pursuing college, she may perhaps qualify for a low pay job some day. Given unemployment statistics, her personal style, life circumstances and lack of qualifications, her chances are slim.

The standard means of taking control promoted by counselors, policy makers and researchers, tend to be individualistic and most effective for a privileged slice of society. Trusting social institutions, maximizing interpersonal supports, and engaging in self disclosure are strategies most appropriate for middle class and affluent individuals whose interests are served by those institutions, whose social supports can multiply available resources and contacts and for whom self-disclosure may in fact lead not only to personal change, but to structural change [28, 36].

Unable to trust existing institutions, for Altamese self-disclosure would have exposed wounds unlikely to be healed. Responsible for a network of kin, Altamese could not rely on but had to protect her social supports. Resisting social institutions, withholding information and preserving emotional invulnerability emerged as her strategies for maintaining control [27]. Expecting God to prosecute, loss of memory to insure coping and fantasy to anesthetize reality, Altamese is by no means helpless.

While her social and economic circumstances are such that Altamese cannot change the basic oppressive structures which affect her, the social and psychological strategies she employs are mechanisms of control–protection for self and others [38]. An abstract pursuit of justice was not possible given her social context, commitments and concerns. She organized the realities of her life so as to manage effectively the multiple forces which *are* out to get her and her kin. Like Gilligan's concept of women's relational morality, Altamese exhibited what may be considered relational coping.

With little attention paid to relational concerns and a systematic neglect of power relations, psychologists have prescribed ways to cope as if a consensus about their utility had been established; as if there were no alternatives; as if universals could be applied across contexts, and as if these strategies were uninfluenced by our position in social and economic hierarchies. As the creators of what Foucault calls power-knowledge [33] psychologists have an obligation to expose the dialectics of psychological control and structural control, as experienced by women and men across lines of social class, ethnicity and race, levels of physical ability and disability and sexual preferences. In the absence of such knowledge psychologists impose, as healthy and universal, what may be narrow and elitist strategies for taking control.

One particular strategy, examined below, involves the prescription that persons treated unjustly or confronted by tragedy utilize available social programs. If Altamese is any indication such social programs are likely to be severely underutilized so long as they are designed top-down *for* (and not by) the persons supposedly served.

COPING WITH OPTIONS

One way to take control over adversity, supported by much psychological research (including my own), is to do something to improve one's own life circumstances; to use available options. To battered women, it may be suggested that they leave their abusive homes; to the unemployed, that they enroll for skills retraining; to the underpaid, that they learn to be assertive; to rape victims, that they "ventilate" and prosecute. Social programs have proliferated to offer individuals these services. These programs are generally designed by relatively high power individuals for persons who have what are considered personal problems. Offered as *opportunities* to improve the quality of life experienced by low power persons, these programs generally aim to correct presumed deficits [35, 39, 40]. Some disabled persons have the *opportunity* to work in sheltered workshops, often earning less than minimum wages, trained for non-marketable skills [41]. Some battered women have the *opportunity* to be sheltered in facilities which exclude women with drug or alcohol addictions, are located in unsafe neighborhoods, and limit a maximum stay to two weeks, promising an alternative to violent homes [42]. Some Black high school dropouts have the *opportunity* to earn their Graduate Equivalency Diplomas, promising greater vocational mobility, despite the fact that Black adolescent unemployment figures range from 39 percent to 44 percent for high school graduates and dropouts, respectively [43].

Efforts to fix people and not change structures, many of these options reinforce the recipient's low power position [39]. It is therefore most interesting that when such persons dismiss these options as inappropriate, ineffective or as decoys for the "real issues," these persons are often derogated [9, 23]. Individuals who reject available options, such as disabled adults who picket the Jerry Lewis Telethon claiming it to be condescending and reinforcing of the worst stereotypes, are viewed as ungrateful, unappreciative and sometimes even deserving of their circumstances [35]. The same option that appears valuable to a high power person may be critiqued as a charade by low power persons.

To demonstrate: there exists substantial evidence that high power persons do see social options (e.g., an appeal, grievance procedure, opportunity to flee) as more potentially effective than low power persons do. Experimental and survey data document that in social contexts in which an option to injustice is available, victims are more likely than nonvictims to consider their circumstances unjust, but nonvictims are more likely to rate *the option as powerful to promote change* [44]. Victims see injustice; nonvictims see the potential for change. But, victims are *not* more likely than nonvictims to use an option to change their circumstances. Why would victims reject an opportunity to avenge injustice?

To investigate this question, victim and nonvictim responses to open-ended questions about injustice and appeals were reviewed [9]. Victims claim to be reluctant to appeal an injustice not because they do not recognize injustice, they do; not because they felt they deserved to be treated unfairly, they do not; not because they respect victimizers who commit injustice, they don't. Victims appear to be reluctant because they are in fact less likely to win an appeal, and usually have more to lose than nonvictims who would appeal. The appeal procedure in this study was designed as an *opportunity* for the victim to redress inequity, but actually offered her only a remote chance of success.

To appeal successfully, the victim or nonvictim had to convince at least one other member of a three person group that an inequity had occurred. If she appealed, a victim 1) would appear self serving, 2) could not be sure she would be supported in her appeal, 3) could, if she lost the appeal, get double confirmation that her treatment was justified, and 4) could indeed have much to lose by initiating an appeal.

In marked contrast, a nonvictim who appeals on behalf of the victim 1) would appear benevolent, 2) could be relatively sure of support from the victim, 3) could enjoy public praise for her benevolence, and 4) could gain psychologically and socially from the appeal. It is little wonder, then, that observers view options as more viable for victims than victims do themselves. It is perhaps in this role as observers that psychologists have encouraged victims' utilization of available programs and services. By not understanding how disempowering it may be to be offered an inappropriate option, while reminded that this-is-your-last-chance, even the most benevolent observer/helper can create secondary injury [45].

CONCLUSIONS

> At fifteen life had taught me undeniably that surrender, in its place, was as honorable as resistance, especially if one had no choice.
>
> Maya Angelou
> *I Know Why The Caged Bird Sings,*
> 1969, Bantam Books, p. 212

As social scientists generate master strategies for taking control and promote them as universally applicable, the paradox of "therapeutic hegemony" emerges. Those individuals with the least control over the causes of their problems, much less the means for structural resolution, are prescribed psychological models for individual efficacy. As long as individual victims (or survivors) act alone to improve their circumstances, oppressive economic and social arrangements will persist. The effects of such acts of psychological control may ultimately be indistinguishable from the effects of surrender. Even acts of resistance, if initiated individualistically, ultimately buttress power differentials. Altamese's unwillingness to use the justice system, her non-reliance on kin, and her trust that God will provide or punish, do nothing for the women that these rapist(s) will attack next. Nor do they stem the wave of violence against women. What these behaviors accomplish is that they give Altamese a control strategy by which she can survive, with her remaining child, her mother, and her brothers, in a community where she can get some support. Unfortunately these behaviors also allow psychologists to continue to weave the fantasy that Altamese needs to be educated about options available to her and taught to be assertive about her needs. Psychologists can remain ever convinced that if *only* Altamese would learn to use it, the system would work to her advantage. . . .

EPILOGUE

And so as psychologists we are faced with a conceptual dilemma. Should we expand the definition of "taking control" to incorporate the lived experiences of women and men across class, race, and ethnic lines? Or, do we dispense with the concept of "taking control" totally, rejected as too narrow to be salvaged? I would argue the former. Taking control is undoubtedly a significant psychological experience; knowing that one can effect change in one's environment makes a difference. How individuals accomplish this, however, does vary by economic and social circumstance, gender and perhaps personal style. The phenomenology of individuals like Altamese need be integrated into our conceptions of taking control in order for the concept to have meaning for those persons most likely to confront injustice, tragedy or other life crises. A feminist psychology needs to value relational coping and to contextualize, through the eyes of those women affected, the meaning of victimization and taking control. The continued assessment of "women's coping" as helplessness need be reframed.

AUTHOR'S NOTE

Encouraged by the editor of this book, I have included this note to describe methodological and ethical dilemmas faced in writing this chapter as a social psychologist. I also hope to persuade others, particularly clinicians interested in using this "method," to consider its inherent ethical dilemmas.

This manuscript, which reflects critical thinking about social psychological theory, was provoked by a discussion with a woman I have chosen to call Altamese. This conversation was between me, as a volunteer rape counselor (not as clinician–which I am not–nor as researcher) in an urban hospital and Altamese, an emergency room patient. The conversation took place because I work at the hospital in this capacity, not because I intended to do research on the topic of rape. The information reported does not, therefore, conform to the traditional standards of ethical practices of data collection.

The ethical dilemmas, as I see them, arise in a way not addressed by the 1983 Ethical principles (APA): Altamese was not "informed" because at the time there was no research to be informed of; she was not "debriefed" because our only conversation took place in the course of my offering her support, not through the use of a pre-defined research instrument. Because of these factors, I remain somewhat ambivalent about the presentation of this material.

The problem is, simply, what to do with information gathered in a context in which research was not being conducted, in which the assumption is one of privacy, from which a publishable article evolves two years later? Three issues need to be examined: anonymity, informed consent, and assumptions about privacy.

Anonymity concerns appear to be the easiest to satisfy in both the present work and any other which utilizes a similar methodology. In the present work, names, demographics and life circumstances have been changed radically so that anonymity is well guarded. The details of the rape and reactions to it have been omitted so that no one could identify this woman—perhaps not even she herself. When information provided in any private setting is subsequently introduced in a manuscript, revealing data should be deleted, changed and/or "checked back" (if possible) for use.

Informed consent is more complicated. In this case, there was no presumption of "doing research." There would have been no reason, therefore, to request such consent. And two years later, with neither telephone nor forwarding address available, it is impossible to ascertain consent today. Of course, as someone suggested, it is possible that Altamese did sign a statement upon entering the emergency room which "OKed" the research use of relevant information, but one cannot assume this to be *INFORMED CONSENT.*

In thinking about informed consent it must be clear that 1) if a researcher is explicitly interested in gathering clinical information for research purposes all clients need to complete informed consent forms non-coercively (so that they have the option to receive services even if they do not agree to be involved in research); and 2) even if informed consent is provided, clients have the right to delete certain quotes or information from a manuscript if they feel revealed or betrayed by that section of the manuscript.

The third issue is for me the most complicated—what to do when information is provided in a context presumed to be private and confidential. Do researchers have a right to use this information for research/theoretical ends? I want to say a blanket "no" but again my own work leaves me wanting a more qualified response. A central consideration, here, is the issue of risk. In the present case, I can see no risk. Clearly, if Altamese were prosecuting these rapists, the potential risk would be enormous and publication out of the question.

This legal aspect of risk acknowledged, however, we still need to consider how we would feel if information we provided confidentially showed up in a journal article. The more explicit we can be with clients about the potential research purposes and the more we can involve clients in the importance of writing about this material (e.g., to make "public" what are experienced as "private" and "personal" problems), the less damage we will do to the trust levels between ourselves and our clients/informants; the better we will understand how clients/informants view violations of confidentiality and breaches of contracts, and presumably the better the information we will gather (perhaps too optimistic).

This chapter is about an encounter between two women and incorporates my impressions of that encounter. I have elected to use the material, while trying to describe my ambivalent feelings about the encounter and about this chapter based on the encounter. In this note I have tried to reflect on the ethical dilemmas I have confronted and offer suggestions to individuals who may be interested in utilizing such a methodology systematically and intentionally:

1. Develop informed consent procedures so that all clients/potential informants are aware that information could be used for research purposes, providing services even if research consent is denied, and recognizing that introducing the topic of informed consent may systematically alter the nature of the relationship. The question needs to be asked: are there some counseling relationships in which counselors cannot simultaneously be collecting research-relevant information?
2. Beyond this safeguard, the potential risks to clients of using their information for research purposes need to be weighed, and discussed with clients.
3. Our responsibilities to people who provide us information need be respected. Researchers need to be particularly careful about abusing information provided when people assume the exchange to be private, confidential and safe.

ACKNOWLEDGMENTS

Many people deserve thanks for the production of this manuscript. David Surrey was helpful in reviewing, and listening about this material. His theoretical contributions and support are most appreciated. Dell Hymes provided invaluable outside analytic insight. Rhoda Unger and two anonymous reviewers have been supportive and conceptually most helpful. Theresa Singleton typed through numerous versions, until we got it "right." Her patience and good will are appreciated. Altamese Thomas, a pseudonym, and the millions of women who have been raped, have taught me a lot about being a psychologist and being a woman.

REFERENCES

1. P. Brickman, V. Rabinowitz, J. Karuza, D. Coates, E. Cohn, and L. Kidder, Models of Helping and Coping, *American Psychologist, 37,* pp. 368-384, 1982.
2. A. Burgess and L. Holstrom, Coping Behavior of the Rape Victim, *American Journal of Psychiatry*, *133*, pp. 413-418, 1976.
3. R. Janoff-Bulman, Characterological versus Behavioral Self Blame: Inquiries into Depression and Rape, *Journal of Personality and Social Psychology*, *37*, pp. 1798-1809, 1979.
4. R. Janoff-Bulman and C. Wortman, Attributions of Blame and Coping in the 'Real World': Severe Accident Victims React to Their Lot, *Journal of Personality and Social Psychology*, *35*, pp. 351-363, 1977.

5. D. Schorr and J. Rodin, The Role of Perceived Control in Practitioner-Patient Relationships, in *Basic Processes in Helping Relationships*, T. Wills (ed.), Academic Press, New York, 1982.
6. R. Schutz, Effects of Control and Predictability on the Physical and Psychological Well Being of the Institutionalized Aged, *Journal of Personality and Social Psychology*, *33*, pp. 563-573, 1976.
7. S. Cobb and S. Kasl, *Termination: The Consequences of Job Loss* (Publication #LR 77-224), Department of Health, Education and Welfare, Washington, D.C., 1977.
8. C. Dweck and B. Licht, Learned Helplessness and Intellectual Achievement, in *Human Helplessness*, J. Garber and M. Seligman (eds.), Academic Press, New York, 1980.
9. M. Fine, The Social Context and a Sense of Injustice: The Option to Challenge, *Representative Research in Social Psychology*, *13*:1, pp. 15-33, 1983(a).
10. R. Janoff-Bulman and G. Marshall, Mortality, Well Being and Control: A Study of a Population of Institutionalized Aged, *Personality and Social Psychology Bulletin*, *8*:4, pp. 691-698, 1982.
11. H. Lefcourt, Personality and Locus of Control, in *Human Helplessness*, J. Garber and M. Seligman (eds.), Academic Press, New York, 1980.
12. C. Peterson, S. Schwartz and M. Seligman, Self Blame and Depressive Symptoms, *Journal of Personality and Social Psychology*, *41*, pp. 253-259, 1981.
13. B. DePaulo, Social Psychological Processes in Informal Help Seeking, in *Basic Processes in Helping Relationships*, T. Wills (ed.), Academic Press, New York, 1980.
14. M. Fine, When Nonvictims Derogate: Powerlessness in the Helping Professions, *Personality and Social Psychology Bulletin*, *8*:4, 637-643, 1982.
15. T. Antonucci and C. Depner, Social Support and Information Helping Relationships, in *Basic Processes in Helping Relationships*, T. Wills (ed.), Academic Press, New York, 1982.
16. C. Solano, P. Batten and E. Parish, Loneliness and Patterns of Self-Disclosure, *Journal of Personality and Social Psychology*, *43*:3, pp. 524-531, 1982.
17. C. Swenson, Using Natural Helping Networks to Promote Competence, in *Promoting Competence in Clients*, A. N. Maluccio (ed.), Free Press, New York, 1981.
18. R. Silver and C. Wortman, Coping with Undesirable Life Events, in *Human Helplessness*, J. Garber and M. Seligman (eds.), Academic Press, New York, 1980.
19. R. Unger, Controlling Out the Obvious: Power, Status and Social Psychology, paper presented at American Psychological Association, Washington, D.C., 1982.
20. J. B. Miller, *Toward a New Psychology of Women,* Beacon Press, Boston, 1976.
21. M. Seligman, *Helplessness: On Depression, Development and Death*, W. H. Freeman, San Francisco, 1975.
22. W. Ryan, *Equality*, Pantheon Books, New York, 1981.
23. M. Fine, Perspectives on Inequity: Voices from Urban Schools, in *Applied Social Psychology Annual,* L. Brickman (ed.), *4,* Sage, Beverly Hills, 1983(b).

24. C. Gilligan, *In a Different Voice*, Harvard University Press, Cambridge, 1982.
25. E. Sampson, Cognitive Psychology as Ideology, *American Psychologist, 36*:7, pp. 730-743, 1981.
26. E. Cagan, Individualism, Collectivism and Radical Educational Reform, *Harvard Educational Review*, *48*, pp. 227-266, 1978.
27. J. Anyon, Intersections of Gender and Class: Accommodation and Resistance by Working Class and Affluent Females in Contradictory Sex-Role Ideologies, in *Gender, Class and Education*, L. Barton and S. Walker (eds.), Fatiner Press, England, 1982.
28. L. Furby, Individualist Bias in Studies of Locus of Control, in *Psychology in Social Context*, A. Buss (ed.), Irvington Publishers, New York, pp. 169-190, 1979.
29. A. Buss (ed.), *Psychology in Social Context*, Irvington Publishers, New York, 1979.
30. C. Wortman and J. Brehm, Responses to Uncontrollable Outcomes: An Integration of Reactance Theory and the Learned Helplessness Model, in *Advances in Experimental Social Psychology*, Vol. 8, L. Berkowitz (ed.), Academic Press, New York, 1975.
31. R. Sennett, *Authority*, Vantage Books, New York, 1980.
32. H. Giroux, *Theory and Resistance: A Pedagogy for Opposition*, J. F. Bergin and J. Garvey Publishers, South Hadley, Massachusetts, 1982.
33. M. Foucault, Intellectuals and Power, *TELOS*, *16*, pp. 103-109, 1972.
34. P. Gurin, G. Gurin, R. Lao, and M. Beattie, Internal-External Control in the Motivational Dynamics of Negro Youth, *Journal of Social Issues*, *25*, pp. 29-53, 1969.
35. L. Kidder and M. Fine, The Justice of Rights versus Needs, paper presented at the meeting of the International Society for Political Psychology, Washington, D.C., 1982.
36. E. Apfelbaum, Relations of Domination and Movements for Liberation: An Analysis of Power Between Groups, in *The Social Psychology of Intergroup Relations*, W. Austin and S. Worchel (eds.), Brooks/Cole, Monterey, 1979.
37. B. Hooks, *Ain't I a Woman?*, South End Press, Boston, 1981.
38. E. Genovese, *Roll, Jordan, Roll: The World the Slaves Made*, Vintage, New York, 1972.
39. W. Gaylin, I. Glasser, S. Marcus, and D. Rothman, *Doing Good: The Limits of Benevolence*, Pantheon Books, New York, 1978.
40. P. Green, *The Pursuit of Inequality*, Pantheon Books, New York, 1981.
41. C. Vash, Women and Employment, L. Perlman and K. Arnseon, *Women and Rehabilitation of Disabled Persons*, Report of the Sixth Mary Switzer Memorial Seminar, National Rehabilitation Association, Washington, D.C., 1982.
42. S. Schechter, *Women and Male Violence*, South End Press, Boston, 1982.
43. A. Young, School and Work Among Youths During the 1970s, *Monthly Labor Review*, *9*, pp. 44-47.
44. M. Fine, Options to Injustice: Seeing Other Lights, *Representative Research in Social Psychology*, *10*, pp. 61-76, 1979.
45. M. Symonds, The 'Second Injury' to Victims, *Evaluation and Change*, Special Edition, pp. 36-38, 1980.

PART III

Innovative Strategies for Examining Social Constructs

In some ways this part of the book is the most traditional in terms of psychological methodology. However, all of these studies vary from the "norm" in some way. For example, all but one study examined only women and all but one selected subjects with a concern for situational or circumstantial context. Although nonrandom sampling may limit the generalizability of results in some ways, examination of particular groups of women may produce findings that enable us to understand more about how sex and gender operate in real life. The studies in this section were also concerned with multiple response measures. They attempted to avoid experimenter bias produced by the use of predetermined questions and the accompanying limitation of the individual's freedom to make unstructured responses.

Unger's study using the *Attitudes about Reality Scale* illustrates one strategy for avoiding methodological constraints. Thus, although the scale appears to be a traditional psychological instrument comprised of statements with which the individual can agree or disagree to a varying extent, many of the items in the scale are deliberately ambiguous. Responses may differ depending upon the beliefs about the way the world works that the person brings to the item. For example, an item such as "The facts of science change over time" will be responded to differently depending on whether one defines a fact as an "enduring truth" or a "probabilistic conjecture." Findings using this methodology suggest that ideological identification may be a more important predictor of personal epistemology than is a person's biological sex.

Sanders and her colleagues used multiple measures to investigate women's response to stories involving traditional life choices among married career women. They found that even in a religiously orthodox group of women, the responses to such decisions varied depending on whether they used rating scales or open-ended questions. Although these women appeared to concur with traditional decisions when objective measures were used, more subjective responses revealed that they were angry and/or unhappy with such decisions.

Frieze and her associates used a more elaborate subjective methodology—the generation of daily life scripts about women in various non-traditional and traditional roles. They found that women college students can put themselves much more easily into the role of housewife than that of the lawyer or businesswoman despite being more negative toward the former role. There has been little concern about the effect of familiarity upon the career choices of college women. Both studies raise important issues about the way we ask our questions and how they determine our answers. For example, which measure accurately reflects a woman's beliefs and which better predicts her behavior when she herself has to make family-career choices?

Schwartz asked her respondents for subjective information about their own lives. She found sex-related differences in earliest memories with men reporting more positive memories than do women. Her study went beyond the question of sex differences, however, by looking at people in different life circumstances. Thus, sex differences disappear when women and men in graduate school are compared. LaFrance presented the same questions to subjects at different points in their lives. She found that the explanations women give for job changes have little temporal consistency. Both these studies suggest that we reconstruct our memories about past events depending upon our present life circumstances.

Some of the questions raised by papers in this section include: Why are subjective methods considered less desirable by psychologists than are objective methods? What can we learn by examining populations that differ from "standard" ones (the white middle-class college student—female or male) in various known ways? What is the relationship between familiarity with information, our affect about this information, and our behavior? How can we find out whether people redesign reality throughout the course of their lives and what factors are related to their reconstructions?

FURTHER READINGS

Dion, K. L. and K. K. Dion. Romantic Love: Individual and Cultural Perspectives, in *Anatomy of Love*, R. J. Sternberg and M. L. Barnes (eds.), Yale University Press, New Haven, in press.

Mishler, E. G. Meaning in Context: Is There Any Other Kind? *Harvard Educational Review*, *49*, pp. 1-19, 1979.

Sherif, C. W. Bias in Psychology, in *The Prism of Sex*, J. Sherman and E. Beck (eds.), University of Wisconsin Press, Madison, 1979.

Stewart, A. J. Some Consequences of the Things Our Mothers Did and Didn't Tell Us: Social and Individual Change in Women's Lives, invited address, Eastern Psychological Association, Washington, D.C., April 12, 1987.

Wallston, B. S. What Are the Questions in Psychology of Women? A Feminist Approach to Research, *Psychology of Women Quarterly*, *5*, pp. 597-617, 1981.

CHAPTER 14

Explorations in Feminist Ideology: Surprising Consistencies and Unexamined Conflicts*

RHODA K. UNGER

There are probably as many definitions of feminism as there are feminists. However, little effort has been made to determine whether feminists agree on anything beyond the concept of political, economic, and social equality of the sexes. The only measuring instrument in general use, the Attitudes toward Women Scale developed by Spence and Helmreich is designed to measure attitudes only in the aforementioned areas [1]. Nevertheless, over a decade's experience with the conflicts engendered by even such an apparently simple legal statement as the Equal Rights Amendment suggests that the concept of the equality of the sexes masks more fundamental conflicts in ideology and values.

This chapter represents an attempt to determine whether feminists share a community of values distinct from nonfeminists and to categorize domains in which distinct value differences occur. I have argued elsewhere [2, 3] that personal ideology reflects an epistemological framework explaining how the world works. This epistemology is concerned not with the question of whether individual differences exist, but with how (biologically, socially, interactively, etc.) such differences may be explained. Personal epistemology is also concerned with the relationship between the individual's behavior and its outcome and with the relationship between personal and structural aspects of society.

In brief, I have argued that one can measure epistemological predisposition in terms of a person's place on a continuum ranging from belief that reality constructs the person to belief that the person constructs reality [3]. In order to

*An earlier version of this chapter was presented at the meeting of the American Psychological Association, Toronto, August, 1984.

analyze such predispositions I have constructed a forty item, 7-point Likert scale called the Attitudes about Reality Scale encompassing four conceptual domains: power as a personal versus a societal construct; preference for biological versus social explanations for individual and group differences; acceptance of the societal status quo versus belief in the legitimacy and efficacy of individual efforts to change society; and belief that science (as a major force in today's society) is value-free and objective versus relativistic and subjective [3]. I hypothesized that feminists and other social activists would be more likely to subscribe to statements that represented the latter part of each dichotomy.

Results indicated that students enrolled in courses on women are more likely to endorse statements indicating that the person constructs reality than are students enrolled in equivalent level courses without political content [3]. Students who designate themselves as feminist (independent of the course in which they are enrolled) have significantly lower scores on the Attitudes about Reality Scale (in the direction of the personal construction of reality) than do nonfeminists enrolled in the same courses. Exposure to courses on the psychology of women or social issues significantly reduced scores as compared to students enrolled in social psychology courses with the same instructor.

One would expect, of course, that individuals intensively involved in feminist activities on a professional and scholarly level would have even lower scores on this scale than feminist studies. Data for this chapter were, therefore, collected from twenty individuals who were identified as leaders in feminist activities within the American Psychological Association or the Association for Women in Psychology. All of these individuals have held offices within Division 35 (Psychology of Women) or AWP and most of them have written one or more scholarly papers on the psychology of women. The sample includes six past or present presidents of an APA division (not always Division 35) and includes two men. All of the individuals studied self-identified themselves as feminists on an information sheet included with the scale. It may be argued that this group is a representative sample of the feminist leadership within APA although one certainly cannot argue that it is representative of psychologists as a whole.

Total scores on the Attitudes about Reality Scale were obtained for this group and compared to scores obtained from students enrolled in courses on women at a state college in the eastern United States. Data from individual items in the scale were also analyzed and compared. In order to determine whether differences between feminist leaders and students were not a function simply of age, academic training, or professional versus student status, an additional comparison group of nine individuals on the psychology faculty at the state college was also examined. Although the two professional groups were of comparable age and professional experience, it is important to stress that they were not comparable in a number of important ways. The local sample consisted of six men and three women, the individuals identified themselves as teachers rather than researchers or teacher/researchers as did the feminist leadership group, and were less invested professionally than the feminists. Both groups, however, did include some representatives from the major areas of psychology; e.g., experimentalists, clinicians, etc.

The purpose of this study was to determine whether and in what ways active feminists within psychology differ from students becoming interested in the psychology of women. Epistemological predispositions are particularly interesting in this area because they are rarely explicitly acknowledged or examined, but may impede the acquisition of information seen as self evident by those with other epistemological assumptions [4].

RESULTS

As predicted, feminist leaders had significantly lower scores on the Attitudes about Reality Scale (M = 108.55, s.d. = 22.08) than did students enrolled in courses on women (M = 143.43, s.d. = 19.80). Their scores were similar to another sample of eleven academic feminists collected at a women's studies conference in New Jersey (M = 115.73, s.d. = 18.63). Feminist leaders in psychology also had significantly lower scores on this scale than a sample of faculty members in psychology (M = 134.89, s.d. = 16.34).

Instead of looking at the total scores on the scale, however, it is more interesting to examine specific items to see if there are any patterns of similarities and differences between committed feminist scholars and students who are enrolled in courses in which the work of these scholars is extensively cited. If differences in epistemological assumptions exist, they may alert us to areas where communication between groups will be particularly problematic.

In this analysis a one way analysis of variance was used to test for significant differences between groups on each item of the scale as well as for the scale as a whole (see Table 1). Local faculty in psychology and students enrolled in psychology of women courses at the college were more similar to each other than either group was to the group of academic feminists. They differed from each other on only nine items on the forty item scale. These results tend to support the conclusions of a recent investigation by Lori Sussman using total scores on the Attitudes about Reality Scale to compare faculty and students in humanities, social science, and science [5]. She found that with the exception of faculty in sociology, there were no significant differences between faculty and students in the same disciplinary domains. A similar conclusion has been drawn by King comparing faculty and students on values about theoretical orientations within psychology [6].

In contrast, feminist psychologists and students in the psychology of women differed from each other on thirteen items and ten of these differences were not found in any other faculty-student comparison. More intensive analysis of the items revealed interesting patterns. Virtually all of the items in which feminist leaders differed from students enrolled in a course that used much of the

Table 1. Mean Score on Each Item in the Attitudes about Reality Scale for Selected Groups

Item #	*MSC Faculty (N = 9)*	*Students (N = 64)*	*Feminists (N = 20)*	*F*	*P*
Total	*134.9*	*143.4*	*105.6*	*16.97*	*.0001*
*1	2.2	2.6	1.5	4.24	.018
2	3.3	3.3	2.4	2.57	.083
3	4.8	4.4	2.6	11.88	.0001
*4	1.6	2.0	1.5	1.44	n.s.
*5	1.5	2.9	1.2	13.18	.0001
6	4.4	5.0	4.8	.87	n.s.
7	2.6	2.8	2.2	.93	n.s.
8	4.1	3.5	2.4	4.60	.013
9	3.7	3.8	3.1	1.23	n.s.
10	5.6	4.1	3.5	5.49	.007
11	4.3	3.9	3.3	1.54	n.s.
12	3.7	3.4	3.2	.32	n.s.
13	2.6	2.2	1.5	3.36	.040
14	2.9	2.9	2.1	1.72	n.s.
15	2.7	3.1	2.8	.24	n.s.
*16	1.6	3.4	1.8	9.60	.0001
17	3.1	4.0	2.8	4.32	.017
18	3.8	3.6	3.2	.52	n.s.
*19	2.1	1.6	2.1	3.72	.029
20	3.6	4.9	2.6	12.03	.0001
21	4.7	3.2	3.2	3.76	.028
22	4.5	5.4	5.2	1.66	n.s.
23	3.7	4.0	3.1	2.59	.081
24	3.2	3.9	2.5	4.66	.013
25	4.2	5.2	3.6	7.44	.002
26	3.4	2.4	2.1	3.87	.025
*27	3.7	2.0	2.9	9.14	.001
*28	1.9	2.6	2.5	1.02	n.s.
29	4.4	4.4	2.9	4.96	.010
*30	2.2	3.0	2.8	.98	n.s.
31	4.8	4.5	3.9	1.21	n.s.
32	5.1	4.4	3.4	3.98	.023
*33	2.9	3.0	2.05	3.73	.029
34	5.4	5.4	3.6	12.91	.0001
*35	2.1	2.5	2.1	1.16	n.s.
*36	2.9	3.2	2.7	.61	n.s.
37	2.3	2.2	1.6	1.69	n.s.
38	3.1	3.8	3.0	2.02	n.s.
*39	2.8	3.0	2.7	.24	n.s.
40	3.3	3.4	1.98	8.46	.001

Note: (High scores equal agreement with a statement except for items marked with * where scoring is reversed and high scores indicate disagreement.)

former's theory and research could be classified as involving views about biological versus social causality or about the nature of science. Feminist leaders had more socially constructionist viewpoints in these areas than did students. For example, leaders were more likely to disagree with each of the following statements:

#3. Science has underestimated the extent to which genes affect human behavior.
#8. Most sex differences have an evolutionary purpose.
#20. Personality characteristics account for most differences in human behavior.
#24. Biological sex, sex role, and sexual preference are highly related to each other in normal people.
#34. A great deal can be learned about human behavior by studying animals.

Feminist leaders also differed from students in a number of statements involving perceptions about how science works. Feminist scholars are more likely to view science as a human enterprise and to believe that it works less well and is less fair than students view it. Thus, feminists agree more than students with statements such as:

#33. It is important to decrease the distance between the 'real world' and and the scientific laboratory.

They also disagree more than students with the statement:

#40. Most social problems are solved by a few very qualified individuals.

Not surprisingly, feminist leaders are also more sensitive than students to issues involving personal and social power. They are more sensitive to power inequities among individuals and less likely to view negatively attempts at social change. Thus, they endorse more than students statements such as:

#1. Who has power is a central issue in understanding how society works.

And, they disagree more than students do with the following statements:

#17. The United States has the most egalitarian society in the world.
#29. Society must protect itself from those who do not accept its rules.

Feminist leaders also differ from their less active professional peers in these areas although some items appear to indicate a faculty-student divergence in epistemology rather than an activist/non-activist one. For example, both of the faculty samples appear to hold more socially constructionist views on some items than do students. They agree more with statements indicating that science is relativistic and subjective:

#5. The way scientists choose to investigate problems is influenced by the values of their society.
#16. The facts of science change over time.

Faculty members are also less certain about the importance of early childhood experiences than are students.

#25. The mother-infant relationship is a key to understanding adult behavior.

It is important to stress that there is considerable agreement among all these groups on a number of items on the scale (15 items show little difference in mean scores between groups). In general, all of these groups seem to concur with statements relating to persons' ability to deal effectively with their world. Thus, they agree with statements such as:

#6. If one works hard at solving a problem, one can usually find the answer.
#22. Effort can often make up for an absence of talent in an area.

There is also a surprising amount of agreement on statements indicating lack of satisfaction with the societal status quo and positive perception of those who attempt to change it. All of the groups tended to concur with statements such as:

#4. Some nonconformity is necessary for social change to occur.
#35. Those who are nonconformists during one period of history are often found to be innovators by future eras.

They all tend to disagree with statements such as:

#9. People who achieve success usually deserve it.
#15. People who demand social change are usually those who have been ineffectual in present society.

If one looks at the data in another way–in terms of statements in which feminist leaders diverge most from other groups– a similar pattern emerges. The biggest differences between activist feminist psychologists and other faculty and their students are in statements involving biological causality and scientific values. In addition to the items discussed previously, these include lower evaluation of the value of technology for science and less belief than others that scientific merit is determined by the excellence of the work done. In these two items (as well as in items #3, 8, 10, 25, 29, and 34) feminist leaders differ from all other groups by scoring on the opposite side of the theoretical neutral point.

DISCUSSION

These data indicate that feminist leaders within psychology possess a coherent world view that differs in some respects from that of their students and probably that of most of their professional peers. Since much information about the value structures of psychologists has been published recently, I will discuss feminist divergence from the psychological "norm" first.

In an extensive investigation of the personal and professional viewpoints of psychologists, Coan found that they tended to manifest a belief in impersonal causality and a view that laws and principles should be expressible in physical terms [7]. He found no differences between the viewpoints of men and women in his sample. More recently, Kimble [8] and Krasner and Houts [9] have noted differences in belief structures between groups of individuals within psychology who are very involved in professional and scholarly issues within a particular sub-disciplinary domain. Both those classified as experimentalists [8] and behaviorists [9] showed consistent and systematic differences from comparison groups in basic assumptions about psychology and scientific epistemology.

Similar to findings with students [3] belief in biological determinism was associated with sociocultural conservatism among both behaviorists and comparison psychologists [9]. Officers of the Society for the Psychological Study of Social Issues (Division 9 of APA)–the group within APA most concerned with social issues–(and the group most similar to the present sample of feminist leaders–a number of whom have also been active in Division 9) were distinguishable from the experimentalists by their position on the environmentalist side of the "nature-nurture" controversy despite their agreement with that group on the importance of objectivity rather than intuitism in science [8]. SPSSI leaders also affirmed the importance of human values over scientific needs, the worth of field studies, and the need to look at the whole person rather than elemental parts. These values are similar to those found for feminist leaders using the Attitudes about Reality Scale.

Kimble has suggested that intra-group socialization combined with an initial preference for particular philosophical positions can lead to the formation of groups with mutually incomprehensible epistemologies [8]. Since epistemological positions exist on a level beneath awareness and are rarely the subject of discussion, scholarly groupings may remain unaware of how their differing assumptions and different definitions of the same terms interfere with the process of communication between them.

Evidence of differing epistemological systems between faculty and students may have even more important implications in terms of the communication of information that is seen as "self-evident" by the communicator. Students enrolled in courses in the psychology of women appear to be aware of the political issues of sex inequality, but are as conservative as their peers and professional mentors on issues involving biological determinism and the value-free nature of science and its worth in the solution of human problems. These assumptions are not likely to be discussed in the classroom. And, these areas appear to be the key data base from which issues of political and social inequality are decided.

Unexamined assumptions may also produce communication problems among feminists as well as between them and their students. The reason for the connection between biological determinism and conservative political assumptions is not clear and is a product of a group effect rather than being subscribed to by all individuals. Thus, some feminists may argue for group equality and still acknowledge a biological basis for some differences between groups. Acknowledgment of differing assumptions would allow the discussion of some conflicts which currently engender more heat than light.

Contradictions within unexamined belief structures may also cause intrapersonal conflicts for feminists as well as others working within professional structures. On one hand, a person may perceive that outcomes are not always the product of individual competence and merit. On the other hand, that person may be committed to social change and appear to share with their professional peers a belief in the efficacy of individual effort and the value of individual efforts to produce such change. Such conflicts may contribute to some of the "burn-out" problem that is increasingly common within the feminist community.

This perspective of differing world views is important in terms of both interpersonal as well as intrapersonal conflict. It is clear from previous research that psychologists with different scholarly orientations all possess unexamined assumptions about how the world works. These personal epistemologies may reflect early experience and may relate to sociocultural positions seemingly distinct from theoretical orientation [3,10,11]. They are rarely overtly acknowledged or discussed. They may help to explain why concepts about the person and society take such a long time to alter even when the evidence supporting these beliefs has been thoroughly discredited.

REFERENCES

1. J. T. Spence and R. Helmreich, *Masculinity and Feminity*, University of Texas Press, Austin, 1978.
2. R. K. Unger, Hidden Assumptions in Theory and Research on Women, in *Women Therapists Working with Women*, C. Brody (ed.), Springer, New York, 1984.
3. R. K. Unger, R. D. Draper and M. L. Pendergrass, Personal Epistemology and Personal Experience, *Journal of Social Issues, 42,* pp. 67-79, 1986.
4. R. K. Unger, Through the Looking Glass: No Wonderland Yet! (The reciprocal relationship between methodology and models of reality), *Psychology of Women Quarterly, 8*, pp. 9–32, 1983.

5. L. E. Sussman, "Attitudes about Reality in Faculty and Students in the Social Sciences, Natural Sciences, and Humanities," Unpublished master's dissertation, Montclair State College, 1985.
6. D. J. King, Values of Undergraduate Students and Faculty Members on Theoretical Orientations within Psychology, *Teaching of Psychology, 7*, pp. 236–237, 1980.
7. R. W. Coan, *Psychologists: Personal and Theoretical Pathways*, Irvington, New York, 1979.
8. G. A. Kimble, Psychology's Two Cultures, *American Psychologist, 39*, pp. 833–839, 1984.
9. L. Krasner and A. C. Houts, A Study of the "Value" Systems of Behavioral Scientists, *American Psychologist, 39*, pp. 840–850, 1984.
10. J. J. Sherwood and M. Nataupsky, Predicting the Conclusions of Negro-White Intelligence Research from Biographical Characteristics of the Investigator, *Journal of Personality and Social Psychology, 8*, pp. 53–58, 1968.
11. N. Pastore, *The Nature-Nurture Controversy*, King's Cross Press, New York, 1949.

CHAPTER 15

Taking the Traditional Route: Some Covert Costs of Traditional Decisions for the Married Career Woman*

AUDREY SANDERS
JANICE M. STEIL
JANET WEINGLASS

A dramatic increase in women's participation in the U. S. labor force occurred in the decade of the 1970s. The largest increase (9.2%) occurred among the married. Over half of married women over twenty were employed in 1980 as compared to 41.3 percent nine years earlier [1]. This increased participation has been paralleled by an increase in the literature on women's careers. Among the topics discussed are issues related to gender differences in aspiration and achievement levels [2-4], characteristics of dual-worker and dual-career marriages [5-8] and descriptions of the problems specific to women who undertake careers in corporate and professional settings [9-11]. Throughout the literature we find consistent evidence of a differential valuing of the careers of married women as compared to married men and an unequal sharing of the responsibilities of multiple roles.

Studies from the dual career literature consistently show that employed wives are more likely than their husbands to curtail their career involvements in favor of family demands and that both partners seem to accept as inevitable the idea that women will bear the main brunt of child care and domestic organization [8, 12]. Families receive positive support from others when the wife interrupts her career for the sake of husband and children [11, 13] and negative sanctions when she does not [8]. Despite the wife's participation in the career world, she is still expected to give her primary attention to the needs of husband, home and family [10]. Yet the literature suggests that there is minimal dissatisfaction

*An earlier version of this chapter was presented at the meetings of the Eastern Psychological Association, Philadelphia, Pennsylvania, 1983.

among married career women who are experiencing such demands. More than likely, for example, wives will give up their own jobs and relocate because of their husbands' careers [14]. Furthermore, the marital satisfaction of high-level career women has been reported to be unrelated to the number of times they have moved for their husbands' advancement [15]. Other studies suggest not only that a great deal of satisfaction is reported but that a sense of discrimination is rarely felt [16].

We wonder whether this is the whole story. Are there really no psychological costs incurred by the employed woman, who moves for the sake of her husband's career? Conscious thoughts and feelings about a particular situation often differ from less conscious affect. This is virtually a truism in psychology which has been discussed extensively in both psychoanalytical and experimental literature.

The purpose of this study then, was to explore the relationship between reported satisfaction levels and less conscious affect regarding career decisions in a sample of women likely to experience internal conflict. Modern orthodox Jewish women were selected because they are exposed to both the religiously sanctioned belief system of strict role prescription for women and the concept of equal opportunity for both sexes. As a consequence we predicted that internal conflict should be particularly high in such a sample.

SUBJECTS

Subjects were 123 women between the ages of sixteen and twenty-seven, who were either students at an orthodox Jewish women's college or members of an orthodox Jewish social and educational organization.

PROCEDURE

Data from two sections of a larger questionnaire were used. Respondents' future career goals, attitudes and aspirations were assessed as well as their responses to two vignettes pertinent to the topic of careers. The inclusion of open as well as closed-ended questions allowed for more diverse and in-depth examination of affective responses.

Questions in the first section asked the respondent to answer as she would "seven years from now."

1. Do you hope to be working?
2. How much time do you hope to devote to your work? (part-time, full-time (9-5), greater than full time (9–5+).
3. What annual earnings do you personally expect to be receiving?
4. How seriously do you hope to be pursuing a career seven years from now? (9-point scale: Not at all to extremely seriously)

5. Do you want to have children?
6. If you have children, what do you most hope to do regarding children and work outside the home? (stop working altogether; stop working until the children are in school; stop working briefly then resume part-time or full-time work; continue working without interruption except for maternity leave).

The second section included the vignettes and relevant questions.

Vignette 1

Carol, an orthodox Jewish woman, has just completed her Ph.D. in Psychology, but has been unable, despite sending out fifty job applications to obtain a university position. Recently, she was offered a position teaching in a local private high school at a salary of $6,000 annually and she has decided to accept that position.

1. How satisfied or dissatisfied do you think Carol feels regarding her new position? (9-point scale; extremely dissatisfied to extremely satisfied).

1a. Briefly, tell why you gave the answer you did.

2. If you were Carol, how satisfied or dissatisfied would you feel? (9-point scale).

Vignette 2

Bernice, an orthodox Jewish woman was recently given tenure as a professor at the prestigious university at which she works. Her husband was offered an excellent job in another city. It was decided that his position was a really exceptional opportunity and so they are both moving.

1. Describe how you think the decision was made. What were the deciding factors?
2. How satisfied or dissatisfied do you think Bernice feels? (9-point scale: extremely dissatisfied to extremely satisfied).

2a. Briefly, tell why you gave the answer you did.

3. How satisfied or dissatisfied would you feel if you were Bernice?

The two vignettes present different kinds of career-related issues, parallel in the sense that each character is a Ph.D. who has chosen a career in academia, and who has been presented with a decision that may be contrary to the pursuit of those career goals. They are not parallel because the actor in vignette 1 is apparently a single woman who has not yet begun her career, while the actor in vignette 2 is married and has already achieved a position of tenure. In addition, the married woman in vignette 2 faces a more ambiguous situation. She has given up a satisfying career for an uncertain outcome. This contrasts with the single woman in vignette 1 who is presented with a certain outcome: she is underemployed.[1]

CODING

Open ended responses were coded for the presence or absence of: 1) specific words of affect; 2) implicit or explicit indications of anger; 3) statements indicative of rationalization; 4) statements indicative of resignation and 5) indications of feelings of discrimination or unfairness. Twenty-five affective words were used. These were subsequently subdivided into three categories: 1) negative active words (e.g., furious, incensed); 2) negative passive words (e.g., unhappy, sorry) and 3) indications of negative loss (e.g., loss of identity, loss of self-esteem).

Original agreement between two coders on the items related to vignette 1 ranged from 74 percent to 92 percent with an overall average of 85 percent. Agreement in the items related to vignette 2 ranged from 76 percent to 95 percent with an overall average of 84 percent. Discussion of the differences led to consensus on all items.

DESCRIPTION OF THE SAMPLE

The mean age of the respondents was 18.5 years, with a range of sixteen to twenty-seven years. All but four of those who answered the question "Do you want to have children?" ($n = 111$) replied in the affirmative. Of the remaining four, three answered negatively and one was undecided. Eighty-three percent of the respondents reported that they expected to be working seven years hence. Forty-seven percent of the sample planned to work part-time. Forty-one percent planned to work full-time (9–5) and 12 percent expected to be in positions that would require more than a 9–5 commitment. Expected income ranged from $5,000 to $50,000 with a mean of $15,500. Eight percent of the respondents expected to stop work altogether after the birth of their children. Forty-three percent planned to stop working briefly, and 42 percent planned to stop working until their children started school. Only 6.5 percent planned to work continuously taking time off only for normal maternity leave. Respondents were divided into three groups on the basis of how seriously they expected to pursue a career. Those responding at or below the scale mid-point were categorized as not serious and comprised 18.6 percent of the sample. Those

[1] We thank an anonymous reviewer for identifying this point.

circling the two numbers above the midpoint were categorized as somewhat serious (34.3%) and those circling the two furthermost points were categorized as very serious. By this criterion nearly half of the respondents (47%) expected to be pursuing a career very seriously seven years hence.

RESULTS

Extreme dissatisfaction was voiced in response to the single woman's decision to accept the low paying position. Subjects' dissatisfaction was high whether they responded on behalf of the actor in the vignette ($\bar{x} = 1.92$) or for themselves ($\bar{x} = 1.95$). Significantly less dissatisfaction was expressed for the married woman's decision to give up her tenured professorship and move with her husband ($t\ (95) = 11.00, p < .001$). Again, this was true whether the women responded for themselves ($\bar{x} = 4.34$) or the actor in the vignette ($\bar{x} = 4.21$). Thus, the single woman's decision was viewed as more dissatisfying and was also more likely than the married woman's to be perceived as unfair ($t\ (95) = 2.46$, $p < .05$).

Consistent with this pattern, only three respondents (3.1%) expressed any positive affect regarding the single woman's decision to take the teaching position. By contrast, twenty-four respondents (25%) expressed positive affect regarding the decision that the married woman will give up her position and move with her husband. Closer examination, however, revealed that in every instance the positive affect was expressed on behalf of the woman's husband rather than herself. Phrases such as "she's happy for her husband" and "what he shall achieve would make her to a certain extent happy" are typical of what was written.

Turning to the negative affect, we find a pattern that stands in opposition to respondents' reported satisfaction levels. Significantly more negative affect was expressed in the open-ended responses to the decision of the married woman (58%) than to the decision of the single woman (30%) ($t\ (95) = -5.72, p < .001$).[2] When the negative affect was examined by category types it was found that few negative active words (e.g., "furious" or "enraged") were used overall (See Table 1). There was also no difference in the number of negative active responses to one vignette as compared to the other ($t\ (95) = 0.82$, NS), nor were there differences in the frequency of expressions of resignation ($t\ (95) = -1.51$, NS) or anger ($t\ (95) = 0.77$, NS). Negative passive affect (e.g., "sorry" and "unhappy") was the most frequently used category type and overall differences were due to the greater use of negative passive words in response to the married as compared to the single woman's dilemma ($t\ (95) = -3.35, p < .001$). There were also significantly more indications of feelings of loss (loss of identity, career, importance, self-esteem, self-respect and a "personal" sense of loss)

[2] The *t* statistics reported here are results of correlated *t*-tests.

Table 1. Differences in Coded Responses to the Open-Ended Questions[a,b]

Variable	*Mean*	*% of Responses*	*T Value*	*df*	*P*
Vignette 1 — Negative Affect	0.2813	30%	−5.72	95	.001
Vignette 2 — Negative Affect	0.7604	58			
Vignette 1 — Positive Affect	0.0208	3	−4.53	95	.001
Vignette 2 — Positive Affect	0.2604	25			
Vignette 1 — Negative Active Affect	0.0417	5	0.82	95	NS
Vignette 2 — Negative Active Affect	0.0208	2			
Vignette 1 — Negative Passive Affect	0.1667	20	−3.35	95	.001
Vignette 2 — Negative Passive Affect	0.3542	33			
Vignette 1 — Negative Loss	0.0729	6	−4.80	95	.001
Vignette 2 — Negative Loss	0.3854	33			
Vignette 1 — Rationalization	0.1771	20	−2.09	95	.05
Vignette 2 — Rationalization	0.3021	28			
Vignette 1 — Resignation	0.0729	9	−1.51	95	NS
Vignette 2 — Resignation	0.1354	14			
Vignette 1 — Unfair	0.1979	21	2.46	95	.05
Vignette 2 — Unfair	0.0833	9			
Vignette 1 — Discrimination	0.0417	5	0.00	95	NS
Vignette 2 — Discrimination	0.0417	5			
Vignette 1 — Anger	0.0938	10	0.77	95	NS
Vignette 2 — Anger	0.0625	6			

[a]Vignette 1: Carol, Single Woman
[b]Vignette 2: Bernice, Married Woman

(t (95) = -4.80, $p < .001$), as well as a tendency for more rationalization (t (95) = -2.09, $p < .05$) on behalf of the married woman.

Respondents' indications of the deciding factors in the decision to move were also coded. Four categories emerged. The one used most frequently (by 28% of the respondents) was labelled "husband's job comes first." Responses typical of this category included "they decided that the husband's job was more important than Bernice's." "He (or the husband) usually should have a better paying job—being the breadwinner." The second category was labelled "consideration of male ego." It included responses such as "I think it is important that the male should hold the main job in (the) family. He needs it for his ego and pride." "A man is more sensitive when it comes to earning more money. His pride comes before her position." Twenty-five percent of the respondents gave reasons that fell into this category. Twelve and one-half percent of the respondents gave reasons which fell in the third category labelled "wife should consider the family first." Examples typical of this category included "They may have considered future plans for a family and decided that there would be a significant amount of time she wouldn't be working;" and "Factors in the decision were Bernice's ultimate duty to raise the family and her husband's obligation to support." The final category was labelled "rewards of the husband's new position." Responses characteristic of this category were reported by 11.5 percent of the subjects. A typical example was "Apparently her husband had the better opportunity—factors such as room for advancement, salary, prestige (were considered)."

The deciding factors, affective responses, and reported satisfaction levels were analyzed in relation to respondents' expected career commitment (e.g., expected work seriousness). No differences were found on any of the measures. It seems that a similar pattern emerges among all respondents independent of the expected level of their commitment to a career. Projecting themselves into a married life style, respondents report minimum dissatisfaction at giving up a valued position. They assert the importance of traditional roles and express some positive feelings on behalf of their husbands. Yet despite the assumption of the traditional perspective, negative affect, particularly negative passive affect is expressed.

CONCLUSIONS AND IMPLICATIONS

On behalf of the single woman (Carol), respondents freely express dissatisfaction ($\bar{x} = 1.92$). The lower level of dissatisfaction ($\bar{x} = 4.21$) expressed by the respondents on behalf of the married woman (Bernice) is coupled with a greater evidence of negative passive affect. Dissatisfaction is expressed for both of the actors, since both scores were below the midpoint; nevertheless, the difference is highly significant ($p < .001$).

The situation of the married woman in our study typifies the dilemma that many women face. Bernice is a woman who is apparently committed to both family and career. Faced with a conflict between these roles, the choice made is a traditional one. Opting for the conservative female role elicits minimal dissatisfaction on the part of our respondents. The choice is rationalized by statements which acknowledge and sometimes justify the valuing of the husband's position above her own (e.g., "husband's job comes first;" "wife should consider family first;" "considerations of male ego;" "rewards of new position.") Yet, the presence of negative passive emotionality points to the limited effectiveness of this tactic. Among the factors that limit the expression of overt dissatisfaction on the part of the married woman is her perception that this is an issue that involves choice and she has participated in the decision making process. Seventy-four percent of our respondents said that the decision for the married woman in vignette 2 had been arrived at mutually. The reason given for the decision clearly reflect the social values that give disproportionate importance to the husband's as compared to the wife's career. Yet, there was little to suggest that these values were perceived as unfair. Nor was there any discussion of the extent to which these values tend to predetermine the outcome of the decision-making process. The perception of choice may be, in many instances, somewhat illusory. Yet, the perception of choice and participation limit overt dissatisfaction. As a result, negative reactions emerge covertly.

Indeed, the single most striking aspect of this study is the examination of the difference between women's covert and overt expressions of dissatisfaction. Had our study simply focused on our respondents' overt feelings, the married woman would have emerged as more satisfied than the unmarried woman. Because we examined less conscious affect as well, we were able to tap an undercurrent that other research has not found. In investigating populations such as ours—women likely to experience internal conflict—it seems particularly important to utilize methodologies that allow such complexities to emerge. Further research on role strain in general, and on females and role strain in particular, could benefit from the use of similar strategies.

Our sample are college students who did not face immediate career-familial decisions. When projecting about a single woman, they express clear dissatisfaction. Yet, in their projection about how they would adapt in a family situation, they take a secondary role, express less dissatisfaction and more underlying distress. While the situations are hypothetical, they can have a powerful impact. A woman who does not conceive of equality in marriage, even in her projections, is unlikely to take the risks that could lead to equality in real life.

This research should also add further insights to the literature that reports low aspirations of women [17]. At the mean age of 18.5 years, this particular sample of college women have already made some important personal predictions. If they know, as young college women, that in a few short years they may be confronted with a career conflict that could abort that career, we can expect a psychological self-limitation at the outset.

ACKNOWLEDGMENTS

We wish to thank Andrew Sahara for his assistance with some of the data analysis. The data for this study were collected as part of a larger survey conducted in 1979.

REFERENCES

1. D. N. Westcott and R. W. Bednarzik, Employment and Unemployment: A Report on 1980, U. S. Department of Labor, Bureau of Labor Statistics, *Monthly Labor Review, 104:*2, pp. 4–14, February 1981.
2. E. M. Almquist, S. S. Angrist, and R. Michelson, Women's Career Aspirations and Achievements: College and Seven Years Later, *Sociology of Work and Occupations, 7:*3, pp. 367–384, 1980.
3. F. L. Denmark, B. K. Baxter, and E. J. Shirk, The Future Goals of College Woman, in *Women – Volume 1, A PDI Research Reference Work,* F. L. Denmark and R. W. Wesner (eds.), Psychological Dimensions, Inc., New York, 1976.
4. T. G. Alper, Achievement Motivation in College Women – A Now-You-See-Now-You-Don't Phenomenon, *American Psychologist,* pp. 194–203, 1974.
5. F. Pepitone-Rockwell, *Dual-Career Couples,* Sage Publications, Beverly Hills and London, 1980.
6. D. G. Rice, *Dual-Career Marriage: Conflict and Treatment,* The Free Press, New York, 1979.
7. J. B. Bryson and R. Bryson, *Dual-Career Couples,* Human Sciences Press, New York and London, 1978.
8. R. Rapoport and R. N. Rapoport, *Dual-Career Families,* Penguin Books, London, 1971.
9. ______, *Dual-Career Families Re-Examined,* Harper and Row, Harper Colophon Books, New York, 1976.
10. R. M. Kanter, *Men and Women of the Corporation,* Basic Books, New York, 1977.
11. T. N. Garland, The Better Half? The Male in the Dual Profession Family, in *Toward a Sociology of Women,* C. Safilios-Rothschild (ed.), Xerox College Publishing, Lexington, Massachusetts, 1972.
12. R. L. Coser and G. Rokoff, Women in the Occupational World: Social Disruption and Conflict, *Social Problems, 18,* pp. 535–554, 1971.
13. J. M. Steil, Marriage: An Unequal Partnership, in *Handbook of Family and Marital Therapy,* B. B. Wolman and G. Stricker (eds.), Plenum Press, New York, 1983.
14. M. M. Poloma, Role Conflict and the Married Professional Women, in *Toward a Sociology of Women,* C. Safilios-Rothschild (ed.), Xerox College Publishing, Lexington, Massachusetts, 1972.
15. B. S. Wallston, M. A. Foster, and M. Berger, I Will Follow Him: Myth, Reality or Forced Choice–Job Seeking Experiences of Dual-Career Couples, *Psychology of Women Quarterly 3:*1, pp. 9–21, 1978.

16. S. K. Houseknecht and A. S. Macke, Combining Marriage and Career: The Marital Adjustment of Professional Women, *Journal of Marriage and the Family, 43:*3, pp. 651-661, 1981.
17. M. M. Poloma and T. N. Garland, The Married Professional Woman: A Study in the Tolerance of Domestication, *Journal of Marriage and the Family, 33,* pp. 531–540, 1971.
18. S. L. Sutherland, The Unambitious Female: Women's Low Professional Aspirations, *Signs, 3:*4, pp. 774–794, 1978.

CHAPTER 16

Perceptions of Daily Life Scripts and Their Effects on College Women's Desires for Children

IRENE HANSON FRIEZE
SCOTT BAILEY
PATRICIA MAMULA
MIRA MOSS

As increasing numbers of women are entering the labor force, understanding the types of career choices women make becomes increasingly important for understanding the lives of women. Labor force participation rates for women have risen dramatically in the last thirty years. While only 20 percent of adult women in this country were employed outside the home in 1900, 51 percent of adult women were working outside the home by 1979 [3]. One of the largest changes in women's labor force participation has been the employment of married mothers. By 1980, 57 percent of mothers with children under eighteen were in the labor force [4]. This means that employment outside the home is becoming increasingly acceptable for women, and is probably expected for many women.

Women are found in a wider range of jobs too, especially since 1970. However, most women still choose female-dominated occupations. Although some women do go into male fields, few men choose female fields. Thus, the labor force is largely sex-segregated. An unfortunate correlate of this job segregation for women is that female-dominated jobs tend to pay less than male jobs requiring equal amounts of skill and training.

In the last few years there have been a number of studies on the determinants of women's career and family aspirations. These have generally taken a nontheoretical approach and relate various demographic predictor variables to

* Portions of this chapter were presented at the annual meeting of the Society for Experimental Social Psychology, Pittsburgh, October, 1983.

whether women aspire to a career and the type of job they want. There is still no well developed theory of career choice for women [5].

Research on career attainment in women [6-9] has suggested that having a supportive father, a mother who was happily career oriented, and upper middle class or upper class family background, and being the oldest child are especially predictive of a woman's having high career aspirations for herself. Researchers have also looked at various personality or motivational variables in trying to understand female achievement, but this approach has been less successful than many had hoped. More important factors appear to be the attitudes and beliefs of the women [10]. One study which explicitly compared the relative effects of demographic variables, personality factors, and attitudinal and belief variables found that the latter category of variables accounted for 27 percent of the variance in career aspirations of college women while demographic and personality factors together explained only 21 percent of the variance [11].

This chapter is an attempt to empirically investigate the role of women's fantasy and beliefs about various careers and major life choices (such as being a full time housewife) in their own decision making. Techniques borrowed from script theory are utilized to assess these beliefs. The role of beliefs in occupational choice was pointed out many years ago by Ginzberg, Ginsburg, Axelrod and Herma [12] who suggested that as people choose their ultimate careers, they move from fantasy to tentative choices and then to realistic decisions. However, this work was largely theoretical and little attempt was made to actually study the types of fantasies involved in this decision making (see [13]). A more recent study [14] has attempted to look at daydreams about occupational choices and has found that college women do fantasize about the careers to which they aspire.

SCRIPT THEORY

Two lines of research have been developed somewhat independently which rely on the concept of the "script." These might be considered as macro and micro analyses of scripts in people's lives. First is the clinical psychological literature which sees scripts as life plans [2, 15] or as recurring episodes in a person's life [16, 17]. Based on his clinical work, Steiner suggests that, "People make conscious life plans in childhood or early adolescence which influence and make predictable the rest of their lives" [2, p. 28].

According to Steiner, one method of choosing a script is to first select a model or heroine [15]. This role model may be, and often is, a mythical figure. Typical scripts for women at the time of his work included Mother Hubbard, the Plastic Woman, the Woman Behind the Man, the Fat Woman, the Queen Bee, the Nurse, or the Tough Lady. According to Steiner's analysis, girls choose one of these or another in adolescence and proceed to attempt to live out this role as fully as possible the rest of their lives. Having a career or working in a particular field may or may not be a part of such a script. Presumably, any career choice would have to be consistent with the general script outline. Steiner was primarily concerned with the negative effects of scripts on the person's life. He saw these life scripts as restricting life choices. The model which we will propose shortly draws upon this work in assuming that women think about various life options or scripts and make career decisions which are consistent with what they perceive as the more positive and realistic scripts for their lives. However, we further suspect that people keep other possible scripts as part of their self concept or self-schema and that such scripts are fantasized often in people's lives and provide a source of satisfaction [18].

Cognitive psychologists have generally used the concept of "script" to mean something quite different from the global conceptions of Steiner. For example, in trying to understand how people understand textual material, Bower, Black and Turner found that although many details of activities are routinely missing from stories, people have no trouble understanding the action of the text [19]. Scripts are seen as sequences of expected activities or actions which are part of our cultural knowledge [1]. Bower *et al.* found that college students showed high agreement on restaurant scripts as well as for scripts for attending a lecture, getting up in the morning, grocery shopping, and visiting a doctor. Such script knowledge is part of our understanding of how society operates. We learn to expect certain sequences of activities or sets of related activities. We are likely to be upset or even shocked when these expected scripts are violated [1, 20].

Although Schank and Abelson suggest that script knowledge influences our plans and daily activities, they are working within a very narrow framework of planning where it is assumed that one has knowledge of goals and that plans follow logically from these goals [21]. In attempting to understand the role of individual script conceptions in career choice, one cannot assume that the goals of the individual are known. In fact, we are assuming that one's goals are derived from one's beliefs about various life scripts.

Our use of scripts is perhaps closest to the conception of Ashmore and DelBoca who have suggested that eliciting scripts may be one approach to studying behavioral stereotypes [22]. Specifically, Ashmore and DelBoca argue that once one knows the particular role that an individual occupies, a set of behavioral expectations for that individual is assumed. These expectations or scripts might also be thought of as stereotypes for particular social groups.

A THEORETICAL MODEL OF CAREER CHOICE

Using the various conceptions of scripts discussed earlier, we propose a model for women's decision making about career choices. (See [23] for a similar model for social decision making). According to this model, the first stage in career choice is the development of job schema or conceptions of various types of jobs and the people who hold these jobs. Although learning of job schema goes on throughout life, it is those schema formed in childhood and adolescence which probably have the most impact on initial career choice. Role models, personal experiences in late adolescence and the early adult years, and the media may also be highly influential [4, 24].

At the same time that children are forming conceptions of jobs, they are also forming a general self concept or self schema [25]. Our model assumes that there is an initial matching of the self schema to the various job schema of the individual. Unless there is some overlap in the schemas, the job would never even be considered as a possibility for the person. One's sense of oneself as female or male is part of the self schema. Girls who think of themselves as highly feminine would probably not consider jobs that they feel are too "masculine" [26]. We also assume that for all but the most masculine of women, the housewife job would be one job possibility that would be tentatively accepted or rejected, but always considered by young women.

Next, once the woman begins to seriously consider various occupational choices, she would imagine herself in the role of a person with each possible occupation. Such fantasizing might take the form of imaging oneself living a typical day in that script. Or, one might project oneself into a particular part of daily life script. By doing this fantasizing, the person would then have a feeling for what her life would be like if she were living that script. Evidence of such fantasizing in adolescents is seen in a TAT study by Elder and MacInnis [27]. Presumably, the career script which "felt" the best would be chosen. (Other research by Anderson [28] has also indicated that the process of imaging oneself in a script may make that script subjectively seem more likely to actually occur.)

Once the person has rejected the jobs which don't "feel right," there will probably be at least some initial movement toward preparation for that occupation. As one learns more about the job, one may modify one's self schema to be more consistent with the developing image of what occupants of this role are like. If this increased knowledge is too discrepant with one's self schema, then the person may instead reject this occupational choice and go on to repeat the process of career choice.

CAREER IMAGES AND CAREER CHOICE

In order to empirically investigate the effects of script knowledge on career choice in women, we have asked women to generate daily life scripts for women in various life situations. We felt that it was important to describe the occupations and the family situations of the women in our stimuli in order to allow the participants in the study to focus on whatever aspects of the daily life they felt were most important. The scripts included a traditional housewife with two children, a married woman lawyer with two children, and a secretary who dropped out of college, and is married with two children. All three women were described as being thirty-four years of age. Young college women were asked to generate a typical daily life script for one of these three women. These scripts were coded for overall positivity or negativity as well as for specific script elements. As an initial test of the proposed model of career choice, this article is concerned with three basic questions:

1. How do college women today view the typical lives of the traditional housewife, the professional woman, and the secretary?
2. Do college women with more ambitious career aspirations have differing views of the traditional housewife, the professional woman, and the secretary?
3. Are these three life choices viewed differently by college women aspiring to traditional female jobs as compared to nontraditional male jobs for themselves?

METHOD

Procedures

The data for this study were based on a questionnaire that was administered during class time to several lower level psychology classes (social psychology, developmental psychology, and psychology of women). Other data was collected from students in beginning psychology classes who completed the questionnaires as part of an experimental participation requirement for their course. This was done in small group settings outside of class.

Questionnaires included questions about the women's year in school, age, marital status, and number of children. Each person also was asked about her aspirations for how much education she would complete and the type of job she wanted and why. In addition, they were asked to briefly describe a typical day in the life of two different women. One of this pair was either a housewife, a secretary, or a lawyer. Asking about how these women spend a typical day was seen as an unobtrusive measure of stereotypes or occupational schema. The sample includes twenty-seven women in housewife condition, twenty-eight for the secretary, and thirty for lawyer.

The scenario about Mary, the housewife, was described as follows:

> Mary graduated from college and married soon after that. She worked for two years as a secretary, and is now staying home full time to care for her husband and two small children. She is thirty-four.

Other scenarios were:

> Jane dropped out of college after completing her second year. She is currently working at a local telephone company as a secretary. Jane has been married for six years, and she recently had her second child. She is thirty-four.

> Ellen is a lawyer and has been working for a large law firm for several years. She got married when she was twenty-six, and now at the age of thirty-four, she has two children.

For each scenario, subjects were asked:

1. Briefly describe a typical day in Mary's (or Jane's or Ellen's) life.
2. What parts of her life would you guess she likes most? Least?
3. If you (or your spouse) were in Mary's (or Jane's or Ellen's) situation, how would you see your life developing or changing?
4. How easy is it for you to imagine yourself (or your spouse) in Mary's (or Jane's or Ellen's) situation? Very easy, easy, unsure, difficult, very difficult.

Study Participants

In order to look at the life plans of women who had not already made significant life choices, we analyzed data from college women between the ages of seventeen and twenty-two who had no children. As noted earlier, these women were selected from a variety of types of psychology classes, including some Women's Studies classes. This broad selection allowed us to study more traditional women as well as a group of women we felt were likely to have quite high career aspirations.

Initial analyses of the study participants indicated that consistent with other recent studies of college women, this group had quite high career goals as well as wanting to marry and have children [7]. There were no significant demographic or attitudinal differences in the three script groups. The majority of the sample is under the age of twenty, white, and single. Most want to get married in about five years, want to have two or three children beginning about the age of twenty-six. Most also plan more education than a bachelor's degree.

Coding

Major dependent variables in this study were the level of career choice and the female or male-dominated nature of the planned job. The women in the sample were asked what job they would like to have and why. The job choice was coded on a 5-point scale from 1 (Unskilled) to 5 (Professional) which was derived from two standard job rankings [29, 30]. Jobs were also assigned as female if the majority of those working in the field were women, male if most were male, and neutral if there was not a clear predominance of either sex.

Another major variable was the perceptions of the daily life scripts. A number of possible script elements were identified after reading through a sample of the scripts. Once this list was established, each script element was coded for absence or presence. If present, the affective context was further coded as positive, negative or neutral. An overall affect (positive, neutral or ambivalent, or negative) was also assigned to each script by the rater. Two trained raters coded the data. Both were reliable with one another at a level of more than 80 percent complete agreement. Coders were not aware of the career choices of the women when they coded the script data.

Another coded variable was the reasons for the job choice. These were coded into three major categories: money or economic factors, intrinsic interest in the type of work, or allowing one to help others.

RESULTS AND DISCUSSION

Career Choices

Career choice data was coded for the level of the job and whether it was a male or female-dominated profession. Reasons for the particular choice were also coded. In all 43 percent choose male jobs and 49 percent female jobs. Other choices were jobs with equal numbers of males and females. The most common female job was nursing and male job was computer-related.

Overall, the reasons for choosing a male job were similar to the reasons given for choosing a female job. Students wanted interesting jobs. However, consistent with other research [4], there was a trend for male jobs to be more often selected for monetary reasons. Female jobs were more chosen because of good job opportunties and because they allowed one to work with women and/or children.

Looking next at the status of the jobs selected, most of these women chose semi-professional jobs (66%). Professional jobs accounted for most of the remaining choices (29%) and 3 percent were skilled (most commercial artists) and 3 percent in the arts. Skilled jobs were most chosen for interest. Semi-professional for interest, ability to help others and opportunities. Professional jobs were most often selected because they were seen as interesting.

Views of Other Women's Lives

The daily life script technique yielded rich data. Some sample scripts generated by participants of this study for Mary, the housewife, were:

> Mary probably gets up around 7:30 each day to get her oldest child off to school. She prepares breakfast for her family and then sends her husband off to work and her daughter off to kindergarten. She then dresses her three-year-old and gets him settled for a day at nursery school and after she has done her housework, Mary reads a newspaper and then calls her girlfriends to get the latest gossip about which marriages are breaking up. (Twenty-year-old single black woman who plans to adopt a child but not to marry. She wants to work as an industrial psychologist after receiving her doctorate. ID = 106.)

and

> She gets up in the morning to make her hubby breakfast. As the kids watch cartoons, she cleans up the breakfast dishes, and makes the beds. After gathering a few loads of wash, she'll sit down for a coffee break. She makes the kids some lunch and catches up on her favorite soap. Getting the mail gives her a little break in her day. She plays with the kids for awhile then starts to prepare dinner. Around 5 her husband comes home

and they sit down to eat. After dinner they both do the dishes. They retire to the living room to play with their kids. A few hours later they put the kids to bed. (Twenty-one-year-old single white woman who plans to marry and who wants two children. She intends to be a systems analyst after earning a master's degree. ID = 107.)

A sample scenario generated for the secretary script was:

> Jane gets up in the morning, feeds her children and husband, gets herself and the children dressed, and leaves for work when the babysitter arrives. She comes home from work and begins preparing dinner. She feeds her family again and then probably does some cleaning or washing while her husband plays with the children. Then it is time to put the children to bed. She probably bathes the children, and gives the baby a bottle and then puts them to bed. She then either goes to bed herself or spends about an hour watching TV with her husband. (Twenty-two-year-old single white woman who wants to marry and have three children before the age of thirty. She wants to work in hotel management after getting her bachelor's degree. ID = 109.)

Some sample scripts generated for lawyer script included:

> Ellen and her husband wake up at 6:30. Her husband jumps in the shower and she goes to wake her children—a four-year-old girl and a seven-year-old boy. By the time she has them both dressed, her husband is out of the shower and also dressed, and takes the kids downstairs to have breakfast.
>
> Ellen showers, comes down and grabs a cup of coffee, then greets Mrs. Smith, the woman who comes every day to stay with the four-year-old.
>
> Ellen goes to work and immerses herself in several cases, taking a break only to have a quick lunch with a new client. At 5:00 she says goodbye to her secretary and her colleagues, meets her husband at 5:15. They have a quick drink in a nearby bar—hurry home to relieve Mrs. Smith, greet the kids—and since it is Friday and her husband's night to cook—he makes dinner. Ellen cleans up the kitchen while her husband watches TV with the kids—then she takes them upstairs to get ready for bed. Her husband comes up to help tuck them in. (A nineteen-year-old white woman who wants to marry and have two children. She plans to work in an art or English field after receiving an advanced degree. ID = 105.)

and

> Ellen gets up at 7, has breakfast and is ready to go to work by 8:30. She has a sitter care for the kids so she doesn't need to worry about them. After working from 9 until 4, she gets home at 5 and plays with the kids, reads, or watches TV. At 6 she fixes dinner for the family and they eat at 7 when her husband gets home. After doing the dishes and straightening the house, Ellen is tired and goes to bed early. (Twenty-year-old white woman who wants to get married in the next two years and begin her family of three children. She plans to earn her bachelor's degree and work as a psychiatric nurse. ID = 121.)

Looking across all three scripts, the most common script elements involved being with or caring for children and husband, housework and meal preparation, and leisure activities. For the employed women, going to work was almost always mentioned, although there was very little imagery about specific work activities. Thus, the housewife script does appear to be well known and is applied to all married women [31]. Many women mentioned that the housewife should go back to work. Thus, for this college sample, being a full time housewife is not viewed positively. Lott reported similar findings several years ago [31].

In order to mathematically assess the differences in the scripts, we used a method from Tversky [32] called similarity analysis. This analysis has been used previously to assess prototype similarity [33]. In our application, we first deleted idiosyncratic responses (script elements mentioned by only one person) from the list of script elements. Then, each pair of scripts was analyzed across all the subjects responding to that script for the shared and for the unique elements for each script. Similarity is represented by the ratio of shared elements to the total number of elements. Larger ratios represent greater similarity between scripts.

By using the similarity analysis, we were able to make general comparisons across the three scripts. A similar type of analysis was used to compare the script descriptions of the subjects who desired female as compared to those who wanted male jobs. Results of the similarity analyses are shown in Table 1. As can be seen, the secretary was seen as similar across both job preference groups; the housewife was most different across groups. Those who wanted a female job saw the housewife and the lawyer as most different. However, the differences across the groups were smaller than expected. Thus, the situations themselves appeared to determine more of the variance in the mention of specific script elements than any individual differences (which we were able to assess) across the study participants.

Individual Differences in Views of Women's Lives

Another prediction we had made was that the women in our study would have different *emotional* reactions to the three scripts as a function of their own career plans. Analyses of the overall affect ratings were done to assess this possibility. One way analyses of variance across the three scripts showed first that the lawyer script was liked most and the housewife least ($p < .001$). On a 1 (negative) to 3 (positive) scale, the housewife = 1.4; the secretary = 1.6; the lawyer = 2.3.

Next, stepwise multiple regression analyses were done to predict the script affect. Initial analyses attempted to identify the ability of the coded career choice and imagination variables to predict affective reactions to each of the three scripts. Affective ratings were regressed on subjective ratings of how easy it was for the subject to imagine herself in the script, which sex dominated the career chosen, and what level job was chosen.

Table 1. Degree of Similarity Across Scripts

	Housewife	*Secretary*	*Lawyer*
Overall			
Housewife	–	.50	.41
Secretary	–	–	.52
Male Job Choice			
Housewife	–	.43	.38
Secretary	–	--	.62
Female Job Choice			
Housewife	–	.35	.29
Secretary	–	--	.78
Male vs. Female Job Choice			
Housewife	.67	.41	.35
Secretary	.36	.82	.63
Lawyer	.32	.70	.70

For both the secretary and the lawyer scripts, affect was best predicted by the ease with which respondents reported being able to imagine themselves in the script. The second variable to enter the equation for both scripts was the level of job chosen by the subject. Those desiring lower levels of jobs for themselves were more positive about the secretary script and less positive about the lawyer script. This fits the career choice model proposed earlier although these regression coefficients were not statistically significant.

In contrast, the best predictor of affect for the housewife script was the coded sex-domination of the job preferred. Contrary to what we expected, those desiring careers in male-dominated areas were more positive about the housewife script. Perhaps these women felt less negative about this script since it was so discrepant with their own goals that they perceived no conflict with this alternative lifestyle. While the second variable to be entered in the equation was the imagination variable, it failed to reach statistical significance.

These data suggest that the scripts for the two employed women, the secretary and the lawyer, were similar with regard to affective predictors. For both scripts, the easier the subject reported being able to imagine herself in the script, the higher the affective rating given that script. This was not the case for the housewife script, perhaps because most women can imagine themselves in this script, and it is the affect associated with this script rather than being able to image it that determines one's own career and family plans.

Being able to image oneself in a career may be more related to feelings about the career. Exposure to possible careers and the lifestyles which they imply may lead to differential affect toward those careers among women [24]. If women spend more time rehearsing their possible role in a preferred career, we would expect them to have developed a broad script regarding that career. This increased rehearsal and script development may then result in relative ease in imagining oneself in that scenario. Of course, the correlational analyses used do not permit the conclusion that ease of imagination leads to more positive affect. It is plausible to suggest that the more positive we feel about a given situation, or lifestyle, the easier we find it to imagine ourselves in that situation.

We were also interested in the relationship of the attitudinal information collected from the study participants to overall script affect. A series of stepwise regression analyses with these variables indicated that consistent with previous research, demographic and attitudinal factors did a poor job of predicting feelings about the various scenarios. Other regression analyses done for job choice also found few relationships between attitudinal factors and job choice. Those who aspired to female jobs desired less education, were older and wanted more children. Thus, not surprisingly, they were more traditional. Similar findings emerged for the level of the job aspired to. Those who planned on more education also wanted higher level jobs. Other predictors were not significant.

CONCLUSIONS

As our results have indicated, our theoretical model of career choice did not function quite as predicted. The model does appear to work best for the lawyer scenario, perhaps because this was the only one of the three scripts about which there was positive affect. An expanded study using more occupations might better test our model, especially if we could find occupations which the college women were themselves aspiring to. It does appear, though, that the college women do not have trouble imaging the housewife script. These women had been exposed to this script through their experiences with their own mothers or other adult women. Perhaps, these women have considered the housewife role for themselves, but have rejected it in most cases before going to college. For many of these women, the housewife role may no longer be a possible self—a self image in which they could easily imagine themselves. If this is the case, the script elements and affect for this script may no longer be relevant for their career choices. Support for this interpretation is given by findings in a recent study by Anderson regarding self-referent scripts and behavioral intentions [28]. Using a task in which subjects portrayed themselves, a friend, and a disliked person as the actor in a cartoon drawing of a behavioral scenario, Anderson found that only self-referent scripts resulted in a significant effect on intentions to perform the depicted behavior. Imaging someone else doing something did not make the person more willing to do the behavior, but imaging oneself doing the task did make the event seem more likely. As most of the present sample involved college women who are planning on more education than a bachelor's degree, the lawyer script may well be the most self-referent script for these women.

We feel that the daily life script technique employed in this study is a valuable procedure for studying beliefs about various life styles. More research using a similar technique might be done. A potential problem with this study is the small sample size and the small number of scripts used. Although subjects were more positive about the lawyer, their average affect even for this script was only slightly more positive than neutral. A more diverse set of occupations would be useful. In future studies, participants might also be asked to describe daily activities at work. This would tell us if the lack of work imagery found in the results reported earlier truly indicates lack of script knowledge about work activities or merely that such activities are seen as less relevant than what happens in the home. In any research using daily life scripts, though, it is important to describe the person as well as the situation. As this research and other work [33] has shown, unique schema are associated with a particular person in a specific situation. Very different findings would be expected if the sample had been asked to describe the daily life activities of male lawyers or clerical workers or even of househusbands.

Another question for future research is the issue of the relative importance of cognitive versus affective beliefs about various life choices. Other research has shown that affect rather than cognitive beliefs are most related to political preference [34]. Perhaps this is also the case for career choices.

Finally, it would be important to look at the career scripts of job counselors as well as those of young adults. These counselors may be very influential and there is evidence that they may have quite stereotypic beliefs about women's role choices [13].

ACKNOWLEDGMENTS

The authors would like to thank Judith Meece for her assistance with the early stages of this project and Jacob Birnberg, Audrey Federouch, Barry Lewis, Linda Price, Craig Russell, and Esther Sales for their helpful comments on an earlier version of this article.

REFERENCES

1. R. P. Abelson, Psychological Status of the Script Concept, *American Psychologist*, *36*, pp. 715-729, 1981.
2. C. M. Steiner, *Scripts People Live: Transactional Analysis of Life Scripts*, Grove Press, New York, 1974.
3. United States Government, Bureau of Labor Statistics, *Employment and Earnings*, January 1979 and September 1979.
4. J. S. Eccles and L. W. Hoffman, Socialization and the Maintenance of a Sex Segregated Labor Market, in *Research in Child Development and Social Policy*, Vol. 1, H. W. Stevenson and A. E. Siegel (eds.), University of Chicago Press, Chicago, 1984.

5. L. F. Fitzgerald and J. O. Crites, Toward a Career Psychology of Women: What Do We Know? What Do We Need to Know?, *Journal of Counseling Psychology*, *27*, pp. 44-62, 1980.
6. R. C. Barnett and G. K. Baruch, *The Competent Woman*, Irvington Publishers, New York, 1978.
7. E. R. Greenglass and R. Devins, Factors Related to Marriage and Career Plans in Unmarried Women, *Sex Roles*, *8*, pp. 57-71, 1982.
8. D. R. Kaufman and B. L. Richardson, *Achievement and Women: Challenging the Assumptions*, The Free Press, New York, 1982.
9. R. K. Unger, *Female and Male: Psychological Perspectives*, Harper and Row, New York, 1979.
10. M. Komarovsky, Female Freshmen View their Future: Career Salience and Its Correlates, *Sex Roles*, *8*, pp. 299-314, 1982.
11. J. E. Parsons, I. H. Frieze, and D. N. Ruble, Intrapsychic Factors Influencing Career Aspirations in College Women, *Sex Roles*, *4*, pp. 337-347, 1978.
12. E. Ginzberg, S. W. Ginsburg, S. Axelrad, and J. L. Herma, *Occupational Choice: An Approach to a General Theory*, Columbia University Press, New York, 1951.
13. W. W. Falk and A. G. Cosby, Women's Marital-Familial Status and Work Histories: Some Conceptual Considerations, *Journal of Vocational Behavior*, *13*, pp. 126-140, 1978.
14. J. G. Touchton and T. M. Magoon, Occupational Daydreams as Predictors of Vocational Plans of College Women, *Journal of Vocational Behavior*, *10*, pp. 156-166, 1977.
15. C. Steiner, *Games Alcoholics Play: An Analysis of Life Scripts*, Grove Press, New York, 1971.
16. R. Carlson, Studies in Script Theory: I. Adult Analogs of A Childhood Nuclear Scene, *Journal of Personality and Social Psychology*, *40*, pp. 501-510, 1981.
17. S. S. Tomkins, Script Theory: Differential Magnification of Affects, in *Nebraska Symposium on Motivation*, Vol. 26, H. E. Howe, Jr. and R. A. Dienstbier (eds.), 1978.
18. H. Markus and P. Nurius, Possible Selves, paper presented at the annual meeting of the Society for Experimental Social Psychology, Indiana, 1982.
19. G. H. Bower, J. B. Black, and T. J. Turner, Scripts in Memory for Text, *Cognitive Psychology*, *11*, pp. 177-220, 1979.
20. E. Goffman, *The Presentation of Self in Everyday Life*, Doubleday, New York, 1959.
21. R. C. Shank and R. P. Abelson, *Scripts, Plans, Goals and Understanding: An Inquiry into Human Knowledge Structures*, Lawrence Erlbaum, Hillsdale, New Jersey, 1977.
22. R. D. Ashmore and F. K. DelBoca, Sex Stereotypes and Implicit Personality Theory: Toward a Cognitive-Social Psychological Conceptualization, *Sex Roles*, *5*, pp. 219-248, 1979.
23. P. M. Niedenthal, N. Cantor, and J. F. Kihlstrom, Prototype Matching: A Strategy for Social Decision Making, *Journal of Personality and Social Psychology*, *45*, pp. 575-584, 1985.

24. S. S. Angrist and E. M. Almquist, *Careers and Contingencies,* Dunellen, New York, 1975.
25. H. Markus, M. Crane, S. Bernstein, and M. Siladi, Self-Schemas and Gender, *Journal of Personality and Social Psychology, 42,* pp. 38-50, 1982.
26. A. C. Huston, Sex Typing and Socialization, invited address for the American Psychological Association Annual Meetings, Washington, D.C., 1982.
27. G. H. Elder, Jr. and D. J. MacInnis, Achievement Imagery in Women's Lives from Adolescence to Adulthood, *Journal of Personality and Social Psychology, 45,* pp. 394-404, 1983.
28. C. A. Anderson, Imagination and Expectation: The Effect of Imagining Behavioral Scripts on Personal Intentions, *Journal of Personality and Social Psychology, 45,* pp. 293-305, 1983.
29. J. H. Goldthorpe and K. Hope, *The Social Grading of Occupations: A New Approach and Scale,* Oxford University Press, London, 1974.
30. A. J. Reiss, *Occupation and Social Status,* The Free Press, New York, 1961.
31. B. E. Lott, Who Wants the Children? Some Relationships among Attitudes toward Children, Parents, and the Liberation of Women, *American Psychologist, 28,* pp. 573-582, 1973.
32. A. Tversky, Features of Similarity, *Psychological Review, 84,* pp. 327-352, 1977.
33. N. Cantor, W. Mischel, and J. C. Schwartz, A Prototype Analysis of Psychological Situations, *Cognitive Psychology, 14,* pp. 45-77, 1982.
34. R. P. Abelson, D. R. Kinder, M. D. Peters, and S. T. Fiske, Affective and Semantic Components in Political Person Perception, *Journal of Personality and Social Psychology, 42,* pp. 619-630, 1982.

CHAPTER 17

Earliest Memories: Sex Differences and the Meaning of Experience

ADRIA E. SCHWARTZ

The study of Earliest Memories first became of interest to dynamic psychologists with the publication of Freud's paper on "Screen Memories" in 1899: He treated early childhood recollections as he did dreams, assigning little value to the manifest content and attending, instead, to the latent content which Freud maintained could only be completedly extracted through his then newly evolving technique of free association [1]. In 1937, Alfred Adler took issue with Freud by treating the content of the memory directly as a manifestation of the workings of the individual's character and lifestyle [2]. Further explorations of Earliest Memories by clinicians have generally followed either one of the above paths, with most agreeing that Earliest Memories seem in some way to reflect core conflict areas and modes of coping.

Kohlberg has suggested that self-categorization by gender, that is the child's recognition at the age of two to three years that "I am a girl/boy" is the most fundamental of cognitive organizers [3]. More recent work by Gilligan [4] and Chodorow [5] suggest that male and female differences in cognitive and relational styles have far-reaching impacts on their ways of Being-in-the-world. One might hypothesize, then, that self-categorization by gender and the consequent attribution of traits, values and style would have a significant effect on earliest memories as a reflection of that matrix of individual and social reality which constitutes personal experience. However, a recent review of the literature from 1967 through July of 1983 revealed no published studies of sex differences in early memories.

METHODOLOGY

The current study is exploratory in nature. It attempts to delineate through phenomenological inquiry the basic categorical dimensions of Earliest Memory and to see if those dimensions differ in female/male experience. The phenomenologist, much like the early introspectionists, seeks to examine the data of conscious experience. Then, by a process of synthetic analysis, an attempt is made to arrive at the essence(s) of that experience. This is in keeping with prior research which demonstrates that the most productive and most reliable means of using earliest memories is through the utilization of thematic groupings [6-10]. More recently, Bruhn, Rahn and Schifman in a methodological critique of Early Memory studies determined that "In this research area, a priori clinical predictions, uses of procedures validated for other purposes (e.g., non-specific scoring manuals) are likely to be inappropriate or invalid." [11, p. 267]

In the current study, Earliest Memories were collected orally and in written form from two samples, A and B, each consisting of equal numbers of females and males for a total *n* of 180. Sample A was composed of sixty graduate students attending a large urban university in the field of Clinical and Counseling Psychology. In Sample B Earliest Memories were elicited from sixty male and sixty female undergraduates who attended a small suburban college within commuting distance of their homes. In Sample A the mean age of the males was 27 and females 27.2 years. In Sample B the mean age of males was 20.5 years, females 22.1 years.

Participants were asked to recall Earliest Memories as well as affective associations. Thematic categories were generated which for the purpose of the analysis became mutually exclusive response categories.

A Chi square test was performed upon the frequency distributions of the content thema generated by female and male subjects to assess sexual differences. Inter-rater agreement between two scorers was .87.

RESULTS[1]

Synthetic analysis of the early memories which included affective associations and the individual's own exploration of why a particular memory stands out amidst his or her early experiences, resulted in six categories which describe the thematic content.

Positive Interpersonal Interaction

These include memories where the individual reports interacting with someone else in an apparently satisfying manner. It may include passive nurturance (being held, fed, etc.) or more active involvement on the part of the participants. "I remember sitting on my father's shoulders as he was walking down the street . . . happiness and love . . . . I must have felt very special. Also

[1] A longer version of this chapter which includes a more detailed explication of the methodology and results is available from the author.

I felt that this was one of the ways my father showed his love for me."

"I was at the train station with my mother and saw a steam engine for the first time . . . waiting for the train to come to the station . . . exciting."

Physical Illness and Injury

This cateogry is for those whose memories refer manifestly to injuries, hospitalization, illnesses, in a thematic manner.

"I was three or four and I fell on the step and hit my mouth and damaged a tooth. I remember that and I remember the incident of tripping and I remember getting the tooth pulled. It's a very scary memory."

"I was four years old sitting in a crib of sorts and I was content playing with an elastic band. I played too much, however, and I poked my eye out . . . confusion and helplessness and frustration. It was traumatic at least, terrifying at best."

Frustration

This rather broad category deals with themes having to do with being rejected or misunderstood in some essential way, being forced to do something against one's will, or generally not being gratified.

"Four years or three-and-a-half–playing house with my father and brother. They were children and I was the mother. They had some sort of alliance between the two of them that they wouldn't listen to me. So I would tell them to do something–take a nap . . . and they would say okay, but I would turn around and they weren't. I remember that I knew they were doing that, playing that game. I was always like that."

"Being locked up in a woodshed because I had thrown a tantrum about something which I cannot to this day recall. I only know my reason for my behavior was not a gross misbehavior . . . because that was the first incident where my parents responded with no obvious understanding of me or my part, for their reasoning."

Fear and Anxiety

Included in this category were those memories involving fear of an external object or force, as well as anxiety over some internalized problem, usually separation anxiety. "I can remember being in a playpen when I was under a year old and a dog jumped in. It looked huge, frightening me . . . I remember green grass and the terror I felt when the dog jumped in."

"Being a really small child (around two years) and being left at a friend's home. I remember being very upset and crying and my mother singing me to sleep in a strange bed."

Mastery and Performance

These were usually proud memories of an accomplishment, some act which won praise and admiration from others, or, more likely, some event which was internally recognized as important for the child's growth and underlying meaning of those memories as a dawning of autonomy.

"I remember standing at my windowsill in the kitchen, mother behind me. I had just realized and was very proud that by standing on my toes I could just look out the ledge and out the window. The significance to me is independence: old enough to entertain myself and turn my back to my mother—self-sufficiency." "Making mud pies in my Easter suit . . . fun and freedom."

Sibling Rivalry

These memories expressed traditional competition and jealousy between siblings.

"Four years old and I remember several events of a trip. I got to go and my older sister didn't. She was crying because she didn't get to go . . . feeling of relief that I wasn't left home. That I was the special one that got to go."

"I had just gotten a new doll and my sister (one year older) threw it down the steps of an old church. The doll's head got smashed to bits. I went home crying and my mom told me she'd get me a new head for the injured doll."

As the results in Table 1 indicate, differences in thematic content for females and males in both Samples A and B were significant at the .01 level.

Generally then, it may be said that the males reported memories in which they perceived themselves to be more firmly embedded in a matrix of positive interpersonal interaction; existentially vulnerable perhaps as manifested by concerns over bodily illness and injury, subject to frustration, fears and

Table 1. Sex Differences and Thematic Content of Earliest Memories

	Positive Interpersonal Interaction	*Illness and Injury*	*Frustration*	*Fear and Anxiety*	*Mastery and Performance*	*Sibling Rivalry*	*Totals*
			SAMPLE A				
Females	3	2	9	9	4	3	30
Males	11	6	7	0	4	2	30
Totals	14	8	16	9	8	5	60
$n = 60$; $\chi^2 = 16.02$ with 5 d.f.; $p \leqslant .01$							
			SAMPLE B				
Females	13	13	8	15	1	10	60
Males	13	10	4	16	14	3	60
Totals	26	23	12	31	15	13	120
$n = 120$; $\chi^2 = 16.87$ with 5 d.f.; $p \leqslant .01$							
			SAMPLES A & B				
Females	16	15	17	24	5	13	90
Males	24	16	11	16	18	5	90
Totals	40	31	28	40	23	18	180
$n = 180$; $\chi^2 = 15.43$ with 5 d.f.; $p \leqslant .01$							

anxieties, but more secure than the females in their ability to master developmental tasks and meet reality obstacles.

In sharp contradistinction, the women present the now all too familiar picture of what might be termed in Ericksonian language, a lack of basic trust [12]. Their positive sense of self seems less well developed, and with a greater proportion of experience dominated by anxiety and frustration, both existential and interpersonal, while they evidence much less of a conviction that these problems were net and mastered successfully.

DISCUSSION

The primary question to be considered is how the difference in emphasis of thematic content of the Earliest Memories reported by the males and females in both samples are reflective of significant differences in psychological concerns.

Perhaps most striking is the difference between the males and females as reported by the undergraduate State College students–Sample B–in their memories concerning Mastery and Performance and Frustration. In this more traditional parochial population, the sex role stereotype remains largely intact, with the males accurately reflecting their socialized belief that they will achieve and be positively reinforced by it. Their sense of competence and effectiveness is intrinsic in their gender role. The young women, on the other hand, reflect no such assurance, with only one memory where Mastery and Performance was a dominant issue. The frequency of "frustration" themes was double that of the men in the sample. For this young women, their "fear and anxiety," "frustration," and "sibling rivalry," were of greater psychic force than recollections of developmental mastery.

For the graduate students in Sample A, the primary issue seemed to be the dynamic opposition of "Fear and Anxiety" to "Positive Interpersonal Interaction." Thus, the major differences here fell not in the realm of Mastery and Performance as it did for the undergraduate students, but competency as it excels in the Interpersonal sphere. The women in Sample A are older, Doctoral candidates, more advanced in their careers. They have achieved, are achieving and can expect to achieve; and they are being reinforced for it. It is understandable, then, that the issues of "Mastery and Performance" are not gender differentiated in this group.

For these women the salient issue appears to be their strength in relation to others and to themselves. What is their experience of Being-in-the-World? They are vulnerable to frustration and uncertainty and subject to abandonment both physical and psychological. Rarely do they report interacting positivity with others. The men, again, report a far greater number of such experiences. They, too, experience frustration but seem more firmly rooted in a sense of what Laing has described as a position of ontological security: "that his identity and autonomy are never in question . . . having an inner consistency, substantiality, genuineness, and worth. . . " [13, p. 41].

Ontological security also entails firm sense of our bodily selves. The early memories dealing with themes of "Physical Illness and Injury" reflect concern over our biological vulnerability. Existentialists talk of the problem of finitude, and Freudians of castration anxiety; Adlerians treat the related concept of organ inferiority. It seems that any comprehensive theory of personality must account for our knowledge of our frailty, epitomized most concretely in our physicality. The men and women of Sample B were not differentiated by the frequency of memories in this area, whereas those in Sample A were; males reported 20 percent of their memories with this theme as compared to not quite 7 percent for the women.

Bodily integrity, as suggested above, is often experienced as a concretization of a more elusive sense of emotional wholeness, or integrity of self-hood. It might be inferred then that somatization is a more acceptable means of expressing fear and anxiety for these men than the more vocal experiential statement of the women. Thus, in Sample B, where the males express their fear and anxiety more directly, they do not significantly differ from the women in their memories of physical illness or injuries. In Sample A, men reported no memories dealing primarily with fear and anxiety, but they did report a significant number of memories dealing with illness and injury.

Thus it is possible that these two categories are tapping internal experiences which are selected out of the psychic repertoire in different ways depending on the expressive style and defensive structure of the individual. Moreover, the data suggest, in keeping with current feminist theory [4, 5] that these styles are gender related.

Psychiatric epidemiologists have recently questioned evidence that women experience and report more symptoms and general emotional discomfort than do men [14]. Phillips and Segal suggest that this difference is not attributable to real differences in frequency, but rather "man's reluctance to admit certain unpleasurable feelings and sensations." [15, p. 69] They suggest that "women may be more likely than men to report certain acts, behaviors and feelings because it is more culturally appropriate and acceptable for women to be expressive about their difficulties." [15, p. 59]

The remaining thematic category to be discussed is that of Sibling Rivalry. Here the lack of a priori assumptions, the spirit of "disciplined naivete" underlying the pilot presents a significant problem. No data on the number or sex of siblings were collected from the subjects as there was no way of anticipating that this would arise as a major thematic category. With a relatively small *n* it is likely that the differences between the sexes is reflective merely of a sampling artifact.

However, a brief look at the situation of the majority of the women in Sample B reminds us that they live, for the most part, at home within the nuclear family and often with younger siblings. In fact, it is not uncommon for these young women to assume much responsibility at home from an early age, often adopting a role of surrogate mother . . . a role which is by definition conflict ridden. The women of Sample A, on the other hand, lived apart from their parental home and were, at least, spatially autonomous. They were not faced with the day-to-day competition with family members for love and other nurturant favors.

If, indeed, early memories do reflect current conflicts then the difference between the women in the samples is most understandable. What remains to be explained is why the men in Sample B, also living within the nuclear family did not evidence similar concern. In the more traditional families from which these young women spring it is their status more so than that of their brothers which is altered by the presence of siblings, as they become mother's helpers, and take second place to any new males in the family. It is interesting to note here that seven out of the ten memories reported by these women had to do with male siblings.

CONCLUSIONS

The phenomenological analysis of a relatively small sample of Earliest Memories strongly suggest that Earliest Memories serve a most valuable guide to the structure of experience. The thematic analysis of 180 Earliest Memories has elucidated six areas of vital concern to our Being-in-the-World.

Positive Interpersonal Interaction

This theme refers to experience which reflects a firm sense of trust in being-with-others. Whether adopting a passive stance of being nurtured and cared for, or a more active involvement, the interaction of self and others is viewed as positive and gratifying.

Fear and Anxiety

In contrast to the interpersonal trust and strength of self reflected in experiences of PII, themes of Fear and Anxiety reflect a threat to the security of Being-in-the-World. Although some of these memories dealt with threat of external dangers, the majority of the memories reported concerned themselves with anxiety over being left alone, abandoned, either figuratively or literally. Being-in-the-World, as reflected by these constellations is precarious. Neither the resources of the self alone, nor significant others seemed strong enough to ward off imminent danger.

Mastery and Performance

Here, experiences reflecting a sense of competence and effectance suggest a way of Being-in-the-World whereby the individual projects various aspects of his or her self meaningfully through action on to a more objective natural and social reality.

Frustration

Themes of frustration, lack of gratification or communication, the perception that one is being "forced" to give up or is being violated are all included in this category. It is a way of Being-in-the-World whereby individual self-expression and growth is blocked somehow in his or her being-with-others.

Physical Illness and Injury

Threats to the integrity of our corporeal selves is most vividly expressed in these experiences whereby our biological vulnerability and, by extrapolation, the very tenuousness of our Being at all, is at issue.

Sibling Rivalry

This category of experiences differs most sharply from the others in that they seem most reflective of a particular cultural situation; that of a small nuclear family where there is intense competition for love and protection from significant others. It remains a task of further research to see if this theme remains central to peoples of different socio-cultural backgrounds.

A comparison of Earliest Memories by sex found differences consonant with current role patterns of socialization and expectations so long entrenched in majority culture of American society. The women appeared through their early memories to be more anxious, frustrated, and generally less secure in their basic individual and interpersonal effectance. The males in the sample, in contrast, evidenced a more fairly developed sense of Self which encompassed both their personal competence and interpersonal relationships. It became obvious through the analysis that the young men and women experienced very different ways of Being-in-the-World which reflected their Being-with-Others as well as their integral sense of self [16].

The data suggest a confirmation of Kohlberg's theory that gender identity and consequent role attribution occurring in early childhood is a significant determinant of future emotional/cognitive development. The strikingly different constellation of thematic content elicited from the females and males of this sample suggest that gender difference is significant and reflective of a major imbalance in the social/emotional construction of gender in our current society.

REFERENCES

1. S. Freud, Screen Memories, *Collected Papers*, *5*, Hogarth Press, London, 1950.
2. A. Adler, The Significance of Early Recollections, *International Journal of Individual Psychology*, *3*, pp. 283-287, 1937.
3. L. Kohlberg, A Cognitive Developmental Analysis of Sex-Role Concepts and Attitudes, in *The Development of Sex Differences*, E. Maccoby (ed.), Stanford University Press, California, pp. 82-173, 1966.
4. C. Gilligan, *In a Different Voice*, Harvard University Press, Cambridge, Massachusetts, 1982.
5. N. Chodorow, *The Reproduction of Mothering*, University of California Press, Berkeley, California, 1978.
6. L. Saul, T. R. Snyder, and E. Sheppard, On Earliest Memories, *Psychoanalytic Quarterly*, *25*, pp. 228-237, 1956.

7. H. Mosak, Early Recollections as a Projective Technique, *Journal of Projective Techniques*, *22*, pp. 302-311, 1958.
8. M. Kramer, C. Winset, and R. Whitman, A City Dreams, *American Journal of Psychiatry*, *127*:10, pp. 1350-1356, 1971.
9. R. J. Langs, M. B. Rothenbend, J. R. Fishman, and M. F. Reiser, A Method for Clinical and Theoretical Study of the Earliest Memory, *Archives of General Psychiatry*, *3*, pp. 523-534, 1960.
10. R. J. Langs, Earliest Memories and Personality, *Archives of General Psychiatry*, *12*, pp. 379-390, 1965.
11. A. Bruhn and H. Schiffman, Invalid Assumptions and Methodological Difficulties in Early Memory Research, *Journal of Personality Assessment*, *46*:3, pp. 265-267, 1982.
12. E. Erickson, *Childhood and Society*, W. W. Norton and Company, New York, 1950.
13. R. D. Laing, *The Divided Self*, Penguin, Baltimore, 1965.
14. M. Guttentag, S. Salain and D. Belle (eds.), *The Mental Health of Women*, Academic Press, New York, 1980.
15. D. Phillips and B. Segal, Sexual Status and Psychiatric Symptoms, *American Sociological Review*, *34*, pp. 58-72, 1969.
16. A. Schwartz, Being-in-Time: A Phenomenological Exploration of the Existential Past, Present and Future, *Review of Existential Psychology and Psychiatry*, *15*:1, 1977.

CHAPTER 18

She Has Her Reasons: Women's Explanations for Job Changes*

MARIANNE LaFRANCE

Women are frequently in the position of having to explain themselves, of supplying "good" reasons for what they have done or failed to do. Reasons are typically intended as explicit disclosures, changing what might be seen as nonsensical or suspect into something that is sensible and reasonable. In fact, the reasons for acting in a particular way often count for more than the actions themselves. Goffman has gone so far as to argue that, "we see that there is no act whose meaning is independent of reasons understood for its occurrence; and there seems to be no act for which radically different reasons cannot be provided, and hence radically different meanings" [1, p. 110].

Having reasons thus seems an ubiquitous and public aspect of social life. Reasons provide information not only about particular deeds but also more broadly about the person performing those deeds. To know something about a person's reasons is to understand something about how that person sees herself. Further, there are grounds for believing that people adopt reasons which they understand will be acceptable to others. This chapter describes a study of the reasons that a group of highly educated women gave for changes in their employment situation over the course of their careers. By looking closely at these reasons, we have at hand a method for uncovering the images that women have and are expected to have of themselves at various points in their lives.

A study of replies to a request to supply reasons can also be informative about whether these explanations relate to other events or experiences in the respondents' lives. For example, reasons for present job changes might influence

* This research was supported in part by funds from The Andrew W. Mellon Foundation given by Radcliffe College for research at The Henry A. Murray Research Center of Radcliffe College.

future work experience or might be the result of prior work experience. In other words, one's stated reasons for acting in a particular way may affect subsequent actions or may themselves change as a result of past actions. Having experienced the outcome of a decision, one may modify the description of what went into the decision in the first place.

Despite the fact that the literature on self-attributions is quite voluminous [2], research efforts have hardly begun to explore systematically the role of this variable as either a contributor or an outcome in the dynamics of work experience. In order to examine reasons as cause and/or effect, time series data are required. Without longitudinal data, it is not possible to examine the nature or direction of the relationship between social psychological processes and work experience. The purpose of the present chapter is to help fill this void by utilizing an existing longitudinal data set that allows these issues to be directly addressed.

An important conceptual caveat is in order before more detail is provided on the rationale and method for the analysis. The present investigation will not be concerned with the "truth" of a particular explanation—that is whether the reason provided accurately describes the event according to an objective standard or even whether it is a veridical representation of the respondents' private beliefs. The "real" reason is notoriously difficult to pin down. For example, Epstein reported that women say they are motivated to work because they need money [3] yet when asked if they would leave their work if economic pressures lessened many say they would not. What is of concern are the kinds of reasons that women express when inquiries are made. It is then an empirical question to determine the psychological import of the explicit rendering.

When individuals speak of having a "good" reason for an action, they seem to mean that they can provide an account that is passingly acceptable. Goffman has suggested in this context that, "the goodness or badness of an account must, of course, be distinguished from its trueness or falseness. True accounts are often good, but false accounts are sometimes better" [1, p. 112]. In regard to employment in particular, women's explicit justifications for why they work can be made to fit in with normative expectations. For example, Oppenheimer wrote, "In sum I would argue that, on the whole, people are not unqualifiedly enthusiastic about married women working outside the home. But if the work goals can be defined in an acceptable fashion (as really familial goals for example) . . . attitudes are flexible enough to permit a considerable proportion of married women to work" [4, p. 51].

RATIONALE FOR STUDYING REASONS

Before turning to the reasons given by a sample of women for their employment changes, let me describe in more detail my reasons for studying them. As is the case in reason-giving more generally the rationale is based on a number of considerations.

One reason for studying reasons has to do with exploring the employment experience of an important, and until recently, neglected population – namely the careers of employed women. Women have and are entering the work force in record numbers [5] yet we know little about how they see their employment histories. Explanations are frequently offered to explain why women start and stop work but these tend not to come directly from the women themselves. Consequently there is need to probe how women explain these career moves.

The decision to take or leave a certain job is simultaneously a personal one and a social one. C. Wright Mills suggested that our actions are guided by remembering the various ways in which we could subsequently justify them to others [6]. Reasons thus may be important because they indicate to self and to others what one considers to be legitimate factors in making a decision. Attributions are worth noting because they suggest how women are socialized to explain their work lives to others. Further, these justifications may come to direct the way an individual thinks and decides even when alone.

A second reason for studying reasons derives from research in social psychology that suggests that attributions concerning why events have happened may be instrumental in affecting feelings about those events and in influencing expectations about future actions. Attribution processes are assumed to be central to the individual's construction of personal reality. Moreover, attribution theory assumes that personal reality is made up in good measure by the predisposition to see things in causal terms [7]. Presumably if one can explain why something has occurred, can locate its cause, then that person may be in a better position from which to exert control and thereby to increase one's sense of personal efficacy.

Take the example of accounting for a job change. Was a particular job taken because it was perceived as the "only thing available" or because the actor "was seeking a way to learn something new?" Having attributed the reason to an external constraint such as "only thing available" rather than to a personal goal, a woman may be less likely to feel personally responsible for the work undertaken, to feel less pride if the job goes well, and to anticipate less future progress [8]. What is of interest here is the effect on future behavior of attributing one's actions more to one set of reasons than to another. In particular, reasons for employment decisions may affect a woman's subsequent orientation to whether she works or how much. The present chapter aimed to test the validity of this hypothesis.

Third, studying reasons over time may contribute to our understanding of temporal and real-life aspects of attribution. Attributions are frequently studied in laboratory contexts as one-time occurrences, with the implication that once made, they do not change. Research is needed to explore reasons given over time [9] and about non-contrived situations. In that way it will be possible to chart the role of attributions as either contributing to or resulting from meaningful personal decisions. To a considerable extent, research efforts into issues such as these have been hampered by the unavailability of longitudinal data which permit investigation of the unfolding of the relation between reason giving and real world outcomes. This study describes results showing change in reasons for taking and leaving various jobs as a function of change in labor force participation. Further the present study afforded the opportunity to study the reasons for taking the same job when the same question about the same job was asked twelve years apart.

A final set of reasons for studying reasons centers on the issue of how to categorize types of reasons. Reasons are frequently quite complex and are deserving of greater scrutiny in their own right. To date, psychologists studying attribution processes have seen everyday social perception, including self-perception as analogous to scientific understanding [10]. In other words, in asking why a particular outcome occurred, attribution researchers have tended to assume that lay people think in causal terms and that the significant question is whether the cause is seen to be external or internal to the actor. More recently, this approach has been criticized [11] for being insensitive to the need to distinguish between lay reasons and scientific causes. The argument is that people do not so much articulate the causes underlying their own actions as they seek to justify them via reasons.

Philosophers have long distinguished between reasons and causes [12-15]. The approved, objective, scientific way of explaining human behavior, as with other occurrences, is to observe it from the outside and to look for empirical regularities between particular behaviors and various features of the actor's history or the environment. This is contrasted with the more familiar, if less respectable, tactic of simply asking people why they behaved as they did. In reply they tend to cite those aspects of their present or even anticipated future situation, themselves, the action or its consequences that persuaded them to behave in that way. These are their *reasons* for so acting. The contrast is sometimes made this way: between explanation without justification (cause) and explanation via justification (reason). Or as Toulmin put it, all behavior is explicable; some actions are also justifiable [16].

In an effort to reconcile the various positions on whether actors give reason or casual explanations for their own behavior Locke and Pennington [17], proposed a three tier organization of attributions. The topmost tier makes the distinction between internal and external causes. Under that heading, internal causes are then subdivided into reasons and other internal causes. The lowest tier then divides reasons into two types: psychological and situational reasons. In other words, reasons provided by actors for their own behavior are by definition internal attributions but ones which can refer either to psychological or situational factors.

This distinction between psychological and situational reasons is roughly analogous to conceptualizations which separate reasons into those which are *justifications* and those which are *excuses* [18-20]. Justifications are seen to be attempts by actors to maximize desirable aspects or minimize any undesirable aspects of an event, while directly acknowledging the commission of an event. For example, a woman may acknowledge leaving a good job but justify it by noting that it was in the service of securing a better one. In contrast, excuses are seen to be attempts by actors to minimize negative evaluation by pointing to reduced freedom and the presence of extenuating circumstances. Excuses thus allow an actor to claim less than the normal amount of choice. For example, a woman might indicate that she left a good job due to having been transferred.

Kelley also has made the distinction between explanations that are justifications and those which are excuses [19]. The former type of account justifies behavior by defining it as being: 1) in conformity with known values or norms or 2) as something made acceptable because one's intentions were honorable or 3) as being desirable in its own right. Excuses, however, attribute behavior to: 1) extenuating circumstances or 2) other people or objects or 3) the actor's physical or psychological state.

Consequently, one of the objectives of the present study was to develop a more fine-grained way to code actors' reasons for their own job changes. It seems characteristic of actors to go to some pains to point out the particular factors that influenced their actions. Further, it seems reasonable to suppose that the distinctions that actors make when they account for their actions are psychologically meaningful and that a simple bifurcation into internal or external factors may not sufficiently capture what goes into providing an explanation for one's own behavior.

DEVELOPMENT OF THE CODING SYSTEM FOR REASON TYPE

In order to differentiate between different types of reasons, the present study elected to begin with "a careful analysis of language expressions" in order "to arrive at concepts that will enable us to clarify the implicit relations among words referring to psychological phenomena" [7, p. 10]. In other words, the way in which a reason is phrased seems to be an important factor in understanding what tack the actor is taking with respect to justifying her action. Take the reason for leaving a job as being centered on having a baby. Initial review of the responses showed that this apparently simple fact could be variously phrased including, "I wanted to have a baby" or "pregnancy" or "I got pregnant." The locus is internal in all these cases yet the psychological orientation appears different in each one. In the first case, a deliberate goal is stated, whereas in the third case, a passive, almost happenstance occurrence is described. Indeed there is evidence from sociolinguistics [21] that stylistic aspects in a verbal account can convey a great deal about an actor's engagement or disengagement with the thing that he or she describes. Consequently, a coding strategy was devised which sustained the initial concern with cataloging several types of reasons and which based the distinctions between categories on the wording of the response as well as its content.

The resulting coding system consisted of seven categories:

1. Extenuating Circumstances (EC) which describes extenuating circumstances or existing states that prompted or inhibited the job taking or leaving but which were not aspects of the job itself such as "my husband was transferred" or "motherhood." Also included were instances in which the respondent was the object or recipient of some action such as having been transferred or phrased in a passive voice such as "doing what I was trained for."
2. Respondent's Physical or Psychological State (PS) which describes some ongoing physical condition such as illness or pregnancy or some relatively enduring psychological condition such as "depressed" or "bored."
3. Other People (OP) describes the reason as being the result of some action by specified others that affected the job leaving or taking, such as "my boss took me with him" or "my husband felt better about my not working."
4. Intent/Purpose/Goal (IPG) describes the reason as being a goal or a means to a goal such as "to go to college" or "I wanted more experience." The purpose or goal need not be job related. For example, the reason "to take some time off" or "to be with my family" would also be coded as IPG.
5. Job Characteristic (JC) describes some aspect of the work itself that was influential in making the job change including, but not limited to salary, schedule, working conditions or location. Examples would be "it was closer to home" or "a good supervisor." Also included in the job characteristic category were assessments of the job's advantages or disadvantages without a direct personal reference such as a "fine opportunity."
6. Actor's Preference/Belief/Judgment (APB) describes the respondent's preference, considered judgment, or evaluation stated in the first person such as "I preferred teaching to administration" or implied personal assessment such as "I liked staying at home." Also included in this APB category would be statements indicating respondent's values or beliefs such as "I thought it was the best thing to do at the time" or "it was my duty."
7. Job Definition (JD) describes some feature inherent in the job description usually implying some limited aspect such as "medical residency" or "summer job" or "one year visiting appointment."

In sum, each reason was coded into one of these seven categories on the basis of the actual language used by the respondent in the reply. In terms of the earlier example of having a baby, the response was coded as Intent/Purpose/Goal if the reason was phrased as "I wanted to have a baby," but was coded as Physical or Psychological State if the reason was cast as "pregnancy." If the reason was stated instead as "I got pregnant," the Extenuating Circumstance category was coded.

PROCEDURES

Respondents

The data for the results presented here were drawn from a longitudinal study entitled, "Life styles of educated women" [22]. Subjects for the study were female fellowship recipients and members of honorary societies selected from among those women graduate students enrolled in academic departments and professional schools at Columbia University in the years between 1945 and 1951. Respondents were sent lengthy open-ended questionnaires first in 1963 and again twelve years later in 1975. Two hundred and thirty-eight women constituted the sample for the first wave of the study (a response rate of 75%) and 169 (71%) of the original respondents were available for the second wave in 1975. Analysis of the non response bias of the second sample, based on data collected in the first survey, indicated no differences between those who were and were not available for the followup.

At the time of the initial survey, the subjects' median age was forty years and the median educational attainment was master's degree or equivalent. Sixty-nine percent (69%) of the respondents were married and 86 percent of those married had children. Seventy-two percent (72%) of the total sample were employed outside the home (51% full time) and had worked outside the home for an average of twelve years.

Both surveys included extensive inquiries into respondents' family, educational and employment background as well as probing current circumstances.

Reason Coding

The reason giving responses were coded from sections in both data sets which asked the respondents to give their employment history in the years preceding 1963 and between 1963 and 1975. Alongside each job description, space was provided for indicating the reasons for taking and leaving it.

Each reason was coded into only one of the categories but respondents could have more than one category for each job taking or leaving due to the fact that more than one reason could be offered for each choice. A respondent thus received a score on each of the seven possible categories at both testing points which was the product of dividing the total number of times each category was mentioned by the total number of job takings and leavings described.

RESULTS

Letting the Reasons Speak for Themselves

The assumption behind multiple category coding of reasons was that a single internal-external causal distinction was inadequate to encompass how the reasons were actually expressed. Correlation and factor analyses were performed on the reason scores to check on the validity of this assumption. Results supported the distinctions. For example, on face value the EC (Extenuating Circumstances) category is external as is the category JC (Job Characteristics), yet the correlation between them was non-significant ($r = .12$). Similarly the PS category (Physical or Psychological State) apparently refers to an internal state as does Attitude/Preference/Belief (APB), the correlation between them however was also non-significant ($r = .07$). The one significant correlation between IPG (Intent/Purpose/Goal) and EC ($r = -.40$) does however lend support to the idea that these two categories may represent opposite ends of a single intentionality dimension. Additional support for this idea comes from results which show that respondents appealed to the EC category significantly more frequently when leaving as opposed to taking a job; IPG in contrast was used significantly more frequently when taking a job than when leaving it. The untested notion here is that in leaving a job one has or is seen to have less freedom than in taking one. It is worth noting as well that these two categories were the most frequently applied codes with the EC category cited most often followed closely by PIG and JC, then at some distance by APB, JD, PS, and OP respectively.

Revising Reasons

Longitudinal data have a number of advantages and these data proved to be no exception. First, it was possible to ask at the aggregate level whether respondents tended to use the same kinds of reasons across time. Alternatively, one could also inquire as to whether there were cohort or historical trends in the kinds of reasons being cited. At the individual level, this longitudinal data set also afforded the opportunity to look at how taking the same job was explained on two occasions separated by twelve years.

The results show little temporal stability in the reason categories. The correlations among reasons given in 1963 and 1975 were low and non-significant. Similarly analysis of variance using cohort (under or over age 40) and year of testing (1963, 1975) results revealed few main significant effects. Both results can be interpreted to mean that respondents did not stay with the same kinds of reasons over the course of the study but that neither respondent age nor time of testing could account for the observed variability.

At the individual level some interesting changes were in evidence. In 1963 the most recent job taking was explained along with all the jobs that had preceded it. Frequently, this same job was explained again in 1975 although now it was listed as the least most recent in the employment history. If reasons are somehow seen to be attached to the reality of the event at the time that it occurred rather than to the present reformulation of that event then there should be little shift in the reasons given. If however, reasons get revised in the service of the present or in light of subsequent fallout from the original rationale, then one might expect more changes.

In the present case, over a third of the analyzed sample described the same job at the two testing points and of these over half (56%) used *different* reason categories in 1975 than they had originally used in 1963. An example of a change is the following: In 1963 an editor of a small poetry magazine wrote that the reason for taking that job was "an office, a secretary and money for my magazine," each component of which was coded JC. Twelve years later in 1975 she wrote of the same job that the "univeristy offered to subsidize the magazine" which was now coded as OP. Even though the content is similar, the shift in phrasing seems to represent movement from a direct description of the job's benefits from her perspective to a more passive stance of having accepted another agent's intervention. In Kelley's model this corresponds to a shift from a justification to an excuse [19].

Shifts also occurred in the opposite direction, such as from an EC code in 1963 to an IPG code in 1975. In taking a job as an instructor in economics one respondent wrote first that she was "invited to do so" coded as OP; in 1975 she wrote that the reason was that she had "wanted to teach" (coded as IPG). Finally, there were cases of substantial shift in category and content apparently reflecting other changes. A lawyer taking a job in 1963 as a clerk/treasurer in a small town wrote that it was "an ideal way to occupy free time" (coded as JC). In 1975 she said that her reason for taking that job was "an unhappy marriage" (EC).

Changing Situation Meant Changing Reasons

In order to examine the relation between reason giving and work experience across the two testing times of 1963 and 1975, regression analyses were performed on the data using change scores as the dependent and predictor variables. (Separate regression analyses of each time point yielded few significant effects.)

The results showed that the reasons which highly educated women give for job changes are systematically related to labor force participation. Specifically, four different reasons were found to change as the number of hours worked changed. For those women who *increased* the number of hours they worked in a week between 1963 and 1975, there was a significant *decrease* in two reason categories to explain job shifts. Both Extenuating Circumstances and Physical/Psychological State declined as reasons cited. On the other hand, this same increase in hours worked resulted in increased use of IPG (Intent/Purpose/Goal) as well as greater use of JC (Job Characteristic). In other words, more time on the job was associated with less reference to extenuating circumstances and more reference to personal goals and aspects of the job itself.

There were a couple of interesting effects with regard to change in marital status. Getting married resulted in the falling off of IPG and more use of both JC and APB. Those who got married between 1963 and 1975 made less reference to personal goals and more to assessments of the job itself.

CONCLUSIONS

In conclusion, these findings have implications for a number of issues. In the first place, the reasons provided by this group of highly educated women were as varied and extensive as the careers they described. Not infrequently, respondents went considerably beyond the space allotted for the responses. Such elaboration not only provides face validity for studying reasons given in real life contexts but more importantly perhaps, suggests that respondents felt some pressure to provide a satisfactory explanation for the work changes that they made. The fact that many of these women occupied jobs for which they were clearly overqualified may have had something to do with that.

Secondly, the present results show there is validity to a strategy which catalogues reasons multi-dimensionally according to both their content and their formulation. This is in line with recent criticisms of attribution theory which have argued that insufficient attention has been brought to how people actually explain themselves. When ordinary language is taken into account both a greater complexity and cogency emerge. To further distill the range of reasons used by these highly educated women would result in a noticeable loss of external validity.

One implication that derives from this attention to "lay explanations" is the need to know more about how they get adopted and formulated, that is how they come to be part of one's social repertoire. There was enough repetition of reasons across types of jobs to suggest that people learn how to explain themselves. Further, there appears to be a rule which states that job taking decisions should be justified but that job leaving decisions should be excused.

Third, these data provide considerable support for the hypothesis that self-attributions bear an ongoing relationship to actual work experience and so change when it changes. Analyses of the longitudinal data have shown that self-perceptions are less a contributor to real work experience (as attribution theory would have predicted) than they are an outcome of that experience. A change in objective circumstances calls for a change in the subjective rendering of relevant events. Reason giving is dynamic and responsive to work life. For those women who worked less, the profferred reasons reflected their predicaments and plights; for those who worked more the reasons reflected instead their purposes and preferences.

Finally, it appears also that the past is being rewritten by a significant proportion of the respondents. Over half gave different reasons for the same job change when asked on two separate occasions. The fact that there was a twelve year gap may explain some of the variance but evidence from research on the psychology of the self indicates also that as historians of our own lives we are revisionists [9]. Reasons for prior actions may thus be more statements about a person's present than a trustworthy report of her past.

The usual psychological interpretation of changes in personal history is to see them as distorting the facts. However, it might be argued that changes in reasons may reflect warranted reconstruction rather than distortion of the past. At a general level, feminist critical practice points to, and even calls for reevaluation and redefinition of cultural history [23]. At the level of individual history, these data suggest that individual lives are continually being re-viewed and hence hold the opportunity for revision.

REFERENCES

1. E. Goffman, *Relations in Public*, Basic Books, New York, 1971.
2. J. Suls and A. G. Greenwald (eds.), *Psychological Perspectives on the Self (Vol. 2)*, Lawrence Erlbaum Associates, Hillsdale, New Jersey, 1983.
3. C. F. Epstein, *Women's Place: Options and Limits in Professional Careers*, University of California Press, Berkeley, California, 1970.
4. V. Oppenheimer, *The Female Labor Force in the United States: Demographic and Economic Factors Governing Its Growth and Changing Composition*, University of California Press, Population Monograph Series No. 5, Berkeley, California, 1970.
5. R. E. Smith, The Movement of Women into the Work Force, in *The Subtle Revolution: Women at Work*, R. E. Smith (ed.), The Urban Institute, Washington, D.C., 1979.
6. C. Wright Mills, Situated Actions and Vocabularies of Motives, *American Sociological Review*, *5*, pp. 904-913, 1940.
7. F. Heider, *The Psychology of Interpersonal Relations*, Wiley, New York, 1958.
8. H. M. Lefcourt, Internal Versus External Control of Reinforcement: A Review, *Psychological Bulletin*, *65*, pp. 206-220, 1966.
9. A. G. Greenwald, The Totalitarian Ego: Fabrication and Revision of Personal History, *American Psychologist*, *35*, pp. 603-618, 1981.
10. J. H. Harvey, W. Ickes, and R. F. Kidd, *New Directions in Attribution Research (Vol. 1)*, Lawrence Erlbaum Associates, Hillsdale, New Jersey, 1978.
11. A. R. Buss, Causes and Reasons in Attribution Theory: A Conceptual Critique, *Journal of Personality and Social Psychology*, *36*, pp. 1311-1321, 1978.
12. K. S. Donellan, Reasons and Causes, in *Encyclopedia of Philosophy (Vol. 7)*, Macmillan and Free Press, New York, pp. 85-88, 1967.
13. A. C. MacIntyre, Determinism, *Mind*, *66*, 28-41, 1957.
14. A. I. Meldon, *Free Action*, Routledge and Kegan Paul, London, 1961.
15. R. S. Peters, *The Concept of Motivation*, Routledge and Kegan Paul, London, 1958.
16. S. Toulmin, Reasons and Causes, in *Explanation in the Behavioural Sciences*, R. Borger and F. Cioffi (eds.), Cambridge University Press, London, 1970.
17. D. Locke and D. Pennington, Reasons and Other Causes: Their Role in Attribution Processes, *Journal of Personality and Social Psychology*, *42*, pp. 212-223, 1982.

18. J. Austin, A Plea for Excuses, in *Philosophic Papers*, J. L. Austin (ed.), Oxford University Press, London, 1961.
19. H. H. Kelley, *Personal Relationships: Their Structures and Processes*, Lawrence Erlbaum Associates, Hillsdale, New Jersey, 1979.
20. B. Schlenker, *Impression Management: The Self Concept, Social Identity and Interpersonal Relations*, Brooks/Cole, Monterey, California, 1980.
21. A. Mehrabian, Verbal and Nonverbal Interaction of Strangers in a Waiting Situation, *Journal of Experimental Research in Personality*, *5*, pp. 127-138, 1971.
22. E. Ginzberg et al., *Educated American Women: Life Style and Self Portraits*, Columbia University Press, New York, 1971.
23. S. M. Gilbert and S. Gubar, *The Madwoman in the Attic: The Woman Writer and the Nineteenth-Century Imagination*, Yale University Press, New Haven, Connecticut, 1979.

PART IV

Dichotomizing Sex and Gender: The Use of Fiction

The chapters in this section represent a more interdisciplinary synthesis than those in other sections of the book. They were written by scholars from psychology, human development, literary criticism, and sociology. What they all have in common, however, is the use of fiction. Fiction is particularly useful for social constructionism because it enables us to examine multiple viewpoints without having to sustain a belief in one true reality. Fiction permits us to examine sex and gender as forms of negotiated understanding in contrast to a view of them as fixed and universal properties of individuals independent of social or temporal context.

John and Sussman manipulated informational cues relevant to gender in the course of a fictional narrative about the interaction of two persons whose sex was unspecified. They found that people constructed sexual categories for the two stimulus persons which reflected cultural ideology about the opposite nature of the two sexes even at the expense of available objective information to the contrary. It seems that people prefer to be misinformed rather than deal with ambiguous categories in these areas.

Datan examined the concept of androgyny by reconstructing the *Bacchae* from a gendered point of view. She suggests that coming to terms with androgyny may be an important life crisis in the middle years. She suggests that the tragedy of the young king may be seen as a tragedy provoked by cultural definitions of maleness and femaleness as separate and opposite. Datan also points out that androgyny is not a new concept, but one that has been rediscovered and lost as cultural beliefs about sex have changed.

Hartman analyzed the female characters in some of George Eliot's novels in terms of their inability to surmount their century's beliefs about sex and gender. She suggests that although Eliot's female characters appear to have a more multifaceted sensibility than her male characters, they are unable to function independently in the public domain. Although Eliot was aware of unfair societal constraints on women and in a limited way was able to circumvent them, she was not able to offer her female characters a freedom she, herself, was not able to achieve.

Fiction offers a way to consider societal constraints in a non-threatening arena—the not here and not now. Fine and her associates offer an annotated bibliography of some past and current speculative fiction examining sex and gender. While such fiction indicates alternatives to current domestic and societal arrangements, even feminist "professional speculators" have difficulty envisioning a future unconstrainted by the constructs of the present.

In a final chapter, Farganis asks us to think about the uses and limits of social constructionism. Through her examination of Margaret Atwood's dystopia, *The Handmaid's Tale*, Farganis cautions us that if any aspect of life can be socially constructed, the problem becomes whose social constructs will be the accepted ones. Those who have power in society also have the power to impose their definitions upon us all. Farganis is particularly concerned about current reconstructions of the female body as a vehicle for childbearing.

These chapters also raise many questions. Under what circumstances will people stop trying to preserve their belief structures at the expense of objective information contrary to their beliefs? Why are we so resistant to any definitions of sex and gender which attempt to transcend dichotomies? Does the awareness of a constraining reality make it easier to bear? Does the awareness of alternative potential realities make one more receptive to social change? What are the societal implications of social constructionism? Finally, is there any such thing as a truly "safe" conceptual change?

FURTHER READINGS

Becker, H. S. Whose Side Are We On? *Social Problems*, *14*, pp. 239-247, 1967.

Helson, R. Through the Pages of Children's Books and What a Psychologist Found There, *Psychology Today*, *7*:6, pp. 107-112, 1973.

Jagger, A. M. *Feminist Politics and Human Nature*, Rowman and Allanheld, Totowa, New Jersey, 1983.

Kaufman, D. R. and B. L. Richardson. *Achievement and Women: Challenging the Assumptions*, The Free Press, New York, 1982.

Lorber, J. Dismantling Noah's Ark, *Sex Roles*, *14*, pp. 567-580, 1986.

CHAPTER 19

Initiative Taking as a Determinant of Role-Reciprocal Organization

BERTRAM A. JOHN
LORI E. SUSSMAN

Asch suggested that we tend to organize bits of information about a person into cohesive, stable units. These units or person percepts are not unlike the units formed when we perceive "things." [1] Two principles emerged from the early person perception literature:

1. the notion that there are some central, densely organized traits around which impressions are formed; and
2. the notion that the order in which information is received will influence the way in which impressions are formed.

Typically, there is a strong primacy effect when impressions are formed from serially presented information.

Much of the early work on person perception focused on the person as the appropriate unit of study and impression formation as the dependent variable. As such, theories in this Gestalt tradition tend to explore and to explain patterns of impression formation in terms of information presented serially about a single individual [2].

With the growing influence of cognitive approaches to impression formation, and particularly with the interests derived from developmental approaches to social cognition, it has become important to explore whether impressions once formed remain stable over time or are transformed as they interact with other impressions (in memory or in the flow of information) and whether under more appropriate conditions (i.e., when there is an ambient flow of information) the centrality of traits and the order effects noted by Asch remain effective.

Cognitive approaches to social cognition have traditionally stressed that the individual constructs reality by acting on or interpreting events in the environment. As such, the individual's knowledge both affects and is affected by the *interaction.* Bartlett utilized the concept of schema to describe an inherent structure through which stimulus information is reconstructed as it is interpreted. For him, the schema represented a dynamic constructive process which was uncovered through a method utilizing serial reproductions of stories. Bartlett's research suggested that structures can best be understood in their temporal context. This suggestion echoed a position taken by the Gestaltists (Koffka, 1935) that organization is temporally extended transformation based on the interaction among the parts which comprise the whole and between the parts and the whole [3].

Piaget makes explicit the importance of the interactions within internal (structures) schemata and between these schemata and the external world to the process of development. As he points out, these interactions lead to reorganization and reconstruction [4]. The development of social constructs has been further explored by several investigators, particularly in the domain of perspective taking [5-7].

What is interesting about this line of research is that it begins to connect social cognition to its developmental roots. There is growing evidence that children move through a series of stages in perspective taking abilities roughly equivalent to the development of conservation abilities reported by Piaget.

The idea that social cognition depends upon how we interpret, or construct, the role of the "other" relative to the "self" in some self-other configuration led some researchers to examine the emergent organization of children's understanding of social roles [5-7]. This approach has proved valuable in the investigation of ontogenetic development.

A further direction in social cognition also utilizing schematic assumptions is the growing area of "schematic processing." Neisser suggests that schemata provide ideas or hypotheses about stimuli, so that no information can be handled by the organism if there is not a schema through which it can become meaningful [8]. The effort to understand the role of social schemata has been undertaken in several ways, e.g., script schemata, person schemata, schemata for complex stories, and person memory, which examines the value of personality traits as temporally extended organizing structures [9-12].

These approaches share a common assumption that there are inherent structures (schemata) which provide a commonly shared frame of reference for certain social episodes. Such an interpretation bears striking similarity to Asch's idea of organization, and suggests an underlying theoretical unity among the various approaches to the study of social cognition.

The research undertaken in the present study emerges from the neo-Gestalt view that

a. The principles of organization described by Wertheimer can be understood in terms of grouping by belongingness, and this "belongingness" can be perceptual or conceptual so it can be seen in both spatial and temporal terms [13].

b. Temporal organization requires the integration of new information into the existing Gestalt, but there is a problem posed by the fact that not all new information is likely to fit the existing structure. In such cases one of two possibilities exist, either the new information is distorted to fit the existing structure (Asch's central trait and Bartlett's cultural schema) or the existing structure is reorganized. Evidence for this pattern has been demonstrated by John and Komada recently, and bears a relationship to Piaget's notion of accommodation [14].

c. The organization of information must be studied contextually. In such a way the rules underlying the continuity of experience can be better appreciated [15]. To study experience contextually, we must appreciate the role of the self as an integral aspect of the context. This issue is particularly pertinent to current efforts in social cognition to describe the role of the self in our knowledge of the surround, and was posed by both Koffka and Asch [16]. Recent efforts to explore the relationship have been undertaken by Komada and John in a study of social cognition and by John in a study of visual memory [17].

Recent findings from research into self-presentational processes suggest that individuals will adjust their behavior in accordance with the stereotypic views they assumed were held by the other person in a dyadic relationship. Zanna and Pack demonstrated that female undergraduates will describe their behavior in a manner consistent with the stereotypes suggested by the ideology of a "desirable" male Princeton senior [18]. Von Bayer, Sherk, and Zanna found that expectations about the social beliefs of male interviewers were related to the behavior and appearance of female job applicants [19]. Skrypnek and Snyder found that perceivers' beliefs about the sex of a target influenced the direction of the behavior of the target on a gender-based division of labor [20]. These studies focused on the relationship between belief and action, but they also demonstrate that assumptions about the "other" in a social interaction will influence the shape of the overall flow of information. They also suggest an importance methodological consideration for research into social cognition, i.e., the importance of the context in which role-reciprocal organization emerges.

THE ROLE-TAKING TASK

Role taking has been used as a measure of ontogenesis in social cognition on the assumption that Piaget's concept of decentering can be applied to levels of role-taking activity. Evidence in support of this assumption has been provided by Feffer and Gourevitch in an empirical test of the relationship between the degrees of balanced decentering in children's performance on the role-taking task (RTT) and intellectual performance across Piaget's stages of cognitive development [21]. Further demonstrations of ontogenesis utilizing role-taking have been provided by Chandler and Kohlberg [7].

The rationale for the RTT is that levels of role-taking can be measured by the degree of balance in decentering activity, that a positive correlation exists between age group and level of role taking, and that this corresponds to the relationship between the degree of balanced decentering and stage level as measured by Piaget's impersonal cognitive tasks. Feffer and Gourevitch describe a hierarchial series of performance levels ranging from:

a. simple refocusing – the subject can take the perspective of a given story character and have that character reflect on herself or himself;
b. character elaboration – the subject can refocus on a given story character and have that character refocus on another character;
c. perspective elaboration – the subject in addition to the above must indicate the appropriate inner-oriented framework for the role being taken, and an outer-oriented framework for the other character(s); and
d. change of perspective – the subject must be able to reverse the perspectives described in c. above with appropriate shifts in the inner-outer orientation.

Two important considerations must be examined here. First, any role-taking task is a projective task. As such, we might assume that to take a role means that qualities of the self are being projected onto that role. Degrees of decentering would essentially mean that different patterns of interaction between the self as the subject and as the object of experience can be observed. Secondly, since the patterns of development described by Feffer and Gourevitch apply to the ontogeny of role-taking ability an examination of the more subtle changes which emerge in adult processing of the flow of social information requires a microgenetic approach. Such an approach was undertaken by Phillips, Broverman and Zigler who found patterns of differentiation and integration in Rorschach responses. (These patterns were consistent with the hierarchial organization proposed by Werner.) [21-23].

We are – in the present investigation – utilizing a measurement based on this microgenetic approach. We can therefore describe the patterns formed by the interaction between self-as-subject of experience and self-as-object of experience in the temporal context, the story. Here, integration can be understood to involve the development of sufficiently flexible decentering to coordinate both elaborated perspectives across the transitions in our story. Differentiation can be understood to involve the elaboration of one perspective (along with the rigidification of the other, such that this perspective becomes egocentric). This pattern may vary across transitions such that while each perspective may be elaborated at some point, the schema is insufficiently flexible to coordinate both perspectives. Finally, globality can be understood to involve the mutual isolation of perspectives such that the interaction is characterized by rigidity of the schema.

This approach also allows us to describe the strategies which might be utilized to achieve the patterns of organization described above and the relationship they bear to organization.

THE STUDY

The present study explores the evolution of subjects' constructions of role-reciprocal relationships in a story involving two protagonists who were differentiated only by the colors of their shirt buttons and by the initiatives each took across three transitions in the story. At each transition, a change occurs in the identity of the protagonist who takes an initiative. In this context, initiative taking can be defined as the expression of a point of view which changes the direction of a social interaction. In the present case, these interactions involved a potential romantic encounter in the course of which the interchange between two protagonists undergoes a series of adjustments characterized by shifts in the degree of initiative-taking exhibited by each protagonist (see Figure 1). We were interested in how subjects attributed gender and intention to each protagonist and whether those constructions permitted them to maintain intra-role and inter-role consistency as well as integrity of the story line.

We reasoned that any characteristic attributed to our ambiguous protagonists would represent the schemata through which subjects made sense of them. As such, we would be able to examine and measure the pattern of change in subjects' descriptions of the protagonists after each transition in the story. Such changes would represent transformations in schemata. We could therefore detect the pattern of stability and fluctuation between and within role schemata. Furthermore, we could examine the relationship between roles and the story, so that we could determine whether role schemata are at times sufficiently rigid to cause distortion in the details of the story. Finally, we expected that this format would allow us to examine the role of primacy in the organization of social information presented over time.

Method

Fifty-four subjects (twenty-seven female and twenty-seven male undergraduates at Montclair State College) volunteered to participate in the study. They were tested in random groups of approximately ten. Subjects were provided booklets containing the story with the baseline information and each of the three transitions in the story on separate pages. They were instructed to pretend to be each of the protagonists in the story (see Figure 1) and to answer the questions that followed in the first person, as though they were the relevant protagonist. (A trial run with a different story segment was utilized to ascertain that the instructions were well understood.) Each phase of the story was read aloud by the experimenter and subjects were asked to read along subvocally.

The scene is a "singles" bar located in a middle-sized town. Some people are dancing in one section of the room. Others are sitting or standing around the bar drinking and socializing. An individual with brown shirt buttons (Brown Buttons) walks purposefully towards a person with gray shirt buttons (Gray Buttons) and begins a conversation. After a few minutes, Brown Buttons asks Gray Buttons to dance. Gray Buttons agrees, and they begin to move to the dancing area.

Transition 1 [Gray Buttons Initiates Change in the Direction of the Interaction]

As they start to dance, Gray Buttons says to Brown Buttons, "You are a good dancer. I don't come across many people who dance this well."

"Thank you," says Brown Buttons with a slightly embarrassed smile. "I think you dance well too."

"What do you do for a living?" asks Gray Buttons.

"I'm a high school teacher," answers Brown Buttons, "and you?"

"I'm a research technician," says Gray Buttons, "but I'm thinking of getting into computers."

As the music comes to an end, Gray Buttons says, "You *are* a very interesting person. I'd like us to talk some more . . . why don't we sit over here?," motioning to a small table in the corner.

Transition 2 [Gray Buttons Initiates Change in the Direction of the Interaction]

They've been sitting for quite a while. Brown Buttons orders drinks again, and they continue to talk . . . . "I'm really fascinated by your life; I'd like to get to know you better."

"That's interesting," says Gray Buttons. "I find you exciting too, but I'm not sure that I'm able to handle too much familiarity now. I'm really interested in pursuing my career . . . . "

Transition 3 [Gray Buttons Initiates Change in the Direction of the Interaction]

"I understand your position," says Brown Buttons, "but I'd really like to see more of you."

"I'm going to think about it," says Gray Buttons . . . . "Why don't we stop off at my place? Perhaps we'd both get some perspective over coffee and . . . . "

Figure 1. Baseline [brown buttons initiates the interaction].

After the baseline information was presented and at the end of the story subjects recorded the age and sex of each protagonist. They also indicated which protagonist was more like them (with explanations).

After each transition subjects recorded the age and sex of the protagonists and answered questions about the thoughts, feelings, plans and expected resolutions from the perspectives of both protagonists.

Results

Gender assignments and shifts across transitions – Eighty-nine percent of all subjects (89% of male subjects and 89% of female subjects) described Brown Buttons (BB) as male and Gray Buttons (GB) as female. Three male subjects and two females reversed this description, and a single female saw the protagonists as indeterminate regarding sex (Table 1).

At Transition 1, 63 percent of female subjects described BB as female and GB as male, i.e., 67 percent of those who initially described BB as male and GS as female now switched their descriptions.

Twenty-four percent of the female maintained their original descriptions (BB = male; GB = female). Two subjects who initially described BB as female and GB as male and the subject who assigned no gender maintained their original descriptions.

For male subjects a different pattern emerges. Sixty-three percent maintained the original gender assignments; 30.7 percent now represented BB as female rather than male and 3.7 percent switched from female to male (Table 2).

At Transition 2, 36.7 percent of male subjects and 54 percent of female subjects switched gender assignments of BB from female to male, and at Transition 3, 18.5 percent of male subjects and 7.7 percent of female subjects switched BB's gender from male to female. (When subjects switched the gender assignments for BB a reciprocal switch was made in the gender assignment for GB).

Across transitions, then, there was a decreasing tendency to switch genders. However, it is significant that substantial proportions of subjects were willing to switch genders on the basis of the initiatives taken by the protagonists.

Age shifts across transitions – At Transition 1, a majority of female (50%) and male (59.4%) subjects increased the ages assigned to BB. At Transition 2, 32 percent of the females and 52 percent of the males continued to increase BB's age. However, at Transition 3, 20 percent of the females and 26 percent of the males increased BB's age. There was an increasing tendency across transitions to report the ages as equivalent. This tendency to shift ages in relation to the initiatives taken by both protagonists shows similar characteristics to the shifts in assigned gender noted above.

Role consistency – Loss of role taking was measured by failure to respond in the first person. Our results show that at Transition 1, 30 percent of subjects show some loss of role taking. This figure falls to 17 percent after Transition 2

Table 1. Gender Assignments across Transitions (Percentages Rounded Off)

	Percentages											
	Baseline			*Transition 1*			*Transition 2*			*Transition 3*		
	M	*F*	*(None)*	*M*	*F*	*(None)*	*M*	*F*	*(None)*	*M*	*F*	*(None)*
Male Subjects												
BB	89	11		63	37		96	4		82	19	
GB	11	89		37	63		4	96		19	82	
Female Subjects												
BB	89	7	3	27	70	4	81	19	0	77	23	0
GB	7	89	3	70	27	4	19	81	0	23	77	0

Table 2. Shifts of Gender Assignments across Transitions

	Percentages		
	Transition 1	*Transition 2*	*Transition 3*
Male Subjects			
BB	M → F 30.7%	M → F 0%	M → F 18.5%
GB	F → M 3.7%	F → M 36.7%	F → M 0%
Female Subjects			
BB	M → F 69.9%	M → F 0%	M → F 7.7%
GB	M → F 0%	M → F 54.0%	M → F 3.9%

and to 4 percent after Transition 3. Loss of role taking was never accompanied by confusion with role assignments or with the information in the story.

Microgenetic analysis – Role-taking activity was measured for degree of decentering (see Figure 2). Three categoires, consistent with the orthogenetic principle, were outlined:

1. Global – Roles were constructed independently, i.e., while intra-role consistency might be maintained throughout the story, the self as subject did not interact with, or take the perspective of, self as object, or vice versa. In Piagetian terms, we might refer to this construction as mutual egocentrism.
2. Differentiation – Roles were constructed such that self as subject *or* as object could reverse perspective, but both could not do so during the same transition.
3. Integration – Roles and their reciprocals reversed perspectives in the same transition and exhibited balanced decentering in both cognitions and affect.

To explore the possibility that transformations occurred in role-taking activity, we tabulated the proportion and direction of change across transitions. We found that over 44 percent of those role-reciprocals that were constructed

1. Globalization (Without Character Elaboration)

Transition 1	*As BB*	*As GB*
What are you thinking?	"fun"	"relaxed"
Why do you think that?	"I'm at a bar"	"nice place"
How do you feel?	"good"	"having a nice time"
Why?	"drinking"	"nice place"

2. Globalization (With Character Elaboration)

Transition 1	*As BB*	*As GB*
What are you thinking?	"sex"	"horny"
Why do you think that?	"She came on"	"I've been drinking"
How do you feel?	"willing"	"a little drunk"

3. Differentiation

Transition 2	*As BB*	*As GB*
What are you thinking?	"She really broke my bubble"	"my career"
Why do you think that?	"She was leading me on"	"because of what I just told him"

4. Integration

Transition 2	*As BB*	*As GB*
What are you thinking?	"I guess she isn't too sure about me. It's too early."	"I really want him to be aware about how important my career is."
Why do you think that?	"She's pulling away"	"He seems interested. I want things to be clear."

Figure 2. Samples of role-taking activity at various orthogenetic levels.

independently of each other at the first transition were differentiated in the second transition. This same proportion remained differentiated at the third transition (Table 3). We further found that when we distinguished between those global organizations with one character elaborated (CE) and those with neither character elaborated, 100 percent of the non-elaborated organizations remained so at Transitions 2 and 3, while 61.5 percent of those character elaborated organizations were transformed to differentiated organizations at Transitions 2 and 3 (Table 4).

Organizations in which roles and their reciprocals were differentiated at Transition 1 showed an interesting pattern of change at Transitions 2 and 3. Over 14 percent of these organizations became integrated at Transition 2 and 32 percent became integrated at Transition 3. At Transition 2, 3.6 percent were transformed into global organizations, but none maintained this organization at Transition 3 (Table 5).

Finally, organizations at Transition 1 in which roles and their reciprocals were integrated substantially remained so across Transitions 2 and 3. Only 12.5 percent of these organizations were transformed to differentiated role-reciprocals at Transition 2, and none changed at Transition 3 (Table 6).

We next examined those conditions where consistent patterns of gender assignment occurred throughout the story. We found two such patterns. One of these involved stability in gender assignments across transitions, $N = 21$ (Men = 66.6%). We found a relationship between the gender of the participant and the degree of change in organization across transitions. For example, women's initial organizations (at Transition 1) invariably involved differentiated role-reciprocals, and demonstrated substantial transformation towards integration – from 43 percent differentiated at Transition 1, to 71.4 percent integrated at Transition 3. For men, 57.1 percent constructed global organizations at Transition 1, and only 9 percent constructed integrated organizations at Transition 3.

The second popular pattern of gender assignments involved a shift at the first transition and then stability across Transitions 2 and 3. In the more common of these patterns, $N = 21$ (Women = 13%), BB was described as a male at baseline, as female at Transition 1, and as male at subsequent transitions. Here, a similar pattern emerged in organization across transitions. Women's initial organizations were predominantly differentiated role-reciprocal, 92.3 percent. These reduced across Transitions 2 and 3, from 84.6 percent to 54 percent, respectively, while integrated organizations increased from none at Transition 1 to 15.4 percent and 46.2 percent at Transitions 2 and 3, respectively. Males' initial organizations tended to be globalized, 71.4 percent at Transition 1, and change was primarily towards differentiation (43% at Transitions 2 and 3).

These results suggest that while males were more likely to maintain gender assignments, these assignments were rigid, and little influenced by new information. In this case, the primacy effect served the interest of stability rather than of development.

DISCUSSION

The results indicate that subjects utilize particular schemata for organizing information over time. It is significant that all subjects inferred a heterosexual interaction so that shifts in the assignments of gender to one protagonist were accompanied by reciprocal shifts in the assignment of gender to the other. In

Table 3. Change in Role-Reciprocal Organization across Transitions 2 and 3 When Role-Reciprocals Are Global at Transition 1

	Percent		
N = 18	*Integrated*	*Differentiated*	*Globalized*
Transition 2	–	44.4	55.6
Transition 3	–	44.4	55.6

Table 4. Change in Role-Reciprocal Organization across Transitions 2 and 3 When Global Role-Reciprocals at Transition 1 Are Separated by Degree of Character Elaboration (CE)

	Percent					
	Integrated		*Differentiated*		*Globalized*	
N = 18	*One CE*	*No CE*	*One CE*	*No CE*	*One CE*	*No CE*
Transition 2	–	–	61.5	–	38.5	100
Transition 3	–	–	61.5	–	38.5	100

Table 5. Change in Role-Reciprocal Organization across Transitions 2 and 3 When Role-Reciprocals Are Differentiated at Transition 1

	Percent		
N = 28	*Integrated*	*Differentiated*	*Globalized*
Transition 2	14.3	82.1	3.6
Transition 3	32.1	64.3	–

Table 6. Change in Role-Reciprocal Organization across Transitions 2 and 3 When Role-Reciprocals Are Integrated at Transition 1

	Percent		
N = 8	*Integrated*	*Differentiated*	*Globalized*
Transition 2	87.5	12.5	–
Transition 3	100	–	–

effect, the stability of these reciprocals was often achieved at the expense of intra-role consistency and story integrity. It can be argued that the organization of the flow of information around gender assignment was most salient so that tolerance for distortion was considerable.

In the present case, information was reorganized by existing social schemata into gender determination based upon the strength of the initiatives taken by one protagonist *vis a vis* the other. This pattern of organization was consistent through the first two transitions in the story. However, another factor in social cognition has emerged here. There is a strong tendency towards stability in the assignment of gender and age as the story progresses. This would suggest that as the event unfolds, each protagonist becomes more stably represented in consciousness and, as intra-role consistency increases the consistency in the relationship between roles, the integrity of the story line also increases.

The pattern of role-taking loss supports this argument. Subjects demonstrated decreasing loss of role-taking consistency as the story unfolded. By itself, this finding might be explained as simply a case of increasing familiarity with the task. However, it seems noteworthy that the loss of role taking occurred when shifts in gender and age assignments were most dramatic (i.e., when the roles were most unstable).

When we examine the task facing our subjects, some of the components of organization become tangible. In order for a structure to become transformed, some interaction had to take place between characters from the perspective of at least one of them. No change occurred when one character was not elaborated sufficiently to view the other character "from the inside out." A deeper understanding of this type of cognitive interaction would provide an explanation of how cognitive "belongingness" is determined in relation to temporal context. The fact that our subjects were required to make sense of what was occurring at a given transition in conjunction with what occurred previously meant that considerable flexibility would characterize the organization (schema) that coordinated these sometimes ambiguous, sometimes contradictory characters' experiences. The pattern of microgenesis seems to represent an unfolding of increasingly integrative organizations, but we think it premature to suggest that this pattern is unidirectional. Patterns of fluctuation do occur, and these need to be explored systematically. A microgenetic approach seems advantageous for such a task.

With respect to temporal effects on role organization, we can argue that the assignment of age and gender reflected hypotheses being generated by the system. When these hypotheses were tested against the flow of information, appropriate adjustments were made and these adjustments led to increasingly stable constructs which were more inclusive.

We think it fruitful to characterize the patterns of stability we have observed (see Tables 3 through 6) as temporally more extended interactions produced by the flexibility of the organization, or by the elimination of new information.

Some subjects utilized distortion (either adding or subtracting information) at either or both the character and story levels.

The consequence over time for the self when information is distorted seems to represent a significant applied research issue.

This approach has the advantage of providing insights into the dynamic nature of social cognition, but its limitations are evident. A systematic definition of terms is required. We are aware that a task such as this elicits certain expectations from our subjects, but our interest is in the *constructive* process as it applies to social knowledge. In this approach, we are more concerned with the description of change itself, rather than in the shape produced by change at some arbitrary point. We suggest that the relationship between ontogenesis and microgenesis needs to be empirically defined. Our results suggest that there is both a theoretical and methodological basis for exploring this option. Apparently, some continuity exists among the various aspects of cognitive development. The relationship between the self and the impersonal world has been theoretically proposed by Piaget that between the self and the interpersonal world has been demonstrated by Kohlberg [24], Feffer, Chandler and others. The context for examining the interactions which comprise these experiences has been formulated by the Gestaltists and neo-Gestaltists. We have attempted to demonstrate that a focus on the emergence of knowledge in the social/interpersonal context represents an ecologically viable approach to discovering the rules which apply to the study of the self in its total relation to knowledge.

REFERENCES

1. S. E. Asch, Forming Impressions of Personality, *Journal of Abnormal and Social Psychology, 41,* pp. 258-290, 1946.
2. F. Heider, *The Psychology of Interpersonal Relations,* John Wiley and Sons, New York, 1958.
3. F. C. Bartlett, *Remembering: A Study in Experimental and Social Psychology,* Cambridge University Press, Cambridge, United Kingdom, 1932.
4. J. Piaget, *The Moral Judgement of the Child,* Harcourt Brace and World, New York, 1932.
5. M. Feffer, The Cognitive Implications of Role-Taking Behavior, *Journal of Personality, 27,* pp. 152-168, 1959.
6. A. J. Sameroff and M. J. Chandler, *Review of Child Development Research,* F. Horowitz (ed.), University of Chicago Press, Chicago, Illinois, 1975.
7. M. J. Chandler, *Social Cognition and Life-Span Approaches to the Study of Child Development,* unpublished paper, University of Rochester, New York, 1976.
8. U. Neisser, *Cognition and Reality: Principles and Implications of Cognitive Psychology,* Freeman Press, San Francisco, California, 1976.

9. R. C. Shank and R. P. Abelson, *Scripts, Plans, Goals and Understanding,* Earlbaum, Hillsdale, New Jersey, 1977.
10. N. Cantor and W. Mischel, *Advances in Experimental Social Psychology, Vol. 12,* L. Berkowitz (ed.), Academic Press, New York, 1979.
11. G. H. Bower, J. B. Black, and J. T. Turner, Scripts in Text Comprehension and Memory, *Cognitive Psychology, 11,* pp. 177-220, 1979.
12. R. Hastie and P. A. Kumar, Person Memory: Personality Traits as Organizing Principles in Memory for Behaviors, *Journal of Personality and Social Psychology, 37,* pp. 25-38, 1979.
13. M. Wertheimer, *Productive Thinking,* Harper Torchbooks/Harper and Row, New York, 1959.
14. B. A. John and K. A. Komada, *Microgenesis in Social Cognition: A Role-Reciprocal Analysis,* unpublished manuscript.
15. D. Dinnerstein, Previous and Concurrent Visual Experience as Determinants of Phenomenal Shape, *American Journal of Psychology, 78,* pp. 235-242, 1965.
16. K. Koffka, *Principles of Gestalt Psychology,* Harcourt, Brace and World, New York, 1935.
17. B. A. John, Context Effects on Memory for Form, *Dissertation Abstracts International, 41,* p. 1141B, 1980.
18. M. P. Zanna and S. J. Pack, On the Self-Fulling Nature of Apparent Sex Differences in Behavior, *Journal of Experimental Social Psychology, 11,* pp. 583-591, 1975.
19. C. L. von Bayer, D. L. Sherk, and M. P. Zanna, *Impression Management in the Job Interview: When the Female Applicant Meets the Male (Chauvinist) Interviewer,* unpublished manuscript, University of Waterloo, Canada, 1978.
20. B. J. Skrypnek and M. Snyder, *On the Self-Perpetuating Nature of Stereotypes about Women and Men,* unpublished manuscript, University of Minnesota.
21. M. H. Feffer and V. Gourevitch, Cognitive Aspects of Role-Taking in Children, *Journal of Personality, 28,* pp. 384-396, 1960.
22. L. Phillips, I. K. Broverman, and E. Zigler, Sphere Dominance, Role Orientation, and Diagnosis, *Journal of Abnormal Psychology, 73,* pp. 306-312, 1968.
23. H. Werner, *The Comparative Psychology of Mental Development,* International Universities Press, New York, 1948.
24. L. Kohlberg, *Moral Development, New Directions for Child Development, No. 2,* W. Damon (ed.), Jossey-Bass, San Francisco, California, 1978.

CHAPTER 20

Androgyny and the Life Cycle: The Bacchae of Euripides

NANCY DATAN

This chapter is an effort to bridge the gap between life cycle views of androgyny, as seen in the work of Jung, Gutmann, and others, and trait views of androgyny, as found in the work of Sandra Bem and others. This bridge will span not merely sub-fields of psychology but centuries of literary criticism. My thesis is twofold: first, I shall suggest that the incorporation of Greek tragic heroes into the literature of developmental psychology, as well as the literary interpretation of Greek tragedy, are subject to all the constraints imposed by any sociology of knowledge, and can be shown to reflect selective blindness as well as selective incorporation; second, I shall argue that evidence for the lifelong adaptive value of androgyny can be found in The Bacchae of Euripides, a drama of intergenerational strife and the war between the sexes.

ANDROGYNY AND ADAPTATION

Developmental and social psychological views of androgyny proceed from a common premise: that the androgynous individual is responsive to adaptive demands placed by the environment. These views differ with respect to the nature and timing of these demands. The developmental view is distinguished by the premise of innate bisexuality, shaped into age-related sex roles or sex role transcendance. Jung has remarked that the second half of life is compensation for the first; Gutmann argues that the birth of a child ushers in the "chronic emergency of parenthood," with its bureaucratization of sexuality [1]. At this stage of the life cycle, Gutmann proposes, the child's needs for nurturance are best served by a mother who surrenders her aggressive, managerial needs to the father, who in turn must surrender his passive, dependency needs to the mother in order to secure a living for the family. As the child's dependency comes to an end, and with it the chronic emergency of parenthood, the period of "the normal unisex of later life" begins, in which the middle-aged woman reclaims her aggressive and managerial self and the middle-aged man gives expression to his own needs for passive, dependent nurturance.

The social psychological view of androgyny is based on the study of traits associated with typically masculine or typically feminine behavior. Bem's androgyny scale was developed on the assumption that these traits could be measured independently; she defined androgyny as a relative balance between the masculine and the feminine. It has subsequently been argued that relative balance alone is not enough: as Unger puts it, "A truly androgynous person has a large measure of the characteristics of both sexes," with the obvious adaptive advantage of access to a wider range of behaviors [2, p. 163].

For some developmental psychologists then, the emergence of sex-typed behaviors is an adaptive response timed by events in the family life cycle; social psychologists suggest that the androgynous individual is at an adaptive advantage at any point in the life cycle. In this chapter, I shall seek to reconcile these points of view by suggesting that while androgyny may be adaptive throughout the life cycle, sexual anxiety—and with it, sex-stereotyped behavior—may be maturationally timed, and that the "normal unisex of later life" may be the consequence of the ebbing of sexual anxieties of young adulthood.

As each of us remembers from the schoolyard, however, and as Deaux [3] and others have shown, masculine and feminine traits are not equally valued: a girl may be a tomboy and win some grudging praise, but woe to the gentle boy who is called a sissy. We might expect, then, that an admixture of masculine and feminine traits is more easily achieved by women, who take on some of the preferred traits of masculinity, than by men, for whom androgyny means incorporation of the devalued traits of masculinity. As the discussion of The Bacchae will show, Euripides wove this truth into the fabric of his tragedy: indeed, the overvaluation of masculinity in young adulthood will be seen to be the flaw on which the doom of Pentheus hangs.

THE INCOMPLETE LESSONS OF GREEK TRAGEDY

Psychological interest in Greek tragedy has been selectively stimulated by the counterintuitive ever since Aristotle wrote the Poetics and singled out Oedipus as the epitome of the man with the tragic flaw. Aristotle's insights were carried forward into the twentieth century by Freud, who recognized that classical drama survived if it contained eternal tension—in the case of Oedipus Rex, the unconscious tension of the incestuous boy, whose appeal presumably reached the lustful five-year-old in everyone's heart.

So far, so good. But a number of significant characters in Greek tragedy have failed to make the grade in psychological literature despite the fact that evidence for eternal tensions, which they might reasonably be considered to represent, abounds. Among these are King Laius, the father of Oedipus Rex, who sets the drama of his own demise in motion with the intentional murder of his infant son–his intentions thwarted by the compassion of the servant charged with the deed–and his wife and widow Jocasta, whose reported suicide is prelude to the tragedy's conclusion, and whose voice lives on through a messenger's report after her death, telling and retelling her dreadful deed, her sexual congress with her son. Clinical evidence for the Oedipus complex can be marshalled, to be sure; but evidence that children are the victims of their parents' sexual passions and murderous rages is no less abundant. Thus the reading of Greek tragedy, I suggest, has been self-serving, guided perhaps by the wounded vanity of the adult who recognizes the latent strength of childhood passions but considers the superior strength of adult passion no more than the adult's just reward [4].

Exclusion of The Bacchae from the group of tragedies and tragic heroes which are part of popular consciousness, such as Oedipus and Medea, represents, I suggest, a special case of self-serving selective vision. If Oedipus represents a wound to the vanity of the adult, the wound is easy to bandage. This son grew up to murder his father, but after all, he tried not to–a fact which contributes to the dramatic tension of the tragedy but detracts somewhat from the psychological thesis–and when his tragedy is ended, he has been suitably punished. A father would not go home from a performance of this drama fearing his son.

The message of The Bacchae is less comforting. The Bacchae reaches its tragic climax with the murder of the young king Pentheus by his mother Agave–thus it is one more instance of the murder of children by parents, a relatively unremarkable event unlikely to perturb an adult audience. However, the dramatic events which lead to the bloody climax of The Bacchae are somewhat more unsettling than the domestic quarrel between Jason and Medea which brings Medea to murder her children. The Bacchae has been interpreted as a drama of tension between the rational and the irrational, at a particular point in the history of Greek religion. I will here propose that The Bacchae is a record of intergenerational strife and of the war between the sexes. Furthermore, the dramatic tension in this play, the tragic flaw in Pentheus, is his rejection of androgyny.

ANDROGYNY AND THE LIFE CYCLE: THE BACCHAE OF EURIPIDES

I turn now to the tragedy of The Bacchae [5], the reveling women who keep the rites of Dionysus. Unlike Oedipus Rex, who gave his name to a stage in human development, or Medea, who though not yet part of life-cycle theory is someone we know, The Bacchae play their part in a drama unfamiliar to most of us outside classical literature. The brief summary which follows bends the drama to my purposes, and, it is hoped, will also send the reader to the original source.

Dionysus, the god of wine and revelry, opens the drama; from him we learn that King Pentheus has prohibited Bacchic rites in the city of Thebes. Thus the entry of Dionysus—who has come to avenge his worshippers—strikes a sinister, forboding note on which the tragedy of The Bacchae opens. As Dionysus speaks, we learn that he is the son of an adulterous union of Zeus and Semele, the daughter of King Cadmus of Thebes. A Greek audience would also know that Semele was struck by lightning in childbed, and that Zeus saved his son's life from the wrath of Hera by sewing the infant into his thigh—the first life-giving androgynous note to be sounded in the tragedy.

In the critical canon of The Bacchae, the next scene is a puzzle. Two old men, King Cadmus and the seer Teiresias, enter wearing the fawnskins of the Bacchic ritual—in women's dress. The critic William Arrowsmith remarks: "Teiresias and Cadmus . . . are more problematic . . . two doddering old men in fawnskins off to the dances on the mountain" [5, p. 343]. Yet The Bacchae is universally acclaimed as "the most perfect" of all the tragedies of Euripides, the crown of his old age [6, p. 1]. I shall not argue the dramatic merits of this scene, but rather suggest that it is the second sounding of the androgynous note, and the first time androgyny is linked to later life.

Of Teiresias there can be no doubt; legend tells us he assumed a woman's body and then a man's, and having taken sexual pleasure in both, told Zeus that there were ten parts to sexual pleasure; a woman had thrice three, and a man only one. A man was therefore entitled to take his sexual pleasures wherever he could find them. Hera struck Teiresias blind in her fury, but Zeus compensated him with second sight, the prescience of the seer, and a lifetime seven times longer than that of an ordinary man [7, p. 11].

In this scene Cadmus invites Teiresias to join him in paying homage to the god Dionysus, his daughter's son; then they are interrupted by the arrival of the young king Pentheus, also a grandson of Cadmus and heir to the thone of Thebes. We are told by the stage directions of Euripides that Dionysus is young, beardless, beautiful, even effeminate; his long blond hair curls over his shoulders. Pentheus too is young and beardless, but athletic where Dionysus is slight, clothed in tradition where Dionysus is wreathed in ivy. Though the two young men have not yet met, the very sight of each forewarns the audience that one must bring doom to the other.

Pentheus condemns the Bacchic revels of the women, and then seems suddenly to turn to another matter: "They tell me that a stranger out of Lydia has come to Thebes,: he says, "with long yellow curls smelling of perfume . . . His days and nights he spends with women and girls . . . By god, I'll have his head cut off!" Then Pentheus discovers Teiresias and his grandfather Cadmus, and mocks them, condemning "the feasts of women." Teiresias begs him to accept the divinity of Dionysus, creator of wine and slumber, comfort to humanity, second of the two supreme blessings of which the first is the harvest of Demeter, mother earth. To no avail: Pentheus rejects the Bacchic worship and turns once more to the problem of the Lydian stranger: "Go and scour the city," he instructs his attendants, "for that effeminate stranger, the man who infects our beds." Teiresias begs Cadmus to join him in prayer for Pentheus and the city of Thebes.

The capture of Dionysus is the beginning of doom. He is led before Pentheus, offering no resistance. "So," says Pentheus, "you *are* attractive, stranger, at least to women . . . Your curls are long. You do not wrestle, I take it." Thus the world's first hippie is brought in chains before the world's first jock. The irony of the confrontation which follows is sharpened by our knowledge that both–one mortal, the other divine–are grandsons of Cadmus, and thus are cousins–two sides, we may say today, of a divided self, one a lover of women, the other their enemy.

In the dialogue which follows, Pentheus cuts off the long curls of Dionysus, takes his wand of ivy, and commands the attendants to imprison him. To this Dionysus replies:

> You do not know the limits of your strength.
> You do not know what you do.
> You do not know who you are.

–a sinister echo of Jocasta's warning to Oedipus Rex, "Ah, may you never find out who you are!"

From the prison of the palace, Dionysus summons an earthquake which fells the palace and frees him. Soon Pentheus discovers Dionysus walking free among the ruins of his palace, and the final steps toward tragedy are taken. A messenger comes forward to tell the king that the Bacchae are reveling out on the mountainside, led by the king's own mother Agave. Pentheus commands his troops to march against the Bacchae: "Affairs are out of hand when we tamely endure such conduct here."

But Dionysus intercedes. He volunteers to lead the women back to Thebes without bloodshed. Pentheus refuses, calls for his armor, and strides away; but Dionysus calls him back: "*Wait*! Would you like to see their revels on the mountain?" he asks, and Pentheus confesses to a hunger to see the revels of the women. Dionysus urges Pentheus to put on a woman's long robe and a wig with long hair. Pentheus wrestles with shame, lust, and curiosity, and exits to ponder the advice. With his departure Dionysus turns to the chorus of Bacchae and declares: "Women, our prey now thrashes in the net we threw. He shall see the Bacchae, and pay the price with death."

When Pentheus reappears he is robed as a woman and utterly bewitched; Dionysus leads him out to the mountain, promising that his mother will bring him home as an example to all men. And this proves true: his mother finds him spying on the revels, and, though he rips off his disguise, in the madness of the Bacchic revels she dismembers him and brings his head back down the mountainside to Thebes. There Cadmus greets her with horror, but she is still mad with Bacchic revelry and replies:

> How scowling and crabbed is old age
> in men. I hope my son takes after his mother . . . .
> But all my son can do is quarrel with god.
> He should be scolded, Father, and you are the one
> who should scold him.

Then Cadmus brings her to her senses, she recognizes her son's head in her hands, and knows herself his murderer. Dionysus pronounces the final doom: banishment, for blasphemy.

ANDROGYNY AND ADAPTATION: SURVIVING INTO OLD AGE

At the conclusion of The Bacchae we find three categories of survivor: The assertive, managerial, agentic women who revelled on the mountainside; the nurturant old men who put on women's clothes and felt no shame; and the graceful, feline, feral Dionysus, a friend to women and girls. Pentheus, the angry young man who denied the women their revels, is dead at the hands of his own mother. Fearful of women's power, he perishes at the hands of women; lustfully curious, he dies of curiosity; after mocking Cadmus and Teiresias for wearing women's clothes, he puts on women's clothing and dies in his disguise.

Agave, Cadmus, and Teiresias have their contemporary counterparts in adult developmental psychology, where Neugarten and Gutmann [8] have found that aggressive and managerial traits are attributed to the older woman in a two-generational family scene, a TAT stimulus developed especially for the study of middle-aged adults' projective responses; the older man is described as passive, nurturant, and if an authority, benevolent.

Gutmann has subsequently suggested that the androgyny of later life suggested by these findings is an outcome of an earlier adaptive response [1], in young adulthood, to the "chronic emergency of parenthood," which calls for a woman to surrender her aggressive needs to her husband in order to shelter the child, while the man in turn gives up his dependency needs to become the family breadwinner. With the departure of grown children from the home, the middle-aged parents are able to reclaim the lost portions of themselves; midlife ushers in the "normal unisex of later life" [1, p. 180].

The social psychologists who argue the case for the adaptive value of androgyny as a trait would dispute the life cycle model of androgyny suggested by Gutmann–and so, if I read him correctly, would Euripides. The so-called comic scene in which old men dress up in women's clothes, which has so troubled some contemporary critics [5, p. 353] did not trouble the Athenian judges of tragedy: The Bacchae, the last of the tragedies of Euripides, written in his old age, was the first to win first prize at Athens, after his death. Carolyn Heilbrun, arguing for a hidden river of androgyny in classical literature, points to Euripides as an "obvious . . . source for the androgynous vision" [9, p. 14], and finds in Dionysus the unbounded, indefinable embodiment of androgyny [9, p. xi].

If we consider the life cycle with its unfolding of developmental tasks, if we accept in part the "chronic emergency of parenthood," if we accept as well the adaptive value of androgyny, we need not fear that androgyny is the exclusive prerogative of the gods. The old men of The Bacchae, with whom we must suppose Euripides felt some kinship, had no fear of women. Nor did the old men fear Dionysus, the young man driving the women to revel on the mountainside. Rather, they feared Pentheus, who threatened to confine the women. And Pentheus found his doom in stages: first when he shrugged off the wisdom of old men, next when he denied the women, once again when he refused the counsel of Dionysus, and finally when Dionysus led him to discover the woman within himself–to put on women's clothes when curiosity conquered shame, and thus to die. Writing in his old age, Euripides seems to suggest that it is not androgyny which is paced by the life cycle, but the fear of androgyny: the young man Pentheus feared the woman within himself and died of his fear; the old men put on women's clothes and felt no shame. Those who seek to reconcile the adaptive features of the trait model of androgyny and the developmental model of androgyny might do well to begin with a careful reading of The Bacchae, as the discussion which follows will propose.

NOTES ON THE SOCIOLOGY OF KNOWLEDGE

The implicit dissent suggested in this chapter between social psychological trait models of androgyny and the life cycle model, in which androgyny emerges in later life, is partially reconciled by the proposal that it is sexual anxieties and the fear of androgyny–specifically, the fear of the woman within the man–which are developmentally paced.

The reconciliation proposed, however, is not new–though if its fate resembles that of previous reconciliations, it will be short-lived. In 1954 Bruno Bettelheim wrote *Symbolic Wounds*, suggesting that penis envy in girls had its complement in womb envy in boys–manifest in primitive cultures in male initiation ceremonies, replicated unknowingly by the schizophrenic boys under Bettelheim's care at the Orthogenic School [10]. The book had a generally hostile reception. One exception was David Riesman, who commented, ". . . on the whole, men, by virtue of the very patriarchal dominance which puts them on top, must repress the extent of their longing for the . . . indisputable potentialities of being a woman, whereas women are much freer to express their envy of the male's equipment and roles" [10, p. 11].

The long-term reception to the revised edition was worse than hostility: it was indifference. For scholars interested in androgyny, *Symbolic Wounds* is a book of major significance; for historians of science, its significance is even greater. Many feminist critics of psychoanalysis writing today fault Freud for ever supposing a woman could envy a man (see, for example, Ruth [11]); none mention Bettelheim, who showed that a man could envy a woman.

The history of androgyny in literary criticism seems to have had a similar fate: Carolyn Heilbrun notes that Colebridge remarked, "The truth is, a great mind must be androgynous," more than one hundred years ago, and comments that her own essay on androgyny, if it succeeds at all, "will, in a short time, be considered too obvious to be interesting" [9, p. xx]. The more unhappy but more probable outcome is that her thesis will be accepted and then forgotten.

Thus the initial question which prompted this exploration of androgyny, the effort to bridge the gap between social and developmental psychological theories, has given way to a larger question: namely, why have so many efforts to recognize androgynous potential gone unrecognized? If great minds are androgynous, perhaps they are also scarce; lesser minds may be afraid, as Pentheus was, of the unknowable other within, and fail to discover, until it is too late, that denial is the forerunner of doom.

ACKNOWLEDGMENTS

An earlier version of this chapter was presented as a portion of an invited address at a Festschrift honoring thirty years of contributions by Bernice Neugarten to the field of gerontology.

I am grateful to Bruno Bettelheim for his critical reading of the earlier version, to the participants of the C. V. Ramana Saturday Seminar, whose comments and suggestions guided me to the conclusion of this chapter, and to Rhoda Unger for helping me through the finishing touches.

REFERENCES

1. D. Gutmann, Parenthood: A Key to the Comparative Study of the Life Cycle, in *Life-Span Developmental Psychology: Normative Life Crises*, N. Datan and L. H. Ginsberg (eds.), Academic Press, New York, 1975.
2. R. Unger, *Female and Male: Psychological Perspectives*, Harper and Row, New York, 1979.
3. K. Deaux, *The Behavior of Women and Men*, Brooks/Cole Publishing Company, Monterey, California, 1976.
4. N. Datan, After Oedipus: Laius, Medea, and Other Parental Myths, *Journal of Mind and Behavior, 3*:1, pp. 17–26, Winter 1982.
5. Euripides, The Bacchae, in *The Complete Greek Tragedies*, Vol. 7, D. Grene and R. Lattimore (eds.), Modern Library Editions, New York, 1958.

6. G. S. Kirk, *The Bacchae of Euripides*, Cambridge University Press, Cambridge, 1979.
7. R. Graves, *The Greek Myths*: Vol. 2, Penguin Books, Middlesex, England, 1955.
8. B. L. Neugarten and D. Gutmánn, Age-sex Roles and Personality in Middle Age: A Thematic Apperception Study, in *Middle Age and Aging*, B. L. Neugarten (ed.), The University of Chicago Press, Chicago, 1968.
9. C. G. Heilbrun, *Toward a Recognition of Androgyny*, Alfred A. Knopf, New York, 1973.
10. B. Bettelheim, *Symbolic Wounds*, Revised edition, Collier-MacMillan, New York, 1962.
11. S. Ruth (ed.), *Issues in Feminism: A First Course in Women's Studies*, Houghton-Mifflin Company, Boston, 1980.

CHAPTER 21

The Pier Glass and the Candle: Reality, Perception, and Gender in the Fiction of George Eliot

JOAN E. HARTMAN

> Your pier-glass or extensive surface of polished steel made to be rubbed by a housemaid, will be minutely and multitudinously scratched in all directions; but place now against it a lighted candle as a centre of illumination, and lo! the scratches will seem to arrange themselves in a fine series of concentric circles round that little sun. It is demonstrable that the scratches are going everywhere impartially, and it is only your candle which produces the flattering illusion of a concentric arrangement, its light falling with an exclusive optical selection. These things are a parable. The scratches are events, and the candle is the egoism of any person. . . .
>
> George Eliot, *Middlemarch* [1]

Eliot's parable of the pier glass and the candle mediates between two paradigms of cognition, that persons construct reality and that reality constructs persons. The minute scratches on the steel pier glass cannot be apprehended without the optical selection provided by the candle; there is no perception unmediated by the self. But the impartial scratches are there to be perceived by moving the candle; changing selves apprehend more of reality than fixed, unchanging ones. Eliot had a keen sense of the reciprocal interactions of selves and worlds her parable points to, and fiction gave her the space to record them. In novel after novel she registers the cognitive strategies of her characters, their habitual, *characteristic* strategies.[1] Her narrative presence is extensive and her commentary is often directed to grounding character and behavior in perception.

[1] See Baruch Hochman's defense of character in literature against various modernist critical positions that subvert or ignore it [2].

In Eliot's fiction, seeing widely and seeing well are moral acts: because selfhood is grounded in perception, Eliot extends her judgment of character to judgment of cognitive strategies. Heroic characters are not, as she ironically puts it in her parable, little suns flattering themselves with the illusion that the world is concentrically arranged about them. They are open to a range of impartial scratches and to the cognitive dissonance that results when perceiving new scratches calls into question familiar constructs of self and world and requires the construction of new ones. Invariably, in her fiction, characters who enlarge their perceptual field take in other selves, selves who resist their desires and imaginations and exert claims on them. To recognize them, to take them in, is to alter one's sense of oneself and the world, to put one's identity at risk.

In addition, heroic characters in Eliot's fiction, the characters, that is, who enlarge their perceptual field to take in other selves, are, more often than not, women.[2] Eliot explores, from a woman's point of view—George Eliot is the pseudonym Mary Anne Evans adopted when she began to publish fiction—the construction of gendered selves in nineteenth-century England. Women were restricted to half the pier glass, the private and domestic half. The other, public half was closed to them: they might hear of it from their fathers and brothers and husbands, read of it, and imagine it, but they were unable to exert themselves in it—which is to say that women in Eliot's novels are constructed by experience that is more limited than men's and have less experience to apprehend. They may be safe or at risk because of the narrowness of their experience, unheroic or heroic, but all of them exist in a state of social and psychic deprivation. The heroines of this essay—Maggie Tulliver of *The Mill on the Floss* and Dorothea Brooke of *Middlemarch*—are at risk and rebellious, as Eliot herself was. Nevertheless, she did not permit her female characters to trespass into the public world, as she did in her career as a writer, or to transgress the conventions of the private world, as she did in her liaison with George Henry Lewes.

Eliot was born in 1819 into a provincial family in Warwickshire and educated at schools and at home. In London she wrote for and managed the *Westminster Review*, an important intellectual journal. When she was thirty-five, she and George Henry Lewes, a writer and scientist, began to live together; Lewes was unable to divorce his adulterous wife. Eliot considered herself Mrs. Lewes. She mothered Lewes's sons and he mothered her and sustained her creativity—she did not begin to write fiction until after their liaison began. She was, to a considerable degree, ostracized for living with him. Her choice of a masculine pseudonym was not unusual for the time (see, for example, the Bronte sisters),

[2] Those who are men tend also to be outsiders: Adam Bede, the rural carpenter in *Adam Bede*, Silas Marner, the outcast linen-weaver in *Silas Marner*, and Daniel Deronda, whose parentage is unknown, in *Daniel Deronda*.

but it also kept readers from associating the author of her novels with the disreputable Miss Evans.[3]

The Mill on the Floss (published in 1860) is the most autobiographical of Eliot's novels [6] ; a female *bildungsroman*, it reflects in Maggie Tulliver and her brother Tom elements of Eliot's own childhood and her estrangement from her brother Isaac. It also enables Eliot to contrast gendered childrearing in a single family, to depict the constellation of factors that produce, in the son, security, privilege, and freedom, and in the daughter, rebellion and insecurity. When the novel begins, with Tom twelve or thirteen and Maggie eight or nine, Maggie's preferred activities are roaming the reaches of her father's mill and fishing with Tom, when he permits her to. She is the despair of her mother and her Dodson aunts and recognizes guiltily how far her behavior falls short of her cousin Lucy's; Lucy's fair hair is always curled and her dress tidy. Once Maggie defies her placid but peevish mother by ducking her head in water to prevent her hair's being curled; once, in a burst of elation, she cuts it short, which she quickly regrets. Dark like the Tullivers, she is her father's pet; he dotes on her quickness and spirit. Intermittently he shields and defends her, but he does not protect her from the constraints against which she rebels or even understand why she rebels against them. Rather he contributes to her vulnerability, which stems from her need for approval and love and her despair when they are withdrawn.

Maggie is an impulsive and tempestuous child whose rebellions are short-lived. When she encounters the disapproval of her mother or the intermittent but more damaging disapproval of her father and brother, she retreats to the attic of the Tulliver house, where she frets out "all her ill-humours" and keeps a "Fetish," a wooden doll that she punishes and then comforts [6] . Three nails in its head commemorate "as many crises in Maggie's nine years of earthly struggle"; she grinds and beats its head against the bricks of the chimneys that rise through the attic. The nails Eliot attributes to her remembering "the picture of Jael destroying Sisera in the old Bible." But Maggie's treatment of her doll is also a powerful enactment of bad mothering and her childish vulnerability.

The pattern of action, reproach, and self-reproach that characterizes Maggie's life, as well as her dependence on her brother Tom, appears in early episodes of the novel. His behavior toward her is less predictable than that of her parents: he seems to encourage her misbehavior and then, when her parents express their displeasure, to forsake her in her misery and even join them in censuring her. Differences in their identities that will persist into adulthood appear in the episode of the jam puff. Tom, who cuts it, is unable to divide it evenly, and Maggie, thinking it to her advantage to please him—for such is her insecurity—

[3] Haight's is the standard biography [3], Redinger's the more illuminating study of the making of the woman and the writer [4]; see also Knoepflmacher's essay on Eliot and Lewes [5].

wants him to take the larger piece. He, however, insists that she close her eyes and choose, which she does, thereby acquiring the larger piece. Again she offers it to him, still mindful of pleasing him, and again he refuses it—fair is fair in his code. But as he watches her eat the last bites of her piece he feels aggrieved: "He was conscious of having acted very fairly and thought she ought to have considered this, and made up to him for it." He reproaches her for greediness and leaves her in tears. Maggie, greedy for love and approval rather than for jam puff, discovers that what is fair for Tom is not fair for her.

Maggie is wrong no matter what she does. The young Tom has recourse to a code, to rules that legitimate his rights as well as his responsibilities.[4] It makes him self-assured and self-confident and solidifies his character: his face, Eliot observes, "in which it seems impossible to discern anything but the generic character of boyhood," conceals "some of her [Nature's] most rigid, inflexible purposes, some of her most unmodifiable characters; and the dark-eyed, demonstrative, rebellious girl may after all turn out to be a passive being compared with this pink-and-white bit of masculinity with the indeterminate features." Tom measures himself against rules, rules of the game like playing fair (and despising cheaters), and is satisfied when he reviews his actions, though he expects approbation for them as well. Maggie, insecure and needy, lacks clear direction; she seldom satisfies others and, propped by no rules, seldom satisfies herself. Her imperatives disenable her: she must anticipate the expectations of those she loves and curb her impulses to earn the approval she craves. Tom's ethics are princpled, hers situational and improvisatory, and Eliot depicts the link between her contingent ethics and her contingent and vulnerable identity. The one period Tom goes without the approval his mother lavishes on him and his father accords him as his son and heir makes him vulnerable, more like Maggie. Sent by his father to study with a clergyman, he is introduced to geometry and Latin under Mr. Stelling's brisk tutelage and cannot master them. He "became more like a girl than he had ever been in his life before"; "his pride got into an uneasy condition which quite nullified his boyish self-satisfaction and gave him something of a girl's susceptibility." Both Tom and Maggie need approval, but he, in the ordinary course of events, gets it, while she does not.

Maggie, who has the "power of apprehending signs and abstractions" that Tom is deficient in, could excel as a student were she given the opportunity. She is a voracious reader and, though her quickness is subject to her father's general censure—"a woman's no business wi' being so clever"—he quite approves of it. When she is invited by the Stellings to visit for a fortnight, she rather self-importantly expects to help Tom with his studies. Euclid defeats her; Latin she finds interesting because she discovers the English key at the end of the book

[4] Carol Gilligan discusses the rule-based behavior of boys and the relationship-based behavior of girls, and I am indebted to her analysis [7]. She also discusses *The Mill on the Floss.*

and is able to puzzle out sentences. But Tom regains his superiority by assailing her pronunciation: "I told you girls couldn't learn Latin." Mr. Stelling ratifies Tom's view of the sexual division of intellectual labor: girls have "a great deal of superficial cleverness; but they couldn't go far into anything. They're quick and shallow." Maggie, accustomed to praise for her quickness and cleverness, discovers that in the public world, which Tom's education is supposed to initiate him into, they are devalued commodities. Rapidly assimilating this new information, she sees its consequences for herself and is "so oppressed by this dreadful destiny that she had no spirit for retort." Educated for the private and domestic world at Miss Furniss's boarding school, Maggie will never experience her intellectual ability as valuable and will never value it herself.

Both Maggie's and Tom's worlds are constricted when their father, as the result of a lawsuit he rashly initiated, loses his property, his occupation, and his health. But their father's losses paradoxically empower the sixteen-year-old Tom by expanding his sphere of action from the classroom, where he is accustomed to fail, to his uncle's warehouse, where he learns to succeed. As he tells Uncle Deane, Lucy's father, he wants "a manly business, where I should have to look after things, and get credit for what I did"; he works hard and earns both money and approbation. Maggie, however, is disempowered by confinement to home, her sphere of failure, where she experiences a "still, sad monotony" that throws her "more than ever on her inward self." Her experience of her own misery has schooled her to apprehend the misery of her parents; her rebelliousness is tamed by pity and sorrow for her father's dumb suffering and her mother's bewildered loss of status and household comforts. But she receives no return of love from either her parents or Tom for her disciplined renunciation of her wishes and desires. She has conformed to their–and society's–expectations of daughters and sisters and gets no credit for doing so.

Maggie, who is frightened by the cost to her identity of this conformity, seeks external props to sustain her. She turns first to her schoolbooks and then to Tom's, but does not find them answerable to her needs. The voice that speaks to her condition is that of Thomas à Kempis: "it flashed through her like the suddenly apprehended solution of a problem, that all the miseries of her young life had come from fixing her heart on her own pleasure as if that were the central necessity of the universe, and for the first time she saw the possibility of shifting the position from which she looked at the gratification of her own desires–of taking her stand out of herself, and looking at her own life as an insignificant part of a divinely-guided whole." Maggie, who knows nothing "of doctrines and systems–of mysticism or quietism" as a religious discipline, finds a cosmic principle to dignify her conformity to society's gendered expectations of her. It seems to come to her across the centuries unmediated by anything except her experience of need and sorrow, and it helps her to order her perception of herself in relation to both the world that she is closed off from and the world she lives in. That is to say, she has looked for and feels strengthened by a code, even though it is a code that negates her rights—as opposed to Tom's code, which balances rights and responsibilities.

Maggie's regimen of principled renunciation is disrupted some three years later when she encounters Philip Wakem, whom she knew as her brother's schoolfellow at Mr. Stelling's and whose father the Tullivers hold responsible for their ruin. Philip, who is severely crippled, has travelled abroad and studied painting; he has experienced a world Maggie knows only through the books she no longer reads, and is eager to share it with her. It is to him that she articulates her sense of her trials—the loss of everything she loved and her self-denial. When he offers to lend her the book he is reading, she perspicaciously declines: "Because I should want too much." But her resolve not to see him again does not hold, and their clandestine meetings both relieve her loneliness and make her impatient: it is easier to renounce a world that is not present to one's consciousness, even at second-hand. Eventually Philip owns up to his love for her. So habitual is Maggie's repression of her needs that she thinks first of making him happy, only then of the fact that he has made her happy. But marriage is impossible, given her family's enmity toward his.

When Tom discovers her meetings with Philip, Maggie experiences not conflict between rights and responsibilities but rather conflict among responsibilities, to her father, to Tom, and to Philip. Tom threatens exposure, with the pain it will give their father, unless she gives Philip up, and she agrees to. But when Philip appears, Tom berates him for taking advantage of a handsome but inexperienced girl whom he, with his physical deformity, could never win by "fair means"—I hear in his words the vocabulary of games. Tom is cruel but, he thinks, just: as Eliot observes, he "did not know how much of an old boyish repulsion and of mere personal pride and animosity was concerned in the bitter severity of the words by which he meant to do the duty of a son and a brother." Satisfaction with his principled behavior has led Tom to construct an identity that is proof against introspection; habitually assuming his ends to be just and his motives honorable, he overrides complexities. Nor does he imaginatively enter into the feelings of others, which is, for Maggie, a source of her compassion and a motive of her renunciations.

Maggie, as she listens to Tom, is aware not only of the pain he is inflicting on Philip but also of elements of his character she has hitherto ignored or repressed, since they relate to his treatment of her. Her perception leads to a rapid reconstruction of their past: "you have always enjoyed punishing me," she tells him; "you have always been hard and cruel to me." This new perception administers a shock to her identity: it would have been simpler for her to recover her "inward harmony" if she could believe Tom entirely right, herself entirely wrong, but "now her penitence and submission were constantly obstructed by resentment that would present it to herself no otherwise than as a just indignation." Yet she is unable to sustain her indignation, especially when Tom, shortly afterwards, pays off their creditors in full with money he has amassed by speculation in commodities and makes their father happy. Maggie, in a characteristic move, forgives him at the cost of reproach to herself: "she felt that all the faults he had to pardon in her had never been redeemed, as his faults were." Tom's wider sphere of action gives him more opportunities than Maggie has to succeed, to win approbation, and to think well of himself.

The possibility of Maggie's growing apart from Tom and attaining a sense of her own worth is cut off by the catastrophe that ends the novel: the river Floss rises, the boat Maggie and Tom are in capsizes, and when the flood subsides their bodies are found in a close embrace. But Maggie's trip on the river with Tom is preceded by a more placid but equally dangerous trip with Stephen Guest, a young man who is her cousin Lucy's suitor. Maggie comes to visit Lucy after two years of independence: she has chosen to earn her own way by teaching, rather than, as Tom wishes, to live dependent on one of her aunts. A visit with Lucy introduces her to the life of a young lady: at the Deane home there is comfort, society, and music. Her return activates both her memory of the past and her imagination of the future; she feels "a sense of privation too keen to let her taste what was offered in the transient present" and finds "the image of the intense and varied life she yearned for, and despaired of, becoming more and more importunate." Equally vivid to her is the presence of Stephen Guest: each "was oppressively conscious of the other's presence, even to the finger ends." As Maggie's habitual disciplining of her desires lessens, aspects of herself she has repressed overwhelm her: she is "absorbed in the direct, immediate experience, without any energy left for taking account of it and reasoning about it." Balanced against her love for her cousin Lucy and sense of obligation to her is a powerful sexual attraction such as she has never experienced, certainly not with Philip Wakem. When Stephen asks her to marry him, she declines, though acknowledging her love and the happiness she would experience with him were it not achieved at Lucy's expense. But when they find themselves on the river together she abandons herself to him, "yearning after that belief that the tide was doing it all—that she might glide along with the swift, silent stream, and not struggle any more"—her yielding to the river is a powerful image of the sexual surrender that does not take place.[5]

Maggie's sin against social decorum—she and Stephen were together unchaperoned for a day and a night—could be patched up, for Stephen urges marriage. But Maggie, aware of the pain she has inflicted on those she loves, is brought back to her principled self. She refuses Stephen and returns to live out the reproaches leveled against her, especially Tom's, and most disenabling of all, her own. Fearful of the impulses she has given in to and the apparent fragility of her renunciatory ethics, she accepts Tom's vision of herself as wayward and lacking in self-control, telling him, "I want to be kept from doing wrong again."

[5] Gilligan also interprets the image of drifting as an evasion, a refusal to take control of situations where the choice is between selfishness and responsibility for others [7].

He refuses her even a home; only her mother and Lucy try to support her in her misery. The pattern of action, reproach, and self-reproach has been repeated. Confronting the intense and desperate consequences of her action, she recollects a passage from Thomas à Kempis that she once committed to memory—his acceptance of the cross laid upon him that he will bear to his death—just as water coming through the door rises about her. The consummation of Maggie's love for Tom in a death that is a virtual apotheosis of their childhood seems forced and arbitrary, though Eliot planned it from the start of the novel; what seems more forced and arbitrary is her limiting Maggie's opportunities for development not simply to marriage—that is a convention of the nineteenth-century novel—but rather to two unsuitable suitors, Philip Wakem and Stephen Guest. The catastrophe violates our sense of Maggie's extraordinary potential and Tom's decently limited one. Yet Eliot, with a substantial novel completed, had to bring it to a close, and with what fictional integrity could she reverse Maggie's characteristic cognitive strategies to show her asserting her right to satisfaction and happiness at the expense of others? All Eliot herself admitted was that "the tragedy is not adequately prepared" [8].

Eliot, perhaps for biographical reasons that remain a matter of speculation, invests Maggie's love for Tom with resonance so extraordinary as to preclude her sustained analysis of how it disempowers her. But Maggie's disempowerment is social as well as psychic. Although both she and Tom are confined, he at least escapes into a public world that, though narrow, is wider than hers, a world that offers him opportunities to assert himself and yields him approval other than that of those he loves. The limitations Maggie shares with Tom throw into relief the limitations consequent upon her gender: Tom has power that she lacks and can neither claim nor even imagine for herself. On the one occasion she expresses her contempt for him, she observes, "you are a man, Tom, and have power, and can do something in the world." Maggie needs, at least, a wider domestic world and some power to play out the impulses and desires and capacities that her life, confined as it is to her family, leads her to mistrust and repress. The constraints on her imagination—and perhaps on Eliot's imagination as well—I think account for the harrowing power of *The Mill on the Floss*.

Middlemarch, subtitled *A Study of Provincial Life*, was published in 1872, twelve years after *The Mill on the Floss*; Middlemarch is the name of a town. In it Eliot extends the study of gendered selves begun in Maggie and Tom Tulliver through two courtships and two marriages, that of Dorothea Brooke and Edward Casaubon and that of Rosamond Vincy and Tertius Lydgate. Neither couple lives happily ever after; rather all four enter into marriage imagining a future in accord with their various internalizations of society's gendered expectations.

Dorothea Brooke challenges comparison with Maggie Tulliver. Motherless, fatherless, and brotherless (she and her sister Celia were raised by their genial and ineffectual bachelor uncle Arthur Brooke), she is less emotionally vulnerable than Maggie; well-connected and an heiress, her world is larger. But it is still private and domestic, not large enough for her to play out or even test her vaguely-conceived aspirations. Eliot contrasts her with Saint Teresa of Avila, whose "passionate, ideal nature demanded an epic life," that is, a life of action in the public world, and achieved one; turned back as a child from seeking martyrdom among the Moors, she nevertheless "found her epos in the reform of a religious order." Dorothea thinks to realize her yearning for a life of wide knowledge infused with spirituality, if not a life of service, by marrying a clergyman twenty-seven years her senior, Edward Casaubon. Whereas Celia perceives him as ugly, Dorothea, looking "deep into the ungauged reservoir of Mr. Casaubon's mind, seeing reflected there in vague labyrinthine extension every quality she herself brought," perceives him variously as the living incarnation of Augustine, Bossuet, Hooker, Locke, Milton, and Pascal, all of whom she has at least heard of through an education "both narrow and promiscuous," first in residence with an English family and then with a Swiss family in Lausanne.

Nothing Casaubon does during their brief courtship and short engagement serves to check Dorothea's imagination of him; indeed, it is her imagination that fills up "all blanks with unmanifested perfections, interpreting him as she interpreted the works of Providence, and accounting for seeming discords by her own deafness to the higher harmonies." But after marriage her perceptions of him change "with the secret motion of a watch-hand." The dissonance between her expectations and her experience of him she is at first barely able to recognize, much less admit. Over time, however, as she recognizes the distance between expectation and reality, she revises her opinion of him—he is cold, distant, timid, and disguises his timidity behind a grave facade of age and learning—and also her opinion of herself. Sick at heart when she imagines her marriage extending into the future, she recognizes that she mistook Casaubon and that she, not he, is to blame for the mistake. She takes responsibility for it and for the principled renunciation of her spontaneous needs and desires that she expected to be fulfilled in marrying. What she achieves is domestic martyrdom, not the heroic martyrdom she vaguely aspired to.

But Casaubon's "suspicious interpretation" of her wifely devotion leads him to withdraw from her and makes their marriage even less rewarding to her, at which point, momentarily but fiercely blaming him rather than herself, she experiences "the jar of her whole being," which she reconstitutes by willing her imagination to act as Casaubon's advocate. Less dependent than Maggie, with less experience of pain to enable her intuitively to apprehend the suffering of another, she consciously makes Casaubon's suffering as vivid to her as her own; she wills the sympathetic identification that comes naturally to Maggie, and this disciplined exercise enables her to turn to Casaubon with a gesture of loving reconciliation. Both Dorothea and Maggie take their ethic of responsibility as a mandate to alter their perception—to work on outer reality as it is present to their inner reality; outer reality they take as impartial and irrevocable.

But Dorothea's revised opinion of Casaubon's life work, the *Key to All Mythologies* that so impressed her before their marriage, is unalterable, and when he, in failing health, asks her to continue it after his death, she resists. Early in her marriage, Will Ladislaw, Casaubon's young cousin, tells her that Casaubon, by ignoring German historical scholarship, is "groping about in woods with a pocket-compass while they have made good roads." Dorothea, as she learns to help her husband in his work, is instructed not only in his views concerning Dagon and other fish deities and Warburton's interpretation of the Egyptian mysteries but also in his pedantry and intellectual timidity; she correctly assesses the *Key to All Mythologies* as "questionable riddle-guessing" rather than "high knowledge which was to make life worthier." The promise Casaubon asks of her requires more than her imaginative sympathy: "Neither law nor the world's opinion compelled her to this—only her husband's nature and her own compassion, only the ideal and not the real yoke of marriage." Nevertheless, she accepts the "ideal" yoke of marriage (her version of a code that negates her rights in conformity to society's gendered expectations of her) and represses her distaste for a commitment that will extend her unrewarding and unrewarded submission beyond her husband's death. Dorothea, less dependent on the approval of others than Maggie, is demanding of herself and lives by a code that privileges responsibility over rights. But Eliot, though she cast Dorothea in the heroic mold of Maggie, managed to spare her a life of principled renunciation, not by having her alter her outer reality but by altering it for her: just as Dorothea is ready to accede to Casaubon's wishes, Eliot sees to it that he dies.

After Casaubon's death, no longer responsible for behaving with compassion toward him, Dorothea is able to stand apart from him; his demeaning suspicions of her, manifested in a codicil to his will in which he disinherits her if she marries Will Ladislaw, help the process. One change, however, "terrified her as if it had been a sin"—"a violent shock of repulsion from her departed husband." But changes in the reality that constructs Dorothea and the Dorothea who constructs reality coincide and she is conscious, on the one hand, "that her life was taking on a new form, that she was undergoing a metamorphosis in which memory would not adjust itself to the stirring of new organs," and on the other that, reciprocally, her world was "in a state of convulsive change." This radical unsettling of self and world liberate Dorothea—up to a point. During her widowhood she tries to exert herself for the wider good but is unable to find a serious project; the religious orders that gave Saint Teresa her sphere of action are closed to a young Protestant. Eliot provides her with an opportunity to assert her rights to satisfaction and happiness through a second marriage, to Will Ladislaw, who fortuitously combines the ardent imagination of a Philip Wakem—he, like Philip, has traveled abroad and studied painting—and the sexual attractiveness of a Stephen Guest. Will enlarges Dorothea's world by becoming a barrister, entering parliament, and exerting himself in the public interest, and Dorothea, happy in her private and domestic world, is also satisfied in effacing herself to support Will in the public world from which she is excluded. This resolution is more than the conventional marriage plot of the nineteenth-century novel. Eliot, raising the question of whether "so substantive and rare a creature should have been absorbed into the life of another and be only known in a certain circle as a wife and mother," puts it aside with the realistic caveat that nineteenth-century England, Dorothea's age (and hers), does not permit new Teresas and new Antigones to assert themselves in the public world. Eliot, though she endowed Dorothea with strength unsapped by the rebellious struggles and emotional dependence of Maggie Tulliver, tamed Dorothea's imagination of satisfaction to domestic happiness and vicarious experience of the public world. Dorothea's situation somewhat resembles Eliot's own after she began to live with Lewes: great domestic content and a partial withdrawal from the public world of journalism into fiction-writing, with Lewes standing between her and her publisher.

Not all Eliot's female characters see widely and see well, and *Middlemarch* contains a full-scale presentation of one who does not, Rosamond Vincy, daughter of a prosperous Middlemarch manufacturer. Through her Eliot explores the construction of a female identity whose safety lies in the narrowness of her experience and whose cognitive strategies protect her from risk. Rosamond is fair, elegant in person, and accomplished–"the flower of Mrs. Lemon's school." Accustomed to the admiration of Middlemarch, she is also aware of its limitations, and her vague imaginings of greater distinction for herself take on particularity when Tertius Lydgate comes to Middlemarch to establish a medical practice: he is reputed to be talented, personable, and the nephew of a baronet. After their first meeting she imagines their marriage, at least to the details of her wedding costume and the visits they will pay to his relatives. They do marry (Lydgate had planned to defer marriage) and set up housekeeping (on a somewhat grander scale than he had expected), but Lydgate believes he has found perfection in womanhood, "instructed to the true womanly limit and not a hair's-breadth beyond–docile, therefore, and ready to carry out behests which came from beyond that limit," and Rosamond fancies herself in love. Over time, however, Lydgate discovers her "terrible tenacity" and realizes she has mastered him without ever quarreling with him or seeming to set herself against him; when keenly offended she sits quietly, her hands folded in her lap, and leaves him to interpret the signs of her displeasure.

What interests Eliot is Rosamond's mode of "establishing sequences:" "to see nothing except the desirable cause and close upon it the desirable effect rids us of doubt and makes our minds strongly intuitive." This mode of intuition, Eliot observes, is not unique to women but more prevalent among them than among men, simply because the narrowness of their domestic world keeps them ignorant of many details in linked chains of cause and effect; their intuitiveness is thus another manifestation of their social and psychic deprivation. Rosamond, however, wills her ignorance: she resists involvement in Lydgate's concerns and he, made short-tempered by them, stops telling her about them to avoid the exacerbation of spirit that comes from her resistance.

Her tenacity—and her mastery of Lydgate—is illustrated when she goes riding with his cousin while pregnant with her first child and loses the baby. She rides the first time without telling him and then, declaring her health better for the exercise, tells him "with full reliance on his consent that she should go riding again." When Lydgate forbids her and waits for her to promise not to, she deflects his force by enlisting his help in pinning up her hair. In face of her silence he says he will take the matter up with his cousin, to which Rosamond objects that he treats her like a child, an objection whose justice he allows. He ends up promising not to tell and Rosamond's promise remains unmade. As Eliot observes, Rosamond has "that victorious obstinacy which never wastes its energy in impetuous resistance"—as do Maggie and Dorothea. "What she liked to do was to her the right thing, and all her cleverness was directed to getting the means of doing it." Rosamond, like Tom Tulliver, has constructed an identity that is proof against introspection by assuming that her ends are just and her motives honorable. Eliot shows her extending her sequences backward as well as forward, to avoid both reproach and self-reproach: she forestalls recrimination over disobeying her husband by observing that she would have lost the baby anyway because she had experienced before riding the symptoms that produced her miscarriage.

Rosamond directs her cleverness to getting what she wants without seeming to assert her rights instead of considering what she ought to want because she has internalized the admiration of Middlemarch and the approval of her family. Maggie and Dorothea are cognizant of selves set against the world and of behavior as a negotiation between the self and the world's expectations. Rosamond is not: her egotism has locked her into a reciprocal interaction of world and self in which the world is virtually her own creation and the self continuous with it.[6] Eliot makes this point in a complicated parenthesis. When Rosamond first meets Lydgate, she is acutely aware of his awareness of her: "Every nerve and muscle in Rosamond was adjusted to the consciousness that she was being looked at. She was by nature an actress of parts that entered into her *physique*; she even acted her own character, and so well that she did not know it precisely to be her own." (*Physique* suggests consciousness that falls short of cognizance.)

What, then, would happen if a different part entered Rosamond's "*physique*?" Eliot manages the plot of *Middlemarch* to see that one does, through the agency of Will Ladislaw. Lydgate, tender of Rosamond's feelings and accepting responsibility for them, is gentle with her; Ladislaw, with whom she carries on a flirtation that initiates, in her mind, sequences terminating in his lasting admiration, is not sufficiently involved with her to restrain himself. Feeling

[6] The parable of the pier glass and the candle quoted as epigraph Eliot applies to Rosamond: she is the little sun who flatters herself with the illusion that the world is concentrically arranged about her.

compromised when Dorothea Brooke discovers him with Rosamond, goaded into fury by her suggestion that he has a "preference" for Dorothea, he rounds on her: "What another nature felt in opposition to her own was being burnt and bitten into her consciousness"–into her *physique*. Her sequence shattered, "her little world was in ruins, and she felt herself tottering in the midst as a lonely bewildered consciousness." (Eliot's repetition of *consciousness* to signify both Rosamond's awareness of the world external to her and her identity suggests the continuity between them.) But Ladislaw's radical unsettling of Rosamond's self and world does not liberate her as it does Dorothea; accustomed to avoiding the pain of cognitive dissonance, she turns to Lydgate to reconstitute her domestic world, a world that gives her as much identity as she requires. Rosamond is scarcely heroic–abstractly considered, she is a monster of egotism–but Eliot's delineation of her sense of herself and her cognitive strategies gives her a claim on Eliot's sympathy and ours. Without suffering, she also exemplifies the social and psychic deprivation of women.

Whereas Dorothea Brooke and Rosamond Vincy live in one world, a private and domestic world, Edward Casaubon and Tertius Lydgate live in two, one private and one public and professional, and Eliot's experience of the latter world undoubtedly contributes to the authority of her presentation, to the force of her parallel lives. Casaubon and Lydgate appear in *Middlemarch* in their maturity; we do not see them, as we see Tom Tulliver, take on their identities as boys in a domestic world and grow into their identities as men in a public world. Rather we see them, when they marry, move their professional identities into the private world of marriage, which they share with their wives without sharing their wives' perceptions of it. They also live in a larger public world than Tom, who matures from a schoolboy into a tradesman. Casaubon, nominally a clergyman, is a classical scholar, and Lydgate not merely a medical man but also a scientist whose training in Edinburgh and Paris as well as in London was superior to that of most nineteenth-century doctors. Both have experienced what the young Maggie thinks of as "real learning and wisdom, such as great men knew"; Eliot, mindful of Maggie's impoverished education, describes her as left "with no other part of her inherited share in the hard-won treasures of thought, which generations of painful toil have laid up for the race of *men*, than shreds and patches of feeble literature and false history" (emphasis added). Dorothea also venerates the "provinces of *masculine* knowledge" as "a standing-ground from which all truth could be seen more truly" (emphasis added). Both *The Mill on the Floss* and *Middlemarch* permit Eliot's quizzical scrutiny of the role of masculine knowledge in the construction of male identities.

As Dorothea comes to recognize the aridity of Casaubon's cross-cultural study of myths, it alters her perception of him. The other perception of self staked on a *Key to All Mythologies* is Casaubon's own. Its belated completion is more than a matter of procrastination. The bits of it, the pamphlets he has launched into the world, have met with small notice, and he is impeded by his fears of what the great minds of the day—the scholars of Brasenose—will say about it; that is to say, he is less than comfortable in the public world of classical scholarship he has chosen to exert himself in. But, like Rosamond, he has established sequences of cause and effect, interpreting his need to read yet another document as scholarly scrupulosity, and he works in solitude, with no one to reflect back to him an image of himself he does not wish to take cognizance of. Until he permitted Dorothea to help him, he had never had a secretary, for, as Eliot explains, he was "nervously conscious that he was expected to manifest a powerful mind." When, early in their marriage, Dorothea urges him to bring the *Key* to completion, she gives "loud emphatic iteration to those muffled suggestions of consciousness which it was possible to explain as mere fancy, the illusion of exaggerated sensitiveness." He expected her, in her ignorance of masculine knowledge, to reflect back to him an image of himself with which he would be comfortable; that is to say, he did not expect to put his scholarly self at risk by marrying her. As he suspects her of perceiving in him the inadequacies he perceives in himself he withdraws from her.

Dorothea makes Casaubon uncomfortable in his public identity but not in his private identity as a husband, a role he is equally if not more unsuited to. His education had at least taught him what classical scholarship is and he measured himself, albeit intermittently and with a muffled consciousness, against greater minds than his. It had taught him nothing about matrimony, nor had he cared to investigate so commonplace a subject. When he chose to marry he expected "family pleasures" and an heir, "that copy of himself," Eliot ironically puts it, "which seemed so urgently required of a man—to the sonneteers of the sixteenth century." "Society never made the preposterous demand that a man should think as much about his own qualifications for making a charming girl happy as he thinks of hers for making himself happy": this commonplace obviated the need for introspection about his long bachelorhood and what it signified concerning his desire or his fitness to share his life with another. While the rest of Middlemarch was startled by Dorothea's acceptance of him, he was not: he assumed himself to be a proper man. When his response to Dorothea's emotion turned out to be rather less than he expected it to be, "there was nothing external by which he could account for a certain blankness of sensibility which came over him just when his expectant gladness should have been most lively." Dissonance between his expectations and his experience is present to him but, accustomed to tolerating dissonance in his public identity by submerging it, he tolerates it in his private identity as well. In addition, the dissonance in his private identity discomforts him less because he values his private self less and stands in no fear of judgment—it is Dorothea, not the scholars of Brasenose, who will assess his domestic accomplishments. Consequently he risks less of his identity in the private world than in the public. He also has a code to fall back on, a code of correct husbandly behavior that exempts him from the loving work of imagining Dorothea's feelings and leaves him nothing to reproach himself with.

Tertius Lydgate, like Edward Casaubon, brings to marriage a store of easy assumptions, considering himself "amply informed by literature and the traditional wisdom which is handed down in the genial conversation of men." In his professional life, unlike Casaubon, he is bold and innovative. He intends to reform medical practice: he wishes to understand the causes of disease rather than treat its symptoms by indiscriminate medication, and he refuses either to dispense drugs himself (to his profit) or take a percentage on his prescriptions from the local apothecary (as many doctors did). And he wishes not simply to keep abreast of current research but also to contribute to it by investigating "new connexions and hitherto hidden facts of structure which must be taken into account in considering the symptoms of maladies and the actions of medicaments." Eliot herself investigated what was the state of medical knowledge in 1829 [3] and illuminated what she learned with a description of the perception required by scientific research, "that delightful labour of the imagination which is not mere arbitrariness, but the exercise of disciplined power—combining and constructing with the clearest eye for probabilities and the fullest obedience to knowledge; and then, in yet more energetic alliance with impartial Nature, standing aloof to invent tests by which to try its own work." Lydgate, she writes, "was enamoured of that arduous invention which is the very eye of research, provisionally framing its object and correcting it to more and more exactness of relation."

Eliot's description of the ego-decentered perception necessary to science stands in thematic contrast to her description of ego-centered perception through the metaphor of the pier glass and the candle. Scientific perception, self-consciously decentered, is provisional, framed and reframed, and tested against reality, "impartial Nature," which is proof against our wishes and desires. Perception, in Eliot's vision of scientific labor, is a singularly pure compromise between both paradigms of cognition, that reality constructs persons and that persons construct reality. Scientists on the one hand stand apart from nature to exercise imagination and power upon it, and on the other hand, their perception is clear-eyed, their power disciplined, and their construction of reality submitted to rigorous testing. Lydgate does derive satisfaction from his scientific research, but that satisfaction is distanced from the acts of perception he performs in the research itself; his public identity is also involved in his scientific research, but at a similar distance. When he does science, whatever cognitive dissonance there is between his imagination of reality and his testing of it leads to discoveries, discoveries that, on the one hand, advance science, and on the other, do not put at risk his stable self.

But as the cognitive strategies Casaubon employs in his professional life are related to those he employs in his private life, so too are Lydgate's. As he comes to recognize the dissonance between his expectations of marriage and his experience of it, he confronts it rather than, like Casaubon, ignoring it. That Rosamond is an immovable force is painful for him to recognize; that the behavior he took to be an expression of her love is dependent on his gratifying her desires is even more painful. He moves from the certainty "She will never love me much" to the fear "I shall love her no more." His clear-eyed vision of her, however, becomes the ground of his principled renunciation of self—or selves, both private and public. He accedes to his obligation to cherish her knowing the limited satisfaction to be derived from his marriage, and to pay off his debts he takes up a fashionable London practice and writes a treatise on the gout, a disease that afflicts his wealthy patients. But he "to the last occasionally let slip a bitter speech." Expecting to assert himself in the service of larger goods and public causes, he finds it difficult to efface himself in the service of smaller goods and the immediate needs of others. His bitterness evidences his resistance to an ethic of responsibility, however clear-sighted he is about his responsibilities. Dorothea suffers in silence, with Eliot making it clear that her renunciatory ethics, expected of her by society, indeed involve suffering; Lydgate is much less patient.

"Man's love is of man's life a thing apart; / 'Tis woman's whole existence," Byron cheerfully opined [9]. George Eliot, reading Byron's lines, might well have paused.[7] Her fiction undermines his brisk masculine generalizations. She is attentive to the ways reality constructs persons: to the two worlds that construct the persons of men and to their double identities, different yet subtly connected by the cognitive strategies by which they apprehend their private and public worlds, and to the single world that constructs women and the cost to them of their confinement to it. She is equally attentive to the ways persons construct reality and to the risks of cognitive dissonance. Her attentiveness is made visible in plots that manifest perceptual habits and cognitive strategies and in incisive and finely-honed analyses of them; the temptation to quote her formulations is irresistible.

In a profound sense, however, Eliot subscribes to the renunciatory ethics of Maggie Tulliver and Dorothea Brooke. Self-assertion in the private and domestic world, where female self-assertion invariably takes place, takes place, in her view, at the expense of others; it is, to her, selfishness. She judges men's as well as women's domestic conduct by these renunciatory ethics. She records and recognizes how men's selfishness enforces upon women, particularly women like Maggie Tulliver and Dorothea Brooke, peculiar and intense privation. But she cannot imagine for women another world, a public world in which they might stand free of domestic intimacy and fearful imaginings of the pain their acts of self-assertion are likely to inflict on those to whom they are bound by love. Her own escape from the confinement of the private world was costly: until her liaison with Lewes she was deprived of domestic intimacy and all her life she was pained by her estrangement from her brother. Her identity

[7] Eliot, an avid reader of Byron in her younger years, observed (in 1869, when she was fifty): "He seems to me the most *vulgar-minded* genius that ever produced a great effect in literature" [8].

constructed by a gendered upbringing that internalized society's expectations, Eliot was a trespasser in the world of men and felt herself to be one. Her fiction manifests her understanding of the sources of male egoism and the construction of male reality. It also manifests her understanding of the sources of female vulnerability, the limited resources they have to construct female reality, and the self-denying and self-wounding pain of female heroism.

REFERENCES

1. G. Eliot, *Middlemarch*, D. Carroll (ed.), Clarendon Press, Oxford, 1986.
2. B. Hochman, *Character in Literature*, Cornell University Press, Ithaca, New York, 1985.
3. G. S. Haight, *George Eliot: A Biography*, Oxford University Press, New York, 1968.
4. R. S. Redinger, *George Eliot: The Emergent Self*, Knopf, New York, 1975.
5. U. C. Knoepflmacher, On Exile and Fiction: The Leweses and the Shelleys, in *Mothering the Mind*, R. Perry and M. W. Brownley (eds.), Holmes and Meier, New York, 1984.
6. G. Eliot, *The Mill on the Floss*, G. S. Haight (ed.), Clarendon Press, Oxford, 1980.
7. C. Gilligan, *In A Different Voice: Psychological Theory and Women's Development*, Harvard University Press, Cambridge, 1982.
8. G. Eliot, *Selections from George Eliot's Letters*, G. S. Haight (ed.), Yale University Press, New Haven, 1985.
9. G. Gordon, Lord Byron, *Don Juan* 1.194.

CHAPTER 22

Imaging Feminist Visions: Comments on a Bibliography

MICHELLE FINE
LOUISE KIDDER
JOANNE BOELL

> And how do you look backward. By looking forward. And what do they see. As they look forward. They see what they had to do before they could look backward. And there we have it all.
>
> Gertrude Stein
> "Thoughts on an American Contemporary Feeling"
> *Reflections on the Atomic Bomb*, I, 1932.

Feminist visions critique the distribution of social power, child-rearing responsibilities, material resources and interpersonal care in our society. Stretching to imagine societies not stratified by social class, race, and gender; not segregated by sexuality or disability, but organized toward collectivity, cooperation and nurturance, a literature on feminist visions has recently proliferated. Through this chapter all readers—even those initially not "inclined"—are encouraged to imagine social arrangements in which people's experiences are not structured by their gender.

The analysis of "vision" appears central to understanding the relations between imagination, cognition and consciousness. Without imagining alternative arrangements, cognitions about current arrangements remain narrow. Without thinking about what "could be," critical consciousness of "what is" is limited. Without embracing a vision, political struggles for change prove often frustrating. This chapter, then, represents a case study of the difficult process of accumulating visions as a critique of current realities.

To bring together this rudimentary collection of written feminist visions, members of a Task Force of Division 35, American Psychological Association assembled an annotated bibliography.[1] Although the task was initially viewed by some with skepticism, it proved to be an opportunity to integrate visions of a feminist tomorrow with versions of a feminist today.

THE ENTRIES

The breadth and contradictions inherent in this bibliography reveal how democratic the inclusion criteria were. Compiled by a Task Force, there are claims to be neither comprehensive nor internally consistent. Zillah Eisenstein's *Capitalist Patriarchy and The Case for Socialist Feminism* [1] sits neatly beside Betty Friedan's *The Second Stage* [2]. The bibliography includes a range of writings which use gender as a means to critique economic, social and/or psychological arrangements. The entries were organized alphabetically for ease of locating entries by authors' last names.

The bibliographic entries could have been organized in a number of ways, however. A number of themes appear throughout many of the entries, and these themes underlie feminist questions about gender arrangements. For example, parenting: Is it given any consideration? Do the authors advocate dividing it equally between men and women? Is it viewed as a private or public responsibility?

Alternatively, the entries could have been organized by how presumed *sex differences* are explained: Does the author attribute observed differences to genetics? biology? the effects of socialization? the prevalence of androgyny? the influence of object relations? the impact of power differentials?

Or, the entries could have been organized by *divisions of labor.* We could examine the generally understood concept of paid labor and unpaid housework as well as other aspects of "women's work" such as responsibility for nurturance, healing, role modeling, challenging, mentoring, emotional housekeeping and so on. In a "labor framework" most entries could have been classified as to whether the author recognized these activities as the province of women, men or both, the responsibility of individuals or social collectives.

In one simple utopian vision equality between men and women is no longer a problem. Unpaid reproductive and paid productive work are not separated. Gender does not determine wages, rights, nor duties. This vision is achieved in a world of all women—simultaneously strong and nurturant.

Charlotte Perkins Gilman creates this society in her novel *Herland* [3]. Most of the novel is clearly science fiction, and much of it is very funny. Children are conceived parthenogenetically, and only girls are born. Child rearing, the most

[1] Many women contributed to the bibliography who individually and collectively deserve credit. Some were members of the Division 35 Task Force on Feminist Visions and others were members of the Delaware Valley Women's Studies Consortium. The bibliography may be purchased for $1.00 from Louise Kidder, Psychology Department, Temple University, Philadelphia, Pennsylvania 19122.

highly honored work, is entrusted to specialists, not necessarily the biological mothers. While Gilman wrongly assumes that all women would *like* to bear children, she correctly recognizes not all would enjoy or excel at the work of mothering, particularly in the solitude of their own homes. The story is told through the encounters of three men who, upon arriving at Herland in disbelief, have their assumptions about women disrupted with each encounter.

Other authors urge women to "master" those "labors" exclusively associated with male power [2] . Often classified as liberal feminism, these writings assume current economic and familial arrangements to be fair, even desirable. Capitalism and the nuclear, heterosexual, monogamous family need only be reformed to "equalize" women's and men's outcomes. The structures themselves are presumed intact and necessary.

Still other authors assert a more radical position on labor. Gender, social class, racial and heterosexist-based inequities are recognized as interdependent, sustaining capitalist, racist, patriarchal institutions. These analyses trace the webbing of these "isms" as they shape women's lives.

Yet even a cursory review of the individual entries reveals that they vary broadly in their analyses of gender and feminism. Further, the bibliography does not provide analysis of any of the entries. This collection therefore in many ways reproduces the substance and tattered edges of feminism today. In some respects this is unfortunate—a critical analysis would have enriched the bibliography. But as it stands, the Task Force's bibliography permits a review of how the threads were woven together and where the entries, like contemporary political divisions within feminism have frayed.

SOURCES OF FEMINIST VISIONS: WOMEN ON THE MARGINS

From where do feminist visions arise? While it can be said that feminist visions, because they are cultivated within patriarchal structures, are imbued with aspects of domination, power and inequality, it is also true that visions enable movement beyond current structures, even as they are formed through resistance to those structures.

This bibliography aims to cultivate the pluralism which defines women's lives. Feminism of the 1960s/70s/80s is captured in a popular literature dominated by the writings of middle class, usually heterosexual, almost always non-disabled, white women. Excluded have been the experiences and analyses of Black, Hispanic, Asian and Native American women, lesbians and bi-sexual women, poor and working class women, and women with disabilities. Often put out "as if" they represented the experiences of all women, the more privileged voices obscured the diversity of women's lives.

Women who reside on the margins of "mainstream" North American traditions provide rich material for alternative futures [4] . These authors emerge as critics of current gender arrangements, offering alternative models for organizing women's lives. Drawing from cross cultural and multi-ethnic ethnographies and autobiographies, the bibliography weaves analyses of women's resistance to patriarchal constructions (see Morga and Anzaldúa, *This Bridge Called My Back* [5], an anthology of writings by Radical Women of Color which combine poetry and prose, anger and affection; Ethel Phelps, *Tatterhood and Other Tales* [6]).

Voices of women long viewed as "deviants," such as lesbian women (see Radclyffe Hall's *Well of Loneliness* [7], Jill Johnston's *Lesbian Nation* [8], Lillian Faderman's *Surpassing the Love of Men* [9]); women long viewed as "neutered," such as women with disabilities (see Fine and Asch, "Disabled Women: Sexism without the Pedestal" [4]), and women long dismissed as "traditional" (see Lillian Rubin, *Worlds of Pain: Life in the Working Class Family* [10]) diversify the images.

By examining personal diaries and writings on social movements for economic change (see Emma Goldman, *Living My Life* [11]) and restructured gender arrangements (see Simone de Beauvoir's *The Second Sex* [12]), the analysis of how capitalism and patriarchy structure inequities between women and men is deepened. Journeys into cross cultural and science fiction literatures (e.g., Ursula Le Guin's *Left Hand of Darkness*, or *The Word for the World Is Forest* [13, 14]) challenge what is assumed "natural," "transhistorical" or "necessary." By imaging the future, one can reinterpret the present (see Zillah Eisenstein, *The Radical Future of Liberal Feminism* [15]; Marily Ferguson, *The Acquarian Conspiracy: Personal and Social Transformation in the 1980's* [16]), taking note of assertive, strong, kind and vulnerable behaviors women have always engaged in, which have previously gone unnoticed.

Locating Injustice

Feminist visions, while sharpening a critique of current inequities, can propose strategies for confronting these inequities. Some writers locate the source of the problems and therefore the solutions in *economics*. Meredith Tax describes, for example, socialist feminist trade unions coalitions organized around re-allocation of resources and re-analysis of social conditions (e.g., *The Rising of the Women* [17]). Others frame the problem in terms of mothers *being exclusively responsible* for child care and nurturance. Nancy Chodorow [18] and Dorothy Dinnerstein [19] advocate the collective redistribution of child rearing responsibilities. Carol Gilligan calls for the societal infusion of nurturance, caring and intimacy as fundamental to social relationships (e.g., Carol Gilligan, *In A Different Voice* [20]). Finally, some target the intractable core of *patriarchy* as the transhistorical source of women's oppression.

As a collection, the bibliography demands a commitment to critical analyses and restructuring of social arrangements so that women can control their reproductive sexual lives; in which social collectives participate in decisions about allocations of material, child rearing and emotional resources. The astute reader will recognize, however, that the bibliography is fraught with contradictions in analyses and solutions.

THE DYNAMICS OF INJUSTICE

Entertaining alternative visions of gender, race and class arrangements enables an examination of the dynamics which sustain current inequities. Nancy Chodorow, in *The Reproduction of Mothering* [18], documents how the exclusive use of women as primary child rearers limits the development of women, as well as their sons and daughters. Advocating a social commitment to child rearing by men and women, she frames this problem as one of a skewed allocation of child rearing responsibilities. In a society committed to public child care by men and women, personality development of boys and girls might be less sex-typed.

Jean Baker Miller, in *Toward a New Psychology of Women* [21], explicates how power relations of domination-subordination characterize male female relations. Women as "subordinates," are expected to help men deny their own vulnerability. Women keep secrets for men[2], saving men from knowing their emotional, soft and weak selves. Women thereby carry an emotional double-load. The exposé of these secrets, Miller argues, would free women from the burden of warehousing society's emotions, and would perhaps force men to share responsibility for emotional work. The inequity is framed as one of social power and psychological care-taking by women of men.

Nancy Henley, in her book, *Body Politics: Power, Sex and Nonverbal Communication* [22] also provides critical commentary on the power dynamics between women and men. For her the unit of analysis is behavior. She demonstrates that patterns of touching, eye contact, familiar address, and other interactions between the powerful (men) and powerless (women) masquerade as intimacy. She argues that women need to touch men, stare, use first names, take up physical space and be nonverbally assertive to disrupt these nonverbal reproductions of power inequities.

These authors analyze the processes by which social inequities are reproduced in today's child rearing practices, responsibility for psychological nurturance and in the enactment of nonverbal behaviors. Another group of writers has begun to consider more equitable allocations of power and resources. Dolores Hayden writes about, "What would a nonsexist city be like?" [23]. Zillah Eisenstein [2] edits a forum on the contradictions of capitalism and patriarchy/socialism and feminism. Diane Ehrensaft, in her article "When Women and Men Mother" [24] provides a powerful analysis of co-parenting, arguing that women may not

[2] For instance, men describe to women their fears, and women are responsible to not tell anyone about these areas of male vulnerability.

willingly share child rearing responsibilities with men until women have an equal share of economic rewards and responsibilities.

These authors, who have experimented with and thought about alternative arrangements, illuminate today's inequities, tomorrow's fantasies and the dilemmas encountered in times of transition—from vision to reality.

FEMINIST VISIONS EXPOSING PSYCHOLOGICAL ASSUMPTIONS

> For those who are concerned with generating radically different possibilities for the future, the technique of brainstorming . . . is designed to jog people loose from their customary mental ruts and help them imagine wildly different 'somethings.'
>
> Elise Boulding
> Futurology and the Imaging Capacity of the West

As the visions introduced in this bibliography identify social inequities, the limits of social science, research and theorizing are also exposed. The bibliographic entries reject some assumptions essential to psychological thinking—e.g., individualism, meritocratic beliefs, and privatization of women's lives. Instead, women's collective endeavors are documented (see Meredith Tax, *The Rising of Women* [17]); women's anger examined (see Audre Lourde on the "Uses of Anger" [25]) and women's perceptions of discrimination (see Robert and Jane Coles, *Women in Crisis* [26]) recognized as requisite to social change. Demanded are *public* commitments to issues long considered personal and shouldered by women as if they were indeed private (see Rayna Rapp, Ellen Ross, and Renate Bridenthal, "Examining Family History" [27]).

Transcending the assumptions of today, the bibliography offers worlds without male authority (see Paula Webster, "Matriarchy: A Vision of Power" [28]), without gender (see Suzanne Kessler and Wendy McKenna, *Gender: An Ethnomethodological Approach* [29]), without economic inequity (see Zillah Eisenstein, *Capitalist Patriarchy and the Case for Socialist Feminism* [2]) and without interference (see Virginia Woolf, *A Room of One's Own* [30]). Many of the works present radical analyses of capitalism (see Susan Strasser, *Never Done* [31], on American housework under capitalism), racism (see Maya Angelou, *I Know Why the Caged Bird Sings* [32]), sexism (see Shulamith Firestone, *The Dialectics of Sex* [33]), religion (see Mary Daly, *Beyond God the Father and Gyn/Ecology* [34, 35]; Ann Matter, "The Virgin Mary: A Goddess?" [36]) and heterosexism (see Moraga and Anzaldúa, *This Bridge Called My Back* [5]) and show how they combine to make women mad (see Charlotte Perkins Gilman, *The Yellow Wallpaper* [37] and Marge Piercy, *Woman on the Edge of Time* [38]).

Through these writings it is clear that ideologies about women's passivity and fears of success notwithstanding, women have responded to injustice with strength, resistance and in numbers: through collective separatism [33], progressive coalitions [17], structural reform [39] and varied psychological coping mechanisms [40].

Women have actively created networks and structures, by choice or not, in which nurturance and pooling of resources are social values: in theology [41]; among kin [42, 43]; in love and sexual relationships [44]; at work [45]; and in how women relate to themselves [46, 47].

One major question about feminist futures which lingers is what to do about women's traditional work; nurturing at home and on the job. The secretary at work, expected to do much more than is written in a job description, will frequently have to coordinate office parties, serve coffee, remember birthdays, shop for other people's presents, and tend to details that make life in the office more pleasant and efficient—for everyone but her. Though aspects of the job are undoubtedly exploitative, some are fundamentally nurturant activities—the social and emotional housekeeping at the office. How are these to be managed? A few feminist visions call for nurturant work to be depersonalized and bureaucraticized. In others, shared by men and women; in still others, reimbursed financially.

Like with this question of nurturance, through imaging alternatives a variety of feminist contradictions emerge which deserve attention. Many are current in today's feminist discourse:

- To what extent should feminists introduce "nurturance" as a prevailing social value? Will this responsibility, as it has in the past, fall to women as "emotional and relational experts?"
- How can social groupings and structures be made responsive to human needs for intimacy, commitment and community to challenge the ideological function of the traditional family? Can a radical politic incorporate privacy needs, for example?
- What is the role for men in feminist futures, e.g., in decisions about child caring and child rearing?
- How can a feminist politic incorporate the multiple sources of oppression, (e.g., gender, class, race, sexual orientation and disability) and sustain a rich gender-based critique of social institutions?
- Is sexuality a site of oppression, liberation or both for women?
- From what bases do women get power today (e.g., in rearing children or in building relationships); to what extent do the strategies for "empowering women" today narrow the breadth of women's potential power in the future?

Looking across the feminist visions, it is perhaps through discourse about these contradictions that more progressive, less divisive feminist politics develop.

THE FUNCTIONS OF BEING VISIONARY

Imaging feminist rearrangements is not without its problems. Some could say that only a Pollyanna would spin a bibliography of fantasy at a time when the potential for blowing ourselves up with nuclear arms looms so large. Others might insist that visions are not visionable—that people's cognitive abilities may be so constricted by what exists *now* that even "radical" visions are only modifications within, not beyond, current arrangements. Or maybe people's predictive abilities, while adequate to envision continued exploitation, are too primitive to anticipate movements of resistance or change. And what would this feminist future look like, anyway [48]?

In this bibliography, we drew on the privilege of dreamers. We integrated diversity, permitted contradiction and suspended disbelief. We recognized that only with *visions* can work for feminist goals persist. These feminist visions, promoted by scholars, writers and activists, offer no sure fire solutions—only a process to think about alternatives, silenced voices and new visions of justice. Many of these visions bring with them new problems to be managed—probably managed by women. This compilation of visions of tomorrow and versions of today helped move this Task Force of academics, activists, and feminists beyond the constricted view of gender shaped by today's economic, social and psychological arrangements between men and women.

ACKNOWLEDGMENT

We wish to thank Rhoda Unger for her support and encouragement on this manuscript.

REFERENCES

1. Z. Eisenstein (ed.), *Capitalist Patriarchy and the Case for Socialist Feminism*, Monthly Review Press, New York, 1979.
2. B. Friedan, *The Second Stage*, Summit Books, New York, 1981.
3. C. P. Gilman, *Herland*, Pantheon Books, New York, 1979.
4. M. Fine and A. Asch, Disabled Women: Sexism without the Pedestal, *Journal of Sociology and Social Welfare*, *6*:2, pp. 233-248, 1982.
5. C. Moraga and G. Anzaldúa, (eds.), *This Bridge Called My Back: Writings by Radical Women of Color*, Persephone Press, Watertown, Massachusetts, 1981.
6. E. Phelps (ed.), *Tatterhood and Other Tales*, Feminist Press, New York, 1978.
7. R. Hall, *The Well of Loneliness*, Avon Books, New York, 1981.
8. J. Johnston, *Lesbian Nation: The Feminist Solution*, Simon and Schuster, New York, 1974.
9. L. Faderman, *Surpassing the Love of Men*, William Morrow, New York, 1981.
10. L. Rubin, *Worlds of Pain: Life in the Working Class Family*, Basic Books, New York, 1976.

11. E. Goldman, *Living My Life*, Dover Publications, Inc., New York, 1930.
12. S. De Beauvoir, *The Second Sex*, Vintage Books, New York, 1973.
13. U. K. LeGuin, *Left Hand of Darkness*, Harper and Row, New York, 1980.
14. ______, *The Word for the World Is Forest*, Berkley, New York, 1976.
15. Z. Eisenstein, *The Radical Future of Liberal Feminism*, Longman, New York, 1981.
16. M. Ferguson, *The Acquarian Conspiracy: Personal and Social Transformations in the 1980's*, J. P. Tarcher, Inc., Los Angeles, 1980.
17. M. Tax, *The Rising of the Women*, Monthly Review Press, New York, 1980.
18. N. Chodorow, *The Reproduction of Mothering: Psychoanalysis and the Sociology of Gender*, University of California Press, Berkeley, California, 1978.
19. D. Dinnerstein, *The Mermaid and the Minotaur: Sexual Arrangement and Human Malaise*, Harper and Row, Inc., New York, 1976.
20. C. Gilligan, *In A Different Voice*, Harvard University Press, Cambridge, 1983.
21. J. B. Miller, *Toward a New Psychology of Women*, Beacon Press, Boston, 1977.
22. N. M. Henley, *Body Politics: Power, Sex, and Nonverbal Communication*, Prentice-Hall, Englewood Cliffs, New Jersey, 1977.
23. D. Hayden, What Would a Non-Sexist City Be Like: Speculations On Housing, Urban Design, and Human Work, *Signs: Journal of Women in Culture and Society*, *5*, pp. 170-187, 1980.
24. D. Ehrensaft, When Women and Men Mother, *Socialist Review*, *10*, p. 49, January/February 1980.
25. A. Lourde, The Uses of Anger, Keynote Address: The NWSA Convention, *Women's Studies Quarterly*, *9*, p. 3, Fall 1981.
26. R. Coles and J. H. Coles, *Women in Crisis*, Delcorte, New York, 1978.
27. R. Rapp, E. Ross, and R. Bridenthal, Examining Family History, *Feminist Studies*, *5*, p. 1, Spring 1979.
28. P. Webster, Matriarchy: A Vision of Power, in *Toward an Anthropology of Women*, R. R. Reiter (ed.), Monthly Review Press, New York, 1975.
29. S. Kessler and W. McKenna, *Gender: An Ethnomethodological Approach*, Wiley, New York, 1978.
30. V. Woolf, *A Room of One's Own*, Harcourt, Brace, Jovanovich, Inc., New York, 1963.
31. S. Stresser, *Never Done: A History of American Housework*, Pantheon Books, New York, 1982.
32. M. Angelou, *I Know Why The Caged Bird Sings*, Bantam, New York, 1971.
33. S. Firestone, *The Dialectics of Sex*, Morrow, New York, 1970.
34. M. Daly, *Beyond God the Father*, Beacon, Boston, 1973.
35. ______, *Gyn/Ecology: The Metaethics of Radical Feminism*, Beacon, Boston, 1979.
36. E. A. Matter, The Virgin Mary: A Goddess? in *An Introduction to the Religion of the Goddess*, C. Olson (ed.), Seabury, New York, 1982.
37. C. P. Gilman, *The Yellow Wallpaper*, Feminist Press, New York, 1973.
38. M. Piercy, *Woman on the Edge of Time*, Fawcett, New York, 1978.
39. *Manual on Pay Equity: Conference on Alternative State and Local Policies*, 2000 Florida Avenue, N.W., Washington, D.C. 20009, 1980.

40. L. M. Glennon, *Women and Dualism: A Sociology of Knowledge Analysis*, Longman, New York, 1979.
41. C. C. Gould and M. W. Wartofsky (eds.), *Women and Philosophy: Toward a Theory of Liberation*, Putnam, New York, 1976.
42. C. Stack, *All Our Kin*, Harper and Row, New York, 1974.
43. L. Gould, *X: A Fabulous Child's Story*, Daughters, Houston, 1981.
44. *Heresies #12: The Sex Issue*, 1981.
45. S. Ruddick and P. Daniels (eds.), *Working It Out*, Pantheon, New York, 1977.
46. M. Gordon, *Final Payments*, Ballantine Books, New York, 1978.
47. ———, *The Company of Women*, Random House, New York, 1980.
48. P. Rosser, "Countdown to the Year 2000: Is There A Feminist Future?," *Ms., IX*, 75-78, February 1981.

CHAPTER 23

The Social Construction of Gender: The Turn to Fiction

SONDRA FARGANIS

Both within sociology and within women's studies, there has been interest, of late, in the social construction of gender, that is, in the ways in which the individual comes to learn of his or her sex and the ways in which the society comes to regard that sexuality. As a counter to theories of biological determinism, with their images of the body as a mechanistic model operating on rather simplistic notions of cause and effect, and as a refutation of Freudian models which have been interpreted as being similarly fixed and rigid in their notions of how anatomy colors actions, social constructionism has emphasized the role that the historical constellations of social and political power play in defining gender and its accompanying sexual and familial relationships. Instead of believing that what we are is set by our bodies which have fixed inputs and outputs, predictable causes and effects, the understanding is that gender is dependent upon the particularities of social circumstance and the accepted knowledge of systems of the time.

The modern statement of the ways in which and the limits on how social forces construct human personalities is to be found in the work of Peter Berger and Thomas Luckmann. The valuableness of their thesis in *The Social Construction of Reality* is its emphasis on the dialectical relationship between self and society. Who we are and how we come to know who we are are socially conditioned; that is, the self is situated in a biology that occupies a moment in *a* time and *a* space.

Unlike social determinism, social constructionism gives credit to the role that individuals play in determining their lives. Through consciousness, persons can change their social structure; that is, they can reconstruct the boundaries around them. The thrust of constructionism is in decided opposition to either biological and/or psychological determinism. For, in introducing existential themes of human freedom to the legacy of a social theory that had emphasized the ways in which factors of class, status and power shape and mold personality, Berger and Luckmann offer a route out of the "gigantic Alcatraz" [1, p. 90] that society, sitting on top of us as it does, appears to be.

If looked at more closely, social constructionism is not so naive as to underestimate the particular patterns of stratification which place and lock people into set social maps. What individuals know they know from society, from the ways in which the groups into which they are born structure their lives. Individuals see what they have been socialized into seeing and the significant question concerns how active individuals are in questioning the socialization processes, that is, in reconstructing their worlds.

Within any given society and at any point in time, there exist institutions—the church, for example, or marriage—which have rules and regulations which establish patterns of behavior, that is, which explain how the individual is to act if he or she is to realize the purposes of the institution. Learning how to act or behave is learning how to play socially sanctioned roles, which are, as in a drama, parts which spell out the rights and obligations incumbent upon one. Individuals in the society take the institutions as being true or real: they are "experienced as existing over and beyond the individuals who 'happen' to embody them at the moment . . . [they] are experienced as a reality of their own, a reality that confronts the individual as an external and coercive fact" [2, p. 58]. Institutions are not abstract; like individuals, they exist in history and are a product and a reflection of concrete interests. It is by understanding these interests that we understand the institutions: "It is impossible to understand an institution adequately without an understanding of the historical process in which it was produced" [2, pp. 54-55].

It is not simply the case that "reality constructs the person" or that "the person constructs reality"—if I may make reference to two distinct paradigms [3], but, rather, that the construction of self occurs in a reality that is *there* and that the "there-ness" and the "one-ness" are in a dialectical relationship with each other. The reality is given meaning by concrete historical actors and it is in this sense that the reality is also an historical reality: "The individual *realizes* himself in society—that is, he recognizes his identity in socially defined terms and these definitions *become reality* as he lives in society" [4, p. 108]. For in our relationships with people in precise and specific societies—in coming face to face with them, in learning their language, in gaining knowledge of the society—we develop ourselves: "the process of becoming man takes place in an interrelationship with an environment [which is] . . . both a natural and a human one" [2, p. 48]. The sociologist, then, always wants to know the historicity of the there-ness, and, sociological inquiries into facts of class, status and power—the indices of social stratification—are ways of understanding the construction of social selves.

One of the continuing concerns of those working within the social constructionist framework is whether there are biological differences relating to childbearing that result in sex-specific behavior that makes it distinct–a relationship between a woman and the child she bears, for example. Just how plastic is the individual? Just how much can a person be molded by social and political constellations? Sociologists and anthropologists tend to stress the ways in which human beings can be shaped by the social order; that is, they stress human malleability and pliability. Across societies, variety is the norm, even though within any given culture set norms or structured patterns of behavior do occur and the values–the ideology–of the society–exist to ensure that people will be socialized to take the norms as the given, the sole reality, the truth. Berger and Luckmann, speaking of sexual variety, write: "The empirical relativity of these configurations, their immense variety and luxurious inventiveness, indicate that they are the product of man's own sociocultural formations rather than of a biologically fixed human nature" [2, pp. 49-50].

While social constraints exist, the individual is not let off the hook in choosing how to behave. Moral considerations come into play insofar as the individual has freedom to say "no" to some demands. Social constructionism walks this tightrope: the society encourages and oftentimes demands the personality traits it requires if the values of the system are to be held intact while some inner voice tells the individual to follow his or her personal values, make his or her own moral choices, choose his or her own sexual arrangements.

Social constructionism, while emphasizing the regularities and patterns of social behavior, posits a special quality to being human. Berger and Luckmann are thus able to avoid the sociological determinism that in lesser hands might overburden social constructionism. Individuals are not locked into a social prison from which there is no escape, even though the social self is, to a large degree, shaped, molded, and controlled by social forces that exist prior to and outside the person. The prison-like quality of society conditions the individual, predisposes him or her to acting in certain ways in much the way that physical and biological forces limit what people can and cannot do: society is decisive for the individual just as much as the individual is decisive for society and just as much as the laws of gravity and hormonal levels are decisive for human action. Yet, institutions as well as individuals change. Under certain conditions, persons can refuse the demands of the system; in fact, for Berger, the individual is guilty, in Sartrian terms, of "bad faith" if he or she refuses to recognize instances where defiance is possible. Berger anguishes over "a flight from freedom, a dishonest evasion of the 'agony of choice'" [4, p. 143]. Paradoxically, then, the knowledge we have of the ways in which society is socially constructed is the route to negation, of refusing to do what the society demands of us: seeing society as a social construct means seeing it as a human product.

In this chapter, I am interested in seeing how one understands sex-specific behavior within the social constructionist perspective. In particular, I am interested in issues concerning mothering and the institution of motherhood, the ways in which these are socially conditioned, the ways in which these are changed, and the political and moral consequences of policies which either advance or challenge the given-ness of children to women born (to alter Adrienne Rich's phraseology somewhat [5]). I have looked at this problem in a traditional way elsewhere [6], using the analytic prism of the sociology of knowledge to see how ideas on motherhood are socially constructed and reconstructed. Here, I should like to turn to a recent work of fiction, Margaret Atwood's *The Handmaid's Tale* [7], and see what we can learn from an artist with vision, while, in turn, bringing her ideas back into the contemporary landscape where issues of what constitutes a mother and what rights, privileges and obligations constitute the relationship between mother and child are being worked out in laboratories as well as in courts of law. More precisely, I am interested in how Atwood sheds light on the ways in which sex and gender are socially constructed and how it might be the case that there is a part of that self that is not subject to social construction. Two particular instances bear looking at: a woman's responsibility for the fetus she is to birth; and the problematic of surrogate mothers.

I have read *The Handmaid's Tale* as the presentation of an artist, a performer, if you will, who presents a story to which we must respond. Take heed, the Handmaid says: this is my tale, a tocsin, a warning signal about the dangerous trends in contemporary society, and by your response I shall know of what stuff you are made. For surely, the Handmaid continues, I intend to play upon your fears of the present by offering you a vision of the future that bears witness to the ways in which certain ideas of the here and now will grow and flourish.

The locale is Cambridge (Harvard, perhaps), sometime around 2020, and the Republic of Gilead, designed by the Sons of Jacob Think-Tank, has been set up in a crisis-ridden America with carefully circumscribed echelons to rule this post-Holocaust, post-nuclear society. There are the rulers, the guardians and educators and the producers, all of which parallels the class structure in Plato's *Republic*. In Gilead, women have been returned to the hearth and home, some to be Wives, some to do the housework (the Marthas), some to breed children (the Handmaids), and some to assist the breeders (the Aunts). The Handmaids are part of the producing echelon, although there are groups below them—colonies of portable populations, prostitutes, enemies, unwomen, unbabies and gender traitors. The Handmaids belong to the commanders (the tale is told by the Handmaid Of-Fred, of her master), are kept in good health, and are wombs through which the masters have children. By lying, at propitious moments, between the thighs of the Wives of the commander, they perform the service of being impregnated by their masters. The Handmaid's job is to bear Fred a perfect baby; if she fails to conceive after three trys, or if the baby is born deformed, the Handmaid will be banished to the Colonies to clean up radioactive nuclear wastes, surviving there three years at best.

As presented by the Handmaid as narrator, visions of George Orwell's *1984* come to mind; but Gilead is more real and, therefore, more frightening because there are references to issues of concern to us now–pornography, nuclear warfare, religious fundamentalism, sexual liberation. Atwood suggests that her allegory will evolve out of our actions on these issues in our own society. The Handmaid is a womb-as-object and the tale concerns the Handmaid's recollections of the past, her hatred and fear of the present, and her efforts to escape across the border to Canada. At the book's conclusion, we learn that her tale has been preserved on tapes which were discovered in the 22nd century; in the concluding coda, familiar sounding academicians attempt to deconstruct the now-past Gilead.

Atwood shows us how things will look in the future and then in the future beyond that. What warnings do we hear when we read the tale of a woman who is a "social vessel," a "two-legged womb," a container for fetuses? On one level, Atwood's "ladies in reduced circumstances" are a warning that we must not take our feminist rights for granted and must not assume that the struggle for equality is over and that we can sit back and relax. We must not ignore instances of rights being whittled away. At another level, Atwood warns about equating sex with procreation or reducing birthing to a biological act. Here she is fearful of emphasizing the uniqueness of women, to wit, their biological potential to bear children. In the Gidlean vision of a woman's culture, the politics of feminine separatism and the ideology of those who emphasize women's distinctiveness contribute to, in the sense of play into, the hands of Gilead's ruling echelon. The Handmaids are sexual vessels without power, ultimately subserviant to the military-industrial-knowledge elite. Because the society fears the declining fertility rate, those women who can bear healthy babies are commanded to produce them. The idea that women are their bodies is given political import: Gilead uses the myth of biological determinism to construct a fusion of sex and gender ("anatomy is destiny"). In other words, the Gileadian elite, knowing that power rests with those who float the myths and institutionalize the idology, use biological determinism to keep the social order in line. Social constructionism becomes social determinism through the myth of biological determinism. "Anatomy is destiny" functions like Plato's Noble Lie.

In Atwood's dystopia, the richness and toleration of diversity is gone. Gilead, whose trappings are a Christian fundamentalist society where the "natural order of things" is followed, allows for no options, no choices, as to how to appropriate one's body. The two realms, embraced by liberalism–public and private–are collapsed into one. Gilead is social constructionism without the tightrope: a society of perfect socialization in which there is only a public persona whose gender is defined by those who have power. Gilead is Herbert Marcuse's "one-dimensional" society [8], peopled by individuals who are atomized, organized and manipulated. If what is unique to the individual, what is his or her essential quality, is the ability to reason–what Berger would see as the freedom to assess and reject–then the Gildean world jeopardizes the continuation of this characteristically human trait. The individual can no longer choose how to live or give self-direction to his or her life. The public and private realms, once fused and flattened into a "one-dimensionality," preclude the presence of forces which could contradict the present set of arrangements and establish a critical perspective for a qualitatively different set of alternatives. In Atwood's tale, Gilead wins out through war, assassination, nuclear devastation, AIDS. Gilead needs armed force and nuclear conflict to establish its power base, in addition to social engineering skills. In Marcuse's "one-dimensional" society, persons become robotized, administered and dulled not by brute force but by social engineering or scientific management selling goods and services while subtly manipulating human needs and human relationships.

Like the sociologist, Atwood is concerned with the ways in which sexuality is shaped, that is, how power constitutes emotions and desires and sexual arrangements. Sex exists within society: a society that devalues women except for their childbearing potentials defines sex in a certain way. Gilead, but another version of a "brave new world," has as its "collective conscience" the morality of righteousness, having invested the power to pronounce on how one ought to live to those who are the guardians of the state. Gilead, in response to the crisis of sexual meanings of the late twentieth-century, came to see the need to regulate and control sexual practices. The leadership cadre of Gilead feared the demystification of sexuality, that is, the calling into question of sexual practices by social movements such as the woman's movement and the gay rights movement. These movements were not prepared to accept the received ideology which envalued a certain kind of puritanical heterosexuality and which acted to constrain certain forms of eroticism. Atwood, through her imagery of the loss of self, of self-direction and self-purpose, warns us of the totalitarianism of righteousness. Gilead is different from the social world we presently know; for in Atwood's New England of the twenty-first century we are not troubled by a plurality of moralities. We are not troubled by pornography or religious diversity or unusual sexual behavior or the decline in fertility. These problems no longer confront us. Answers exist to black and white questions: women are controlled so they can breed; the unproductive are reassigned to the colonies to clean up radioactive and toxic waste, becoming Unwomen; deformed children become Unbabies; enemies are clearly defined. Nothing becomes a problem: the state is conflict-free.

Atwood allows us to understand how Offred the Handmaid, experiences her oppression. Our feminist interlocutors–Atwood and her Handmaid–whom we can trust, tell us of the dangers of allowing those in power (the guardians of Gilead) to determine how we ought to live. Renounce, Atwood is saying, those philosophic voices which have an elitist megastructure. Beware any philosophic system which is not aware of the precise, specific and historically real ways in which sex and privacy are constructed and realized. In other words, it is not enough to abstractly understand the social construction of sexuality; one must also understand who has the power to construct that sexuality *at the moment*. In allowing sex to be named, studied and expertized, we grant sex the status of a discourse and we grant power to those who at that moment of time write the discourses. Those men of knowledge housed in those think-tanks called universities or research laboratories contribute, in no small way, to Gilead and take away from us, in the process, the chance to find out for ourselves who and what we are. Power becomes, as Michel Foucault warns, the power of experts, the power of definition and the power of control: once sexuality becomes a matter for experts and a legitimate subject to be written on—that is, once it becomes totally and completely demystified, "a human being turns him or herself into a subject" [9, p. 208] to be analyzed by others. There is the real invasion of the body snatchers. Foucault is worried that in the name of what Max Horkheimer would call "psychological enlightenment" [10, p. 12]—the Son of Jacob Think Tank, in Atwood's terms—the behavior of people will be manipulated and constructed along lines set by mind-managers.

Yet there is some hope in Gilead, some way beyond the social construction of self. Atwood offers the example of her Handmaid, who like the lesbian Moira resists having lust, that most private of desires, controlled. Moira managers to have her company of women and the Handmaid her Nick, although at a very high price. Neither wants to be a "sacred vessel" or a "two-legged womb" who is to produce the new ruling elite: women, or at least some of them, reject sex on demand or sex as a chore. Each wants sex that is playful, that is, without purpose or production. Each longs for a place to call one's own, a place where one's instinct for the erotic can be given free play, a place where the characters can be left to their own devices to read, and think, and be passionate in his or her own way.

Atwood forces us to get at the heart of social constructionist theory. If we emphasize the ways in which we are a product of the society and stress that personalities are shaped by the nexus of power and ideology, then are there any limitations to this defining process? At what point does social constructionism become social determinism?

Atwood's characters—certainly the Handmaid and Moira—have a self beyond the social self, although it may be known only to the individual. The Handmaid is not one-dimensional: she has consciousness even if the sociopolitical forces do not allow her to realize that self in the concrete. The view that each person has a unique link to his or herself—that only I know who I am and what I think—may not be illusory. Through dialogue with this self I know how to act: I am not dependent upon the church (with fears of salvation or damnation) or the state to tell me how to act. What I must safeguard, then, is this dialogue, or the possibility of this dialogue: to do this I must be able to see beyond social construction, social conditioning and social control—but how do I do this if I am an historical subject grounded in a precise social moment?

One of the reasons why Berger is so valuable is that he postulates a moral view of the person that, like Kant's transcendent subject, is a potential source of negation, a potential resister of social power. Gilead is as close as one will get to that "gigantic Alcatraz" which any society potentially is. Atwood, in describing the Handmaid's efforts to escape as well as by adding a coda in which there are people (however pure-white, sterile and academic they might be) to tell of Gilead, reminds us that political efforts can call into question the values of the dominant social order. Put differently, to insure that social constructionism does not become social determinism, the individual psyche must raise questions and social actors must be linked with social movements which press for public spaces in which to discuss the myths, values and ideology of the society.

One could put this another way and say that social constructionism without limits leads to fascism [11, 12], that a socially constructed society can lead to the intrusion of state power via state ideology into the individual's mind and body and those who instruct us in how to behave, the purveyors of the techniques, become the new agents of social domination. Foreseeing a calamitous future, some social commentators (Horkheimer and Christopher Lasch, for instance [10, 13, 14]) are pessimistic about the "helping professions," the sexologists, and the value-clarificationists who, in leading us toward a conflict-free society, lead us to an inauthentic existence. This age of the expert extracts conformity in the name of scientific rationality: this is a new kind of despotism. The "loss of interiority" results in a new kind of modern man: "As interiority has withered away, the joy of making personal decisions, of cultural development, and of the free exercise of imagination has gone with it. Other inclinations and other goals mark the man of today: technological expertise, presence of mind, pleasure in the mastery of machinery, the need to be part of and agree with the majority of some group which is chosen as a model and whose regulations replace individual judgment. Advice, prescriptions, and patterns for guidance replace moral substance" [10, p. 12].

Throughout *The Handmaid's Tale*, Atwood shows the consequences of losing things which are particular to ourselves, most especially the sense of our body. Gilead by controlling sex has made it meaningless and reduced it to the single act of procreation. Offred, for example, bemoans the passing of "falling in love" and Atwood most certainly worries about the increasing power that social engineers have over the lives of individuals. She wants not a socially free self but a socially mediated self and a socially aware self.

In *Eros and Civilization* [15], Marcuse posits the aesthetic dimension as the principle means by which the present social reality can be called into question. The imagination, realizing or reasonably constructing what is historically possible, can spearhead a political movement whose political weapon would be a new consciousness, in Freudian terms, a new reality principle. This political movement would act to bring into being a new non-repressive reality.

The aesthetic is then the political agent of negation. I understand Marcuse to be saying, following Freud, that the individual comes to understand that he or she cannot have the immediate gratification of needs and must move from the pleasure to the reality principles. Rather than self-destruct, the id becomes the organized ego and reason tests, understands and orders the phenomena of reality. This move from pleasure to reality makes the individual a social animal, one who is capable of consciously recognizing the historical conditions under which the pleasure-seeking instincts must operate. With the addition of the superego, the adoption of a specific moral code, the conscience of the society becomes introjected into the conscience of the individual. The person will now do what the present reality (mediated by the ego) and the past culture (mediated by the superego) orders.

There is a socio-psychological path out of the pact that ego has made with reality, for the pact, if not questioned, leads to a dangerous obedience to authority. Phantasy, or imagination–id-derived and id-satisfied–finds a conscious outlet in art, the real exposition of dreams. Here are played out the truths which existed before the organized reality came into being. Here lies the key to seeing beyond the established or historical reality principle.

The Handmaid, by telling her tale, is acting politically in the only way that she can. Through phantasy, through imagination, through art–the aesthetic realm–the Handmaid sublimates in a manner that is not repressive. The tale survives because it is generated by images that are more satisfying and pleasurable than those which are legitimately, socially and politically constructed. The aesthetic realm must be organized for and controlled by the prevailing historical form of domination. Only a conscience freed from manipulation can seize the initiative and create an awareness of an alternative reality. Only such a consciousness can be genuinely subversive and, in this sense, it is a pre-condition for political action by the historical agent of social change.

Marcuse fears an illusory freedom: Gilead is just that, a place where people are socialized into taking their wants and needs as their own. This is truly Plato's Republic, one might argue. Sex becomes a utility item, not a spontaneous and playful occurrence. It is sex for reproduction, for physical release, for consumer consumption. Once libido is no longer a private affair between the individual and his or her psyche, then the "private space" unique to person is obliterated. The person becomes a public object, a commodity, stripped of reason that can negotiate between id and ego. Reason itself loses its dialectical quality, its ability to distinguish between what social persons and institutions are and what they can historically become. Reason, helpless to pronounce on moral values, becomes the logic of operationalism, the logic of domination.

Richard Sennett reminds us that in modern society the fear of being discrete, of holding onto some things as being of a private nature, is considered retrograde and conservative [16]. For Sennett, "the very idea of self-disclosure, the authenticity event, the open community is destructive" [16, p. 344].

If the only "real" relationships are those in which the other tells you exactly how he or she feels, then the only "real" relationships are ones which glorify the narcissistic personality. Social relationships, which by necessity require restraints and constraints, are seen as repressive: total liberation from the society becomes the goal rather than reformation of legitimate *social* relationships.

In a similar way, a personality that can be constructed and reconstructed at will—Robert Lifton's protean man [17]—has an especially modern appeal in that it denies *a* human nature, *a* set of innate characteristics, a view of the self as somehow beyond history. But, Sennett argues: "A protean man may live a rich immediate life, but only at the cost of accommodation to his environment. By contrast, the person who feels his selfhood to be constant has acquired the will to resist his environment" [16, p. 350]. Whether it is then open-ended malleability or the intrusion of the state into the space where the person needs psychological freedom, Sennett is worried about positing any place that is devoid or spared the social dimension. He wants to avoid conservative or romantic notions of a private sphere just as he wants to avoid the glorification which, conversely, sees the public sphere as, at best, a necessary evil. Quite the opposite, he wants to see not a "liberation of self" which is narcissism but a "liberation from the self" where one can attend to matters of social and political import beyond one's immediate interest. Thus, what is needed is that dialectic between self and society of which Berger and Luckmann spoke.

I started this chapter with an exposition of social constructionism and I intended two things: first, a statement of the importance of a position that emphasizes the role that concrete historical factors play in shaping the person; and second, a concern that the mechanistic model of biological determinism not be replaced by an equally mechanistic social determinism. By building upon Berger and Luckmann's work, I suggested we could see the moral contours that surround social constructionism, that is, see its subsumption within a humanistic framework. By seeing the constructions, the individual can raise questions about the constructions and attain a perspective on the society that alters, or has the potential to alter, that society.

In other words, we must always ask questions about the ways in which people are to be treated both in the future and in the here-and-now. We must understand not an eternal feminine but the concrete historical relationships which color the ways in which women of certain class, and of a certain race, and of a certain sexual orientation are regarded or esteemed. At the same time, we do not want to undersell or, worse still, disregard the biological bases of gender.

The turn to fiction, the reading of Atwood's *The Handmaid's Tale*, allows the social theorist to look at the same kinds of questions from a different perspective, one in which the artist is not bound by the same kind of paradigmatic constraints as is the social theorist. Atwood asks: how is Gilead (society) constructed? how is gender constructed within that society? The reader of the tale understands why and how the Handmaid behaves like a "social vessel," but the reader also sees what dimension of the maid's humanity remains if the reflective mode is kept and the person can question the particular way in which gender is constructed.

Several questions unite the social and fictional accounts of gender: what, empirically, is considered the feminine role now; how is that role legitimated; what critique of that role might be raised. Two cases are before us, as I write this, which merit attention. One concerns a woman who, while pregnant, failed to follow the medical advice of her doctors, continued taking drugs which were potentially dangerous to the fetus, and in so doing is charged with having caused the deformation and subsequent death of her infant. The questions being raised concern the nature of a woman's relationship to the fetus, the same kind of question raised in the abortion debate. As in that debate, where technology has affected the idea of fetal viability on which *Roe v. Wade* rests, prenatal testing and diagnoses, that is, technical knowledge about the fetus and the geographic space (the womb or intrauterine environment) affect the dignity, privacy and freedom of individuals.

George Annas, a bioethicist, has analyzed the case with reference to Atwood's novel, raising the question of whether the woman is to be regarded as she is in *The Handmaid's Tale* as a container or vessel for the fetus rather than as a valued subject in her own right. I have serious problems with the Annas position, but recommend it for the way in which it has framed the issue [18]. Might not the fetus require protection? But are we then not putting the fetus into an adversarial relationship with the woman in whose body it is to be found? Or does the very location of the fetus give a woman a special mediating rule for that fetus?

The second case centers around the custody battle over babies born to surrogate mothers. Here we come face to face with whether being a mother is a biological and/or social condition: what constitutes "mother" in this age of rapid changes in reproductive technology? Are we now able to see parenting as genetic and/or gestational and/or rearing relationships? Might we not have to rethink the entire issue of a "personal identity?" When social constructionism says that the self is embodied in time and space, it implies that mothers, mothering and motherhood are shaped by considerations of class, status and power as well as by technological change. And yet from all that has been said, might we not want to ask if there are limits to the implied malleability in social constructionism, that is, might we not want to say that she who carries and bears the baby has a relationship to that baby that is distinct regardless of time and place? Issues in reproductive technology are colored by concerns regarding the social and ethical aspects of medicine: who bears babies? who has access to the technologies? how is birthing being distributed, funded and transformed?

The question that arises is whether there are limits to how these biological properties (these sex specific categories) can be defined. Are there constraints imposed by the biology itself? What factors (scientific? political?) will alter, or affect, these constraints? In the Berger-Luckmann version of social constructionism, the construction implies the import of human agency—it is a counter to determinism while at the same time indicating the constraints of construction itself (i.e., construct institutions which constrain behavior). The human actor is always free to say no or not comply with institutional demands: i.e., there is such a thing as an individual consciousness free from social constraints. Social constraints alert us to the shifting sands of biological "realities:" changes brought about by human intervention (a new technological device, say, invented by concrete scientists) change realities. We see this most clearly in issues of fetal viability and reproductive technology like surrogate mothering.

I should argue that for Atwood, Mary Beth Whitehead, in the much publicized "Baby M" case, is the Handmaid: she is the one to whom feminist sympathies seemed to have gone. For feminists are concerned with the concreteness of what happens to which women as a result of technological change: how does being a woman change? is the change the same for Third World women, women of color, gay women, poor women? Other feminists might ask if Whitehead was really coerced into becoming a vessel or container? Was her bearing a child for William and Elizabeth Stern not a progressive way of saying motherhood is not biological but social and, therefore, the Sterns are the socially defined parents of the child biologically of Whitehead and William Stern born? Are surrogate practices not a viable alternative to adoption?

Yet, what is happening in the society about which we should be worried? Is the person, here Whitehead, being separated from her baby? Is her body becoming an object, a thing, a container, a vessel, a womb? It is being separated from its subject and is it being seen as a thing not as a process? And are the bodies being objectified not those of a certain (economic) class of women who sell their bodies for money? Not only can women have babies but they can have them for other women; in this sense, they are doing with their bodies what they want. Atwood does not concentrate on the babies. She treats them as if they were commodities: the Handmaid, like Whitehead, is not a mother but a producer who makes a product to be sold or given away to consumers. Atwood forces us to ask if there are any limits to the commodification of human life: does not pornography and the selling of thinness already commodify women?

Gender is limited by what is biologically and socially possible at the moment. You can bear a baby for someone at that point when the technology and the social system give their support. Social constructionism does not believe you can walk through brick walls or on water or defy the laws of gravity; similarly, it recognizes that social facts have a similar "thereness"–class generates money which construct life-chances (education, health care, stocks and bonds) around which one has to operate.

The social construction of gender trains us to recognize that the views we have toward technology are socially and historically defined and that our morality determines how we ought to regard that technology. Therefore, it is not in the abstract that we must look at the relationship that a woman has with the fetus and her body but, rather, how concretely that relationship is constituted now.

ACKNOWLEDGMENTS

I wish to thank Rhoda Unger for her preparedness to read and critique an earlier draft of this chapter. I also wish to thank my former colleagues at Vassar College Nancy McKenzie, Jennifer Church and Audrey McKinney, for the discussions on Atwood which led to the writing of this chapter.

REFERENCES

1. P. L. Berger, *Invitation to Sociology: A Humanistic Perspective*, Doubleday, Garden City, New York, 1963.
2. P. L. Berger and T. Luckmann, *The Social Construction of Reality: A Treatise in the Sociology of Knowledge*, Doubleday, Garden City, New York, 1966.
3. R. Unger, paraphrasing Buss, *Supra*.
4. P. Berger, Identity as a Problem in the Sociology of Knowledge, *European Journal of Sociology*, 7, pp. 105-115, 1966.
5. A. Rich, *Of Woman Born: Motherhood as Experience and Institution*, Norton, New York, 1976.
6. S. Farganis, *Social Reconstruction of the Feminine Character*, Rowman and Littlefield, Totowa, 1986.
7. M. Atwood, *The Handmaid's Tale*, Houghton Mifflin, Boston, 1986.
8. H. Marcuse, *One-Dimensional Man: Studies in the Ideology of Advanced Industrial Society*, Beacon, Boston, 1984.
9. M. Foucault, The Subject and Power, in *M. Foucault: Beyond Structuralism and Hermeneutics*, Harvester, Brighton, 1982.
10. M. Horkheimer, *Critique of Instrumental Reason: Lectures and Essays Since the End of World War II*, Seabury, New York, 1974.
11. R. Lichtman, Symbolic Interactionism and Social Reality: Some Marxist Questions, *Berkeley Journal of Sociology*, *15*, pp. 75-94, 1970.
12. D. Carveth, The Disembodied Dialectic: A Psychoanalytic Critique of Sociological Relativism, *Theory and Society*, *4*, pp. 73-102, 1977.
13. M. Horkheimer, *Critical Theory*, Continuum, New York, 1972.
14. C. Lasch, *Haven in a Heartless World: The Family Beseiged*, Basic Books, New York, 1977.
15. H. Marcuse, *Eros and Civilization: A Philosophical Inquiry into Freud*, Random House, New York, 1955.
16. R. Sennett, Destructive Gemeinschaft, *Partisan Review*, *24*, pp. 341-361, 1976.
17. R. Lifton, Protean Man, *Partisan Review*, *18*, pp. 1-34, 1968.
18. G. J. Annas, Pregnant Women as Fetal Containers, *Hastings Center Report*, *16*, pp. 13-14, 1986.

Biographies

JOANNE BOELL is a doctoral candidate in social psychology at Temple University. In addition to her work on feminist visions, she has done research on the role of social support networks for women in transition and on the dynamics of the teacher/student relationship in personal defense training courses for women. Both of these projects, done in collaboration with Louise Kidder, focused on women's definitions of social reality within various socio-cultural contexts. Joanne is currently interested in Contextualism as an alternative paradigm for social psychology.

STANLEY BRODSKY is a professor of psychology at the University of Alabama. His major interests are in psychology applied to legal issues and settings and in psychotherapy. In 1983 he co-authored the *Handbook of Scales for Research in Crime and Delinquency*. His latest book *The Psychology of Adjustment and Well-Being* appeared at the beginning of 1988.

MARY CRAWFORD was trained as an experimental psychologist (Ph.D., University of Delaware, 1975) and spent several years happily solving intellectual puzzles in associative learning before looking for a research area that could engage the heart as well as the mind. Her current research on gender and language addresses a variety of questions: Are there visible gender differences in language use, and, if so, what do these differences mean? What are the effects of sex bias in language? Are the speech styles of men and women evaluated differently? Does language impede the articulation of women's experiences? As Jane Watson Irwin Professor at Hamilton College (1986–88), she has organized feminist conferences and become preoccupied with studying the relationship between feminist values and methods of scientific inquiry.

NANCY DATAN, to whom this book is dedicated, was Professor of Human Development at the University of Wisconsin–Green Bay at the time of her death on May 10, 1987. She was a graduate of the Committee on Human Development at the University of Chicago and, consistent with that program and with her own personality, her disciplinary affiliation was always difficult to determine. She considered herself a psychologist, a sociologist, an anthropologist, an evolutionary biologist, and, always, an essayist. She was particularly gifted at revealing the universal elements of personal experience and in bringing to life ancient wisdom. Hence, her professional interests focused (if they can be considered focused) on myth, folk, and fairy tales and the message they bore concerning personality and family dynamics in adulthood, on women's experiences in middle age and later life, and, as is reflected in her chapter for this collection, social, cultural, and religious contexts for gender roles.

SONDRA FARGANIS is an Associate Professor of Sociology at the New School for Social Research. She is a past president of the New York State Political Science Association and the author of a recent book "The Social Reconstruction of the Feminine Character" (Rowman and Littlefield, 1986). Out of her concern for the ways in which theory and practice reinforce one another, she has become particularly interested in issues raised by the new reproductive technologies; it is here that she wishes to focus her sociological prism.

MICHELE FINE is Associate Professor of Psychology in Education, Human Development, and Women's Studies at the University of Pennsylvania. She is co-editor of "Women with disabilities: Essays in psychology, culture, and politics" and a public policy consultant on disability, school dropout prevention, adolescent sexuality, and domestic violence.

IRENE FRIEZE is Professor of Psychology and Director of Women's Studies at the University of Pittsburgh. She is the co-author of a text on the psychology of women, "Women and sex roles" and the co-editor of two issues of the *Journal of Social Issues* concerned with victimology. She has published articles in a variety of areas important to women including: achievement, power, rape, feminist methodology, and, most recently, domestic violence.

JOAN HARTMAN is a professor of English (and chairperson of her department) at the College of Staten Island, City University of New York. Her Ph.D., awarded in 1960, is from Radcliffe College – Harvard University began awarding the degree to women in 1964 – and she continues to claim it rather than her retroactive Harvard degree in recognition of the women who made her graduate study possible. She has worked to bring women into positions of authority in the Modern Language Association, to establish women's studies, and to extend opportunities for feminist research and publication in language and literature. From time to time she teaches and writes about the literature of the English Renaissance, her field of specialization. She's been teaching George Eliot's fiction steadily in a variety of courses on women and literature.

RAVENNA HELSON is a personality psychologist at the Institute of Personality Assessment and Research, University of California, Berkeley. She has studied creativity and affective-cognitive patterns in men and women mathematicians and in writers and critics of imaginative literature for children. Though most of her recent work seems to be in a different area – adult development in women the article included in this volume reflects her view that the genre of imaginative literature for children is related to experiences of personality change and renewal in adult authors, and that gender differences in affective-cognitive patterns reflect the different conditions under which men and women build and try to sustain their identities and sense of meaning. This article is atypical of her work in its lack of quantification, but she believes with many other feminists that psychology needs new and multiple approaches for its complex subject of study.

KAREN HOWE received her Ph.D. in social psychology from Princeton University in 1974. She has been teaching at Trenton State College for the past fifteen years, where she is an associate professor of psychology and the coordinator of the women's studies program. She loves teaching the Psychology of Women course, and that experience has generated her current research interest in the psychological impact of women's studies on students.

BERTRAM JOHN received his Ph.D. in social psychology from Rutgers University and was an assistant professor of psychology at Montclair State College when he wrote the article included in this book. He is currently working for the United Nations.

LOUISE KIDDER is currently Professor of Psychology at Temple University. She first developed her interest in exploring other visions in the 1960s when she and her husband traveled to India and she became a participant–observer of the acculturation of Western sojourners in India. Her work since then has focused on feminist and cross-cultural concepts of justice. She has also written about research methods that provide a means to view the word from multiple perspectives. The analysis of feminist visions that she and her co-authors Michelle Fine and Joanne Boell produced is the result of a large cooperative effort among women in the Delaware Valley Women's Studies Consortium. They met for an autumn gathering, with food and friendship as part of the package, to talk about feminist realities and science-fictions. Many women wrote annotations of their favorite books and stories, and out of that came an annotated bibliography from which the three co-authors spun the threads and themes they present in their chapter.

MARIANNE LAFRANCE is Associate Professor of Psychology and Director of Women's Studies at Boston College. Among her many research interests are: gender and nonverbal communication and the theory and practice of mentoring. She is currently on sabbatical at Yale University working on the use of expert systems in artificial intelligence.

M. BRINTON LYKES is an associate professor of psychology at Rhode Island College where she teaches courses in social psychology, the psychology of race and class, and gender issues in psychology. She received her Ph.D. in Social/Community Psychology Program from Boston College in 1984. Prior to that she served as Coordinator of Women's Programs at Harvard Divinity School and designed and implemented nonracist and nonsexist educational models in theological education. Her current research interests focus on cross-cultural theories of the self and on understanding both women's development of consciousness of themselves as social actors and of their resistance to oppression. These issues are explored in her earlier analysis of racism and sexism in the oral histories of older Black women and most recently in her oral history project with Guatemalan Indian women refugees. She is currently working on an applied research project examining the impact of state violence and repression on Guatemalan Indian children. In addition to her research and teaching she is a member of numerous community organizations and boards and serves as a consultant on institutional racism, organizational development and women's issues. She is the co-editor (with Abigail Stewart) of "Gender and personality" (Duke University Press, 1985).

GLENDA MACDONALD is a graduate student in social psychology at the University of Waterloo.

JANET MALLEY is a graduate student in social psychology at Boston University.

LEIGH MARLOWE is New York City born, educated and employed (City University), though intermittently released to suburbs, exurbs and abroad. She is currently a rural-urban bilocal. She has been active in feminist psychology via the Association for Women in Psychology, almost since its beginnings, and at their start in APA's Division 35 (Psychology of Women) and NYSPA's Division of Women's Issues. She is currently Media Reviewer for *Psychology of Women Quarterly* and Editor of DOWI's section in the *New York State Psychologist.*

KATHERINE POPE has a B.A. from Smith College and a Ph.D. from Rice University. She is an associate professor of English at Del Mar College, Corpus Christi, Texas. She is the co-author of "Who am I this time? Female portraits in British and American literature" (McGraw-Hill, 1976) and of "The female hero in American and British literature" (Bowker, 1981).

AUDREY SANDERS was a graduate student in clinical psychology at Adelphi University at the time the chapter she co-authored was written.

ADRIA SCHWARTZ, Ph.D. is a practicing psychologist/psychoanalyst with a longstanding interest in issues of gender and sexuality. Both in her writing and teaching she has spent the last decade in an attempt to facilitate a rapprochement between feminism and psychoanalysis . . . no easy task. In addition to her independent practice, Dr. Schwartz is Adjunct Associate Professor in the Graduate Clinical Program of the City University of New York and Clinical Supervisor in the Ferkauf Graduate Program of Psychology at Yeshiva University.

MARY ANN SEDNEY is an associate professor of psychology at Providence College where she primarily teaches courses in personality and clinical psychology as well as in the psychology of women. She has had a long interest in the concept of androgyny and is the co-author of "Psychology and sex roles: An androgynous perspective" (Little Brown, 1980).

DIEDRICK SNOEK is a professor of psychology at Smith College where he teaches both developmental and social psychology. As co-investigator with the Project on Women and Social Change, he is working on the relationship between gender and ideology based on case studies of the lives of contemporary American women.

JANICE STEIL is Associate Professor of Psychology at the Derner Institute of Advanced Psychological Studies at Adelphi University. Two interests have directed her research since graduate school at Columbia. These are the psychology of justice and psychology and women. Her current research is investigating issues of justice and deserving in the context of marital relationships.

ABIGAIL STEWART is a professor of psychology at the University of Michigan. She served as director of the Henry A. Murray Research Center of Radcliffe College (a center for the study of women's lives) from 1978 to 1980. She received her master's degree from the London School of Economics in 1972 and her doctorate from Harvard University in 1975. She has co-edited two issues of the *Journal of Social Issues* which are devoted to approaches to studying women's lives, and has published a number of research articles in the area. Her main research interest is the study of change at individual and social levels.

LORI SUSSMAN received her M.A. in general psychology from Montclair State College in 1985. She recently received her J.D. from Rutgers.

SHELAGH TOWSON received her M.A. in social psychology from the University of Wisconsin in 1971 and, after living and working on a Northern Ontario Indian Reserve for several years, returned to graduate school at the University of Waterloo where she received her Ph.D. in social psychology. Her research interests include multicultural and cooperative education, attitudinal correlates of academic achievement among Native people, and the role of self-fulfilling prophecy in women's career and life choices. At present, she is an assistant professor in the Applied Social and Developmental Psychology Programs at the University of Windsor.

RHODA UNGER received her Ph.D. in experimental psychology from Harvard University in 1966, but has worked in the area of the psychology of sex and gender since the early 1970s. She is Professor of Psychology and Director of the Honors Program at Montclair State College and has also served several terms as coordinator of women's studies. Her research interests include the perception of women and men, the confounding of gender, power, and social status, methodological issues in feminist scholarship, and the relationship between personal epistemology and various aspects of the person's behavior. Her current focus is on the contradictions and inconsistencies in the definition of behavior–both by oneself and others. During the 1988–1989 academic year she will be a visting professor at the University of Haifa in Israel as a Fulbright scholar.

SUSAN VOLENTINE received her Ph.D. in clinical psychology from the University of Alabama. The work reported in this volume was part of her Ph.D. dissertation.

JANET WEINGLASS was at Adelphi University at the time the article for this volume was written.

MARK ZANNA received a Ph.D. in social psychology from Yale University in 1970. He is a professor of psychology at the University of Waterloo where he has been involved in a series of annual conferences on social cognition. He conducted much of the pioneering research on self-fulfilling prophecies with a particular focus on their application to both the perception of women and the way they present themselves to others.